SHADOWFORCE
ARCHER™
"Through the character of adversity,
the world will know peace."
– Archer Family Motto

CREATED BY
LEAD WRITER • MECHANICS LEAD

Patrick Kapera • Kevin Wilson

LINE DEVELOPER

Patrick Kapera

SYSTEM DEVELOPMENT

Scott Gearin

ADDITIONAL WRITING

Sean Michael Fish, B.D. Flory, Scott Gearin, John R. Phythyon, Jr., Heath Scheiman, Les Simpson, Lucien Soulban

ADDITIONAL CONCEPTS AND ASSISTANCE

Shawn Carman, Steve Crow, B.D. Flory, Brendon Goodyear, Bill LaBarge, Iain McAllister, David Molinar, Michael Petrovich, Omar Topete, Joe Unger

ART DIRECTOR

jim pinto

COVER ART

Veronica V. Jones

COLOR PLATES

Carl Frank

INTERIOR ART

Storn Cook, Jonathan Hunt, A. Bleys Ingram, G.W. McKee II, Richard Pollard, Mike Sellers, Ethan Slayton, Dan Smith, Paul H. Way, Jeff Wright

CONCEPTUAL ART

Cris Dornaus, Carl Frank, Paul H. Way

EDITORS

B.D. Flory, Scott Gearin, Les Simpson, D.J. Trindle, Rob Vaux, KD Yates

INDEXER

Janice Sellers

CREATIVE DIRECTOR

Mark Jelfo

GRAPHIC DESIGNER

Steve Hough

CHIEF EXECUTIVE OFFICER

John Zinser

CHIEF OF OPERATIONS

Maureen Yates

PRODUCTION MANAGER

Mary Valles

IN MEMORY OF JOHN ZINSER, SR. 1938 – 2001

THE SPYCRAFT/SHADOWFORCE ARCHER STORY TEAM IS...

Chad Brunner, Shawn Carman, Steve Crow, B.D. Flory, Paul Nelson, Heath Scheiman, Les Simpson, Steve Wallace, Joe Unger

THE SPYCRAFT/SHADOWFORCE ARCHER DESIGN TEAM IS...

Sean Michael Fish, B.D. Flory, Scott Gearin, Jim Wardrip

SPECIAL THANKS TO...

Janice Sellers would like to dedicate her work on this book to her spooky brother Mark, who works at No Such Agency.

A very special thanks also to Peter Adkison, Monte Cook, Ryan Dancey, Jonathan Tweet, Anthony Valterra, Skip Williams, and our friends at Wizards of the Coast.

WWW.SHADOWFORCEARCHER.COM

Playtest Team XYZZY is...

John Cater, Jason Dyer, David Dyte, Gunther Schmidl, Dan Schmidt, Dan Shiovitz, Emily Short

Playtesters

Dale Adams, William Adley, Ed Alexanian, Brian Anderson, Heath Anthony, Chaz Aris, Steve Bailey, Kevin Ballew, John Ballew, Jon Bancroft, Steve Barr, Jeff Bates, Matt Birdsall, Scott Boding, Cody Branzovsky, Scott Brotherton, William Buckley, Richard Buckner III, Ryan Buesing, Brian and Cynthia Bullock, Michael Burch, Simon Campey, Ryan Carman, Shawn Carman, Cheryl Carmody, Ken Carpenter, Tracy Carpenter, Brian Carroll, Jim Carroll, Aaron Cartels, Rich Carter, Richard Cattle, Chris Celestino, Melissa Childs-Wiley, Neil Christy, Brian Clark, Ryan Clark, Tom Clayton, Casey Cole, Mark Craddock, Joshua Cremosnik, Steve Crow, Gerry Crowe, Scott Cullen, Christine D'Allaird, Tim D'Allaird, Robert Dake, Chris Dauer, Lance Day, John Dees, Julie Dees, Mark Denny, Dana DeVries, Lisa DeVries, Jay Dunkleburger, Rochelle Dvorak, Suzanne Dvorak, Jake Eddington, Richard Eldridge, Tim Elkins, Steve Emmott, Lance Engle, Tim Fletcher, Chris Foley, Joshua Ford, Doug Foster, Mike Franklin, Andrew Franks, Mike Friedl, Mara Valentine Fritts, Thomas Fritts, Ron Gephart, Mark Granquist, Michael Grove, Greg Gruschow, Rob Hall, Jerry Ham, Paula Hershman, Phil Herthel, Steve Heubusch, Marshall Hitch, Mick Hitch, Matthew Hoeveler, Stephen P. Holleran, Nabil Homsi, Nathan Hood, Carl Hotchkiss, Jason Isaac, Sy Hughes, John Henry Jackson, Mike Jackson, Maureen Jackson, Ryan Jensen, Garner Johnson, JD Jorgenson, Sara Jorgenson, Elana Kahana, Kalai Kahana, Brian Kamen, Jeremy Kilburn, Erick King, Paul Kleiman, Bill LaBarge, Karen LaBarge, Nick Lalone, Justin Lewis, Shannon R Lewis, Josh Light, Morgan Littleton, Dave Lockman, Jason Loughmiller, Mark Lowry, Eric Machen, Brian Martinez, M. Leigh Martin, Ray Matthews, George Matzen, Chris McCardle, Matt McGowan, James Hunter McLamb, James McPherson, Mark Means, Shane Meeks, Clint Menezes, Kevin Millard, Ken Mills, David C. Misner, Bill Mize, David Molinar, Jose H. Molinar, J. David Moody, Joshua O'Connor-Rose, Ben O'Leary, Jessica Ocker, Matt Oliver, Sam Ortiz, Glenn Owens, Trey Palmer, Steve Partridge, Miguel A. Perez, Jr., Kent Peet, Bear Peters, Felicia Peters, Michael Petrovich, Stephan Pfuetze, Pat Phillips, John Piziali, Janel Price, Matt Raddings, Tom Reed, Ben Reid, Micah Reid, Dan Reilly, Allen Riley, Lara Rivero, Rolando Rivero, Ken Roberts, Hector Rodriguez, Joseph Rutledge, Steven Rutledge, Patrick Rykwalder, David Salisbury, Mike Sander, Jason Sato, Nancy Sauer, Heath D. Scheiman, Matthew Schenck, Jason Schnell, Bill Schwartz, Craig Scudgington, Kristopher Scudgington, Richard Shaffstall, Crystal Simpson, Les Simpson, Aaron Smalley, Aaron Smith, Abagail Smith, Jeff Smith, Jessica Smith, Mandy Smith, Marshall and Sonya Smith, Gary Sondergaard, John Stapeley, Cynthia Stewart, Simon Stroud, Karl Michael Surber, Taoman, Steve Temple, Adam Thomas, Omar Topete, Heather Townsend, David Trask, Shawn Trevor, Jackie Unger, Joseph Unger, Matt Van Kirk, Randy Vaughn, Isabella Villiani, Frank L. Voros, Garland Walker, James Walker, Sharon Walker, Todd Wallace, Wayne West, Stephen Wilcoxon, Shannon Wiley, Todd Wilkinson, David Williams, Melissa C. Williams, Wayne Williams, Benji Wilson, Sean Winchell, Shaun Witney, Erik Yaple, Mike Zaret, Jay Zicht, John Zinser, Brandon Zuern

Table of Contents

Introduction

Shadowforce Archer is AEG's official world setting for the Spycraft roleplaying game line. In the *Spycraft Espionage Handbook,* we introduced generic rules for roleplaying cinematic espionage games. The plots, characters, and organizations in the Handbook were intentionally devoid of supporting backstory and unconnected to one another to allow the players maximum control over the details of their own games. *Shadowforce Archer* offers you a cohesive world in which to set your missions, and gives the players a collection of organizations to work for, linked together by a common goal – protection from threats of global menace.

But *Shadowforce Archer* is more than just a collection of groups, NPCs and plotlines; it is an ongoing story that you control. The material presented in this book constitutes the first episode of the first season of our interactive storyline, in which you – the players – decide the course of events both major and minor. By including elements of this setting in your own games, making decisions about them, and reporting back to us through the official *Shadowforce Archer* website (www.shadowforcearcher.com), you determine the course of events in this setting, and define the unfolding backstory. You decide who lives, who dies, and why. Visit our website for more information, and to sign up as an agent or Game Control to participate in this exciting new multiplayer experience.

Note: This book does not contain the rules needed to play. You must have the *Spycraft Espionage Handbook* to create and use agents.

A Brief Word About You

More than anything else, *Shadowforce Archer* is about you. Beyond the interactive elements (which aren't for everyone – thus they're limited to the website), we've carefully constructed this book to include only information we felt players could use at the table. NPCs are kept to a minimum, and presented with multiple versions for games of different power levels. Plots are left open for you to adapt as you wish, and every effort is made to limit the story to material you can use as a springboard for your own ideas.

Further, we've included agent options for nearly every story element in the game. All three major psion classes are included, as are rules for mystic agents, playing chemical monsters, and examples of all the major threats in the setting. Future sourcebooks will introduce and develop new concepts instead of fleshing out old ones. We hope you enjoy this approach to world design.

Terms You Need to Know

Many world-specific terms are used throughout this book. If you get stuck and don't know what something means, check out the Glossary *(page 249)* for a definition.

What This Book Contains

All of the material in this book is meant for players. We begin with the **Shadowforce Archer Primer** *(pages 7–32)*, which introduces the core themes behind the setting and describes the Archer Foundation and its subsidiaries. Players can jump start *Shadowforce Archer* games by reading the Primer, though material in Chapters 1-3 are recommended for those who desire greater depth in their games.

Chapter 1 (Shadow History) describes the secret history of the 20th Century which leads up to the setting in your hands. Over one hundred years of saga is detailed here, including events you only think you know the truth about, and many that never made the headlines.

Chapter 2 (Shadow Community) goes into greater detail about the Archer Foundation's structure, resources, personnel, and goals. Sections are included for each of the groups ("Chambers") that train and field agents for the Archer Conspiracy, including details about their allies, enemies, and current plotlines. Inspirations and roleplaying hints for each group can also be found here, along with 2-3 NPCs for each.

Chapter 3 (The Outside World) contains information about world powers outside the Archer Conspiracy (and peripherally linked to it), and threats to the global security of the new millennium.

Chapter 4 (New Agent Options) describes the differences between designing an agent for Spycraft and designing one for Shadowforce Archer, and offers a number of prestige classes for advanced players. Rules for chemical monsters are also found here.

Chapter 5 (Psionics) contains all the basic rules for psionics and playing psionic agents. Included are all three base psion classes (mentalist, physical adept, and telepath), as well as new feats and a healthy number of skills (powers) for your agent to choose from. Finally, many new Psitech gadgets are located at the back of this chapter.

Chapter 6 (The Mystic World) describes how heroes can use the power of the human spirit to perform acts of superheroism, as well as how villains can warp it to dominate the world. A large number of mystic relics and a new prestige class – the shadespeaker – are also described in this chapter.

Chapter 7 (Threats) is a collection of threats you can drop into any ongoing game of *Shadowforce Archer,* with basic descriptions and statistics.

"Let this union of nations usher in a new age of global security, in which the safety of the entire world is placed before the desires of any single body. Let this Pact be our bond, our guide, our mission – to save the world... from itself."
– Raymond Archer,
at the 1950 Conspiracy Caucus

PRIMER

Episode 1: Skypilot

Now.

Kara Stride pulled the ripcord taut for a third time with no response. Her mind raced as fast as the wind rushing past her as she helplessly plummeted to earth.

The second chute's dead, too, she thought, her eyes dancing across the landscape below as she fumbled for a solution. *I'm at 9,000 feet, maybe... 8,000? Thirty seconds or so, no more.*

Three seconds later, Kara derided herself for wondering who rigged her chutes instead of looking for the answer that must be there. *Maybe it was the Foun...*

What the hell is that? Kara's eyes focused on a shape that had darted up from the ground below – a human shape. In seconds, it streaked across the sky, a thin trail of crimson smoke in its wake. Nearly before Kara realized that the shape was a man – a flying man – it rushed into her and scooped her up, arcing toward a lakeshore a half mile away.

He's handsome, Kara noted as her rescuer put down in a clearing beside the lake. The high-pitched whine of the jetpack strapped onto his back lost its urgency and slowed to a quick hum, then faded altogether. Glancing over his shoulder, Kara reached out toward the pack, and–

"Don't touch that!" the flier warned her, then eased back with a charming smile. "It's not hot, but it can still be dangerous."

"And flying isn't?" Kara chided as he dropped her to her feet.

"It's safer than skydiving, apparently."

"Touché," she answered. "You're with the Archer Foundation, aren't you?"

"Let me take you home." A van pulled up behind them and the side door opened. A man within was wearing a ski-mask.

Kara's eyebrow arched. "Not the most welcoming invitation..."

"Him?" the flier asked. "He's harmless. Just the driver."

"Driving," Kara said. "There's an extreme sport."

The flier grinned. "You have no idea."

"So now that I know who you work for," Kara said, slipping into the van, "you think I can know your name?"

The flier entered the van behind her and signaled for the driver to get moving. "Hunter," he responded. "John Hunter."

Seattle, Washington.

"So why are you so fascinated with us?" Hunter asked as the van turned onto Kara's street.

Kara observed him with a combination of intrigue and trepidation. "You're an urban legend. The Foundation: a secret society for the modern age."

Hunter leaned back into the captain's chair as she continued. "Raymond Archer, philanthropic founder of a global government conspiracy to protect the world from itself. Allies in every nation in the world. The truth behind everything from the John F. Kennedy assassinations to the proliferation of movies made by Mario van Peebles and SNL alumni. And," she patted the jetpack, "all these wonderful toys."

"Argus keeps you that well-informed, does he?"

"He does."

"We're here," the driver said, not looking back.

"Thanks for the chat, John Hunter," Kara said, hopping onto her front lawn. "Say hi to the spooks for me."

Hunter grinned again, wondering why Emily couldn't be more like her sister. "Sure."

"We're gonna get you, you know. Blow your secrets on the front page of *The Times.*"

"Looking forward to it." Hunter shut the van door and signaled for the driver to move on. Then he lifted his watch and flipped open the dialface, revealing a tiny video screen, and waited. Seconds later, the fuzzy image of a young man with a crew cut appeared.

"You rang?" the face greeted Hunter.

"Stride made me. I'm heading back to the field office."

"We're on it," the face said, then vanished.

Kara Stride checked her mailbox then fumbled for her keys, taking just long enough to watch the Foundation van turn the corner. As she entered and closed the door, a Jeep Cherokee took its place across the street. Two men got out and walked away, in different directions, one much faster than the other.

The second man wore a freshly trimmed crew cut.

Kara rounded the second floor landing as the house's internal sensors recognized her and brought up the lights in her study and the hall outside to a warm 70 watts. Her computer booted up, the password ready-entered as her fingerprints were confirmed on the door handle, and the entertainment system launched the latest Katt Wilde feature, *Cat's Paw.*

Collapsing into her executive chair, Kara listened to the bold overture over the movie's opening credits and waited for her browser to load. Less than a minute later, the screen was flooded with a sea of pale green binary code in the shape of an eye. She typed in the password – gameafoot – and scanned the news boards for the latest news from her father's associates.

6:13 p.m.

Former U.S. Army Sergeant George Deacon twisted his head around on his shoulders, cracking his neck, and glanced up at the quarry's window. She was still at the computer, just as she'd been for the last two hours.

"Not the most interesting assignment, is it, Deacon," came Dominic Telling's voice as he approached.

"You're supposed to be on the other side of the block," Deacon reprimanded. "We shouldn't be seen together."

"Lighten up, Deac. It's not like we're staking out Carlos the Jackal or anything."

"You watch too much TV."

Deacon resisted the urge to scream when Telling pulled a flask from his breast pocket and offered it to him.

"Why's this one so important, anyway?" Telling asked, taking a long swig of what Deacon preferred to believe was mineral water.

"She's family," Deacon said. "Sister of someone high up over in the U.K."

"Room 39?" Telling chuckled. "I hear they ha–"

Deacon dropped down on one knee almost before Telling's body crumpled into the gutter, three thin trails of blood appearing across his neck. He felt a momentary chill as he pulled his sidearm from the holster at the base of his back, sure it was just a spring breeze.

Deacon immediately homed in on the area to his right, away from where he'd been looking only moments before, and was stunned to find a man dressed in a long trench coat and low-brimmed hat with stylish winter shades facing him. The man's slender fingers gleamed in the early evening moonlight.

"Hello, Agent Deacon," the newcomer crowed.

"Drop your weapon before someone gets hurt," Deacon called out, as loudly as he thought he could get away with on the suburban street. *Can't wake the neighbors,* he thought. *Control woodn' lik thaaaat...*

"I have no weapon," the newcomer replied, lifting his arm so that the coat fell back to reveal five long talons, tipped with a glossy sheen. "And someone has already gotten hurt."

Deacon's vision, now wildly blurred, faded and failed as the toxin raced through his system, lodging in his otherwise healthy heart.

The *Cat's Paw* credits scrolled behind Kara as she hunched closer to the screen.

"Amazing," she commented to no one in particular. She studied the enormous volume of data streaming through her computer and tried to make sense of it. "Coordinates? No, too many variables. Too long to be a password..."

The stress reliever ball she obsessively gripped in her hand slipped from her fingers, bounced off her foot, and rolled across the bedroom, toward the printer stand.

"Damn," she grumbled, stomping over to retrieve it, "now I've lost my train of thought..."

She stared at the stress reliever with a shocking realization. "That's it!" she cried, leaping to her feet and slipping a CD into the computer's burner. "They are coordinates!"

Several seconds later, as the burner's tray slid open, the light dimmed in her bedroom – not much, a mere 10 watts. But it was enough for her to know that someone had entered the house – someone the ID system didn't recognize.

Without a word, Kara retrieved the CD and slipped out the window, jumping down to the lawn below and around the back of the house.

Behind her, a man entered the room and scanned the interior, then approached and studied the workstation. He noted the empty CD tray and smiled. He was about to follow through the window when the first alarm went off outside – a house alarm, preceded sharply by the sound of breaking glass. Moments later, another alarm, this time a car, complete with a metallic voice repeatedly commanding. "Step away from the vehicle."

The intruder's smile widened. *Clever girl,* he mused, lifting a spongy ball in the shape and color of a globe from its resting place on the floor. He lifted the ball and spun it in his talons. *Clever girl indeed.*

London, England.

Emily Savage weaved through the halls of the Omnium Corporation, rushed past the administrative assistant seated in front of a door labeled "Transworld Transport," and bounded towards the office just beyond.

"When were you going to tell me?" She raised her voice even higher than she'd practiced stalking the halls.

"Close the door, please," the twenty-something strawberry blonde perched behind the desk said.

"For God's sake, my sister's under Company surveillance and the Shop gets into her house? What kind of operation are we running that we can't protect a woman in the confines of her own home?"

"Calm down, Emily," Sarah Singleton replied in a mock-soothing voice, rising from her seat and closing the door. "The situation is under control. Kara has evaded their agent. It's just a matter of time before we reacquir–"

"Agent? Singular? How many men did the Company have on this case?"

"Three, as you requested, but their main man was recalled when his cover was blown saving Kara's life."

Sarah Singleton had a way of stating the obvious in such an understated tone that most people wanted to strangle her. Emily was not unlike her peers. "So Hunter just left her there, knowing she was in danger."

"This was a reconnaissance mission, Emily. We never expected Kara to be targeted by anyone but us. How could we know she'd stumble onto something the Shop found important?"

"She's one of Father's blasted Eyes. Of course she'd find something important. That's what they do!" Emily raised her fingers to her forehead in an effort to concentrate, to control the panic welling within her. "I want to go after her," she said, knowing the response before she asked.

"Refused," Singleton clipped. "You know the rules. She doesn't find out about you – she can stay on the outside."

"She's harmless," Emily argued.

"She works for your father," Singleton stated flatly. "That hardly qualifies as harmless."

Emily knew she was right. It was part of the reason she'd moved to Britain. Only distance could keep her sister safe from their family secret – the proverbial thorn in the Archer Foundation's side.

"Now that this is a rescue mission, Hunter's been reassigned. Let him handle it."

"He's the best," both women said together.

Seattle, Washington.

Molly Hendricks left the Stride home with her laptop tucked under her arm, mentally cycling the possibilities. Thirty paces across the street, she was rudely interrupted as someone softly grabbed her shoulder. She whipped around, ready to rail on the interloper and came up short. "Oh, Hunter. You... startled me."

"Got anything yet?" John Hunter asked, his eyes tight and still. That was how you knew he was serious – his eyes lost their humor.

"We have about a gig of data Stride was downloading from what appears to be a Shop domain – at least, it was behind a Shop frontpage. Looks like only a fraction of that's important, though."

"How do you know?"

"That's all she copied onto a CD before she ran."

Hunter opened the cabin door to a semi labeled *Straight Arrow Pest Control* and gestured for Molly to enter, then followed her in. Ducking into the sleeping cabin and through a small door beyond that was normally concealed as the cabin's back wall, Hunter stepped into the body of the semi's trailer – 55 feet of weapons, surveillance gear, and high-tech wizardry compliments of the Company's friends at R&D.

"So what is it?" he asked. "Technical specs?"

Molly shook her head. "Not likely. Too many variables, and the fixed math doesn't make sense for PsiTech."

"May I?" One of the lab technicians lifted Molly's laptop away and another seated both agents in swivel chairs in front of a vast array of computer monitors.

Hunter leaned in close to Molly after the technician was gone and whispered, "I still don't trust 'em, you know?"

"These guys? They're fine. It's the Shop we have to worry about."

"Indeed," came the gravelly voice of Colonel Alan Deitrich from a monitor centered between them. The Company Control waited until both agents were paying attention and then continued.

"This is now a rescue mission. We've confirmed that the man who killed agents Deacon and Telling was a Shop operative who operates under the codename Strik-9."

"Wonderful," Hunter quipped.

"What's wrong? Who is this guy?" Molly asked.

"High-paid, known Shop assassin. Coats six-inch talons over each hand with a mutagenic poison," Control replied. "Uses his own blood on the blades. Cycles through mutations so quickly we can't devise an antidote."

"Oh," Molly sighed. "Sorry I asked."

"Got it!" the female technician called over the chaos

of the battle bus interior. "They're coordinates, but not on earth."

"Where" Hunter asked.

"Outer atmosphere. Likely a satellite or space platform."

"Better and better," Molly smirked as a signature grin spread across Hunter's face. "What are you smiling about?"

"I know where she's going."

"Where?"

"I'll tell you on the way. Come on." Hunter led Molly over toward their custom-built Sagittarius ("with all the usual refinements, of course"), waving bye to the Colonel on his way.

Overwatch Monitoring Station Delta-4.
95 miles northeast of Vancouver, Canada.
10:12 p.m.

"Are you sure about this?" Kara asked, peering through the chain link fence around the innocuous compound. Inside, a few lone guards patrolled the grounds.

"Absolutely," Argus answered. "The coordinates you downloaded from that Foundation site were quite clearly spatial coordinates."

"Spatial. As in space," Kara said, the queasy feeling returning to her stomach.

"As in outer space, my dear."

"Don't be superior, father," Kara admonished.

Argus beamed, the way he only beamed in pictures from his old days in the field, as part of the Archer Foundation's Cold War elite. Pictures Kara was never allowed to see.

"How do you expect us to get into this place, anyway?" Kara continued.

"Elementary, dear," Argus proclaimed, lifting his cane and sliding it open. Within she could make out a long, thin blade, polished to a brilliant silver gleam. He whipped out the sword, slicing through the chain link with incomparable grace. Kara didn't even think she heard the sound of the links splitting apart. "We kindly ask the guards for their keycards, and when they refuse, we knock them unconscious and steal them."

"Ah, yes. Of course."

10:42 p.m.

Hunter pulled into the Overwatch compound driveway and leaned on the horn. "Come on, buddy! Emergency! We haven't got all night!"

"Now see here, sir..." The angered guard came up short as he saw the driver of the rental car. "Yes, sir. Right, away, Mr. Hunter."

Refusing to wait until the gate was completely open, Hunter clipped it with the Saab. The Company would pay for the damage (or rather, the U.S. government would). As the car sped across the open field between the compound's outer perimeter and the launch zone, Hunter saw that the transport rocket was already on the pad and cursed the Company for not having another Sagittarius at the airport as he requested. The improved horsepower of the Foundation sports car might have gotten them here a few precious minutes earlier...

"The rocket's prepped," Molly mimicked his words.

"I know," Hunter spat back at her.

"They're ready to launch."

"I know!"

10:46 p.m.

Kara skidded to a halt as they passed the security station closest to the pad. Displayed on the screen were two figures, running past the slumbering guards Argus had subdued. "We have company!" she screamed to her father, not realizing her unintentional pun.

"There's no time!" Argus called back to her. "We have to leave... now!"

Kara pulled herself away from the station and followed closely behind her father, questioning their actions for the forty-sixth time that evening.

10:51 p.m.

Hunter darted across the enormous field of catwalks leading to the launching pad with the tense ferocity of a charging tiger. Molly, hard-pressed to keep up behind him, made sure he didn't run into anything sharp – or poisonous.

The shockwave from lift-off stopped both agents dead in their tracks, and knocked Molly back off her feet into the hard steel behind her. Hunter crouched to avoid the bulk of the blast, but kept his eyes on the rocket arcing into the sky above them, knowing it was too late.

Molly promised to send a gift basket to the folks who'd failed to have the Sagittarius waiting for them at the airport, and lifted herself to her feet. Shifting her weight, she kicked something small which was lying on the steel weave of the catwalk – a six-inch talon.

Overwatch Space Platform Skypilot. Six hours later.

"How long?" Argus called over the rising din in the central compartment.

"Three minutes," Kara answered. "Maybe less."

"Perfect." Argus' fingers danced gracefully across the keys of the requisitioned laptop. The screen displayed an endless array of commands, responding to the defenses of the station's hidden secondary computer system. The data stream paused for a moment, and he reached back

into the tangle of wires hanging out of the laptop's case and checked for a loose connection.

"Nice." Sarcasm dripped from Kara's words as she launched herself across the compartment, toward the astrologics panel. "Who built this place, a blacksmith?"

Argus smiled, only allowing himself a moment's glance in the direction of his older daughter before refocusing on bypassing the system security. "The Overwatch stations weren't built for looks, dear." His tone was characteristically level. "But utility."

Kara dug her feet into crevices beside the panel and used the leverage to pull it free of the wall. Behind was a pit of electronics – wires and circuit boards meshed together with no apparent rhyme or reason. Kara smiled at the familiar sight. "Well, they could have included an instruction manual for this place," she chided, "a leaflet, maybe?"

"There," Argus smiled ruefully, a moment before the panels around him blinked back into action. He turned back to Kara, who had crawled into the pit and attached a small device to what appeared to be its core. "Coordinates?" he requested.

"...and... gotcha!" Kara exclaimed, pulling the device free and tossing it across the compartment to her father. "What are they targeting?"

"Cities," Argus replied. "Eight cities."

"With what?"

"I don't know." Argus detached the laptop and handed it to Kara, then focused his attention on a new piece of code. "This is promising–a piece of errant code tacked onto the end of the transmission. An email, perhaps?"

"Can you read it?"

"I think so, yes." Argus went still, then pale as the screen in front of him displayed a satellite photo beside an image of a placid island.

"What's wrong?"

"Of course!" Argus exclaimed. "This isn't a Foundation mission."

"Then who?"

"The Shop. And I know what they're after."

"Too bad you'll never have the chance to tell!"

"Strik-9!" Argus screamed as Kara dove to intercept the newcomer. He launched himself toward them, a feral smile spreading across his warped, mutated face. Instinctively, he flexed the fingers and wrist of his right hand, releasing more deadly toxin to trickle onto the gauntlet's talons.

"No!" Argus cried, flinging himself in between them and shouldering Kara toward the airlock below. "You can't have her, you monster!"

Argus caught himself on the station's ribbing, freeing the long blade of his sword-cane.

"One Savage is as good as another," Strik-9 growled, swiping at Argus and leaving a thin trail of poison droplets in the air between them. "Perhaps better."

"There'll be no bounty for you, Strik-9!" Argus swept out at him to keep him at a distance. "Not today!"

Argus didn't expect Strik-9's next move, a low kick to his abdomen, which left him doubled over and tilting backward. His head knocked against the duct frame and he felt light-headed.

"England's greatest secret agent," Strik-9 gloated, preparing to strike. "This is how it ends."

Argus' legs suddenly shot out from where they had curled up to his belly, propelling Strik-9 across the compartment. He twisted a cufflink free and threw it after the villain. "Kara! Close your eyes!"

The cufflink exploded in a shower of sparks, momentarily blinding the villain. Argus looked to Kara, who had righted herself outside Strik-9's capsule. "Take the laptop to John Hunter," he screamed. "The man who saved you. Tell him to give it to Control."

"What about you?" Kara answered.

"Control!" Argus repeated, his voice suddenly bold and sharp. Then he paused, regaining his composure, and smiled warmly. "Don't worry, child. This is only the beginning."

An iris closed between them, cutting Argus off from view. Kara closed her eyes and, focusing on her father's smile, pushed herself into the capsule.

A moment later, she felt the jolt as it broke away from the station and into the turbulence of re-entry...

For the next chapter in the exciting *Shadowforce Archer* saga, pick up *The Archer Foundation sourcebook,* on sale soon and visit **www.shadowforcearcher.com!**

What is Shadowforce Archer?

The world of *Shadowforce Archer* is a fantastic reflection of our own, in which heroic superspies protect the world against criminal organizations, evil geniuses, and many other threats to global security. It is a world in which action and adventure are the name of the game, conspiracy and cover-ups have replaced trust and patriotism, and human evolution has unlocked powers dreamt of only in comic books and science fiction novels.

The world of *Shadowforce Archer* is many things, few of them expected and all of them the stuff of high adventure. You might want to consider them the next time you look outside your window...

Action and Adventure

Think of *Shadowforce Archer* as your favorite espionage movie, television show, or book. Every scene or chapter offers a new challenge, a new avenue for intrigue, suspense, and drama. In the world of *Shadowforce Archer,* every day brings a new mission, bolder and more dangerous enemies, shocking revelations, surprising and exotic locales, and beautiful new temptations that threaten both the agent's wards and the very fiber of his character. Impossible odds are made even through the keen senses and quick reflexes of the world's greatest secret agents (and the occasional laser-watch). Only they stand between the world and those who would destroy or dominate it.

Here, the action is extreme, and the adventure never ends. Russian serum soldiers fight Pan-Asian ninja in helicopters flying wildly out of control over Prague. Company operatives chase villains and their henchmen through the flaming wreckage of their South American strongholds. And agents rarely think twice before diving into the line of fire to save the world.

The first lesson of *Shadowforce Archer:* Spies are nothing if not bold.

Conspiracy and Cover-Ups

On the surface, the world of *Shadowforce Archer* looks just like the one you woke up in this morning, the world you have comfortably grown up in, the world you accept on face value. But that comfort and acceptance comes with a price – one which only the agents of the Archer Foundation are prepared to pay.

Beneath the surface, the world is far more dangerous than anyone suspects, filled with brilliant madmen whose schemes jeopardize the safety of millions, multinational syndicates with the resources to bring governments to their knees, and at times even rogue agents bent upon ruining the fifty-year old pact that safeguards the world from utter destruction.

Perhaps the most important assignment any agent of the Archer Foundation accepts is the one that never ends: ensuring the world is safe, whether it wants to be or not. The conspiracy to keep knowledge of the world's greatest threats (and its greatest champions) a secret is only possible through the efforts of a vast network of specialists and informants, not to mention the media and world governments who support it. But it is ultimately Archer's agents themselves who must make sure that nothing slips through the cracks.

The second lesson of *Shadowforce Archer:* Things are rarely entirely as they seem.

Espionage and Evolution...

The world of *Shadowforce Archer* has diverged from our own in one last all-important way. The dawn of the 21st century has brought with it the realization of true human potential.

...of the Human Mind...

The discovery of psionics has brought with it incredible powers, abilities ranging from reading minds to setting things on fire with a single thought. Mentalism has introduced PsiTech – gadgets which defy the laws of physics and science – physical adepts who regularly exceed the limits of human strength, speed, and endurance, and telepaths who wage a silent war that only they can comprehend, the battles of which are fought across the treacherous landscapes of the human psyche.

...and the Human Spirit

There is one last frontier to be explored – the arcane, which is fueled by the human spirit. Artifacts of lost cultures and occult rituals focus this power as a razor-sharp weapon. Power-mad sorcerers wield ancient powers that can only be countered by the focused strength of mystic agents trained by the Guardians of the Whispering Knife, one of the Archer Foundation's least understood allies.

The final lesson of *Shadowforce Archer:* The future is yours.

Another World, Another War

Shadowforce Archer is set in the world around you. Technology has advanced far beyond anyone's expectations, governments and laws change daily, and the clarity of yesterday has been replaced with uncertainty and fear.

But between the doubts and the dubious policies, a secret war is being waged. This war is rarely ideological, or political, or even personal. The soldiers on its front line call it practical, because the goal of the conflict – at least for them – is nothing short of protecting the entire world... from itself.

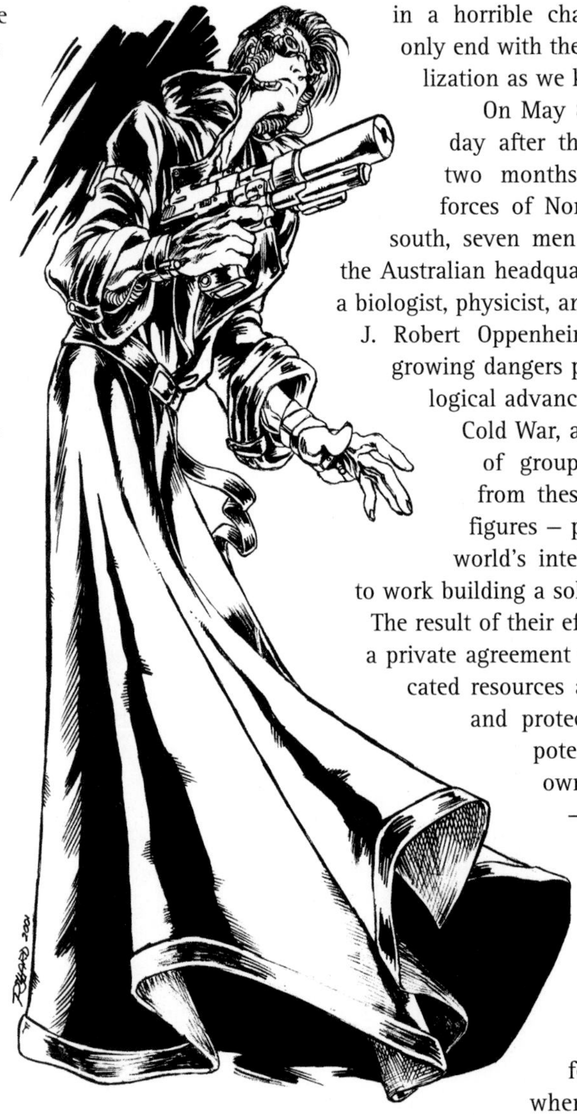

A Century of Change

History is only a shade incorrect. By and large, events occurred as you have been taught by the papers, your teachers, and the government. But there is an underlying truth which has remained hidden from you, a second layer beneath the events – concealed beneath a conspiracy of lies concocted to protect you from the horrors of the modern age.

The dawn of the second half of the 20th century defined this conspiracy. As technological advances made global physical war an obsolete practice, they also engendered a new danger – global devastation. With the creation of "peacekeeping" devices such as the atomic bomb, biological warfare, and industrial espionage, the need to safeguard the world from horrors of its own creation became painfully clear.

The Archer Pact

In the months following the attacks upon Hiroshima and Nagasaki, much of the world cheered the end of what they perceived as the greatest war in human history. But silently, they also mourned the devastating loss of life suffered during the Allied forces' victory, and looked anxiously toward a time when "the Bomb" might be used again. A small group of these wary observers was not content with merely watching, however.

Over the next five years, these individuals observed the spread of Communism through Eastern Europe and Asia, and the birth of what would soon be called the Cold War. It became evident that the world was rapidly spiraling out of control, that the greatest discoveries and victories of all time were merely catalysts in a horrible chain-reaction which could only end with the total devastation of civilization as we know.

On May 8, 1950, five years to the day after the German surrender and two months before the communist forces of North Korea invaded to the south, seven men and women gathered at the Australian headquarters of Raymond Archer, a biologist, physicist, and close personal friend of J. Robert Oppenheimer. They discussed the growing dangers posed by rampant technological advances and the tensions of the Cold War, as well as the proliferation of groups dedicated to profiting from these conditions. These eight figures – prominent members of the world's intelligence agencies – went to work building a solution.

The result of their efforts was the Archer Pact, a private agreement which clandestinely dedicated resources and personnel to policing and protecting the world from all potential threats, including its own governments. This group – the Archer Foundation – is the focus of *Shadowforce Archer.*

The Ecology of Evil

Recently, Archer suffered its greatest setback when the Shop – Archer's PsiTech research and development division – broke away, becoming the world's newest criminal organization. Aside from placing many of Archer's secrets in the hands of a dangerous new enemy, this has jeopardized much of the Conspiracy's structure, as agents now question their every move. Until the break, the Shop pervaded nearly every level of the conspiracy. Its betrayal means that anyone might be a traitor.

This situation drastically altered the way in which the Archer Chambers operate. As the Foundation reels from the news, many of its Agents operate alone, without the guidance or support they have long depended upon.

Storm Clouds Gather

The Shop's succession could not have come at a worse time for the Foundation. Every day, new and more powerful enemies creep into sight, waiting for the Foundation to show a weakness. The Hand of Glory, a threat forged in the fury of World War II, is close to finding the key to ultimate power – a relic lost thousands of years ago, which may unlock the hidden secrets of the universe. And in Russia, allies have become enemies, turning an entire nation of spies against Raymond Archer's protectorate.

Puzzling the World Apart

The Archer Pact carved the world into eight **shadow communities** – pools of spies, soldiers, informants, specialists, political figures, criminals, and others whom the Foundation periodically calls upon in times of need. Each shadow community is administered by a **Chamber,** or branch of Archer operations. Chambers each have a dedicated staff of full-time agents directed by one or more individuals or small groups known as **Control,** who in turn answer directly to the Archer Foundation. This system as a whole is referred to as the **Archer Conspiracy.**

Through its Chambers, the Archer Foundation monitors the activities of the world's shadow communities, as well the actions of the world's governments and the reports of the world's media. When something occurs that threatens the security of the world, agent teams are called in to take care of the problem – usually from the Chamber where the problem is located. The Archer Foundation has the final say concerning these missions (the focus of most *Shadowforce Archer* game sessions), but individual Chambers are usually allowed to direct their own agents without interference.

To keep everyone honest, mission teams are usually formed from more than one Chamber (i.e. agents are summoned from two or more shadow communities to form teams). This practice ensures that no Chamber may operate exclusively of the others, but it also gives players of *Shadowforce Archer* a justification for designing agents from different factions.

Archer's Cloak & Dagger

The Archer Conspiracy operates in total secrecy, shielded from the public it protects by the same network it uses to watch for potential threats. This network is often referred to as the Conspiracy's **Cloak.** When security leaks occur, operatives of the local Chamber are called in to plug them. These agents are often assisted by other members of the local shadow community, who also benefit from the Cloak.

When the Cloak fails, the Foundation calls in its **Dagger** – mission teams directed to shut down or eliminate the leak at all costs. These teams often include the Conspiracy's espionage elite–agents of the very highest caliber, who are prepared to risk everything, up to and including their own lives, to protect Archer's secret.

Chamber Descriptions

The following pages introduce Archer's Chambers – their strengths, weaknesses, brief histories, and functions as part of the Archer Conspiracy.

Each Chamber description includes the following:

Shadow Community: The nations and geographic areas governed and protected by the Chamber.

Focus: The Chamber's primary specialty, and the type of mission they are most often called upon to perform.

Tactics: Common methods and practices.

Organizations: The real-world organizations the Chamber most commonly draws from.

Headquarters: The location of the Chamber's central office.

Control: The name of the Chamber's director.

Additional information about each Chamber is available in Chapter One: World.

A Word About Accuracy

Shadowforce Archer is set in the real world, and includes real-world organizations, persons, and conflicts. But to maintain the style and flavor we desire, many liberties have been taken. In all cases we have tried to remain respectful of the conditions our setting is derived from, but in many cases accuracy has been sacrificed for playability and fun. Agencies have been combined, altered, and augmented to suit the needs of a factionalized roleplaying game, and new goals and biases have been established to fuel the drama and tension commonly seen in spy film and literature. Perhaps most importantly, history itself has been changed in some cases, to support the game's contention of a global, century-long conspiracy, and we have intentionally deviated from the real world as of 2002. Should any of our decisions fail to satisfy, we apologize.

The Archer Foundation

Shadow Community: Technically, Archer's central Chamber guards and observes everything from the Malay Peninsula to New Zealand, and shares all surrounding water bodies with neighboring counterparts, but Pan-Asian Collective operations frequently take place in Archer's northern territories.

Function: Global surveillance and analysis; supervision of all Chambers and direction for all missions (often as field analysts working with teams from other Chambers); financing the Conspiracy; psion research and PsiTech design.

Tactics: Counterespionage; leadership and organization; tactical application of psion powers; "constructive conspiracy" (using the conspiracy as a political and social weapon); heavy use of specialists.

Organizations: Australian Security and Intelligence Organization (ASIO), Australian Secret Intelligence Service (ASIS), International Reporting and Information Service (IRIS), INTERPOL.

Headquarters: The Archer Institute for the Sciences, a stately modern skyrise in Canberra, just a few blocks from the offices of the ASIO.

Control: "Two" *(see below)*, though rumors persist about the existence and identity of "One".

"Through the character of adversity the world will know peace." The Archer family motto has influenced the Conspiracy's growth throughout the last fifty years and can be felt in every office of every Chamber around the world, but nowhere is it more prevalent than in Archer's own backyard. Pitting friends and enemies against one another in order to weaken them all, the Foundation has elevated the motto to an extreme battlefield ethic. Its agents are cunning strategists, hardened spies, and brilliant psions of the highest degree, all trained at the Foundation's front organization, the Archer Institute for the Sciences.

The Institute was operational for some time before the Pact formed in 1950. Raymond Archer's dream of global security was born of the first and second World Wars, and fermented for many years before it became a reality. Prior to the start of the Cold War, the Archer Institute was known as a think-tank specializing in political, military, and social analysis, which world leaders turned to for advice and counsel in times of crisis. This reputation gained the Institute much wealth and influence, as well as the contacts and knowledge required to launch the Pact. Since 1950, the Institute has remained at the cutting edge of scientific development, specializing in biological and medical research – fields in which it has surpassed even the most cutting edge minds outside the Conspiracy. Through its genome and psion investigations, the Foundation has pushed scientific progress farther than anyone else on earth – save some gifted criminal masterminds which their agents face in the field.

The Archer Foundation strives to maintain connections to every intelligence agency, military, corporation, media outlet, secret society, and social group that might provide it with information about global affairs. It also manages the transportation of agents to areas of crisis, communication between Chambers and teams in the field, financing, and recruiting (though Chambers may also recruit on their own).

Necessarily, the Foundation is compartmentalized – some even call its internal structure Byzantine. But it is also terrifically efficient, managing a worldwide network unlike anything since the Roman Empire. It makes the best use of every resource, especially its corps of psion agents, whose minds operate on a level most ordinary humans cannot even comprehend.

Externally, the Foundation operates through Australia's two principal intelligence agencies – the ASIO (an internal, counterespionage group) and the ASIS (which acts abroad). Both were formed mere months before the Archer Pact was established, and have been compromised on a fundamental level by the Conspiracy.

Coincidentally, the authority of both agencies has recently increased several-fold, which makes many outsiders nervous. Though publicly unexplained, this augmentation is part of a calculated Archer stratagem aimed at countering the loss of the Shop, and the myriad problems their betrayal has caused *(see page 55 for more)*.

This Chamber's Control is known only as *Two*. Little is known about this guarded man or his origins, other than his being a veteran of the Cold War. Two has no interests outside the Conspiracy, and is wholly dedicated to Raymond Archer's vision. One of the most powerful psions on the planet, Two has been called "the next step in human evolution."

ARCHER FOUNDATION

The African Alliance

Shadow Community: The African continent, including Madagascar – Egypt and the Middle East are shared with the Guardians of the Whispering Knife *(see page 24);* surrounding seas are shared with other Chambers.

Focus: Special operations *(see below);* spy training.

Tactics: Modern espionage/covert tactics; gunplay; heavy use of physical adepts and interpersonal skills.

Organizations: National Intelligence Agency (NIA), The National Intelligence Coordinating Committee (NICOC), The South African National Defense Force (SANDF), South African Police Service (SAPS), South African Secret Service (SASS).

Headquarters: A private compound on the Comoro Islands ("The Lodge").

Control: Elias "Tendaji" Graham.

Though remote and relatively self-contained, the Chamber known as the African Alliance has a broad scope and an incredible responsibility: they are in charge of what Archer obliquely refers to as special operations. In essence, special operations are what Archer does every day – covert missions in which the scope and threat are both global. But where most Chambers specialize in particular skills and techniques, agents of the African Alliance are broadly trained, offering the most versatile range of options possible when in the field, and therefore the best chance of successfully completing tasks with no clear or immediate objective.

Alliance agents usually begin their education at the NIA's intelligence academy, one of the world's foremost spy schools, but it is the grueling training ground at the Alliance's private island headquarters – the Lodge – where their finest agents are born, or rather *reborn*.

The Lodge's external appearance is very much in keeping with its innocuous name; from the air, the seven-mile island looks like a private estate or vacation resort. But beneath the welcoming paradise is a technological wonder, a sprawling subterranean complex from which the Alliance's operations are staged and the neighboring continent is observed. Supplied with a constant stream of minute-to-minute data by Archer's privately-owned satellite relays, the Alliance remains in constant touch with its territory even while hidden deep beneath the waves.

The African Alliance is the youngest of Archer's Chambers, and was not represented (or even considered) during the 1950 caucus that inspired the Conspiracy. The Chamber was the brainchild of its current Control, Elias "Tendaji" Graham, a South African national and well-known philanthropist. Graham was recruited into the deranged schemes of a genocidal madman known as Helix, a powerful psion who desired to spread the genetic purity of awakened mental powers across the globe.

Helix conceived and built the Lodge (he called it Eden) to cultivate the psion gene, but his tampering accidentally released a psion plague which killed three out of every four people it came in contact with. *(For more about this critical event in the Shadowforce Archer history, see page 41).*

Graham alerted Archer to Helix's plan early enough for them to contain the plague and cover it up, and then lobbied to set up a new Chamber in Helix's base. Graham's argument was sound; with Africa torn by internal strife and often overlooked by outside intelligence agencies, a local Chamber could go largely unnoticed, and help the Foundation bring the tumultuous area back under control.

Since its inception, the African Alliance has grown into one of Archer's strongest, most stable Chambers. With no history or prior allegiances, the Alliance was able to infiltrate every level of the South African government as it reorganized, and covertly helped to rebuild the nation's intelligence agencies after full democracy came in 1994. This stability has earned the Alliance a respect that some other Chambers – notably the Company and the Russian Confederacy – are rarely afforded. Today the Alliance is critically important to Archer's mission, and beyond its special operations, trains many of the Conspiracy's agents.

Elias Graham, who has run the Chamber since its inception, is a rare breed. He maintains a public life outside his Archer duties, working for unilateral freedom and civil rights in his homeland and across the globe. He is fast becoming one of the most respected social reformers in the world, and his extra-curricular activities may soon preclude his responsibilities to the Conspiracy. But until then, Graham remains one of most nurturing and loved of Archer's Controls. His agents are unwaveringly loyal, and accept his commands without hesitation.

AFRICAN

ALLIANCE

The Company

Shadow Community: The Americas, Canada, and Greenland; surrounding seas are shared with neighboring Chambers.

Function: Enforcement.

Tactics: Military and paramilitary action; strategic reconnaissance; sabotage; propaganda; "the business of war".

Organizations: Central Intelligence Agency (CIA), Defense Intelligence Agency (DIA), Department of Defense (DoD), National Security Agency (NSA), National Security Council (NSC).

Headquarters: A training camp southwest of Butte, Montana ("The Kennel").

Control: Colonel Alan Deitrich (Ret.).

The Central Intelligence Agency has long been called "The Company," a moniker promoted only within the organization's ranks. Outsiders are discouraged from using the name, which seems to be reserved as a private term for operatives alone. But there is is another reason for the name, one which has been buried beneath fifty years of fraternity and public acceptance. The Company – the real Company – works for the Archer Conspiracy.

The Conspiracy is more entrenched in the United States than in any other nation, which makes it both very strong and very vulnerable. With the tremendous resources of the world's largest superpower at its disposal, Archer has made great strides in its mission, but the many scandals that have plagued the United States intelligence community – especially the CIA – are a grave danger to Archer. In fact, American scandal nearly destroyed them.

The first nail in what might have been Archer's coffin came in 1961, when the CIA–and parts of the Company, without the authorization or guidance of the Archer Foundation – orchestrated a covert paramilitary invasion of Cuba with the intent of deposing Fidel Castro. This fiasco, known as the "Bay of Pigs," drew the world's attention to the CIA and the Company.

This failed operation was not the only one undertaken by the Company without Archer's blessing. During the remainder of the 1960s and through the 1970s and 1980s, a laundry list of indiscretions were revealed, bringing the Conspiracy closer to the brink of discovery and destruction.

Perhaps the worst of these revelations was Operation MKULTRA, the misguided CIA research project into mind control and genetic manipulation. Again without authorization, the Company privately devoted many of its healthy psions to the project, as well as a quantity of the serum originally used to induce psion powers *(see page 40 for more)*. In the end, MKULTRA resulted in nothing more than several high-profile deaths (often by suicide) and a cadre of psychotics with the power to topple small buildings.

Archer "cleaners" (trouble-shooters) had to be called in to hunt down the psion maniacs and clean up the Company's mess. Though largely successful, the incident still forced Archer's hand. Following in the U.S. government's own footsteps, the Company was methodically removed from public scrutiny. Cutting ties with its CIA roots, the Company withdrew deeper into the U.S. intelligence system and was restructured.

During the last two decades, the Company hid within the U.S. government, offering up its parent organization when necessary to dodge the media or internal auditors. Their current mission is narrow; they are an operations arm, doing what they know best – policing the world.

Even after the scandals, the Company has been unable to completely cut their ties with the U.S., which unknowingly provides the Chamber with funding and personnel – as well as one of their leading training grounds and recruiting centers, the Farm (Camp Perry, Virginia – *see page 76)*. Relying on a core group of conspirators within the U.S. government, the Company siphons resources using forged paperwork, misdirection, and lies. Normally, the Foundation would avoid the danger inherent with such a large-scale contrivance, but the enormous wealth and firepower of the United States government is simply too much to ignore.

Archer's U.S. Control assumed his post when the Shop recently declared independence (an act made possible mainly through the Company's myriad political and military connections). Alan Deitrich is a retired career military intelligence officer, and his sole responsibility is to keep the Company in line. Trained at the Farm and later the Company's own Kennel, Deitrich is more than prepared for the challenge. He'll bring the Company back from the brink – at any cost.

THE

COMPANY

THE EUROPEAN COMMONWEALTH

Shadow Community: Everything west of the Russian Federation except the United Kingdom and Ireland, including France, Germany, Belgium, Greece, Italy, Czechoslovakia, and others; surrounding seas are shared with neighboring Chambers.

Function: Economic espionage; industrial espionage; political levering; conspiracy as a high art form.

Tactics: Disinformation; information and media tampering; mediation; slander; terrorism.

Organizations: *Direction Générale de la Sécurité Extérieure* (DGSE), Central Directorate of General Information (DCRG, for specialists only), Federal Intelligence Service (BND), and various terrorist and criminal elements when necessary.

Headquarters: Mobile (though rumors persist that one or both Chamber Controls have their own strongholds hidden somewhere in Europe).

Control: Stefan Bartolomei (for the European Union) and "Fade" *(see below).*

Conspiracy theorists have long presumed the existence of a shadowy group of power brokers, hidden behind a veil of industrial discretion and polite distance, whose fingers tightly clutch the strings which make the world dance. This group of bankers, media moguls, commercial tsars, political analysts, and outright criminals has been given many names – the Bavarian Illuminati, the Bilderbergers, the New World Order...

In truth, they are called the Gemeinschafft Consortium, and they established the European branch of Archer's espionage and political maneuvering. Their founder, a pre-war capitalist labor baron named Bruno Vangeli, was known to Raymond Archer long before the Pact, and his contacts spoke for themselves. Vangeli operated a vast network of contacts in all levels of European society and government, and offered the Pact its best chance to stabilize the upheavals which had plagued Europe in the past.

Europe has always been a hotbed of political intrigue. The birthplace of modern espionage, Europe epitomized the best and the worst of spying. With two World Wars and four decades of conflict as evidence, it was readily apparent that the area required special attention, especially during the Conspiracy's formative years.

The Gemeinschafft Consortium was already in place, though for how long is still a topic of wild debate. During the 1950s, Vangeli assured Raymond Archer and his allies that the Consortium was still in its "infancy, only a twinkle of greatness..." But urban myth through the streets and markets of Germany and France place them at conferences dating back to the turn of the century, and earlier.

The Gemeinschafft Consortium has guided the last five decades of Europe's growth, rebuilding its unity, independence, and financial security. Lasting improvements such as the European Economic Community (today known as the European Union) and its proposal for universal currency are their designs. The fall of the Berlin Wall, reunification of Germany, and restructuring of corrupt intelligence agencies also reflect their work.

But skeptics still voice concerns about the Consortium's influence upon the European landscape, warning that allowing any single group this much control is asking for a powerful enemy. For now, Archer allows the Consortium to handle affairs in Europe – with the advice of not one but two Controls.

The first is Stefan Bartolomei, a retired member of the DGSE's covert Action Service (the branch of French intelligence devoted to covert military operations), with numerous contacts throughout the French, German, and Italian governments. Stefan filters pertinent information to the Consortium through the global information channel, and organizes most local Archer missions.

Mission teams assigned by Stefan Bartolomei tend to be composed of military and ex-military commandos, toughened espionage agents whose purpose was lost when the Cold War ended, and – much to the Archer Foundation's chagrin – not a few former terrorists. Bartolomei claims that these latter individuals offer him a unique weapon on the criminal's own level, and a window into the world's underbelly, but the leash he has been allowed with them is short... very short.

The second is something of a mystery. "Fade" (as he is known among Europe's criminal elite) was assigned directly by Archer and operates his own agent teams according to his own protocols. Fade's agents are culled from the streets and prisons of Europe, where they are known as thieves (often of quite high-end merchandise) and miscreants of all sorts.

EUROPEAN

COMMONWEALTH

The Guardians of the Whispering Knife

Shadow Community: The Saudi Arabian peninsula, as well as Iraq, Iran, Afghanistan, Pakistan, and northern Africa (including Egypt); surrounding seas (and the Persian Gulf) are shared with neighboring Chambers.

Function: Protectorate of ancient knowledge; paranormal investigation; wetworks (assassination) and infiltration.

Tactics: Mystic warfare (spiritual magic); melee combat (especially with blades); stealth; terrorist and guerrilla warfare; poison, intimidation, and guile; survival tactics.

Organizations: None *(see below)*.

Headquarters: Unknown.

Control: None, and all *(see below)*.

In G'lilot, just north of Tel Aviv, Israel, there is a building called the Center for Special Studies, a labyrinthine stone structure with many courtyards, each dedicated to a period of history in the Arab-Israeli conflict. Engraved on the walls of this memorial are the names of more than 400 intelligence officers who have died in active duty over the last fifty years. A special corner of the memorial is without names, in honor of the men and women whose duties cannot yet be revealed. All of these nameless fallen were members of the Israeli intelligence community.

One of them was more.

In 1944, a woman known only as Umbra died on the island of Crete at the hands of the Nazi party. She was there with a group of psion and mundane secret agents, trying to stop the wife of the most feared man in the world – Adolf Hitler – from unleashing a creature of unimaginable power, an ancient entity capable of plunging the world into eternal hellfire.

The thing that made this woman so much different from her peers is that she was one of a select order, a secret society hundreds or thousands of years old, dedicated to safeguarding it from supernatural threats and knowledge that could drive its inhabitants over the brink of insanity. This group is known as the Guardians of the Whispering Knife.

The Guardians are an ancient people, guided by spiritual forces only they can see. Some are powerful mystics, capable of wielding incredible powers by virtue of their faith alone, others are lethal melee experts whose enchanted knives are forged in the realms of the dead, and still others are shadespeakers, who can commune with the recently deceased and at times even channel them.

Keepers of the secret mystic history of the world, the Guardians know the true rise and fall of kings, countries, and continents. They are privy to whispered truths shielded by thousands of years of lies, and are rumored to know the dark origins of the human soul.

Umbra was the first Guardian to communicate with Conrad Archer and his allies at Room 39, sent to assist them when psionics unexpectedly surfaced again in the early part of the 20th century *(see page 34 for more about the origins of modern psion powers)*. But Umbra was far from the last Guardian to work with the Archer family. Raymond Archer forged an alliance with the society himself when the Pact was established in 1950, sure that their unique experience and skills would be a great asset to the protectorate. He has never been disappointed.

Today, the Guardians are the Foundation's paranormal watchdogs, and those who are sent on missions involving the supernatural and the occult. They are also included when missions require fast and quiet infiltration, and sometimes when an investigation requires... additional information from a body. Finally, they are occasionally (very rarely) asked to call upon certain lethal melee techniques they have carried down through the centuries. Of this last skill, the Guardians are more guarded than anything else – almost as if they are embarrassed by it, remorseful of some horrible atrocity in their long history.

Liaisons from the Guardian homeland are stationed at the home office of each Chamber in the Archer Conspiracy, linked to each other and to their own Control – a woman named Aurora – through what appears to be a mystic/telepathic bond. The transfer of thoughts between them is very fast, and seems to be limited to communication with Aurora herself (or at least that's what the Guardians tell the Foundation).

Aurora is not as secretive as her culture, frequently making her way into the field – sometimes with mission teams, sometimes alone. Four years ago, Aurora was captured by an enemy organization named the Assassins, for reasons as yet unknown. Since her escape, her private forays have become more common, and more pressing.

GUARDIANS OF THE WHISPERING KNIFE

The Pan-Asian Collective

Shadow Community: Everything between Mongolia and the Malaysian Peninsula, including China, Japan, India, and the Philippines; surrounding seas are shared with other neighboring Chambers.

Function: Interrogation; psychological warfare; PsiTech research; reconnaissance.

Tactics: Martial arts; computer espionage; disguise; long-term planning; stealth; telepathy and mentalism.

Organizations: Central External Liaison Department (CELD); Ministry of State Security; New China News Agency.

Headquarters: Beijing, China.

Control: Tien-Kai Tsong.

During the Second World War, the Japanese government employed small bands of secret police called the Kempei Tai. These dogged investigators rooted out subversion and betrayal with ruthless determination, took suspects into custody without warrant or cause, and relentlessly interrogated them – often to death – for information about their perceived acts of sedition.

Following World War II, most of the world was still very nervous about Asia – Japan in particular – and it privately fell to the members of the Archer Pact to ensure that the threat they posed during the conflict wouldn't extend into the Cold War. The Pact decided that Archer's Asian Chamber must take the dangers of its protectorate seriously, and that just as many of its resources be dedicated to looking inward as out.

Thus, for fifty years, the Pan-Asian Collective has been patterned after the now-disbanded Kempei Tai, whose methods – though often overzealous – were perfectly suited for their twofold mission. Though trained in the espionage schools of existing Asian agencies, Collective agents learn the fine arts of disguise and psychological warfare, how to infiltrate any group or government and wrest their secrets from them. Their lessons focus both on potential enemies and on their own governments.

Pan-Asian agents are trained to use their personal willpower to overpower their opponents and their minds to rip information directly from their foes. The Collective makes heavy use of mentalists and telepathic psions, recruiting them whenever possible; after all, how much easier is it to steal someone's secrets when you can rummage through his mind without ever saying a word?

When talk (or thought) fails, however, agents of the Collective have the training to use their bodies to physically overwhelm any and all potential threats. Knowledge of the ancient traditions of the martial arts are imparted to Collective agents, who are often considered near-superhuman by the men and women of other Chambers. From scaling sheer walls without the use of climbing gear (and sometimes without the use of their hands) to flying leaps across impossible distances to breaking bones by force of will alone, agents of the Pan-Asian Collective are considered some of the most skilled unarmed combatants in the world.

The origins of Collective martial arts trace back to the legendary Chinese hero, Wong Fei-Hung. Having saved Conrad Archer's life in 1941 (17 years after his presumed death), Fei-Hung provided the psion (and his philanthropic allies) with intense training and incredible secrets of the eastern disciplines. These became the basis for the wildly powerful martial arts learned by agents of the Pan-Asian Collective to this day.

Divorced from their families and friends (often at a very young age), Collective agents are also trained in the subtle, patient practice of deep cover operations. Once mastery with disguise is achieved, each Collective agent develops several completely different identities, each with its own distinct appearance, voice, history, and demeanor. These are tested in various places where the agent is already well-known (like his home town or former place of employment) to ensure that he is undetectable. Only when an agent can fool his family or a lover is he released into the world.

Collective agents operate alone or in small numbers, infiltrating towns, embassies, government installations, or enemy Agencies for months or years at a time and assuming one of their alternate identities for the duration. They adopt lifestyles in keeping with their assumed roles, their presentations never wavering. Then, one day when their new friends and coworkers least expect it, they strike, complete their assigned task, and vanish into the night.

The Collective's current Control is formerly of China's Ministry of State Security. A rigid military officer and veteran of the Cold War, his goal is to bring Asia out of the isolationism it cultivated after breaking with the former Soviet Union.

PAN-ASIAN COLLECTIVE

Room 39

Shadow Community: England, Ireland, Scotland; surrounding seas are shared with neighboring Chambers.

Function: Cryptography; counterterrorism; industrial espionage; investigation.

Tactics: Electronic warfare (computer hacking); small team tactics; political manipulation; discreet use of strategic force.

Organizations: Defense Intelligence Service (DIS), Government Communications Headquarters (GCHQ), Secret Intelligence Service (MI6), and the Special Air Service Regiment (22 SAS).

Headquarters: The Omnium Corporation, World Headquarters (London, England).

Control: Sarah Singleton, Omnium CEO.

From 1914 to 1919, Room 40 of the Old Admiralty Building in Whitehall was occupied by a band of crack British codebreakers whose function it was to unravel enemy ciphers. These brilliant men and women proved invaluable for the war effort, and earned themselves a permanent place in the history books. But had anyone ever realized what was happening right next door, things might be remembered much differently.

According to Royal Navy records, Room 39 was occupied by a specialized communications project during the War, but in reality the small office was devoted to psion research, with particular interest in ESP and telepathy.

Powers of the mind were considered little more than a crackpot science at the time, and were not revealed to many nations until the Treaty of Versailles in 1919. As a result, Room 39 was allotted few resources and even fewer personnel; only the endorsement of key political and military figures who believed in the operation's potential kept it going. But in time Room 39 proved just as important as its neighbor; by the start of the Second World War, the operation offered Britain more information about psion powers than any other government—and a way to use them.

During World War II, the occupants of Room 39 were moved to a larger, more comfortable headquarters, and were renamed Project MESSENGER. Their mission was also expanded from simply researching psion powers to using them in the field for active espionage. Unofficially, however, the men and women of Britain's psion branch continued to call it Room 39, and their successors have upheld the tradition. (Another name some were fond of was the Dream Suite, and still another was the Blue Room, after the color of the walls in the isolation chambers where early psions were trained.)

In recent years, England's primary role in the world's intelligence community has changed, and her unofficial psion branch has changed with it. With the Cold War over and terrorism on the increase everywhere, it has become necessary for a line of defense to be drawn; Room 39's contribution is the Ultracorps, a covert tactical squad trained to counter threats both foreign and domestic. Operating under the code name PALLADIUM, Ultracorps frequently answers the call for ready combatants in Archer's secret war. Brazen yet perfectly regimented, Ultracorps is a finely-honed weapon with only one credo: "Fortune favors the bold!"

Alongside the commandos of Ultracorps is the second half of Room 39's modern incarnation: the Broken Seal. Almost entirely composed of hacker rebels from Generations X and Y, the Broken Seal's mission is one of electronic warfare and industrial espionage. Jointly a team of computer specialists and field investigators, the Broken Seal can uncover the truth about anything or anyone, and support Ultracorps during its missions. Historically, Ultracorps has been the dominant partner in this relationship, but with the recent appointment of a hacker as Chamber Control *(see below)*, this is starting to change.

Room 39's most dangerous adversary is also perhaps their greatest smoke screen. Britain's counterespionage branch, MI5, has long suspected the presence of a rogue spy operation in the U.K., and has recently acquired reason to believe that such an organization is not only active but deeply rooted in the United Kingdom. With full approval from Parliament, MI5 is now tracking down leads in Britain, searching for their unseen foe. Sooner or later, one of those leads is going to pay off... *(For more about this conflict within the British Chamber of the Archer Conspiracy, see page 130.)*

The British Control at the moment is Sarah Singleton, the youngest Control in the Conspiracy's history and a prodigal find of the Broken Seal division. Gifted with remarkable intelligence and uncanny skill with computers, Sarah is a strong leader, if an impersonal one *(see page 135)*.

ROOM 39

The Russian Confederacy

Shadow Community: The Russian Federation; surrounding seas are shared with neighboring Chambers.

Function: Rebuilding Russia ("cleaning house"); counterespionage; military counsel; equipment and munitions supply.

Tactics: Illicit psion, chemical, and biological research; police techniques, foreign intelligence data collection; healthy black market sales.

Organizations: Federal Agency for Government Communications and Information (FAPSI), Federal Border Service (FPS), Federal Security Service (FSB), Foreign Intelligence Service (SVR), Chief Intelligence Directorate of the General Staff (GRU), Ministry of Internal Affairs (MVD).

Headquarters: Khodynke Airfield, Moscow ("The Aquarium").

Control: Chief Marshal Davros Oleksandre.

Early psion research (before the discovery and exploitation of the human genome) was limited to chemical triggering in the form of a potent serum devised by the field's pioneers *(see page 36 for more about the early awakening of psion powers)*. The serum force-awakened psion powers almost instantly, but used the subject's regular mental faculties to fuel the change. The stress was nearly always too much to bear. In the end, most subjects of this process were dead within a month; the remainder were hopelessly insane, confined for the rest of their miserable lives to hidden sanitariums, or worse.

Reasonably safe methods of nurturing psion abilities were eventually developed by the mentalists of the Archer Foundation, consisting of genetic manipulation, daily training exercises, and rigorous lifelong discipline. These discoveries were distributed throughout the Conspiracy, and serum testing eventually came to a halt. By 1950, the serum was considered obsolete, and inhumane. The Archer Pact included explicit directives ordering the destruction of all serum samples and prohibiting further serum-soldier research.

This was the second rule Russia ignored.

The first was brought to light in January, 1950, when Klaus Fuchs – a scientist at Oppenheimer's Los Alamos laboratory – confessed to being a Soviet mole, and transmitting information about U.S. atomic research to his Soviet handlers. Soon, the rest of the atomic spy ring – and the full extent of Russia's betrayal – was revealed.

The discovery could not have come at a worse time. As part of the Archer Pact, it was decided that the Russian Chamber would itself act as a mole – an entire division of moles – scattered across the nation in every military and intelligence agency. Archer's Russian agents would counter the Cold War from within.

In 1991, revolution shredded the Iron Curtain and toppled the Berlin Wall, and Russia was laid bare before the rest of the world. The image was bleak indeed. Russia's coffers were empty and her people were starving. The great Red Menace had festered from within, neglected until only a bleeding, hollow shell remained.

Of course, the Foundation was already well aware of Russia's condition, and stepped in to help the faltering giant back to its feet (suitably hobbled, of course). But when the Russian intelligence services were disassembled, new indiscretions were revealed: a thriving black market selling off global secrets and weapons of mass destruction; frightening forays into biological and chemical warfare; enemy moles and double agents in nearly every level of government; evidence of continued serum-soldier research; and worst of all, the defection of the entire Chamber under the leadership of a criminal organization dating back to the era of Stalin.

Russia is now firmly in the hands of a criminal organization known as P.E.R.I.L. (the Project for Expansion, Retribution, Iniquity, and Lies), whose roots in the Soviet espionage arena have well prepared them to combat the Archer Foundation. They have a forty-year head start in the area, allies through the government and criminal underground, and worst of all, control of Archer's Russian Chamber *(see below)*.

Archer's mission in the former Soviet Union has changed. No longer caretakers, agents now root out and gouge away corruption wherever they find it, using the nation's own system against itself. Their task is not easy. Russia's society is nearly eighty years behind the times, and many regions have fallen under mob rule. The government is a landscape of lies, treachery, and violence. And Chief Marshal Davros Oleksandre–the man who misled the Foundation for twenty years–refuses to relinquish Chamber Control. Without leaders, the soldiers on this battlefield face an entirely different kind of secret war.

RUSSIAN CONFEDERACY

ARCHER FOUNDATION

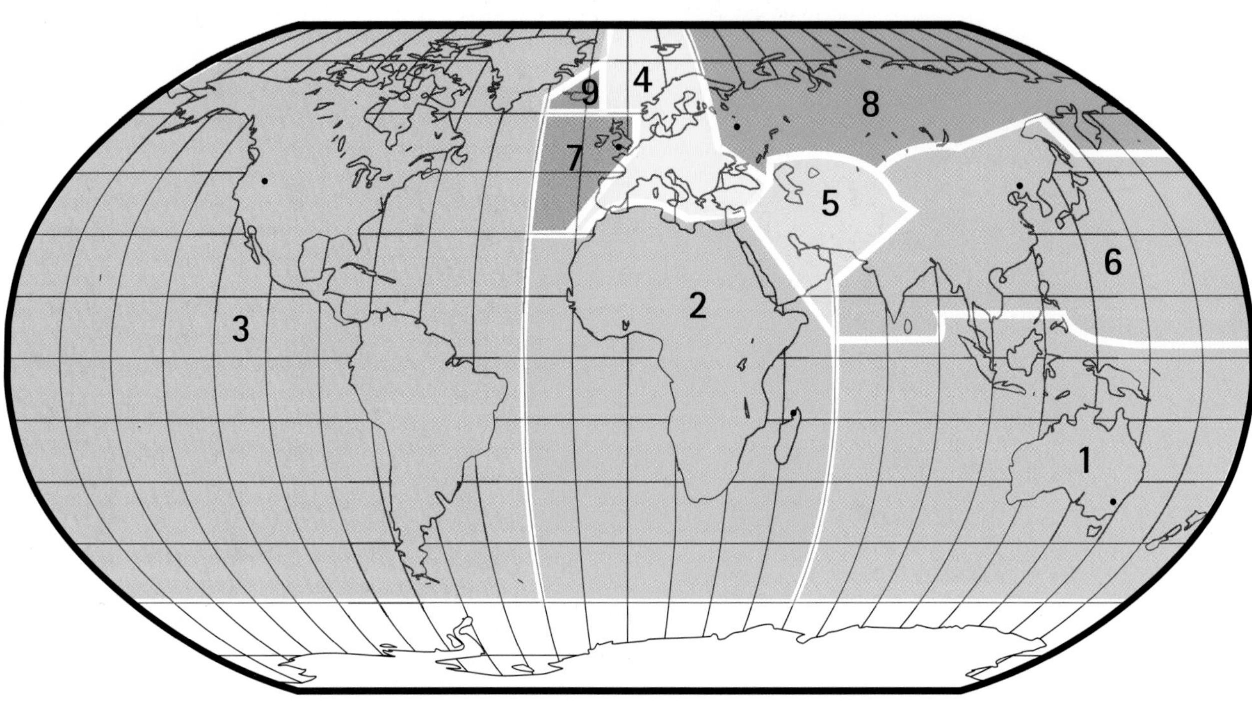

SHADOW COMMUNITY INFLUENCE ZONES

		Chamber	Headquarters
1	=	Archer Foundation	The Archer Institute for the Sciences — Canberra, Australia
2	=	African Alliance	"The Lodge" — Comorro Islands, Africa
3	=	Company	"The Kennel" — Outside Butte, Montana, USA
4	=	European Commonwealth	Mobile
5	=	Guardians of the Whispering Knife	Unknown
6	=	Pan-Asian Collective	Beijing, China
7	=	Room 39	Omnium Corporation — London, England
8	=	Russian Confederacy	"The Aquarium" — Moscow, Russian Federation
9	=	Archer Family Sanctuary	Private Subterranean Base — Iceland

• = Chamber HQ

"It's interesting how one sets out to control the future, and winds up concealing the past."

– Aurora,
The Guardians of the Whispering Knife

SHADOW HISTORY

THE GREAT LIE

For the most part, the alternate history of *Shadowforce Archer* mirrors our own. There are several points at which it deviates, however. The following sections document some of the most divergent events of the last hundred years, decade by decade, focusing on the rise of psion abilities and the birth and spread of the Archer Conspiracy. Additional information about this shadow history will be included in most forthcoming *Shadowforce Archer* supplements.

THE 1900S: DISCOVERY

The most influential divergence was also one of the first, dating back over five thousand years. In 1900, British archaeologist Sir Arthur Evans unearthed the palace of Knossos, the capital of the ancient Minoan civilization, on the Greek island of Crete. Evans recovered many relics of great historical value, including over 2,000 items inscribed with one or both of two previously unknown language systems. He named these languages Linear Scripts A and B.

As far as the world at large is aware, only Linear Script B was ever deciphered – by English architect Michael Ventris in 1953. Ventris determined that Linear B was in fact an archaic Greek dialect, though it was clearly much earlier than any previously found (being 700 years older than the earliest classic Greek). Linear Script B is now considered the oldest known Indo-European writing system in existence.

Linear Script A, on the other hand, has always remained something of a mystery – at least to the world at large. In truth, the method for unraveling it was found several months after Evans' initial discoveries on Crete, during an investigation of a storeroom buried far beneath Knossos. Much by accident, two of Evans' assistants – Sir Avery Schillingsfield and his wife, Evelyn – stumbled onto an even deeper level, previously unknown to the explorers. The area contained a hidden tomb, holding the remains and collected treasures of a ruler preceding the famed Minos, and indeed the whole of the Minoan empire. Among these treasures was a remarkable stone tablet, explaining Linear Script A with startling simplicity.

Being inherently ambitious (though not particularly ethical), Sir Avery concealed the hidden room and kept it from his colleagues as he deciphered bits and pieces of Linear Script A. All the while, his wife, who had mysteriously fallen ill shortly after their secret discovery, grew weak and frail *(see page 36 for more about her)*. Eventually, Avery was forced to return her to the comfort of the British Isles, where he volunteered to continue studying the recovered fragments of Linear Script A, in the hopes of securing a refined translation and a place in history.

What he eventually found would change the world. His work revealed that Linear A was mathematical in nature, intended to measure, define, evaluate, and even explore the world with incredible precision. The script was created by a culture that predated the Minoans, which had made unbelievable scientific leaps before a sudden, unexplained decline. They understood much about science that "modern" thinkers of the late nineteenth and twentieth centuries were only just rediscovering – and even more that had not yet been considered.

One such discovery was, according to the translations, so incredible that the pre-Minoans had buried it in their final years, in the center of a labyrinth deep within a mountain on the Greek mainland. Schillingsfield, now obsessed with unraveling the secrets of the pre-Minoans, pulled every string he had to fund an expedition to the labyrinth's location, and set out for Greece.

In the spring of 1903, Schillingsfield set out for the Greek mainland with European explorer Conrad Archer, where they clandestinely scoured the area until they found an entrance to the subterranean maze. It took another three weeks before Schillingsfield and Archer discovered what they calculated to be the exact center of the maze. Breaking down an ancient stone wall, they entered another room, lost for countless centuries, and carefully picked their way through the darkness. The room was vast, and its odd dimensions confused the explorers, but it was apparently empty.

After several days of searching, the pair finally accepted their fate – either there was no discovery to be made, or Schillingsfield's translations had been wrong. But while gathering their gear to leave, Archer's thumb grazed a sharp spike of rock near the foundation, breaking the skin. The spike was discolored, but appeared harmless, so Archer ignored the minor injury and returned to his packing.

The truth of what had happened to him would not be discovered for eight years.

THE 1910S: STRIFE

The world underwent radical changes during the 1910s. Europe plunged into the first global war, industrialization put an indelible mark upon the nature of combat, and Russia endured a bloody revolution which changed the face of modern politics. The century was really coming into its own, though it was a painful journey and cost humanity many years of peace.

The craft of espionage shared in this sweeping, turbulent change. Though an important part of world affairs in the past, intelligence-gathering took a front seat during World War I (1914-1918), as cryptography and SIGINT (Signals Intelligence) became the new weapons of the age. Transmitting coded messages and deciphering those of the enemy doomed and saved countless lives. Intelligence-gathering agencies, however, were still quite primitive, and some nations (most notably the United States) had no established information centers at all.

Against this backdrop, the drama begun with the discoveries on Crete continued. Conrad Archer now had a son, Raymond, but even fatherhood could not quell his wanderlust, and Conrad soon found himself traveling to the four corners of the earth in search of the past.

In 1911, during an exploratory hike in Peru, Conrad and two others were caught in crossfire during a border dispute. Without hesitation and lacking any weapons, Conrad suddenly burst into action, subduing several gunmen and routing the rest. After the shooting stopped, his companions were shocked at his prowess. They said that he moved "like the fastest, strongest man they had ever seen." Unsure what had happened, Conrad tried to recall the attack without success; the moment was little more than a blur in his mind.

Unable to explain the incident, Conrad focused on the situation at hand. In time, the expedition uncovered the lost city of Machu Picchu, which to this day is heralded as one of the greatest archaeological discoveries of all time. Conrad returned to his home in London with newfound wealth, looking forward to a few quiet years with his wife and son.

Nine months later, while Conrad was visiting a friend in Gravesend east of London, young Raymond wandered off on his own. Conrad noticed a few moments later, just as the boy was stepping out in front of an oncoming motor car, and raced across ten yards and into the path of the speeding auto. A moment later, unaware of what had happened, he found himself behind the vehicle, which had swerved off the road and into a ditch.

The driver and his friend agreed about what they'd seen: Conrad Archer had scooped the child up into his arms, and rushed forward, *up onto and over the moving car!*

Scarcely aware of what he'd done, but somehow sure that it had happened, Conrad Archer stammered out an apology, offering to pay for any damages. But the driver ignored him, pressing for an explanation of his incredible feat. When the explorer could provide none, the driver asked him to see him in his London office, explaining that he was a "doctor of sorts." Archer, unsure and a little frightened by what was happening, agreed to meet with the man, who gave the name "Glentry."

Over the following three months, Glentry's office – the Society for Psychical Research (SPR) – probed Conrad Archer's background, searching for the source of his unusual abilities. They studied him closely and, on three separate occasions, were able to trigger his latent reflexes. Eventually, they decided that Archer's condition was too complicated, too incredible, for the Society to handle alone. They offered him the chance to join a group which could help him, an office within British Intelligence devoted exclusively to the study of psychic phenomena, with whom the Society occasionally worked: Room 39. Archer agreed to the transfer and spent many weeks in the "Dream Suite," under the careful observation of Britain's finest unconventional minds.

Room 39 determined early on that Conrad was "channeling" the abilities of one or more highly-skilled combatants, and that his body was reacting to the experience with increased strength, speed, and durability. But the real breakthrough came that winter, when an unusual woman appeared at the Dream Suite's door claiming to know how Conrad Archer had gained his amazing powers.

The woman called herself Umbra, and spoke with a thick accent. She dressed in dark robes which concealed her form and, as the agents of Room 39 later discovered, a wide array of lethal weapons.

Umbra never revealed how she had entered the Old Admiralty Building undetected, or how she had known to go there in the first place. She merely explained that Conrad Archer was now the vessel of one-third of the greatest power the world had ever seen, and calmly waited to be invited in.

After a lengthy conversation that bred more questions than answers, Room 39 had some idea what was going on. The hidden chamber in the Greek labyrinth had indeed held a great treasure – an alchemical formula which had forever transformed Conrad Archer when he'd nicked his thumb on the stone spike. The change was irreversible and had given him incredible physical abilities. His blood was now a diluted version of the formula, and a serum could be developed from it to temporarily instill the ability in others.

The Dream Suite researchers (not to mention Conrad Archer himself) were stunned, but Umbra continued, telling them that Avery Schillingsfield's discovery on Crete had released a great evil – a mystic creature which was now festering inside Schillingsfield's crazed wife, Evelyn, growing stronger and more insane by the year. If left unchecked, she would eventually become a monster the likes of which no one could possibly comprehend. The being's only weakness was the formula in Conrad Archer's veins, and the two companion samples buried in other ancient sites around the world.

Finally, Umbra delivered the real bombshell: Avery Schillingsfield had heard about Conrad's remarkable awakening and returned to his translations. Obsessed with gaining similar power, he'd traveled to Egypt and scavenged the ruins of Akhenaton IV. The second formula – the key to awakening higher mind functions – was already his.

The Dream Suite researchers questioned Umbra at length, trying to determine where she came from, who she worked for, and how she knew so much about the pre-Minoan formula, but those answers would not come until much later *(see page 100 for much more about Umbra's group)*. Instead, she focused on the third formula, which – until the late 19th century – had been buried on the Kibo summit of Mount Kilimanjaro. German missionaries had collected the relic which held the formula, and sold it off on the black market. Now it could be anywhere.

Umbra offered to remain with Room 39 until the third formula was found and safely locked away again. The agency graciously accepted her, though she never quite fit in; in fact, during the years she worked with them, no one ever saw her face.

For the next three years, Room 39 scoured the markets and museums of the world (legal and illicit), searching for the lost relic: a tribal statue in the shape of a chameleon. But it remained hidden until 1915, when an American collector claimed to have acquired it for his private preserve.

Room 39 purchased the artifact and arranged to have it shipped across the Atlantic on the transport liner *Lusitania*. But as the ship neared the coast of Ireland, it was torpedoed by a German U-Boat and sunk. Over a thousand people died, and the relic was presumed lost at sea. (Unknown to Conrad Archer and his allies in Room 39, the sinking of the *Lusitania* was no accident – it was the work of Evelyn Schillingsfield and her new allies in Germany.)

The sinking of the *Lusitania* is considered a major contributing factor in the United States' entry into the Great War, which brought the conflict into sharp focus for the men and women of Room 39. Many of them desired to do more than just parse codes, and the agency lost many good operatives who volunteered for combat duty at the front.

In 1919, seven months after the fighting ended, one of them did. From the moment he realized his incredible powers, Conrad Archer felt the pressure of responsibility upon him, and Umbra's startling revelations only increased the urge to use his powers in the service of humanity. So, against the better judgment of all involved, he traveled to France and, behind closed doors, offered the serum made from his blood to the assembled leaders at the Treaty of Versailles.

THE 1920S: RESEARCH

Conrad Archer's decision changed the world. With most of the world's nations able to produce psychic soldiers – all but Germany, which was left out of the summit – the landscape of politics and war began to shift. The obvious application of Conrad's physical abilities to espionage made the craft all that much more important, and most of the '20s were spent developing agencies and programs geared to take full advantage of the tools at hand.

Still, knowledge of Conrad's gift remained largely under wraps. As a condition on his offer, Conrad demanded that the world leaders at the summit agree in writing to keep the number of people in the know to a minimum, and threatened to withhold serum samples which could not be generated without fresh samples of his blood if they broke his trust. In effect, one man held the entire world hostage during this decade.

Archer remained with Room 39 throughout the '20s, and together they kept knowledge of the remaining two samples from all others. With Umbra's help, the Dream Suite rapidly grew into the world's premiere "psion intelligence agency" (named after the term Umbra used to describe Conrad's abilities – psion powers), and the hunt for Evelyn and Schillingsfield continued. The former was never seen during this decade, lying low and spreading her tendrils across Europe *(see the timeline for more)*, but the latter eventually emerged in 1923.

Raymond Archer (now twelve) was staying at the Dream Suite, nurturing the abilities he'd inherited from his father. The researchers were keen to determine the extent of his abilities, and the probability of recreating his spontaneous awakening. Equally curious, Avery Schillingsfield infiltrated the Dream Suite – using incredible gadgets his new intellect had devised – and kidnapped the boy.

A rescue operation was immediately mounted by Room 39's commander at the time, Captain Mansfield Cumming ("C"). As one of his last acts with the service (and MI6), Cumming personally led the mission, which also included Raymond's father and the infamous Sidney Reilly, a psion soldier (or *physical adept*, as the thinkers called them) created from the Archer research.

The operation took the team across the English Channel into Holland, where Schillingsfield had perverted an SPR cell into a personal cult dedicated to his twisted vision. Convinced that the physical adept formula could be harvested from Raymond, the first of a new generation of spontaneous psions, Schillingsfield was only moments from performing the operation when Cumming's team arrived.

The battle that followed was short and bloody. None of Schillingsfield's followers were psions, nor were they prepared to face trained operatives. Schillingsfield himself escaped by virtue of a remarkable device that produced an inch-thick rubbery barrier none of the pursuers could break down. The barrier dissolved minutes later, but Schillingsfield was already long gone. With Raymond once again safe, the agents returned to their home office and immediately went about increasing security.

The remainder of the 1920s was quiet, though sad. Within days after returning from the rescue mission, Captain Cumming became seriously ill and retired. He died three months later, the result (it was later learned) of incompatibility with psion serum. Non-latents fuel their abilities, quite literally, with their own lives.

The 1930s: Descent

As the 1930s commenced, it became clear that the world was growing worse. Depression gripped the United States and turmoil rocked Europe. Nations all over the world were rallying toward something big, but no one was entirely sure what it was.

Russian intelligence agencies entered their second major revolution as the NKVD was born, and U.S. espionage endured growing pains, still hindered by rampant isolationism and a cautious administration.

As at the dawn of the century, Europe found itself at the front line of global change, as the Spanish Civil War erupted and a new threat loomed in the future: Adolf Hitler (hereafter referred to as the Demagogue) and his Nazi regime, bent on bringing the world to its knees.

After 1938, when Germany occupied Austria and seized INTERPOL's home office, Room 39 targeted the Demagogue as an especially dangerous foe. It was then, during a routine scouting mission, that one of its agents first sighted Evelyn Schillingsfield at his side.

The Dream Suite immediately went into action, planting bugs and collecting data. Within weeks, they had gathered enough information to make them very, very afraid. Now operating under the name "Eva Kraus," the creature who was once Avery Schillingsfield's wife was apparently using the Demagogue and his war machine to collect items of mystic power for purposes then unknown. She had also convinced the Demagogue that psion abilities were a gift from God, and that he had been cheated out of them by the other nations of the world. "Now," she told him, "it is time we took back what is ours... our birthright!"

The end of the 1930s ushered in the second global war within 25 years, as the Demagogue annexed Czechoslovakia, then invaded Poland. Europe's production of physical adepts increased twice over, and would have tripled if Room 39 had not been so prudent with their serum surplus. Militaries and spy agencies all across the world expanded almost out of control. But the true threat – Avery Schillingsfield – was yet to be seen.

The 1940s: Trial

The 1940s saw the world poised at the very brink of collapse. Psion soldiers operated in the intelligence agencies of every nation in the world (save Germany, which had its own powerhouse in Eva Kraus). The Japanese secret police known as the Kempei Tai operated with impunity thanks to prime minister Hideki Tojo, one of their former operatives. The killer elite SMERSH stalked the icy wastes of Russia, ready and willing to wage the Great Patriotic War. President Roosevelt sent General "Wild Bill" Donovan on a fact-finding mission to Europe, preparing for a conflict America refused to accept. And in England, Winston Churchill organized the Special Operations Executive (SOE) to set Europe ablaze.

During World War II, Room 39 moved, expanded, and received many additional resources to wage the war against the Nazis. It also gained a number of significant allies, each of whom played an important part in the conflict. Raymond Archer, now in his 30s and a full-blown physical adept, was recruited into the agency, as were many German agents turned by Operation DOUBLE-CROSS (the British operation that turned dozens of German infiltrators during the war). The first and most prolific of the turned Germans was codenamed Snow, and volunteered to become a physical adept early on, working closely with the Archers throughout the war.

The 1940s were a wild and uncontrolled period of espionage history, as agents everywhere were swept up in the chaos of war and world change. Especially after the Japanese attack on Pearl Harbor brought the U.S. into the war and Nazi atrocities came to light, it was obvious that nothing would ever be the same again.

The private struggles of Room 39 were drawn into the foreground in early 1944, after the U.S. formed its own covert action and intelligence service, the Office for Strategic Services (OSS). The head of the OSS's Bern office, Allen Dulles, was a known quantity. He'd worked alongside the New York British Security Coordination (BSC) commanded by Sir William Stephenson (codename Intrepid), a trusted Dream Suite operative. These two men assisted each other regardless of the petty rivalries between their agencies, and produced perhaps the most startling intelligence of the war: a direct communiqué to the Demagogue from one of his lieutenants, referred to as Shiva. The message was ENIGMA-coded with the M4 SHARK machine, but the British had cracked even that variant of the cipher by this point in the war.

The transmission was a status report on a secret operation (codenamed AVATAR) taking place on the island of Crete, which the Germans had captured the previous year. According to the report, the lower ruins on the island (where the original Linear Script A tablet was discovered) held the key to locating a "being of equal power to my own, which we are mere weeks or even days from unearthing."

This information was not received well at the Dream Suite, where Umbra confirmed that at least one other being like the one inside Eva was known to exist. Room 39 launched an ambitious operation (codenamed GODSMASHER) to attack the island and eliminate Eva once and for all. Both Archers, Snow, Umbra, and several other "Guardians of the Whispering Knife," along with a unit of mundanes, arrived ready for battle, only to find themselves facing a most unexpected foe: mind-controlled Nazi troops.

Based on information provided by the Guardians of the Whispering Knife, Room 39 had long suspected that the final formula imparted telepathy, including mind control. Now, on the shores of Crete, they could see the result: Nazi shocktroops who would fight to their last breath, and do everything in their power – up to and including sacrificing themselves – to win the war. Beyond their ranks, the increasingly monstrous Eva Kraus stood poised, minutes from unleashing another mystic horror upon the world.

The Archer Foundation still marks the battle waged on Crete during the final months of the war as the most profound use of non-conventional weapons and tactics during the first half of the century. In the end, dozens of Nazi troops lay dead across the island, many of the Cretan ruins were destroyed (including the original pre-Minoan site where everything began), Conrad Archer lay in critical condition, and Umbra was dead.

Eva Kraus still lived, but with the destruction of the pre-Minoan site her search for the companion entity was thwarted for the time being. Also, Operation GODSMASHER had yielded an important prisoner – German General Mannheim Kreipe, whose information about Eva's zombie minions proved invaluable for the war effort. According to his testimony, the dominated troops were controlled by the Demagogue himself, and their instinct, their intuition, was reduced when they were far from him. This gave agents of the Allied psion agencies the edge they needed against the Nazis' secret weapon, but it also meant that Eva had used the third formula not on herself, as previously suspected, but on the Demagogue, transforming the terror of Europe into a menace of global proportions.

There was some hollow consolation. Through Kreipe's debriefing, the Guardians determined that Eva's mystic companion was not found on the island. Her hunt for the god-king would continue.

Through the late spring of 1945, the war in Europe made a decisive turn as the Red Army pushed through eastern Germany. Rumors persisted that the Demagogue had taken his own life in a bunker in Berlin, but Room 39 didn't believe them for a moment.

Then in late April, while recovering from the injuries he suffered on Crete, Conrad Archer received a private summons to a remote location in Italy, signed by Avery Schillingsfield. The note demanded that he alert no one, and warned that millions would die if he failed to answer. Recognizing it as a trap but knowing that Schillingsfield had all the tools to carry out his promise, Archer slipped off to meet the madman alone.

He was never heard from again.

Three months later, Schillingsfield's greatest achievement – the atom bomb – destroyed two cities, ended the war, and ushered in a new and terrible age. The power of the bomb created an atmosphere of global paranoia, which resonated sharply through the halls of Room 39 when another envelope arrived later the same year. It contained a copy of a letter Albert Einstein had written to propose the weapon's fundamentals and a discreet picture of one Julius Preston (a.k.a. Avery Schillingsfield), who'd worked on the Manhattan Project. The message was clear: Schillingsfield had gone completely over the edge, severing all ties with his former life, and was now dabbling in world destruction. He had thrown down the gauntlet that could potentially lead to another World War – a final, terrible war that could only end in the extinction of the entire human race – and he was daring Room 39 to stop him.

The 1950s: Consequence

By the start of the 1950s, the "Cold War" was in full swing. America and Russia stood as polar opposites in a race for strategic and arms superiority, with the rest of the world caught in the middle. But the Cold War would not be fought so much as waged by agents of both nations, trying to outwit, outmaneuver, and outlast each other in a never-ending slow-boil of hysteria.

Raymond Archer, now absolutely dedicated to the cause of world peace – to stopping threats like Schillingsfield, Eva, and the Demagogue from ever endangering anyone again – decided it was time to fight back. On May 8, he and six other members of the world's intelligence community met in the headquarters of his newly-formed front organization, the Archer Institute. The need for an organized defense against Schillingsfield and others like him was obvious, but they still required a plan. This summit provided one.

They started with what the world perceived to be the opposing "superpowers," Russia and the United States. The former head of the Eastern Bloc fell under the purview of the Russian Confederacy, which focused on maintaining order and level heads behind the Iron Curtain. Their goal, at least for the time being, was internal control, with only marginal foreign interest.

The United States Chamber continued the early efforts of Allen Dulles and Frank Wisner, who helped to found the CIA. They paralleled the CIA's organization, function, and intent, but ultimately, the Conspiracy's "Company" answered to the Foundation.

Room 39 continued to monitor the United Kingdom and surrounding water zones, and retained their cryptography and psion research.

The Guardians of the Whispering Knife, already well known to Raymond Archer and his Foundation and bound to Middle Eastern affairs by ancient tradition, were also trusted with guarding Africa and its satellites.

The Asian states (Japan, China, Indochina, Korea, and their neighbors), largely misunderstood by those present at the summit, were grouped together as the "Pan-Asian Collective" and charged with "their own internal affairs."

That left Europe, still a hotbed of rivalry and revolution, torn between East and West with no foothold for peace and security. But Raymond Archer had come prepared – with an old friend of his father's, Bruno Vangeli. A private citizen with no allegiances to any government or political system, Vangeli represented the best hope for the suffering region, and all other Chambers were charged with assisting him in his mission to reunify and strengthen the area.

Finally, the Archer Foundation paid the bills (no one asked where the money came from), kept things running, and supervised the others.

This system was tenuous at best, especially in the early months of the Cold War when nothing was certain and hostilities threatened to erupt anywhere at a moment's notice. Fortunately, however, the first few years of the Cold War were fought away from the public eye, giving the Archer Conspiracy the time it so desperately needed to get its footing.

The 1960s: Scandal

The 1950s is widely considered the "covert action era." In contrast, the 1960s are typically referred to as "the era of disasters." The first came in April of 1961, when parts of the Company, acting well outside their charter and without the permission of the Foundation, involved the Chamber in the "Bay of Pigs," the exile invasion of Cuba intended to kill Fidel Castro. The invasion ended in abject failure, resulting in hundreds of deaths and millions of dollars lost.

It also uncovered revelations about the U.S. Chamber – that the Company was involved in many other unapproved paramilitary operations, and that they had established the MKULTRA research program to study the effects of drugs, torture, and even variants of psion serum on human subjects, many of whom were unwitting or unwilling.

Officially, the Bay of Pigs affair tarnished the reputation of the U.S., and infuriated President Kennedy, who reportedly wanted to "tear the CIA into a million pieces" for their recklessness. But he settled for the resignations of Allen Dulles (the man who made Archer's American Chamber the powerhouse of the Cold War) and Richard M. Bissel, Jr. (the brain trust behind the invasion). Dulles' replacement was John A. McCone, a former chairman of the Atomic Energy Commission, who was completely unaware of the Foundation and its mission. Effectively, this isolated the Company within the U.S. government, making them an agency of moles operating without sanction.

Worse, the Bay of Pigs prompted a reorganization of the CIA, creating a Technical Sciences Division under the Deputy Director of Plans (DDP), who was also uninvolved in the Conspiracy. As a result, much of the CIA's research (including some Foundation secrets) fell into the hands of the uninformed. Loose ends abounded concerning the U.S. Chamber, and many remain today.

Meanwhile, the Soviet Union and the United States vied for the lead spot in the ever-escalating space race, a project that appeared all-consuming on both fronts. To the West, the space race was the pet project of President John F. Kennedy, a man completely uninvolved (though some say not entirely uninformed) with the Archer Conspiracy, while in the East, the race continued under the direction of the Russian Confederacy. Conspiracy resources won the first round of the space race, as Russian astronaut Yuri Gagarin orbited the Earth in the *Vostok I* spacecraft in late 1961. Many more victories would go to the Russians through the next thirty years.

But the real action between Russia and the United States went on behind the scenes. The age of espionage was in full swing, and spies were everywhere. Russians infiltrated the U.S., and vice versa, and both sides spied on everyone else as well. Many such operations were orchestrated (or countered) by the Archer Conspiracy, but many more were not. To maintain the veil of secrecy worldwide required a good deal of distance in many cases, which in turn allowed the unknowing governments of the world plenty of room to continue their own operations. This led to a period of mass chaos, when the Conspiracy's loose structure failed to identify everyone who was a friend – and everyone who wasn't. In the end, most Archer operatives simply lived by their instincts like everyone else, and trusted in the chain of command. The Foundation pulled the strings largely without incident during this decade.

Elsewhere, tensions were rising to a fever pitch. In Africa, racial confrontations spiked, several times erupting into violence and finally sparking into an open civil war with the suspicious death of Prime Minister Patrice Lumumba in 1961. Behind the scenes, the African Alliance strived to keep order, but with less open assistance from Room 39 and the European Commonwealth (following their respective nations' withdrawal from the African continent), the struggle was long and hard-fought.

Racial tensions also ruined the chance for lasting peace in the Middle East, as Israel seized land from its Arab neighbors, inciting the so-called "Six-Day War." It is unknown if the Guardians were involved in this conflict or its UN-assisted resolution.

In Berlin, a concrete wall 28 miles long and 5 feet high was constructed by the Communist party, physically dividing a nation already torn asunder by war and social strife. Until the barbed wire went up, the European Commonwealth's effort to relocate East German refugees saved more than 10,000 lives. After that, early cooperation with the Russian Confederacy saved many thousands more.

The decade showed its worst beginning in 1964, as the Gulf of Tonkin Resolution – settled after North Vietnamese patrol-boats fired upon U.S. destroyers – offered President L.B. Johnson sweeping military power to use in the growing Vietnam War. Four years later, the Vietcong (Vietnamese Communist forces) invaded South Vietnam in a nationwide assault, the "Tet Offensive," prompting an ever-greater commitment to a war many Americans vehemently opposed. Concurrently, several shadows (spies) unaligned with the Conspiracy watched the unfolding horror from the shadow communities of Pan-Asia, and claimed the entire war was unnecessary – the result of friction between the Pan-Asian Collective and the U.S. government (not the Company, who were clearly too busy in the 1960s to launch a war).

Soon enough, the voices stopped, the condemning shadows vanished, and the with the Vietnam War spreading and the world seemingly slipping into the self-destruction the Conspiracy was created to prevent, the finger-pointing stopped and the real work began.

THE 1970S: CHAOS

The Company regained some footing in 1966 with the appointment of Richard Helms as CIA Director. Helms' views paralleled those of the Foundation, and the Company performed many beneficial operations under his watch (including several against the parent organization during the Vietnam War).

All corners of the Conspiracy scrambled to put out fires. The Pan-Asian Collective – whether involved in starting the Vietnam Conflict or not – worked side by side with the Russian Confederacy, Guardians, and Foundation to bring the fighting to a close. The Commonwealth and Room 39 worked together to stabilize the world economy and rebuild the support network the others needed to succeed. The Company prepared to enter the war, to end it if they had to.

But in 1972 another scandal erupted in the U.S. as Nixon office "plumbers" (saboteurs) broke into the National Democratic Committee's HQ. The plumbers relied upon CIA resources, which again put the Company at risk when the break-in was discovered. Helms, who refused to cooperate with Nixon during the scandal, was fired, removing the Company's last major political ally.

Then, following 1974 accusations by the *New York Times* that the CIA was spying on the U.S. populace (among other abuses of power), the Rockefeller Commission was established to review U.S. intelligence services. The Company ducked for cover, surviving only by feeding the CIA to the media wolves. There was talk of pulling out of the nation altogether, but Archer realized that getting back in after the fallout would be practically impossible. So the Company hunkered down and endured the storm; it took years before they could rebuild.

Precious few Company personnel were present for the brutal conclusion to the Vietnam War. Against the stage of the besieged capital of Saigon, the battle raged for days as countless Vietnamese, desperate to flee the approaching Communist forces, fought to obtain a spot on the U.S. helicopters ferrying people to warships waiting in the South China Sea. In the end, thousands of South Vietnamese (and not a few military troops and Conspiracy personnel) were trapped behind the Communist enemy lines. Inquiries about the missing spies fell on deaf ears, and missions into the territory met with armed resistance. Though the Pan-Asian Collective and Russian Confederacy denied any involvement, the impediments should have been a sign of things to come. As it happened, the Foundation and its peers were busy elsewhere.

Avery Schillingsfield – still alive by virtue of the original psion sample and now calling himself "Helix" – resurfaced on an island off the coast of Africa. He'd built a prison for his personal collection of the world's most powerful psions. Helix planned to awaken latent psions across the planet while simultaneously wiping out mundanes; the scheme was countered by an Archer strike team called in by one of his own subordinates (who concluded the operation by taking over the complex as the headquarters of the newly formed African Alliance). The Operation (codenamed POISON APPLE) was one of Raymond Archer's last field missions, and garnered the Foundation pure samples of both the remaining pre-Minoan formulae (which Helix had in his possession when he was captured).

Outside the acquisition of the Lodge, the African situation only declined in the 1970s. Racial strife continued to spark brush wars across the continent, and Steven Biko – political activist and mentor of Elias Graham (*see page 71*) – became one of the most high-profile casualties of the struggle, a victim of South African police brutality. Biko's death was a bitter pill for Tendaji to swallow, following his stint working for the madman Helix, and haunts him to this day.

Decisive victories were made by the end of this decade. First and foremost were the Strategic Arms Limitation Talks (SALT) between the U.S.S.R. and U.S. superpowers, which resulted in unprecedented scale-backs in nuclear arms construction. Second was the continuing space race, now under the joint shadow direction of the Russian Confederacy and the Company, with assistance from the Foundation and others. Great strides were made this decade away from the public eye, including many early experiments that would prove the foundation for today's OVERWATCH project (*see page 56*).

The 1980s: Deconstruction

Acquisition of the two remaining formulae changed the Foundation and its allied Chambers. Telepathic and mentalist psions were trained and incorporated into the ranks, and the Shop was formed to build wondrous technical "gadgets" for use in the field. The power and tools at agents' disposal were more numerous and more versatile than ever before; for this reason, the late 1970s and beyond are now referred to by Archer as the Age of the Superspy.

The 1980s saw many incredible operations, some stemming from very old Foundation concerns. Reagan's "Star Wars" program was aborted (though money would continue to funnel into it until 1993), and Archer launched its first long-term space platform, *Overwatch*. Countless destructive moles, sleepers, and double agents were ferreted out of the system (especially in the U.S.). Archer took steps to reduce the number of nuclear weapons in the world. Parts of Africa were liberated from oppression. And Communism was dismantled, prompting reconstruction in Europe and Russia.

The enemies changed in the 1980s, growing more insidious than ever before. The rise of terrorism and computer hackers gave rise to a revamped version of Room 39, broken into two cooperative halves – the Broken Seal (comprised of computer specialists) and Ultracorps (comprised of counter-terrorists and urban warfare specialists). This change also moved the last of Room 39's psion research and gadget creation into the hands of the Archer Foundation, where it remains today.

There were tragedies as well – the situation in the Middle East worsened considerably, leaving the Guardians in charge of a precarious region; Chernobyl and the Space Shuttle *Challenger* both exploded with lethal results, and the Foundation's best minds came to suspect that several outbreaks of ebola and other virulent contagions might be something more than just medical diseases. But by the end of the decade, it was becoming clear that the Foundation and its Chambers were finally striking a happy balance. At last there was some order.

The 1990s to Now: Rebirth

The modern world has witnessed the passing of many aging foes, slipping away with the dawn of the millennium. Communist Russia is gone and the Cold War is over. Equality has replaced apartheid. And Europe is poised to enter an unprecedented age of community.

But new threats have replaced the old. Ancient hatred fuels violence in Yugoslavia. Religious tension in the Middle East is flaring up. The grim specter of terrorism looms over even the most powerful nations of the world.

The Archer Foundation saw all of these things, and prepared for them. They prevented countless disasters throughout the 1990s, staving off social unrest, political upheaval, and coordinated terrorist attacks, but they could never have envisioned the storm brewing in their own back yard.

In 1991, as the Foundation celebrated the fall of the Iron Curtain and Russia's freedom from the Communist yoke, they instead found themselves at the mercy of an enemy organization which had usurped not only most of the Russian government but their own Chamber in the area as well. The Project for Expansion, Retribution, Iniquity, and Lies (P.E.R.I.L.) had long-since gathered the necessary resources for a protracted secret war, and as liaisons from the Foundation arrived, threw down the gauntlet. All four Foundation representatives were shipped home in pieces. *(For more about P.E.R.I.L. and the current struggle in Russia, see page 136–137.)*

For the last ten years, the Foundation has coordinated operatives within the hostile wilds of P.E.R.I.L. -controlled Russia, a task which has consumed their every available moment. The effort has stolen time from countless smaller projects deserving of the Foundation's attention, including many minor problems festering around the world – and still another problem among their own ranks.

In 2001, without warning, a large portion of the Archer Conspiracy's mentalists – all members of the Research and Development department known as the Shop – broke away, forming their own rival agency.

The reasons for the Shop's secession are as yet unknown, as are their true goals as an independent entity. The Foundation is reasonably certain, however, that they do not intend to bring its existence to light (or they already would have). The Shop has no compunction about fighting and even killing their former allies, and has even left behind some nasty surprises for Foundation agents – from sabotaged gadgets to disloyal agents and specialists.

Thus the Archer Conspiracy has entered a dangerous new era, when friends have become enemies and shades of gray dominate the espionage arena. Now, they must save the world not only from itself, but also from enemies of their own creation.

A Century of Turmoil

This timeline includes both *Shadowforce Archer*-specific information and items of general espionage and world interest.

Before 1900

1881: Kempei Tai and Black Ocean Society formed.

1882: Society for Psychical Research (SPR) established.

The 1900s

1900: Archaeologist Sir Arthur Evans discovers the palace of Knossos on the island of Crete, as well as samples of Linear Scripts A and B.

1901: Sir Avery Schillingsfield and his wife, Evelyn, discover a level beneath Knossos, containing a tablet that can help decipher Linear Script A. Evelyn grows ill and must be returned to London, where Avery secretly continues his researches into the lost language.

Black Dragon Society formed by Ryohei Uchida, a leading member of the Black Ocean Society.

1902: Evelyn Schillingsfield is committed to an asylum after a mental breakdown. Sir Avery, now quite obsessed, focuses his efforts on gaining the knowledge of the culture that created Linear Script A. Within the year, he organizes an expedition to mainland Greece, where "one of their greatest treasures" is buried.

1903: Schillingsfield and European explorer Conrad Archer seek out an ancient labyrinth of Greek myth, where the first of three Minoan alchemical formulae is discovered. Conrad Archer is unwittingly exposed to the formula, and awakens as the century's first psion. His abilities don't immediately manifest, however, and the expedition returns home, seemingly empty-handed.

Evelyn Schillingsfield comes out of her stupor and escapes the asylum. She is not seen again until 1915.

1904–1905: Russo-Japanese War.

1905: U.S. Bureau of Investigation formed.

1906: *HMS Dreadnought*, the first modern battleship, is launched from Britain.

1907: Britain's Room 39 studies the practical applications of psion powers for spying.

1908: Germany launches the Nassau, its version of the *HMS Dreadnought.*

Raymond Archer (Conrad's son) is born.

THE 1910S

1911: Conrad Archer narrowly escapes death during Hiram Bingham's expedition to the Andes Mountains. He only survives by virtue of his newly-awakened psion abilities (he is the century's first physical adept).

1912: Archer's strange case attracts the attention of the Society of Psychical Research, who recruit him as a test subject. Within weeks, his growing power becomes evident, and he is drafted into Room 39 for further study.

Shortly after acquiring Conrad Archer, Room 39 is contacted by agents of the Guardians of the Whispering Knife, who claim to know where his powers come from. They also warn of the danger posed by the mystic creature inhabiting Evelyn Schillingsfield.

The Guardians try, and fail, to prevent Avery Schillingsfield from acquiring the second Minoan formula, hidden among the Egyptian ruins of Akhenaton IV. Schillingsfield takes this sample himself, becoming the century's first mentalist *(see page 179).*

1913: Turkey cedes Crete to Greece as a result of the Balkan Wars.

1914–1918: The Great War.

1914–1919: Room 40 cracks codes and ciphers for the British. Never do they suspect that Britain's psychic research division is right next door.

1915: The third and final Minoan formula is discovered in a relic originally buried high on the Kibo summit of Mount Kilimanjaro. The relic remains hidden until Room 39 tracks it down in the U.S. and arranges for it to be transported to England on board the Cunard liner *Lusitania.*

The transport liner *Lusitania* is sunk by a German U-Boat captured by Evelyn Schillingsfield, who exhibits incredible mystic powers and knowledge. She steals the third formula and scuttles the submarine, leaving the crew for dead. No trace of her presence is found.

1917: Partly due to hysteria generated by the *Lusitania* attack, the U.S. enters the Great War.

Bolshevik Revolution and birth of Communism in the Soviet Union. Cheka is formed.

1917–1934: Soviet intelligence undergoes many revisions. The Cheka become the GPU (1922-1923), and then the OGPU (1923-1934).

1918: Mata Hari ("Agent H-21") executed.

One of Avery Schillingsfield's pet projects produces an unexpected side effect – a Spanish Flu outbreak that kills 20 million people.

1919: Treaty of Versailles. Contrary to the requests of both Room 39 and the Guardians, Conrad Archer presents himself to the world (excluding Germany, where Evelyn Schillingsfield is suspected to be operating from) – "to balance the scales," he says.

Following the Treaty of Versailles, many nations develop their own physical adepts.

League of Nations founded.

German Thule Society founded; Adolf Hitler (the Demagogue) recruited.

The 1920s

1921: Evelyn Schillingsfield – surfacing as Eva Kraus – meets the Demagogue during a Thule gathering. Five months later, she is his mistress.

1922: Mussolini comes to power in Italy.

Raymond Archer manifests as a physical adept and is studied by Room 39.

1923: The National Socialist (Nazi) Party is founded in Germany.

International Police (INTERPOL) founded in Vienna.

Raymond Archer is captured by Avery Schillingsfield, who hopes to harvest the physical adept formula from him. He fails, and Raymond is recovered by Room 39. Conrad Archer vows to see Schillingsfield dead for his actions.

1925: Sidney Reilly – one of Room 39's early physical adepts – is lured across the Soviet-Finnish border by communiqués from a Soviet disinformation organization known as the Trust, who reportedly capture and execute him.

1927: Joseph and Louisa Rhine conduct psychic (psion) research at Duke University. The Rhines, as inspired by Sir Arthur Conan Doyle, focus on experimental psychical research, leaving behind the spiritualist methods of the previous century. They coin the terms ESP and parapsychology.

1929: The Soviet NKVD suffers the first of three purges at the hand of Josef Stalin, who orders the deaths of countless leaders and operatives, trying to remove rightists from the organization.

U.S. War Department's Signals Intelligence Service (SIS) formed.

The 1930s

1930s: As the Demagogue rises to power, his fanatical search for items and knowledge of mystical potence is spearheaded by Eva Kraus, whose own power grows by the year.

Kempei Tai used by Japan's right-wing military movement to intimidate opposing politicians and arrest "terrorists" who campaign against the political order of the time.

1933: The Demagogue is appointed chancellor of Nazi Germany. Eva congratulates him with the third formula. He awakens as the century's first telepath *(see page 196)*, and quickly develops powers of mind control.

Germany leaves the League of Nations.

1934: Russia establishes the NKVD.

J.B. Rhine publishes his early findings but is widely criticized, largely due to the clandestine slander campaign initiated by spies of the nations developing physical adepts.

1935: U.S. Bureau of Investigation is renamed the FBI and given a training academy.

Ignoring his tarnished reputation, Rhine forms Duke University's Parapsychology lab.

1936: Germany occupies the Rhineland, which according to the Treaty of Versailles was to remain a demilitarized zone.

1937–1938: Two more Stalinist purges of the Red Army occur, this time targeting the GRU as well. Many GRU agents run or defect rather than face the savagery in their homeland.

1937: Three hunters sent by Eva Kraus to capture her former husband are incinerated when he arranges the explosion of their transport, the *Hindenburg* zeppelin.

1938: The Nazis occupy Austria, seizing the headquarters of INTERPOL.

1939–1945: Germany invades Poland and sparks World War II, the first major conflict in which psion soldiers play a major role. Room 39 and other intelligence agencies wage a desperate and bloody secret war against Eva Kraus and the Demagogue's mind-controlled mystic warriors.

1939: The League of Nations is suspended.

The GRU is rebuilt after the value of a General Staff is illustrated during the Soviet campaign against Finland.

The FBI is granted authority over matters of espionage and sabotage.

Rhine discovers that the crystalline compound amobarbital inhibits psychic ability.

Dichlorodiphenyltrichloroethane (DDT), a new synthetic insecticide, is used with incredible results, but some worry about long-term effects on the ecosystem. Avery Schillingsfield — part of the scientific team behind the toxin — has already moved onto a new project *(see next)*.

Albert Einstein composes a letter from U.S. physicists to President Roosevelt, explaining the possibility of developing a weapon of massive nuclear power. The option is green-lit and work begins with the British under the codename "the Manhattan Project." A chief British contributor to the project, Julius Preston, is actually Sir Avery Schillingsfield in disguise.

THE 1940S

1940: British Special Operations Executive (SOE) is formed after MI6 stations in Europe are overrun by the Nazis. The SOE is the first intelligence agency to combine intelligence-gathering with clandestine warfare (including support for resistance groups such as the French Maquis). Throughout the war, the SOE performs aggressive sabotage operations all across Europe and incites the wrath of Nazi spy-hunters.

The FBI Academy is moved to Quantico, VA.

Rhine and colleagues publish Extra-Sensory Perception After Sixty Years ("ESP-60").

1941: Pearl Harbor is bombed by the Japanese.

SMERSH ("death to spies") is created by Josef Stalin to track down moles, traitors, and deserters. They are his killer elite, strictly enforcing his "No Retreat, No Surrender" policy.

British codebreakers decipher the German ENIGMA code.

After German tanks roll into Athens, the Allies retreat to the island of Crete. German paratroopers — including Eva Kraus and her mystic relic hunters — stage a spectacular invasion of the island, seizing and holding it for the duration of the war. During the occupation, Kraus searches the Minoan ruins for information that may lead her to a companion mystic entity. Her search is fruitless.

Sir Arthur Evans dies.

1942: The U.S. Office of Strategic Services (OSS) — America's wartime covert action and intelligence agency — is formed, with General "Wild Bill" Donovan at the helm.

The SIS deciphers Japan's version of ENIGMA (the "Purple Machine"), prompting U.S. troops to invade Midway and destroy the Japanese carrier fleet.

Operation UNDERWORLD. The FBI and Mafia work together to protect the U.S. eastern seaboard. This relationship continues with the Company after the Archer Pact of 1950.

1943: (May) BRUSA Agreement. U.S. and Britain's spy agencies establish formal cooperation.

Operation MINCEMEAT. British spies dupe German High Command into thinking that the Allies intend to invade the Balkans instead of Sicily (their real objective) by creating a faux Naval officer ("Major Martin"), planting leading documents on a corpse, and dumping him from the deck of the submarine *Seraph* off the coast of Spain, where he eventually falls into German hands.

1944: British spies — including Conrad Archer and Room 39 — mount a clandestine attack on German-occupied Crete, trying to wrest it from Eva's grasp. They fail, but manage to capture German General Kreipe and smuggle him back to Egypt by submarine.

Operation QUICKSILVER. The Allies create a phantom army called the First U.S. Army Group (FUSAG) to convince the Germans that a massive Allied invasion across the English Channel is imminent. QUICKSILVER is directly commanded by Lt. Gen. George S. Patton.

1945: Victory in Europe. The Red Army seizes Berlin and Germany surrenders.

The Demagogue commits suicide in Berlin, two days before it is seized by the Soviets, and the NKVD takes charge of the city. Eva freezes his body and smuggles it out of Germany using the facilities of ODESSA and Die Spinne ("The Spider"). She is not seen again for many years.

Twenty-two years (and many battles) after vowing to destroy Avery Schillingsfield, Conrad Archer finally corners him in Italy. But it is too late to save tens of thousands as the deviant's supreme project – the atomic bomb – is dropped on Hiroshima and Nagasaki. Conrad Archer disappears.

Japan surrenders, effectively breaking the Axis and ending World War II.

Project PAPERCLIP. U.S. agencies smuggle defecting Germans out of the country after the war.

The United Nations is formed.

The OSS is disbanded.

1946–1949: Project VENONA. Messages sent from Soviet spy handlers in the U.S. to Moscow are intercepted by the SIS and slowly decoded.

After witnessing the power (and threat) of the atomic bomb – and suspecting more devastating advances to come – Raymond Archer begins laying the groundwork for a global intelligence protectorate (realized in 1950). He must do so without the guidance of his father, however.

1946: President Truman creates the National Intelligence Authority (NIA) and Central Intelligence Group (CIG) to coordinate U.S. peacetime intelligence.

1947: The Central Intelligence Agency (CIA), National Security Council (NSC), and Department of Defense (DoD) are formed by the National Security Act, which also places U.S. intelligence agencies under the direct supervision of the CIA's Director (a condition which greatly supports early Archer activities). The CIA absorbs the CIG.

UKUSA Agreement. Australian and Canadian intelligence agencies join forces with those of the U.S. and Britain.

The Rosenberg atomic spy ring hands U.S. Bomb secrets over to the Russians (as orchestrated by Raymond Archer, in preparation for his vision of global guidance).

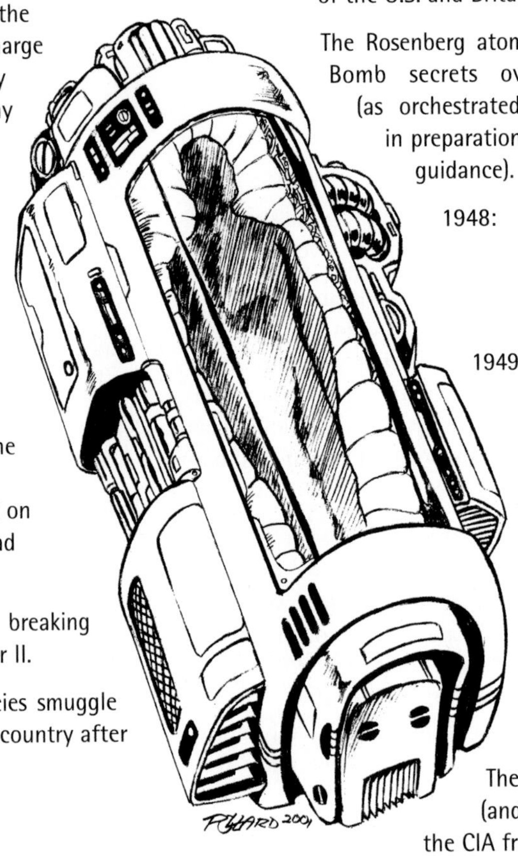

1948: The Central Institute for Intelligence and Security is formed in Israel.

1949: North Atlantic Treaty Organization (NATO) is established.

Reinhard Gehlen, a captured Soviet spy, is promoted to head of the German Federal Intelligence Service in Berlin, where he spearheads Western operations against his former handlers.

The Central Intelligence Act (and Archer's allies) exempts the CIA from disclosure laws (they don't have to reveal how much money they spend, or what it is spent on).

Radio Free Europe and Radio Liberty are organized by the CIA, ostensibly to aid their foreign operations. In truth, these are the first of many communication networks the founders of the Archer Pact set up across the globe.

The Australian Security and Intelligence Organization (ASIO) and Australian Security Intelligence Service (ASIS) are founded.

The Soviets detonate an A-bomb, spurring the CIA to send covert agents into Russia.

THE 1950S

1950s: Operation GENETRIX. The U.S. Air Force uses reconnaissance balloons to photograph targets in the Soviet Union. Nearly three hundred balloons are sent up, but only 44 are recovered. The remainder are secretly retrieved by Confederacy agents, to protect sites incidentally spotted by the balloons that violate the Archer Pact.

1950–1953: Korean War.

1950: The Archer Pact *(see page 39)*. At this time, the Pact includes the Archer Foundation, Room 39, the Guardians of the Whispering Knife, the Company, the Russian Confederacy, the Pan-Asian Collective, and the guarded Gemeinschafft Consortium.

(January) Klaus Fuchs — a scientist at Oppenheimer's Los Alamos laboratory — confesses to being a Soviet mole, and transmitting information about U.S. atomic research to his Soviet handlers.

Project BLUEBIRD. The CIA uses hypnosis and hallucinogens during interrogations and performs mind control experiments, some on North Korean POWs.

John Campbell, editor of *Astounding Science Fiction,* first uses the term "psionics."

1951: Guy Burgess and Donald Maclean vanish from their posts at the British Embassy in Washington, D.C., prompting an investigation which brings the Cambridge Spy Ring to light.

The Company sets up Radio Free Asia, expanding Archer's communications network.

1952: Allen W. Dulles — an ardent supporter of Raymond Archer for many years — is appointed to DCI of the CIA, and starts restructuring U.S. interests as a tool for global protection.

The National Security Agency (NSA) is established by a clandestine Presidential memo (most of which remains classified to this day).

Project ARTICHOKE replaces Project BLUEBIRD. The CIA expands its efforts to include many more questionable techniques, and shifts much of its operations to Europe.

The Pacific Eniwetok Atoll is wiped off the face of the earth by the first H-bomb blast.

1953: The CIA taps East German telephone lines by tunneling under their Army HQ.

Project MKULTRA replaces Project ARTICHOKE. The Company, now fully in charge of this operation, introduces serum samples as part of the drug regimen, which is unknowingly or unwillingly taken by CIA and Company operatives, prisoners, and college students across the nation.

Julius and Ethel Rosenberg, American "atomic spies" (responsible for the theft of U.S. postwar atomic secrets) are executed.

English architect Michael Ventris finds that Linear Script B is actually archaic Greek.

U.S. biologist James Watson and English biochemist Frances Crick decipher the structure of deoxyribonucleic acid (DNA), describing it as a "double helix."

1954: The KGB is established.

The "honorable correspondents" of France's External Documentation and Counterespionage (SDECE) agency are found to be thugs, gangsters, and killers, hired to commit heinous crimes.

With the Soviets developing jet bombers capable of attacking the United States, the CIA authorizes design and construction of the advanced spy plane later known as the U-2.

CIA use of an "exile invasion force" in Guatemala. The mission is a spectacular success and the "exile" model is used again many times (including during the Bay of Pigs debacle).

The U.S. Navy launches the world's first nuclear submarine, the *Nautilus.*

1955: "Gordon Lonsdale" (actually Konon Trifimovich Molody) arrives in Britain and sets up a network of spies for the Soviet Union.

The U.S. Air Force holds a classified commercial competition for spy satellite designs, codenamed PIED PIPER. This endeavor generates incredible results for U.S. space intelligence.

1956: J. Edgar Hoover launches COINTELPRO (counterintelligence programs) to neutralize what he considers destructive political and social movements. These operations directly challenge the freedoms Archer is trying to protect, and consume much of Archer's effort until they are terminated in 1971.

1957: The Soviets launch *Sputnik I*, the world's first satellite. *Sputnik II* is launched a month later.

France, West Germany, Italy, Belgium, Holland, and Luxembourg agree to set up a common trading area: the European Economic Community (EEC) – or Common Market. Some European countries refuse to join, and attempt to create a rival free-trade area. This latter effort is secretly managed by the Gemeinschafft Consortium, who seek to empower their Chamber (known from this time on as the European Commonwealth).

Raymond Archer recruits the services of a shrouded cult icon known as "Fade," and assigns him as a secondary Control in Europe.

THE 1960S

1960: (May) An American U-2 spy plane is shot down over Sverdlovsk when its engine flames out due to lack of oxygen. The pilot, Francis Gary Powers, is captured and admits to being a CIA operative. The Russians put the wreckage on public display to embarrass the Americans.

1961–1975: Air America, the CIA's covert smuggling ring operating out of Southeast Asia, operates at its peak as the largest air force in the world, contracting many ex-military flyers with high wages.

1961: The Bay of Pigs invasion, a disaster for Archer's U.S. Chamber *(see page 39).*

The Berlin Wall goes up in Germany.

A Naval Air Station in Opalocka, Florida – codenamed JMWAVE – is established to organize paramilitary operations against Cuba.

The Company founds Radio Libertad to coordinate Archer's efforts in Cuba.

Satellites are used for photographic reconnaissance. Film is jettisoned and recovered after re-entry (a maneuver called a "bucket drop").

KGB agent Anatoli Golitsin defects to the Company, with information about a Soviet spy ring – codenamed SAPPHIRE – operating deep in de Gaulle's government. Archer turns its attention to Europe, seeking to stabilize the region.

Congo Prime Minister Patrice Lumumba discovered dead; racial strife in Africa.

1962: The Cuban Missile Crisis.

With the treaty banning occupation or exploitation of the South Pole approved, Eva Kraus and her mystic army (now known as the "Hand of Glory") set up a permanent base deep in the ice, where they can work unmolested.

1963: Project MKULTRA is replaced by MKSEARCH. Secretly, the Company maintains hidden resources and personnel, and continues MKULTRA research, focusing on coupling psions to produce more powerful offspring.

The Elysee Treaty resolves some of the issues between France and West Germany, further solidifying the European Commonwealth.

1964: Gulf of Tonkin Resolution offers U.S. President L.B. Johnson sweeping power to deal with Vietnam conflict.

1965: Moroccan nationalist Mehdi Ben Barka is kidnapped and presumably murdered by the SDECE, further discrediting the organization.

During the unexpected blackout sweeping through the upper east U.S. coast, Nathan "Dante" Grier escapes from MKULTRA captivity. Over the following three weeks, he is hunted by Company agents and brainwashed psions (including his parents). He escapes to Asia using stolen Archer communication protocols, sparking an inter-Chamber incident as the Company's continued misuse of its charter is revealed. Grier vanishes shortly thereafter.

1967: "Six-day" war in Middle East raises apprehensions of coming violence in Guardian territory.

1968: Communist North Vietnamese forces mount the Tet Offensive, seizing large swaths of South Vietnamese land. The Vietnam War involves every Chamber of the Conspiracy.

THE 1970S

1970s: Archer uses vaccines to control the psion explosion caused by their own research.

1970: *Psychic Discoveries Behind the Iron Curtain* is published, revealing Soviet experiments with psychic intelligence techniques.

1971: The Russians launch the first *Salyut* orbital laboratory, a predecessor to the *Mir* station.

1972: The Strategic Arms Limitation Treaty is signed in Moscow, limiting the nuclear arms race between the U.S. and U.S.S.R.

1973: The U.K., Denmark, and the Republic of Ireland join the EEC. British feelings about being involved are mixed.

The *Family Jewels* report is issued by DCI James Schesinger, collating all known illegal and improper CIA activities. The 700-page report is still classified.

The U.S. launches the first Rhyolite satellite, which can intercept enemy transmissions.

The price of oil skyrockets, upsetting international trade and employment, as well as the combined Conspiracy effort to recover from the Vietnam War. Rumors persist that the price hike is the result of Gemeinschafft manipulation.

1975: The fall of South Vietnam's capital city, Saigon, prompts the U.S. army to airlift refugees out to warships waiting in the South China Sea.

Operation POISON APPLE. Avery Schillingsfield resurfaces after thirty years under the pseudonym "Helix." Perhaps the world's first criminal mastermind, he plots to simultaneously awaken latent psions and eradicate mundanes across the globe with a rapidly mutating pathogen derived from samples of all three Minoan formulae. The result is a mutagenic plague which awakens latent psions using surrounding mundanes as fuel. One of Helix's lieutenants, Elias "Tendaji" Graham, warns the Archer Foundation, who assault his island stronghold ("Eden") with operatives from several Chambers, including Raymond Archer himself and the mysterious "Fade." Helix is taken prisoner and his scheme prevented. One of his chief test subjects — "Two" — is recruited by Archer.

Fruits from Operation POISON APPLE include pure samples of the two formulae the Chambers are missing, which paves the way for Archer's own mentalists (the "Shop") and telepaths. The age of superspies is born.

Following Operation POISON APPLE, Elias Graham solicits Archer to allow him to form a new Chamber — the African Alliance.

1976: The Senate Select Committee on Intelligence is permanently established to oversee U.S. intelligence organizations.

The U.S. KH-11 satellite instantly beams its images to transmitters on Earth.

1977: The House of Representatives' Select Committee on Intelligence is established to work with its Senatorial counterpart. Together, these organizations forever change the way Archer's U.S. Chamber must function.

Steve Biko, South African political activist, falls victim to police brutality.

THE 1980S

1982: The French General Directorate for External Security (DGSE) is founded.

1983: The Strategic Defense Initiative ("Star Wars") program is considered by Archer too dangerous a weapon for any nation, and derailed.

1984: Project OVERWATCH. Archer launches a long-term space station (named *Orwell*) and global satellite system (named *Big Brother*).

1985: "The Year of the Spy." More than 25 Soviets "walk-in" to offer national secrets to the U.S., and over 55 Soviet moles are expelled.

The Walker family, a productive Soviet spy ring, is captured by the FBI.

1986: Meltdown at Chernobyl power plant.

Space shuttle *Challenger* explodes.

Soviet space platform *Mir* ("Peace").

Spain and Portugal join the EEC.

The German-based Chaos Computer Club starts its electronic reign of terror, hacking into U.S. military and intelligence systems and selling information to the KGB.

1988: The U.S. and the U.S.S.R. agree upon the Intermediate-Range Nuclear Forces (INF) disarmament treaty, reducing the world's nuclear threat.

1989: The Space station *Mir* is briefly unmanned after its three-man crew returns to Earth. Soviet officials cite "technical problems" as the cause.

THE 1990S

1990s: U.S.-Asian industrial espionage.

1991: The Gulf War. The CIA is lambasted when nearly all its wartime operations fail. Fortunately for Archer, the Company is uninvolved.

(December) The Soviet Union falls. The KGB is abolished and replaced by the SVR, the Foreign Intelligence Service, and several agencies for presidential and communications security. The SVR warns that a new type of spy war has begun.

1992: The Open Skies Treaty permits spy planes to conduct overflights (aerial recon) of member territories. By 1996, forty-two nations sign the agreement.

In response to the growing need for specialized anti-terrorist and computer espionage teams, Room 39 reorganizes, founding the Ultracorps and Broken Seal divisions seen today.

1993: The Maastricht Treaty renames the European Community the European Union (EU). There is strong opposition among the members; Britain is the last to ratify the Treaty.

1994: South Africa achieves full democracy and sets about rebuilding its intelligence agencies.

Aldrich Ames is arrested for selling secrets to the Soviets. Many suspect an accomplice.

1996: Swedish hackers change the CIA homepage greeting to "Welcome to the Central Stupidity Agency."

1997: Archer establishes *Aquatica*, its first oceanic operations base, in the Baltic Sea.

1998: Assembly of the *International Space Station* (ISS), the largest cooperative scientific venture in history, begins in orbit in June.

Raymond Archer retires at 88 years of age, leaving the Foundation to his protegé, "Two."

Aurora, the Guardians' Control, is captured by the Chamber's age-old enemies, the Assassins. She is liberated, but thereafter... changes *(see page 110)*.

1999: Archer's Australian (home) Chamber falls victim to a clandestine spy ring among their own shadow community (now known to be a Shop cell). The cell hacks into Archer's systems and counters its domestic operations, prompting the Chamber to arrange for the ASIO to use tracking and monitoring devices, and actively compromise computer systems, without a warrant. This decision upsets many Australian citizens and businesses, though it remains in place today.

The "Euro" currency is established, though it won't be circulated until 2002. Britain, Denmark, Sweden, and Greece remain outside the "euro zone."

NOW

2001: Robert Hanssen is arrested as a Soviet spy. It is possible he worked with Aldrich Ames.

With the *International Space Station* under way, Soviet space station *Mir* is directed out of orbit, splashing down in the Pacific Ocean.

Russia enters into agreement with NATO to combat terrorism around the globe. This momentous step is called "a unique opportunity to build a better, more stable future."

The Shop secedes from Archer.

2002: (April) The *Shadowforce Archer* storyline begins.

"Who are they? The shadows? They're you or me, given half an ounce of ego and the chance to play God!"

– Lord Reginald Savage, The Eyes of Argus

Shadow Communities

The Archer Foundation

"The chess-board is the world; the pieces are the phenomena of the universe; the rules of the game are what we call the laws of Nature. The player on the other side is hidden from us. We know that his play is always fair, just, and patient. But we also know, to our cost, that he never overlooks a mistake, or makes the smallest allowance for ignorance."

–T.H. Huxley

The Australian-based Archer Institute for the Sciences has changed much of the last fifty years, growing and learning with the times, and seeking many new avenues for research and advancement. It has transformed from a war-era think tank into a world-renowned crossroads for scientists of every field. But behind the recognition and the awards, beyond the public service, there is another layer that few ever see – the operations center for a dream of world security, the Archer Foundation.

The Foundation's Mission

In theory, the mission of the Foundation mirrors that of all its supporting Chambers. In practice, it defines them. Ultimately the Foundation has one true purpose – defending the world from any person, group, organization, or government which challenges its freedom and safety. This simple statement is not as simple, however, in a world as complex as ours. Enormous resources and careful planning are required to make the dream a reality.

Function

Archer Foundation agents tend to come in two varieties – those who remain at the Institute full-term, producing PsiTech or keeping one of the Chamber's many internal projects going, and those who venture out into the field as advisors, field executives, and specialists on loan to existing teams. The latter are more likely to become actively involved in missions outside Australia.

Many Archer field agents are psions of great power, hand-selected, trained, and sometimes even surgically or chemically augmented to awaken levels of power otherwise unseen in the natural order. Foundation psions are unrestricted in their training; mentalists, physical adepts, and telepaths all appear within its ranks.

Common Archer Operations

Foundation agents work almost exclusively on missions determined by other Chambers. Only local threats (such as the current espionage crisis between Australia and Southeast Asia) necessitate teams formed solely of Archer agents, and even then outside aid is common.

The Archer Foundation acts primarily as a management arm for the Conspiracy, fielding operatives to remain informed, to keep the other Chambers operating within established protocols, and to maintain their many connections.

Agent Expectations

Players who enjoy careful, plotting agents will find the Archer Foundation appealing. The average Foundation agent analyzes situations thoroughly before acting, and knows when and how to put spin on problems to turn them into assets. Archer agents are cunning, observant, and highly intelligent. And they are usually well-connected, having allies in many levels of government, popular society, and the underworld, not to mention the intelligence community.

Archer Foundation agents are not arbitrarily the leaders of any mission team to which they belong. Often, Archer operatives participate simply because they have special knowledge or training that might be useful on the mission. They might also know a given locale, or have strong connections there (Archer keeps hundreds of agents posted throughout the world, who make sure that data never stops pouring through the arteries of its information network). Finally, many Archer agents are psion powerhouses whose mental abilities are more than sufficient to justify their assignment.

TACTICAL DATA

The greatest tools at the Archer Foundation's disposal are the other Chambers, whom it can dispatch to counter problems anywhere on the globe with a simple encrypted message. But they do not stop there; Archer operatives are the high priests of the information age, cultivating knowledge in all its many forms – including the raw power of unleashed psion ability. If they don't know something now, they can probably dig it up given time, and figure out a way to use it to their advantage.

ARCHER PSITECH

Within the many cloistered research bunkers of their massive subterranean complex, Archer's Bishops *(see the next column)* plumb the secrets of the human mind – and the wondrous inventions it can envision. Though severely hindered by the Shop's recent betrayal, the Foundation's PsiTech laboratories continue to produce the world's foremost technology in every form imaginable, from vehicles to surveillance equipment to advanced technologies like the spy-satellite system called *Overwatch (see page 56).*

CHAMBER ORGANIZATION

The Archer Foundation is divided into five departments, each with its own focus. The Foundation's mindset forms from this bureaucratic mold, a blend of modern corporate philosophy, critical information analysis, and Cold War pragmatism known as "the Game."

THE "PAWNS"

The first, and least secure, department in the Foundation are known as the "Pawns." The Pawns study world affairs, collect data for analysis (which other agents handle), and manage the mundane aspects of the Conspiracy (such as transportation and financing). Pawns operate in the open – which is potentially a great strength – using the Canberra home office of the Archer Institute as their base of operations.

THE "ROOKS"

Rooks handle counterintelligence activities both at home and abroad. They are in charge of physical defenses for all Archer facilities, as well as training and commanding operatives with counterinsurgency techniques. Rook bodyguards are frequently assigned to critical members of the Foundation's information network.

THE "KNIGHTS"

The Knights are Archer's contribution to mission teams (and the Foundation department where player agents most often come from). Usually drawn from the ASIS, Australian Special Air Service, or graduated from the Bishop department, these honored agents are closely protected by the Foundation.

THE "BISHOPS"

The vast majority of Archer's research into psion development and application is conducted by the techno-wizards known as Bishops. Masters of technological espionage, Bishops are the mentalists and genius-level latents who built the first gadget-cars, and – most recently – the underwater stronghold known as Aquatica.

The Bishops are currently under close investigation by the Lords, who suspect that several Shop traitors may still be hiding among them. Until the Foundation is sure that the crisis is over, all Bishops remain suspect.

THE "LORDS"

The final department within the Archer organization are the Lords, the original analysts, strategists, and consultants who formed the Institute. These men and women are the heart and mind of the Foundation, studying the material collected by the Pawns and coordinating Archer mission teams around the world. The Lords are "big thinkers," consumed with their awesome task, and often miss details and overlook nuances.

The Lords are also in charge of the Foundation's "private projects" – those endeavors too sensitive or dangerous to relegate to others. Each private project is codenamed to conceal its true purpose, with one Lord (who shares the codename) placed in charge of the operation. For instance, "Rebus" is a Foundation operative otherwise known as the "Lord of Invention." Her project (also named "Rebus") uses Archer's information network to literally erase known threats from society. Overnight, targets find themselves isolated from their former friends, family, lovers... as if they never existed. Another project – Nostrum – is ministered by a former Bishop known as the "Lord of Discipline," who meets annually with Archer's field teams for extended "training missions" into the Australian Outback. During these meetings, the operatives are evaluated and any potential weaknesses addressed.

"IT'S ALL A GAME"

If the Archer Foundation's structure appears complex and confusing to outsiders, its internal communications system is positively mind-boggling. Based loosely on the moves made in chess, every order issued – no matter how long – can be boiled down to a simple command phrase. An as example, "Bishop to Queen Four" might indicate a transfer of PsiTech to a field team. "Rook to King Bishop Six," on the other hand, could point to an endangered informant seeking assistance.

To make matters worse, the "Game" changes periodically (without warning), creating a constantly recycling cipher shielding Archer's inner workings. Many Foundation operatives wonder if there is more to this than mere security – if perhaps their superiors are playing a different kind of game altogether.

The Game in Australia

The Australian spy world has never really been about monitoring Australia, which is usually left to the Australian Federal Police and their many specialized task forces. In truth, the bulk of Australian intelligence resources is directed at enemy agents operating in Australian territory, or toward those regions which send unsuccessful (and therefore detected) spies to Australia.

One might argue that Australia's relatively isolated intelligence community has little need for extensive covert protection, but the Archer Foundation (which, by and large, runs the Australian espionage arena) has noted an alarming trend in the last two years. Most enemy spies in Australia arrive from Southeast Asia. Some of these can be attributed to the secretive activities of the Pan-Asian Collective, but the rest seem a legitimate threat – apparently unaligned operatives conducting clandestine research into Australian political, economic, and intelligence strength.

The Foundation suspects a greater motive, a Mastermind organization operating out of Asia that knows of the protectorate and wants to ferret it out, if not disable it. Should this group succeed, Archer may find itself fighting a losing war on its home turf – an unsettling prospect, to say the least.

To counter the danger, the Foundation has placed all its local agencies on alert and dispatched a trusted deep-cover operative into the Collective *(see "Dareka" on page 121 for more about this operation)*. Unfortunately, it has since lost contact with its operative and now fears that she may be dead, or worse, turned.

Australian Intelligence Agencies

The Archer Foundation has infiltrated the following agencies, or at least remains involved in their current plotlines. Additional detail is forthcoming in the *Archer Foundation* sourcebook.

Australian Security and Intelligence Organization (ASIO): Partly to counter the Pan-Asian problem, the Archer Foundation has encouraged the continued growth of both of Australia's core intelligence agencies, one of which – the Australian Security and Intelligence Organization (ASIO) – forms the home front of their effort.

The ASIO focuses its efforts on counterintelligence within Australia, which until recently has been rather limited. Until the mysterious incursions from Asia, the nation's principal enemies were the Soviets, whose interest in the country was negligible at best. The most important episode of the Cold War was the defection of Vladimir M. Petrov – an intelligence officer at Canberra's Soviet embassy – and his wife, in 1954. This is only noteworthy because it revealed to the Americans that Project VENONA (the U.S. code-breaking operation leaking information from Russia) was compromised, and that the Soviets were interested in Australian uranium mines.

The ASIO enjoyed a great deal of freedom in its operations, but in 1983 it discovered another Soviet operation. This one targeted powerful individuals in the Australian government, including Labor Party official David Combe. The ASIO brought the penetration to light, but suffered for its efforts; worried about further Soviet infiltration of the Australian government (and the ASIO itself), the agency was ordered to notify the Prime Minister and Attorney General before mounting any major espionage operations.

This decision effectively castrated the ASIO, which for sixteen years was very closely monitored. Then the Asian problem arose and Archer exerted some political sway to renew the ASIO's authority, and give it some not included in its original charter.

Now the ASIO has the right not only to conduct espionage investigations without interference from the government, but also intercept mail and infiltrate computers without a warrant. This shift has of course raised a few eyebrows in Australian parliament, but Archer considers it a calculated risk given the possibility of a full-scale invasion of enemy spies.

Australian Security Intelligence Service (ASIS): The ASIS is Australia's world intelligence arm, the outlet for most globe-trotting spies fielded directly by the Foundation. It currently focuses most of its attention on the Pacific Rim and the unknown Mastermind looming there, but the agency also coordinates frequently with the United States and U.K. By the terms of the UKUSA Agreement of 1946, Australian intelligence services (including the ASIS) share code words, terminology, intercept-handling techniques, and security procedures with those countries.

Like the ASIO, the ASIS is well-staffed and well-funded, thanks to the Archer Foundation's support in 1999.

International Reporting and Information Service (IRIS): Located in New York City, USA, this non-governmental office compiles and sells information gained from a wide variety of sources (most of which are purely legal). The Archer Foundation was introduced to the institution by the Gemeinschafft Consortium, which calls on it frequently for data it can't otherwise get hold of. Archer relies on Gemeinschafft to supplement its own Archives.

INTERPOL: The International Criminal Police Commission is based in Paris, France, and houses the most comprehensive database of law-breakers in the world. It gives and receives information from over 120 member nations, including Australia (and therefore the Archer Foundation).

Playing the Great Game

"I trust that people won't surprise me, though sometimes I wish they would."

– Two

Mission Management: The Foundation's focus is analysis and "big picture" planning, and it tends to shy away from "first contact" missions, depending on the African Alliance to handle the bulk of them. Originally intended to cement the Alliance's place in the Conspiracy and give it the chance for some quick glory, this policy has become a crutch that Foundation directors rely upon when they should be take an active role in exploratory missions. When the Foundation undertakes field missions, Two often calls upon Room 39's twin expertise *(see page 124)*.

Damage Control: The Shops' defection severely impacted the Conspiracy's manpower, stripping away several hundred years of combined experience. Two, ever able to make the most of such crises, seized the opportunity to install his own hand-picked replacements throughout the Conspiracy. Department heads for this new revitalized Shop – nicknamed the "Ego Trust" by those unsure of Two's motives – answer directly to the Foundation's Lords, and operate independently of the Chambers they serve.

Dirty Little Secrets: Two keeps secrets like normal people keep clothes – they pile up like skeletons in his closet until he needs room for more, then he purges them all at once. The Shop's break precipitated one such purge, as Two and his subordinates scrambled to distance themselves from questionable projects and personnel. On most fronts, the Foundation has succeeded in keeping their dirtiest laundry out of sight, but a couple stray items have crept into view. The most damning of these is the Foundation's involvement in the creation of what is now called P.E.R.I.L. In the early 1950s, several Foundation Lords became aware of a growing cancer in the Soviet Union, headed by a Stalinist traitor named Lavrenty Baria. Rather than reveal him to the Conspiracy, however, the Lords supported his activities, helping him develop the shadow government within Russia that would eventually seize control of the entire nation. They also helped to hide the truth from the rest of the Conspiracy – including the Foundation. These Lords – now referred to as the Judas Syndicate – were discovered shortly after the fall of the Soviet Union, and (it is believed) incarcerated in the Foundation's private penitentiary in the Australian outback, prisoners of a shadow war they created.

Leverage: The Lords routinely collect incriminating data on high-ranking officials in the other Chambers, and on each other. As a sharp contrast, Two is completely intolerant of such activities, and shuts them down whenever possible. This is one of the chief reasons that Raymond Archer instituted him as the Foundation's Control – Two is pure, untainted by the corruption eating away at the Conspiracy from within.

Assets: Two directs several private psion-related projects that he feels cannot yet be revealed to the other Chambers. Project TABULA RASA has developed a devastating psionic "Final Trump" – a weapon of mass destruction unlike anything the world has ever seen. (For more about TABULA RASA, see the forthcoming *Archer Foundation* sourcebook.) Further, Two has initiated a personal inquiry into the nature of his own psionic mastery. This project may unlock the potential for other agents to acquire all three families of psionic ability (currently only Two possesses such versatility). At present, this research is still in its infancy, and no hard results have been garnered.

Current Plotlines

Any or all of the following plotlines might make an excellent hook for a Mission or Serial.

Ten Little Indians (Code: Red): Two months ago, Señor Umberto Galt, a Foundation spin doctor, was murdered in his small Rome apartment. An Archer investigation ruled his death the result of random violence, but within two weeks, another Pawn was killed, this time in broad daylight. More deaths followed, and the situation was raised from Code: Yellow to Code: Red *(see page 203 of the Spycraft Espionage Handbook for more about threat codes)*. Seven members of the Foundation's information network have been murdered to date, as yet without a suspect. No formal operation has been authorized.

The Psion Explosion (Code: Red): In the late 1970s, shortly after Archer's final confrontation with Helix, its medical researchers noted a drastic increase in the manifestation of latent psions. Not long thereafter, with the identification of viruses around the world related to Helix's original research, it became terrifyingly clear that the villain's plan had not been entirely thwarted. Since then, the Foundation has devoted significant resources to countering both problems, with only marginal success.

The psion explosion poses an immediate danger. With Archer unable to contact all the psions cropping up throughout the world, many find themselves without guidance, unable to control their blooming powers, or worse, recruited by enemy organizations.

Aquatica (Code: Yellow): The Foundation's latest, greatest achievement is a fully self-contained underwater complex on the floor of the Baltic Sea. All has been quiet since it went operational in 1997, until now. Over the last eleven months, *Aquatica* technicians have observed a gradual rise in local water temperature. At first negligible, it is now reaching alarming levels, leading the Foundation to believe that the inhabitants of *Aquatica* are not alone in the Baltic.

The Foundation Genre

The Archer Foundation is the heart of the protectorate guiding the course of human history for the last fifty years. Byzantine in nature and global in scope, the Foundation is an untrustworthy, unpredictable, and somewhat unkind place far less overt than most other Chambers. Here, explosions are replaced with terse conversations over a leveled pistol and chases become dangerous games of cat-and-mouse.

The most accessible description for the Archer genre is "Cold War spy intrigue." For good examples, refer to any of the classic spy films and novels of the 1950s, 60s, and early 70s.

Archetypes: Bester (from *Babylon 5*), The "Big Three" (Roosevelt, Churchill, and Stalin), Elijah Snow (from *Planetary*), *Men in Black,* Nathan Muir from *Spy Game,* Professor X, Section (from *La Femme Nikita*), Smiley (from several LeCarré novels), The Watchers (from *Buffy the Vampire Slayer*), Alec Leamas from *The Spy Who Came in From the Cold,* the villains from *Enemy of the State* and other conspiracy stories.

Inspirations

Here's an incomplete list of suggested viewing, reading, listening, and playing for Archer players and the Game Control.

Books: *Cryptonomicon* by Neal Stephenson, *ESPERS* (comic book), *The Illuminatus! Trilogy* by Robert Shea and Robert Anton Wilson, *Invisibles* (comic book), *Planetary* (comic book), *Watchmen* (comic book), anything by John LeCarré (especially his Cold War novels, like *The Spy Who Came In From the Cold).*

Movies: *Conspiracy Theory, Enemy of the State, La Femme Nikita, The Man Who Knew Too Much, Men in Black, Presidio, Spy Game, The Third Man, Thirteen Days, Three Days of the Condor, Vertigo, X-Files.*

TV Shows: *The Agency, The Avengers, The Champions, The Gemini Man, La Femme Nikita, The Man From UNCLE, Nowhere Man, The Pretender, Prey, Reilly: Ace of Spies, Smiley's People, SpyTek, Tinker, Tailor, Soldier, Spy, The Tomorrow People, The X-Files.*

Music: Golden Palominos, Orbital, Recoil, anything by Mark Snow (*Disturbing Behavior, X-Files* scores).

Computer and Console Games: *Spider and Web* (an obscure text adventure, a la Zork), *Syndicate.*

Bringing It All Together

With eight core Chambers and hundreds of support cells at its disposal, the Archer Conspiracy may seem like a complex beast that should collapse under its own weight. But in practice, its protocols are painfully simple.

Big Brother

At the forefront of Archer's operations is its observation network, responsible for keeping an eye on the world and sending up a metaphorical warning flare when a situation arises that deserves the Foundation's attention. This network has three primary components.

As described on page 41, the Archer Foundation has its own dedicated satellite hub, Overwatch. Through this hub, Archer's Canberra operations center monitors much of the world's electronic traffic (radio and television frequencies, World Wide Web use, and email). An automated system flags potentially suspicious items for human review. Anything that merits direct action by Foundation agents is immediately sent to the Chamber nearest the event site and copied to the Lords, with a threat recommendation *(see page 203 of the Spycraft Espionage Handbook).* The Lords contact the Chamber directly, usually within 24 hours, with orders and team assignments, redirected through the regional Control to any agents already in the field.

Overwatch's earthbound counterparts are the established intelligence agencies Archer has infiltrated. Though not capable of surveying the same volume of information, compromised analysts in these agencies watch for potential threats, drawing upon hundreds of years of cumulative experience. When operatives within the event area target a situation, word travels back to the Foundation as described above.

Finally, Archer's many informants keep their ears to the ground, passing word of potential situations along to their handlers (who are either agents of a Foundation Chamber, or work for them). Problems filter through the system as described under Intelligence Analysis.

WHICH AGENTS ARE SENT?

When situations arise that demand Archer's attention, one or more agents from the nearest Chamber are automatically dispatched to investigate. This is called a *first contact* mission, and occurs without the Foundation's sanction. First contact agents evaluate the situation and report back to their Control, who determines a course of action. More often than not, the Lords have contacted the Control by this time with their orders, which guide his decision.

If the Lords or the local Control deems the situation worthy of direct intervention, they form a team. Typical protocol dictates that field units accept agents sent by the Lords and flesh the team out with local operatives. Agents are assigned for their talents rather than their proximity to the action, and are called in from foreign territories if needed. Lords often take team dynamics and former assignments into consideration, and group those who work well together into semi-permanent teams.

Game Note: This protocol allows for easy, logical field assignment of your player agent teams, even if they are from different Chambers.

WHO'S IN CONTROL?

Teams are formed with no inherent leader. When situations come up that require a critical and final decision to be made, they defer to the local Chamber Control for leadership. Occasionally, Lords or Archer representatives are assigned to specific missions, whose authority supersedes that of the regional Chamber Control with regards to that mission only.

MISSION PARAMETERS

Mission assignments include many parameters, the most common of which is the acceptable level of "noise" (attention-drawing activity). Most missions are classified "silent," meaning the agents must strive to keep their actions from public view at all times. Operations away from population centers are sometimes "quiet," requiring less discretion. "Hush" is a warning codeword demanding that noise drop immediately.

WHERE DO MASTERMINDS GO?

The Archer Foundation does not actively endorse murder – even of its worst enemies. When masterminds and their henchmen are captured, they are usually incarcerated at one of the Conspiracy's private penitentiaries around the world. The foremost installation in this system is the Panopticon, a subterranean prison beneath the African Alliance's Lodge *(see page 65-66)*.

WHERE DOES THE MONEY COME FROM?

When faced with a global network as complex and invasive as the Archer Conspiracy, it's logical to ask where the money for its often-elaborate operations comes from. Are there shady deals in the mix? Are there private investors? Do tax dollars pay for all this?

In all three cases, the answer is "No. Well, not entirely." Archer Chambers do receive a portion of their operating capital from their patron governments, but only a small part. Early in the twentieth century, many of the organizations that the Foundation has since infiltrated tapped into the industrial market. Telecommunications and other technical fields are closely linked with the espionage world (though those industries are rarely aware of it). Since 1975, certain Shop gadgets which skirted the technological limits of the common market have occasionally been sold to profit the Archer Conspiracy as well.

Many agencies employ a cadre of highly trained and ruthless staff members whose sole job is to manipulate the stock market. These individuals engage in practices that make insider trading seem positively benign, but generate a substantial amount of money to fund the Foundation and its operations.

WORLD LEADERS IN THE KNOW

The Archer Foundation could not maintain its global operations without the aid of many people outside the Conspiracy, including many political, military, and civilian leaders. The following is a brief overview of each region's average understanding of the Foundation, and some means they use to contact the organization in times of need. These notes may be useful to GCs wishing to derive their own information and communication networks on the fly.

AFRICA

The vast majority of Archer's African connections are maintained through the Janus Committee *(see page 64)*, Elias Graham's peace-keeping venture. By and large, the Foundation stays out of African internal politics, though it has recently brought several Janus peace officers into the fold. The most important leading figures in Africa are Graham himself (who has regular contact with the Australian home office, as well as most of the other Chamber Controls) and his immediate staff.

ASIA

Like Russia, Asia has been largely left to its own devices (a condition that Archer now regrets in both cases). The most prominent figures aware of the Conspiracy work within the Ministry of State Security and Central External Liaison Department *(see pages 118–119)*, with only a few exceptions, who remain in infrequent contact with Archer by email.

AUSTRALIA

The most stable of all Archer's constituent nations, Australia is the most heavily indoctrinated into the Conspiracy. Several dozen high-ranking officials in its intelligence community regularly communicate with the Foundation, often simply by picking up the phone. Security protocols are always observed for sensitive situations, however, and personal meetings are often arranged to discuss them.

EUROPE

Once, Archer kept several delegates from Europe's intelligence agencies and political bodies in the loop, but with the many scandals rocking France and other areas, they have scaled their involvement back significantly. Today, most insiders are employed by Gemeinschafft, which stays in contact with Archer through unobtrusive faxes and email.

THE MIDDLE EAST

The Guardians act as an effective barrier between the Foundation and the Middle East, and take sole responsiblity for maintaining relations with the local community. The very few outsiders they let into their circle are all honorary members of their culture. Communication is usually maintained through ordinary means, but occasionally mystical ones as well *(see page 103)*.

RUSSIA

Russian Control has always been responsible for keeping Archer's secrets in the region. Unfortunately, it appears that these details have fallen into the hands of a powerful enemy *(see page 136)*. Agents opposing this enemy stay in contact with Archer through various long-range communication gadgets, such as the Icon ProStar 7 *(see page 207)*.

THE UNITED KINGDOM

Due largely to the adversarial efforts of MI5 *(see page 129)*, knowledge of the Archer Foundation is kept to Room 39 personnel only, who communicate with the home office through the Omnium Corporation *(page 128)*.

THE UNITED STATES

Many U.S. figures know of the Foundation, but the information is contained through media spin and disinformation campaigns. Most in the know fiercely protect their knowledge, seeing the Company as a private reserve or a bargaining chip. All communication from the U.S. goes through Company Control or private channels.

MOSTRUM

Aliases: The Lord of Discipline, Treat Jacobs
Archer Identity Number: 09-692748-893
Nationality: Australian
Gender: Male **Handedness:** Right
Height: 6 ft. 4 in. **Weight:** 220 lbs.
Eyes: Black **Hair:** None
Psion Class: Physical Adept (Grade B)
Place of Birth: Melbourne, Australia
Date of Birth: 1960.09.14
Distinguishing Characteristics: Spider-web tattoo around left eye.

BACKGROUND

Throughout the 1980s and 90s, Treat Jacobs – the Lord of Discipline – has become something of a mythic figure among Archer agents, and a frequent source of anxiety. According to Archer legend, individual agents and occasional mission teams – particularly those whose records are less than stellar – are summoned to his isolated compound in the Australian Outback, where they undergo a grueling battery of physical and psychological tests in a mock-field setting.

Operatives subjected to these tests find themselves faced with an unexpected, unprecedented, and often seemingly impossible situation, without warning, and are evaluated according to their performance, individual actions, teamwork, and a variety of other factors determined by the Foundation. The challenges adapt to the team throughout the testing period, which can last from a few hours to a month or more.

Each test is unique, tailored exclusively for the agents at hand, and many extend outside the compound, and even the nation. For instance, one reported mission-test led the team to a jungle inland of the coastal city of Madras, India, where the operatives (who were primarily an urban task force) faced a colony of terrorist bush predators. Mostrum also reportedly conducts similar tests in the field, under the guise of standard Archer operations.

LOW-LEVEL NOSTRUM

Chamber: The Archer Foundation
Department: Training Ops (11)
Class: Physical Adept
Level: 1

Strength:	14	**Dexterity:**	12
Constitution:	18	**Intelligence:**	14
Wisdom:	12	**Charisma:**	5
Vitality:	14	**Wounds:**	18

Defense: 12 (+1 class, +1 Dex)
Initiative Bonus: +2 (+1 class, +1 Dex)
Speed: 30

Fort: +6 **Ref:** +1 **Will:** +3

Skills: Climb +3, Concentration +5, Driver +3, Intimidate +2, Jump +3, Sense Motive +2

Feats: Adrenal Basics, Metabolic Basics, Vitality Battery

Psion Skills: Control Metabolism +5, Energy Burst +5, Invigorate +5, Pain Transmission +3, Speed Control +5

ATTACKS

12 gauge pump-action shotgun +1 ranged (4d4)

Gear: Per mission-test

Common Gadgets: Sub-cochlear implant

MID-LEVEL NOSTRUM

Chamber: The Archer Foundation
Department: Training Ops (11)
Class: Physical Adept
Level: 8

Strength:	15	**Dexterity:**	13
Constitution:	18	**Intelligence:**	14
Wisdom:	12	**Charisma:**	6
Vitality:	81	**Wounds:**	18

Defense: 16 (+5 class, +1 Dex)
Initiative Bonus: +6 (+5 class, +1 Dex)
Speed: 30

Fort: +10 **Ref:** +3 **Will:** +7

Skills: Climb +4, Concentration +10, Driver +5, Intimidate +9, Jump +4, Knowledge (Archer Secrets) +10, Occult +3, Profession (Spy Trainer) +10, Sense Motive +6, Surveillance +5

Feats: Adrenal Basics, Intense Psi-Training, Metabolic Basics, Point Blank Shot, Sidestep, Vitality Battery

Psion Skills: Control Metabolism +6, Energy Burst +7, Invigorate +8, Pain Transmission +6, Speed Control +6

ATTACKS

12 gauge pump-action shotgun +5 ranged (4d4)

Gear: Per mission-test

Common Gadgets: Sub-cochlear implant

HIGH-LEVEL NOSTRUM

Chamber: The Archer Foundation
Department: Training Ops (11)
Class: Physical Adept
Level: 15

Strength:	16	**Dexterity:**	13
Constitution:	18	**Intelligence:**	15
Wisdom:	12	**Charisma:**	6
Vitality:	147	**Wounds:**	18

Defense: 20 (+9 class, +1 Dex)
Initiative Bonus: +10 (+9 class, +1 Dex)
Speed: 30

Fort: +13 **Ref:** +6 **Will:** +11

Skills: Climb +8, Concentration +15, Driver +8, Intimidate +16, Jump +8, Knowledge (Archer Secrets) +16, Occult +5, Profession (Spy Trainer) +15, Sense Motive +10, Surveillance +5

Feats: Adrenal Basics, Adrenal Mastery, Equilibrium Junction, Expertise, Intense Psi-Training, Metabolic Basics, Metabolic Mastery, Point Blank Shot, Rapid Shot, Sidestep, Vitality Battery

Psion Skills: Control Metabolism +11, Energy Burst +13, Invigorate +10, Pain Transmission +8, Speed Control +11

ATTACKS

12 gauge pump-action shotgun +8 ranged (4d4)

Gear: Per mission-test

Common Gadgets: Sub-cochlear implant

NPCS: WHY THREE VERSIONS?

Each NPC in this book is presented in three versions, one for low-level games (levels 1-7), one for mid-level games (levels 8-15), and a third for high-level games (levels 16 and above). This tradition will continue with all *Shadowforce Archer* products, so that you can insert the NPCs into your game with only minimal modification.

"Two"

Codename: ATLAS
Archer Identity Number: 33-914875-765
Nationality: Undetermined
Gender: Male **Handedness:** Right
Height: 5 ft. 11 in. **Weight:** 180 lbs.
Eyes: Blue-gray **Hair:** Graying black
Psion Class: All (Grade uncharted)
Place of Birth: Undetermined
Date of Birth: 1946.02.18
Distinguishing Characteristics: Icy pale-blue eyes (side effect of gene tampering), rook-topped steel cane with "0010" engraved into side.

Background

In 1998 Raymond Archer retired, leaving the Foundation in the hands of his protegé – an unknown who, as far as anyone knows, spent the last 23 years under the Bishops' microscopes.

"Two" was found during the raid on Eden in 1975. Dragged out of a conditioning tank where prisoners endured force-awakening experiments, Two claimed to have no memory of how he got there. According to the few records Archer recovered, Two was the only latent to survive the project's second phase, the parameters of which were lost in the assault.

Archer searched their Archive for records of a man meeting Two's description, but found none. Two named himself after the number on his tank and has lived with the Bishops ever since, honing his psion ability.

The true extent of Two's powers is unknown. He has mentalist, telepath, and physical adept abilities at striking levels (beyond anything the Bishops have charted before or since), and his power is still growing.

Raymond Archer took a personal interest in Two following the 1975 incident. For reasons he never explained, Archer nurtured Two, spending countless hours playing chess with him to hone his mind and help him come to grips with his missing past – as well as the startling psion abilities he is still discovering.

Low-Level "Two"

Chamber: The Archer Foundation
Department: None
Class: Mentalist/Physical Adept/Telepath
Level: 2/1/1

Strength:	16	**Dexterity:**	16
Constitution:	20	**Intelligence:**	25*
Wisdom:	22*	**Charisma:**	9

*recorded – may be higher

Vitality: 44 **Wounds:** 20

Defense: 15 (+2 class, +3 Dex)
Initiative Bonus: +6 (+3 class, +3 Dex)
Speed: 30

Fort: +7 **Ref:** +7 **Will:** +12

Skills: Balance +2, Bluff +5, Bureaucracy +5, Concentration +11, Cryptography +10, Gather Information +5, Hobby (Chess) +6, Innuendo +5, Intimidate +10, Knowledge (Cold War) +6, Occult +5, Sense Motive +10

Feats: Sidestep + all psion feats

Psionic Skills: All at +5 or above

Attacks

Sword-cane	+4 melee (1d6+3)
9mm service pistol	+4 ranged (1d10)

Gear: Any

Common Gadgets: Any

Mid-Level "Two"

Chamber: The Archer Foundation
Department: None
Class: Mentalist/Physical Adept/Telepath
Level: 4/4/3

Strength:	16	**Dexterity:**	16
Constitution:	20	**Intelligence:**	25*
Wisdom:	22*	**Charisma:**	10

*recoreded – may be higher

Vitality: 115 **Wounds:** 20

Defense: 18 (+5 class, +3 Dex)
Initiative Bonus: +10 (+7 class, +3 Dex)
Speed: 30

Fort: +11 **Ref:** +9 **Will:** +16

Skills: Balance +2, Bluff +8, Bureaucracy +8, Concentration +16, Cryptography +12, Gather Information +8, Hobby (Chess) +16, Innuendo +10, Intimidate +15, Knowledge (Archer Secrets) +11, Knowledge (Cold War) +11, Occult +10, Sense Motive +16

Feats: Sidestep + all psion feats

Psionic Skills: All at +8 or above

Attacks

Sword-cane	+8 melee (1d6+3)
9mm service pistol	+8 ranged (1d10)

Gear: Any

Common Gadgets: Any

HIGH-LEVEL "TWO"

Chamber: The Archer Foundation
Department: None
Class: Mentalist/Physical Adept/Telepath
Level: 6/6/6 *

Strength:	16	**Dexterity:**	16
Constitution:	20	**Intelligence:**	25*
Wisdom:	22*	**Charisma:**	12

*recoreded – may be higher

Vitality: 187 **Wounds:** 20

Defense: 23 (+10 class, +3 Dex)
Initiative Bonus: +16 (+13 class, +3 Dex)
Speed: 30

Fort: +14 **Ref:** +13 **Will:** +19

Skills: Balance +7, Bluff +10, Bureaucracy +10, Concentration +21, Cryptography +15, Gather Information +10, Hobby (Chess) +21, Innuendo +15, Intimidate +20, Knowledge (Archer Secrets) +21, Knowledge (Cold War) +21, Occult +20, Sense Motive +21

Feats: Sidestep + all psion feats

Psionic Skills: All at +10 or above

ATTACKS

Sword-cane	+12 melee (1d6+3)
9mm service pistol	+12 ranged (1d10)

Gear: Any

Common Gadgets: Any

THE AFRICAN ALLIANCE

"Both sides are becoming identical, a perfect blueprint for world order. When the sides facing each other suddenly realize that they are looking into a mirror, they will see that this is the pattern for the future."

–Number 2, "The Chimes of Big Ben"

The criminal mastermind Helix was the greatest threat that Archer faced throughout the 20th Century. The effects of his myriad plots still crop up, but nowhere is his impact felt more sharply than in the bowels of his monstrous island complex, "Eden" (renamed "the Lodge" by its current occupants, the African Alliance). Originally built as the launching pad for his vision of psion domination, the fortress is equal parts scientific laboratory, military bunker, and global operations center, making it the perfect staging ground for Archer's mission.

THE ALLIANCE MISSION

The African Alliance operates like a microcosm of the Archer Foundation itself. With the Lodge's advanced technologies (many of which exceed those of the Foundation, and some of which have yet to be deciphered), it monitors world news, military, and private traffic for signs of trouble, and dispatches teams when necessary. Unlike the other Chambers, the Alliance is self-sufficient, and can operate with or without Archer's support. This is a sore point with some agents of the other Chambers, which have been in business for a quarter century longer than the Alliance. But ultimately, it is the African Chamber's raw idealism and ability to think outside the box that gained them the autonomy they currently enjoy. When the Archer Foundation faces an unfamiliar or global threat, it usually calls in at least one African Alliance agent.

FUNCTION

As the "first-contact" field operations arm for the Archer Foundation, the African Alliance is geared toward dealing with the unforeseen. Agents, freelancers, and Control personnel all regularly run through simulations to enhance their problem-solving skills, and other facets of Alliance training (like social manipulation or gunplay) are presented within the same context. Lodge cadets – especially those of other Chambers, who are not used to the Alliance's frantic methods and pacing – call this method "panic training," and the Foundation values it like no other.

The African Alliance relies heavily upon the other Chambers for support in its missions; an all-African mission is quite rare. Alliance agents' broad training is perfect for field operations – until the problem is identified. Then it is often useful to call in agents of more specialized branches of the Conspiracy to help close the deal. The Company, for instance, might be called in to contend with a military threat, while Room 39 is often consulted about terrorist and urban action, as well as ciphers and other items that require close analysis. The Guardians are called in when mystic or occult problems are encountered, as well as during wetworks and infiltration missions. Prisoners are often sent to the Pan-Asian Collective for interrogation, and so on.

Alliance operatives usually remain on a case through its completion regardless of the involvement of other Chambers. Each agent personally invests himself or herself in the task at hand, and does not consider the job done until the situation is completely resolved and any threat eliminated. The Archer Foundation encourages this attitude (again, often against the arguments of others under their banner).

Common Alliance Missions

Agents of the African Alliance regularly perform important missions for the Foundation, often with little or no clear direction. The majority are included here, along with an idea of how they apply in the *Shadowforce Archer* setting.

Investigation ("First Contact"): The most common mission undertaken by operatives of the African Alliance is to follow up on information and report back with the truth of the matter. For instance, they might be sent in to determine the source and nature of threats against world leaders or Archer affiliates, or search for a missing nuclear submarine, or try to determine the whereabouts of an anarchist during his thirty-year exile. First contact missions often explode into much larger plots, and are the most common way that Alliance agents become involved in other mission types.

Diplomacy: Many Alliance operatives are placed around the world as "diplomatic spies": that is, spies who remain plugged into global affairs and, if necessary, skew perceptions and reactions in a direction favorable to Archer. Diplomatic spies must sometimes perform damage control in times of crisis, but do so *only* if directly ordered by Archer or the Alliance. To act on their own would risk compromising their cover, which has been carefully cultivated and is difficult or impossible to replace.

Archer carefully guards its diplomatic spies, who remain anonymous even to premier agents. Shielded by elaborate communication protocols, code words, and double-blind mail drops, these are the hardest agents to contact or work into typical *Shadowforce Archer* missions.

"Doubling": The Alliance keeps many operatives in key positions within intelligence agencies outside their shadow community, as well as inside foreign governments and known terrorist and villain organizations. When needed, these agents can provide valuable information about their parent groups. It is important to note that – for their own purposes as much as those of Archer – the African Alliance maintains several double-agents in each of the other Chambers as well.

Infiltration: Infiltration is usually only part of a larger mission, but is occasionally required on its own – usually to "seed" agents in a location hours or days before a major operation is conducted there. Infiltration also frequently involves theft. Agents of the African Alliance are perfectly suited to both duties.

One common training scenario which has proven useful in the field involves the agents discovering the remote headquarters of a criminal mastermind, often while on a tight timetable. In such circumstances it is almost always best to call home base or a relay station, report the location, and infiltrate the headquarters, either to gain additional intelligence or sabotage the mastermind's efforts. Consequently, the African Alliance has adopted this as standard practice.

Liquidation: Though it is actively avoided (and many African Alliance agents, including Control, find it distasteful), assassination is sometimes an agent's best option. The Alliance trains a small number of their personnel in the finer points of killing; they call these agents "Lethals." These men and women are sent on missions with the highest estimated casualty rate (the Chamber's way of "balancing the scales"), and are known for leaving long trails of bodies behind them. In response, the Foundation privately assigns at least one Cleaner to each Lethal unit *(see page 64)*, to make sure their messes don't draw too much attention.

Observation: The most basic function of any spy is to remain aware of his surroundings, and more importantly, of the little details he can use to assist his allies or cut down his foes. For the African Alliance, this mission type has become the focus of an entire department, which includes their collection of moles and "Sentries" *(see page 66)*.

Research and Development: Much of Helix's grossly advanced technology has remained at the Lodge (most of it is still part of the facility); a division of technicians work diligently deciphering it. Originally part of the Shop, these mentalists have formally assumed the name "the Daedalus Division" *(see page 65)* since those villains broke away from Archer. Surprisingly, no agents of the Daedalus Division defected with the Shop; whether this indicates that the Alliance R&D department somehow survived the break unscathed or that all Shop infiltrators are keeping their covers intact is as yet unknown.

Sabotage: Interfering with enemy operations is a prime concern of the African Alliance (and, for that matter, all Archer Chambers); all agents have standing orders to conduct sabotage at will, so long as they do not directly risk the security of the Chamber in the process. According to Alliance doctrine, sabotage is most effective when conducted closest to the heart of a villain's organization (which is usually, but not always, closest to the villain himself), though harrying missions can also yield impressive results.

Terminal Action: The African Alliance refers to the final stages of any mission as "terminal action." Several of their agents have become synonymous with this phase of an operation (some of whom are rarely assigned at any other time). These agents are called "Closers," and have the authority to take any steps required in the course of terminal action. Many agents serve as Closers, and indeed it is the most liberating, no-holds-barred position the Alliance has. Some Closers specialize in following a single mission through investigation, bridging operations, and finally bringing the whole thing home; these agents in particular make almost perfect field operatives. But Closers walk the razor's edge between glory and the shame of personally handling a botched operation.

Training: Finally, the Alliance has the privilege of being one of two primary training centers for Archer's agents (the other being the Company – *see page 72*). They use the National Intelligence Agency's academy as a proving ground for raw recruits (none of whom are aware of the Conspiracy until they are inducted) as well as a training bed for basic espionage knowledge, but it is the Lodge itself where a spy's "trial by fire" truly begins. Not only is the base large enough to house several times the number of agents who regularly live there, but many of the lower levels specifically serve to engage minions in mock-field exercises. *(See "The Lodge" on page 65 for more details about the island base.)*

Agent Expectations

Players who enjoy problem-solving, unexpected twists, and over-the-top action will enjoy playing Alliance agents. In general, operatives of this Chamber must be prepared for anything at any time, and go into every situation with an open mind. Alliance operations, though glamorous and romantic, also tend to be poorly defined. Investigation and trouble-shooting are the name of the game here.

Alliance agents must be inventive, confident, adaptable, and broadly trained. These factors generally manifest as a level of sophistication unseen in agents of other Chambers; Alliance operatives understand everything from street-level American and European trends to the finest art and wine of the season. They know the proper clothes, attitude, mannerisms, and banter for every situation.

Finally, Alliance agents must be prepared to face criminal masterminds and deranged madmen on their home turf, without warning. Being part of the first contact with a potential enemy ensures the high level of adrenaline-charged excitement many Alliance agents crave, but it also places them in near-constant danger – danger they must be ready to meet head-on.

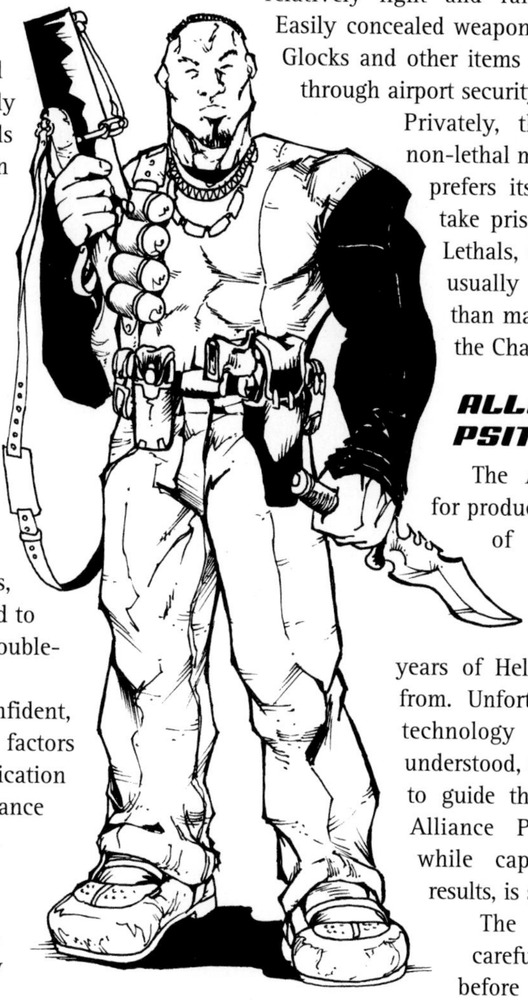

Tactical Data

Alliance operations tend to be broad and global in scope; more often than not, either the problem at hand is too undefined for more specialized units or other teams have already tried and failed. As a result, Alliance agents learn to react quickly and decisively, but more importantly, they know not to tip their hands too early. Typically, they infiltrate and watch until they either gain all the information they need, or the threat escalates to a level where terminal action is required.

Weapons carried by Alliance Agents tend to be relatively light and rarely gadget-enhanced. Easily concealed weapons are the norm, as are Glocks and other items which can be shuffled through airport security.

Privately, the Alliance endorses non-lethal methods of combat, and prefers its agents to subdue or take prisoners rather than kill. Lethals, on the other hand, are usually quite ruthless, more than making up for the rest of the Chamber.

Alliance PsiTech

The Alliance is renowned for producing and fielding some of the most impressive PsiTech in the world, largely because its R&D team has sixty years of Helix's research to draw from. Unfortunately, little of the technology left behind is fully understood, and Helix left no notes to guide the effort. As a result, Alliance PsiTech development, while capable of spectacular results, is slow going.

The Daedalus Division carefully tests its devices before handing them out to agents (usually as part of the simulations held at the lower levels of the Lodge), ensuring a high level of reliability in the field.

Chamber Organization

When describing the internal structure of the African Alliance, one need look no further than the name of its headquarters, "the Lodge." Outsiders joke that Graham chose this name for the size and feel of his organization as much as the surroundings; they may be right.

Control

Elias Graham treats his Chamber much like a spy club, encouraging a convivial tone, close brotherhood between his agents, and a sense of mutual cooperation among everyone on the premises. This is especially prevalent in the offices of the Janus Committee *(the Chamber's front organization and Graham's pet project for world unification – see below)*, where the feeling is not only an attitude, but a credo.

Graham treats all Alliance operatives well; he prefers to keep things informal. Mission briefings take place over morning coffee, and supportive fellow agents often attend their comrades' training sessions. First names or codenames are used more often than not, and members of the Chamber typically know their coworkers personally. Many have become friends, spending their R&R together away from the Lodge.

Of course, these close personal bonds come under fire during field operations, when tempers flare and lives hang in the balance. Too often for Graham's tastes, friends are lost during difficult missions, bringing a dark cloud over the Lodge and reminding everyone of the stakes they play for every time they venture out on a mission. Betrayal bites even deeper than death; Graham invests tremendous effort in every one of his subordinates, and intrinsically trusts everyone he works with. Moles and double agents are not only an injury to the Chamber, but a personal insult to Graham himself.

The Janus Committee

The Alliance's public presence takes the form of the Janus Committee, founded by Elias Graham in 1980. Initially dedicated to bridging the gap between the colors in Africa, the Committee has since spread its message of unilateral acceptance across the seas into Europe, the United States, Asia, and (since the fall of the Iron Curtain in 1991) Russia. But the Janus Committee is far more than a public relations office; it has dozens of offices all around the world which conduct outreach programs, sponsor multi-ethnic activities, and lobby for legislative change.

Beneath the message, however, the Janus Committee is the eyes, ears, and sometimes hands of the African Alliance. Archer superspy Dumisani Tepe and his team all have public personae working for the Committee, cover identities under which they can enter and reconnoiter foreign territories without arousing suspicion. The Committee's private shipping contracts with all the major world couriers ensure quiet delivery of equipment and information in the field. And during times of relative peace, those Janus employees who are aware of the Conspiracy keep an eye out for events that might be important to the Chamber, coding their observations into regular Committee letters and email.

Standard Agents

Most Alliance operatives spend only half their time in the field, and that period includes more than just missions. The Alliance grants generous leeway after the successful completion of a mission, during which the agents may enjoy a little downtime wherever their operation ended, or somewhere they can get to without too much fuss. More often than not, Alliance agents (who are notoriously self-indulgent) gravitate toward stylish locales where posh hotel rooms, lavish casinos, and beautiful people await. Such personal forays generally last up to a week, unless more pressing business prematurely calls them back to base.

On occasion, the Foundation has questioned this practice, unsure of the wisdom of allowing seasoned agents to indulge in potentially reckless public behavior. But Graham has so far successfully defended his policy, citing the Alliance's high success rate and low mortality and defection rates as proof that it works. Archer has so far refrained from pointing out the many times Alliance agents have nearly pierced the Cloak during their terminal action missions, or the high cost of covering them up.

Between downtime and new mission briefings, Alliance agents spend most of their time at the Lodge, training and performing routine functions.

Lethals

Due to their unnerving effect on Chamber morale, as well as the extreme nature of their training and mission parameters, Lethals are typically segregated from their fellow agents. A separate block of living quarters and training areas has been set aside for them several levels beneath the general operations and domestic areas of the Lodge; Lethals even have their own avenues for entering and leaving the complex.

Lethals only go into the field with regular mission teams when it is absolutely necessary. Generally, they accompany Cleaner units (or are trailed by them), following up the investigations of other teams. But sometimes – particularly when dealing with villains of known destructive capability (such as Helix, the Shop, or the Hand of Glory), Lethals work as part of a team.

One peculiar byproduct of the escalation of violence during missions is the perceived need to disguise Lethals for as long as possible, keeping their status a secret from their teammates until their talents are needed. Today, Lethals are often identified during initial recruitment, segregated during their wetworks training, and then slipped in with the non-Lethals as new recruits. This effectively keeps their true talents under wraps until activated in the field.

Agents-in-Training

Until authorized for field missions (after their graduation from the Lodge's training program), Aliiance agents are appointed to positions of secondary importance. Generally, agents can tell how much the Chamber values them at this stage of their career; the higher their security clearance (i.e. the closer their physical place of employment is to the Lodge), the more prestigious their relationship with control. Lodge guards and operations personnel are at the top of this pecking order, while those working in busy or high-profile Sentry Houses *(see page 66)* around the world fall just short. Remote Sentries linger at the bottom, generally forgotten or ignored.

The Daedalus Division

Even deeper in the bowels of the Lodge than the Lethals' quarters lies the Daedalus Division, which conducts research into the many technologies Helix left behind and creates gadgets for field teams. Daedalus personnel are culled from the greatest scientific minds in the world, many of whom requested transfer here after seeing samples of Helix's developments.

Physically, the Daedalus Division consists of several "clean rooms" (sterile environments to test and study electronic devices and biological samples), munitions dumps (where volatile weapons-grade components are kept), and dedicated living quarters for the staff. Vehicles and other devices which require additional room to test usually go through their final paces on the island surface during off-hours, when no one is expected to be around.

Alliance Resources

Though the Alliance can theoretically call upon the resources of the Janus Committee to help bring their missions to a close, Graham has recently taken steps to widen the division between the two, reinforcing the idea that he is considering a return to public life. Outside of keeping a number of agents-in-training on staff at Committee offices and utilizing their shipping contacts, the relationship is quite limited. As a result, the Alliance relies primarily on the resources available at the Lodge.

The Lodge

At roughly 12° east latitude, 44° south longitude – north of Madagascar – rest the Comoro Islands, which are only accessible by ship or air ferry. This small island chain identifies itself as an independent union, but one among them – an otherwise ignored seven-mile strip of light forests, steaming beaches, mangroves, coconut palms, and fruit trees – is privately owned by Elias Graham, and has secretly become the heart of the Archer Foundation's African Chamber.

Externally, there is no indication of the Alliance's presence; the island (which has never been officially named) appears as nothing more than a pleasant rest stop for passersby. But when a helicopter sends a short coded burst over a designated frequency, the island's southern end opens up to permit a landing. Moments later, the helicopter lowers into the Lodge's interior and the landscape returns to normal.

Less obvious methods of entering the secret base are also available. Agents arriving by non-motored boat from the mainland can enter through any of five hidden entrances, all monitored around the clock. (In the rare event that the uninformed stumble onto one of these entrances, they are taken into custody, questioned, and warned that the island is the site of an SANDF biological testing facility; this usually sends the stunned victims packing without inquiry.)

The island can be entered by submarine through a gorge deep beneath the surface of the water. The sub merely follows a careful course under the island and rises inside the complex.

According to sonic bombardments of the island walls near the ocean floor, the Lodge extends at least three hundred feet below the island's surface, but the Alliance's penetration is relatively shallow; agents only occupy the highest fourteen levels. Occupied levels use progressively higher security measures, and break down into the following divisions:

Surface –1: "Biological testing facility" cover
Surface –2 to –4: Agent living quarters
Surface –5: Operations
Surface –6 to –7: Agent training facilities, demolitions and firing ranges
Surface –8 to –9: Lethals camp
Surface –10 to –12: The Daedalus Division and submarine docking gorge
Surface –13 to –17: The Panopticon
Surface –18 and beyond: The "Labyrinth"

The Panopticon

Modeled after Jeremy Bentham's 1791 vision of a humane prison, the Panopticon is a ring of isolated holding cells, all facing in toward a central tower (the only part of the complex connected to the rest of the Lodge). The tower's outer walls consist of one-way mirrors, preventing anyone outside from seeing its interior. The front wall (entrance) of each holding cell is transparent, allowing the tower's occupants to see into any part of any cell at any time without the prisoners' knowledge. The holding cells' back walls are illuminated, floor to ceiling, by pale white light, further reducing their privacy. All are soundproofed, isolating each prisoner in sensory-deprived solitude.

Helix used this place to shake up, interrogate, or emotionally cripple captured psions during the 1970s *(see page 40-41)*. The stark difference helped to throw the psions off balance, to keep them docile, and make them pliable, more willing to accept his direction. The Alliance has found it extremely useful in the detention and interrogation of criminal masterminds and their henchmen.

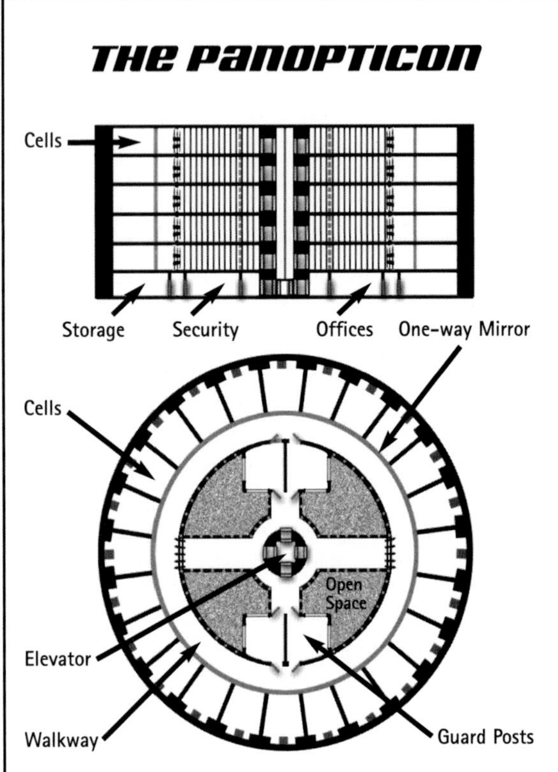

The Labyrinth

At the base of the Panopticon tower a large reinforced trapdoor leads into an area Helix called the Labyrinth. The true function of this multi-level sub-complex is unknown even today, though the Daedalus Division (reasoning from what little it knows of Helix's origins) presumes that the area protects something of great value to the mentalist once known as Avery Schillingsfield.

Attempts to delve into the Labyrinth have met with formidable automated defenses – blast doors, weapons, and complicated death traps responsible for the deaths of 79 agents and technicians (and counting). The effort has been further hampered by the search teams' inability to compile an accurate map, even of the highest level; it appears that the automated defenses include a constantly reconfigured floor plan. Whatever Helix hid at the center of his private maze remains a mystery.

Sentries

Sentry Houses are agent cells set up in the field which constantly observe or protect a specific area. They range from lone operatives huddled in secret basement listening posts, equipped only with a short-wave radio and a pocket knife, to full blocks of agents equipped with state-of-the-art surveillance gear, mobile triangulation units, and impressive armories. Most Sentries have long-term cover identities to conceal their activities, but some are known to the intelligence community in their area as a contact point for the Alliance.

Alliance Sentries are usually Agents-in-Training *(see page 65)*, assigned a Janus Committee office as a contact point for resupply.

The Game in South Africa

Late in 1994, two all-important agreements changed the face of South Africa's intelligence community, starting the continent along the long road to recovery. The National Strategic Intelligence Act (Act 94-39, 02 December 1994) defined the function and structures of African intelligence agencies, and assigned a head of intelligence in the area (the Co-ordinator for Intelligence, who runs the National Intelligence Coordinating Committee; *see opposite*). Meanwhile, the Intelligence Services Act (Act 94-38, 02 December 1994) established South Africa's National Intelligence Agency and South African Secret Service, both of which are critical to the Archer Foundation's efforts on the continent. The Intelligence Services Act also incorporated and redistributed many agents of dissolved organizations and set up strict policies for internal security, discipline, and operations.

African intelligence services have always spearheaded political change in the region, so this sweeping reorganization has had a profound effect on the area. It has also paved the way for a stronger, more unified intelligence front.

South African Intelligence Agencies

Here is a list of agencies that have been infiltrated or affected by the African Alliance. Additional detail is forthcoming in the *African Alliance* sourcebook.

National Intelligence Agency (NIA): As prescribed by the National Intelligence Act, the NIA are responsible for "gathering, correlating, evaluating, and analyzing domestic intelligence, in order to identify any threat or potential threat to the security of the Republic or its people." This broad statement, in practice, boils down to performing the basic practices of counterespionage in South Africa – data collection, research, maintaining domestic security, safeguarding corporate resources and technology, and training operatives.

To perform this function, the NIA has adopted management techniques used in Europe and the United States, and a well-defined chain of command. The NIA answers directly to its own Director-General, the National Intelligence Coordination Committee (NICOC; see opposite), and, through them, the President of South Africa.

The NIA has no official police powers (they cannot arrest, and must obtain permission to enter private property), so they work closely with the South African Police Service (SAPS). They are, however, a powerful organization; equipped with much sensitive information gained during the reorganization – including knowledge of the technological capabilities, professional training, moles, and information networks of African nations, as well as disquieting secrets about the African National Congress (ANC) – NIA stand ready to take on a new and more dangerous period of African spy history.

The National Intelligence Coordinating Committee (NICOC): The NICOC consists of the Coordinator for Intelligence and the heads of all the other services listed here, as well as a few ad hoc appointees. It serves as the central command point for all African intelligence, preparing reports for the President and Cabinet, directing South Africa's spy agencies, and controlling the flow of data between them. NICOC is only broadly involved with the nation's intelligence agencies, focusing more on the priority of cases than the nuts-and-bolts.

The South African National Defense Force (SANDF): The SANDF is a military body limited to gathering military intelligence; its charter strictly forbids it to covertly acquire non-military data unless directed by the NICOC. In addition to external protection and upholding South Africa's treaty obligations, the SANDF also coordinates counterintelligence measures (often with the help of the NIA) throughout the Republic, effectively doing twice the work of military forces in many other nations.

South African Police Service (SAPS): The SAPS underwent perhaps the most radical change during the reorganization of 1994. Eleven separate police services merged to form the modern SAPS, and the autocratic overlording of the apartheid era has been replaced with an agency more involved with and supportive of the African public. Its methods have also improved, and now include a state-of-the-art forensics lab and participation in INTERPOL.

South African Secret Service (SASS): Outside the fact that they operate almost entirely outside the nation, the role of the SASS in national affairs is roughly equivalent to that of the NIA. It collects and analyzes data pertaining to South African security (excluding military intelligence, which is the purview of the SANDF) and answers to the NICOC. This distinction, however, makes it the perfect outlet for Alliance activities through the area.

Playing the Great Game

"I trust we can make the world a better place, but that shouldn't blind us to those who would rather not."

– Elias Graham

Mission Management: Elias's promotion of the African Alliance as a "spy club," coupled with tangible rewards from "on high" for regularly taking on extreme risks, hinders his ability to field agents in low-key roles. Deep infiltration and long term subversion projects are often handed off to agents of the European Commonwealth instead – particularly to Fade's shadow organization. Such assignments would normally be funneled to the Pan-Asian Collective, but the Alliance – and particularly Graham - are skeptical of the PAC's motives, and work with them as little as possible. When delegating over-the-top missions, Elias often teams his own people with operatives from the Company, whose seasoned planners offset Alliance exuberance, and whose heavy munitions can bring such wild confrontations to a successful close.

Damage Control: The Alliance suffered the greatest physical damage during the Shop's departure. The Lodge, former headquarters of the greatest mentalist ever known, was the target of massive destruction during the Shop's break. Upper floor gadget arsenals and entire lab complexes were bombed. Most troubling are the hints that such destruction served as a cover for even more insidious activities – that agents of the Shop launched an unauthorized probe into the island's lowest levels. What they sought down there, and whether they found it, remains a mystery.

Dirty Little Secrets: The Alliance's darkest secret is a gravely personal one. Late during his time as a lieutenant of the infamous mastermind Helix, Elias Graham aided in the capture of Katrina Danilova Savage, an operative of the Russian Confederacy. Seemingly a benign event, Katrina's capture led to her infection with Helix's deadly psion plague, which in turn led to her death at the hands of the Cleaners *(see page 49)*. Ultimately, this tragedy resulted in Lord Reginald Savage – perhaps the Conspiracy's greatest Cold War superspy, and Katrina's husband – resigning his post with Room 39 and going to ground. Elias blames himself for Katrina's death and her husband's departure, as well as the threat Lord Savage has since become. He bears this burden alone.

Leverage: The Alliance's comparative youth has offered its agents few opportunities to obtain leverage, which suits Elias well (after all, leverage isn't his style).

Recently, however, the Alliance Control has found himself intrigued by an unexpected offer. During a post-capture "interview" with Mislav Zane, a Croatian arms smuggler known to supply several of Europe's most prominent criminal masterminds, Elias noticed his guest blanch and acquire a knowing look in his eye. When he asked Zane what was wrong, the smuggler promised to give Elias "the power to change the world" in exchange for his freedom. Blindsided by this wild statement, Elias ignored the proposal, but something about the exchange lingered in his mind. Perhaps it was the smuggler's surprising sincerity, or the excited gleam in his eye (as if he'd just uncovered a remarkable secret), but Elias has more than once considered humoring the prisoner. Maybe someday soon, he will.

Assets: Elias' greatest asset has always been the skill and reliability of his agents - an asset that he is now fostering away from the prying eyes of his fellow Controls. With his extensive training facilities and isolated location, Elias has secretly taken a number of each year's most promising recruits "off the books" for a special project of his own creation. This small, multi-purpose task force, with each of whom knows Graham on a first name basis, is hidden away on Sub-Level 11 of the Lodge, where they can come and go through the island's partially submerged caverns at will. Thus far, Elias has allowed them to cut their teeth in clandestine investigations of Shop activity, but in truth he fears the team may also be needed if other major elements of the Conspiracy should follow in the traitors' footsteps.

CURRENT PLOTLINES

The African Alliance is just as deeply enmeshed in its own plotlines as it is in external matters. The following are three examples, two of which hit the Chamber close to home. Any or all of these plotlines would make an excellent hook for a mission or serial. Many will be developed as part of the official *Shadowforce Archer* storyline.

The Body (Code: Red): Two months ago a 22-year-old Peace Corps volunteer, Robert Mason, was found stabbed to death in an alley in Kinshasa. Originally assumed to be a victim of random street violence, the autopsy revealed traces of an unknown chemical in his bloodstream. The examiner, a specialist and sometime ally of the Foundation, contacted the Alliance and offered them a sample. What they found was startling. The chemical in the body's bloodstream was a pure sample of the missing third psion serum – originally derived from the blood of Conrad Archer.

Unable to secure the body (the powerful Mason family, with many political ties, clamored for it to be brought home to them in Vermont), the Alliance gathered as much information as possible before sending it home. They scoured Robert Mason's last known location – an environmental preserve – but gleaned no new information. Speaking to the other volunteers on site revealed that he had suffered from unexplained migraines for weeks before – ever since a vacation to eastern Europe.

Linking Robert Mason to the alley where he was found has yielded no success. The other volunteers at the preserve thought he was headed home the week he died, and none traveled with him to the airport in Kinshasa. Five hours passed between his last known conversation and his death, during which the Alliance can only assume he met with foul play.

Mission teams in both Africa and Europe are actively assigned to this mission, and the Foundation is watching all world medical disease control services in case new evidence of the pure sample crop up again.

The Freshmen (No Applicable Code): Within the halls of the Archer Institute, strategists speak of the African Alliance with pride. It is the greatest, shining example of Raymond Archer's vision come to life – a fully functional, (as yet) uncorrupted, global observation and protection unit. More and more, the Foundation is coming to rely upon the African Chamber, sending its agents in first to deal with sticky situations, and nurturing its once-meager resources into a world-spanning intelligence conglomerate. Already Archer has assisted the Alliance and its front the Janus Committee in founding over one hundred offices around the world. Critics complain that this increased support only taints the model. Others worry that segments of the convoluted Archer organization have private plans for the Alliance.

Operation COLD FRONT (Code: Red): Africa has always contended with violent weather, but a recent string of meteorological disasters suggest a common source. Several severe cyclones and highly erratic off-shore wind patterns have drenched much of South Africa, causing floods, ruining crops, and leaving countless people homeless. At first considered nothing more than a bad turn, the weather patterns are now considered a little too erratic – as if they are being directed.

Assuming that the African economy or populace is not the focus, the Alliance has looked for other potential targets. So far, the entity most affected by the disasters has been Aurora, Ltd., a diamond export company out of Mozambique. Owned by billionaire playboy Rick Tempest, Aurora's transport facilities have been grounded by the storms, and an undisclosed number of shipments were "misplaced" in the chaos.

The Alliance suspect an even larger scope, however. Aurora, Ltd. is a chief competitor of several companies owned by the Gemeinschafft Consortium in Europe, whose interest in the African diamond market is well known.

The Mystery of the Lodge (Code: Yellow): Throughout the last 25 years, strange, unexplained events have plagued the Lodge. In 1982, a sentry on the island surface, claiming to hear band music, strayed from his post, and was never seen again. In 1990, an agent was startled awake by a man sitting in his room, mumbling nonsense. After a few cryptic exchanges, the visitor left, never to return (though he was later encountered by others). Many agents and visitors report a sense of being watched during their stay. Whether the Lodge is haunted or these events are residual echoes of Helix's plans for the base is a question as yet unanswered.

The Alliance Genre

The genre of the African Alliance is closest to the core *Shadowforce Archer* setting, filled with the bold, ingenious superspies of modern espionage action serials. Alliance agents are classy, stylish, suave, and debonair, capable of slipping into any setting (including nearly all of the other Chamber genres) with minimal effort. Alliance action is fast and cinematic, a blend of movie mayhem and hyperkinetic energy, with spikes into extreme, over-the-top danger. The Alliance world is glamorous and fashionable, filled with beautiful people darting across lavish backdrops to the amped-up beat of an adventure movie score.

Archetypes: James Bond, Deuce and Abbey Chase from *Danger Girl,* Flint from *Our Man Flint* and *In Like Flint,* Han Solo, Jack Colton from *Jewel of the Nile* and *Romancing the Stone,* any strong and independent lead character.

Inspirations

Alliance players and GCs running missions in Alliance territory may find this incomplete list of suggested viewing, reading, and listening, and playing useful.

Books: *Area 52* (comic book), *Danger Girl* and *Kamikaze* (comic books), James Bond novels, *Day of the Jackal* by Frederick Forsyth, *The Human Target* (comic book), anything by Jon Land *(The Alpha Deception, The Gamma Option),* anything by Robert Ludlum (especially *The Bourne Identity* and its sequels).

Movies: Any of the James Bond movies, *Black Box Affair, Cube, Day of the Jackal* (both versions), *Hudson Hawk, In Like Flint, MI: 2, The One, Our Man Flint, Replacement Killers, Ronin, The Specialist.*

TV Shows: *Alias, The Avengers, CI5: The New Professionals, C.S.I.: Crime Scene Investigation, Danger Man/Secret Agent, The Invisible Man* (2000), *MacGyver, The Prisoner, The Professionals, Return of the Saint, Secret Agent Man, Stingray, Spy Game.*

Music: The James Bond scores and theme songs, *Replacement Killers* score, *Speed* score.

Computer and Console Games: *Goldeneye, the Gran Turismo* driving series, *No One Lives Forever, Spy Hunter, Spy Hunter 2.*

Tepe, Dumisani A.

Codename: ARES
Aliases: None
Archer Identity Number: 44-613097-882
Nationality: African (Black)
Gender: Male **Handedness:** Left
Height: 6 ft. 1 in. **Weight:** 185 lbs.
Eyes: Dark Brown **Hair:** None
Psion Class: Non-latent
Place of Birth: Mozambique, Africa
Date of Birth: 1969.08.19
Distinguishing Characteristics: Armani-quality suits, signature items (vehicle, handgun)

Background

Dumisani Tepe is the first man Control Elias Graham turns to in times of need. Having trained with both the Pan-Asian Collective and Room 39, Tepe is an incredible athlete, accomplished driver, and experienced sniper, with the strength and training to tackle almost any physical challenge. His sharp wit and Cambridge-educated mind are primed to make the most of any situation – and the wealth of tradecraft knowledge he has acquired over his many years playing the Great Game.

But beyond this perfect exterior, Tepe is an enigma – particularly to his fellow Alliance agents. His lifestyle is habitual (some call it "robotic"); he is completely monogamous in the pistol he carries (a Mateba auto-revolver), the rifle he uses (a Steyr SBS Tactical Elite), and the car he drives (a Peugeot Oxia), and spends nearly all his time leaping from one completed mission objective to the next, never looking back and never pausing to consider his isolation. His only downtime is the dalliances his playboy facade permits – an endless parade of fast cars, beautiful women, and life-or-death moments.

Deeper still, Tepe served as the primary catalyst in the birth of the Alliance. Captured by Helix for reasons he still doesn't understand, he is the reason that Elias

Graham (the Alliance's founder and current Control) turned on the Mastermind. *(See page 71 for background concerning this event.)*

Low-Level Dumisani Tepe

Chamber: The African Alliance
Department: Home Office (0)
Class: Wheelman
Level: 7

Strength:	14	**Dexterity:**	18
Constitution:	15	**Intelligence:**	16
Wisdom:	14	**Charisma:**	16
Vitality:	65	**Wounds:**	15

Defense: 18 (+4 class, +4 Dex)
Initiative Bonus: +8 (+4 class, +4 Dex)
Speed: 30

Fort: +4 **Ref:** +9 **Will:** +4

Skills: Balance +9, Boating +10, Bluff +5, Cultures +6, Demolitions +8, Disguise +9, Driver +14, Escape Artist +8, Handle Animal +4, Intimidate +4, Languages +6, Open Lock +8, Pilot +10, Spot +10, Surveillance +8, Survival +8, Swim +7

Feats: Drive By, One Hand on the Wheel, Point Blank Shot, Precise Shot, Ride Shotgun, Speed Demon, Speed Trigger

Attacks

Mateba AR (.357 Magnum)	+11 ranged (2d4+1)
Steyr TacElite (5.56×45mm)	+11 ranged (2d8+2)

Gear: Per assignment

Common Gadgets: Sub-cochlear implant, palmprint identifier for both weapons

Mid-Level Dumisani Tepe

Chamber: The African Alliance
Department: Home Office (0)
Class: Wheelman
Level: 14

Strength:	14	**Dexterity:**	18
Constitution:	15	**Intelligence:**	16
Wisdom:	14	**Charisma:**	18
Vitality:	125	**Wounds:**	15

Defense: 22 (+8 class, +4 Dex)
Initiative Bonus: +12 (+8 class, +4 Dex)
Speed: 30

Fort: +6 **Ref:** +13 **Will:** +6

Skills: Balance +15, Boating +15, Bluff +10, Cultures +10, Demolitions +13, Disguise +15, Driver +19, Escape Artist +12, Handle Animal +10, Intimidate +10, Languages +10, Open Lock +12, Pilot +15, Spot +14, Surveillance +12, Survival +12, Swim +7

Feats: A Gun in the Other, Drive By, Far Shot, Lane Dancer, One Hand on the Wheel, Point Blank Shot, Precise Shot, Rapid Shot, Ride Shotgun, Speed Demon, Speed Trigger, Test Lap

Attacks

Mateba AR (.357 Magnum)	+18 ranged (2d4+1)
Steyr TacElite (5.56×45mm)	+18 ranged (2d8+2)

Gear: Per assignment

Common Gadgets: Sub-cochlear implant, palmprint identifier for both weapons

High-Level Dumisani Tepe

Chamber: The African Alliance
Department: Home Office (0)
Class: Wheelman
Level: 20

Strength:	14	**Dexterity:**	20
Constitution:	15	**Intelligence:**	16
Wisdom:	14	**Charisma:**	18
Vitality:	182	**Wounds:**	15

Defense: 27 (+12 class, +5 Dex)
Initiative Bonus: +17 (+12 class, +5 Dex)
Speed: 30

Fort: +8 **Ref:** +17 **Will:** +8

Skills: Balance +18, Boating +18, Bluff +16, Cultures +12, Demolitions +15, Disguise +16, Driver +26, Escape Artist +16, Handle Animal +14, Intimidate +16, Languages +12, Open Lock +16, Pilot +18, Spot +18, Surveillance +15, Survival +15, Swim +10

Feats: A Gun in the Other, Defensive Driving, Drive By, Extreme Range, Far Shot, Increased Precision, Lane Dancer, Offensive Driving, One Hand on the Wheel, Point Blank Shot, Precise Shot, Rapid Shot, Ride Shotgun, Signature Gear (Mateba AR pistol), Speed Demon, Speed Trigger, Test Lap

Attacks

Mateba AR (.357 Magnum)	+25 ranged (2d4+1)
Steyr TacElite (5.56×45mm)	+25 ranged (2d8+2)

Gear: Per assignment

Common Gadgets: Sub-cochlear implant, palmprint identifier for both weapons

Graham, Elias "Tendaji"

Codename: None
Archer Identity Number: 70-804992-611
Nationality: African (White)
Gender: Male **Handedness:** Right
Height: 5 ft. 11 in. **Weight:** 165 lbs.
Eyes: Blue **Hair:** White
Psion Class: Non-latent
Place of Birth: Pretoria, Africa
Date of Birth: 1949.01.28
Distinguishing Characteristics: Monocle worn over right eye.

Background

Elias Graham is the most fatherly of Archer's Controls. A strong and nurturing role model, his personal approach has developed incredible bonds with each of his agents, most of whom would die for him if the situation arose.

Graham's parents were killed during a riot in his home city of Pretoria, but rather than blame their deaths on the "lesser" blacks, he looked to the rift between the classes, vowing to eradicate it. This goal has become his life-long passion, and even threatens to overshadow his work with the Archer Foundation.

It was this passion which led to the darkest period of Graham's life. Deluded by Helix that joining forces could lead to a resolution of Africa's social ills, Graham remained ignorant (perhaps consciously) of the madman's cruelties for many months, until one case – that of Dumisani Tepe *(see page 70)* – hit a little too close to home.

Tepe was a prisoner on Eden, much like a hundred others, but he was not a psion; Helix had captured him for some other purpose. The madman wanted to break Tepe, and used many psychological trials to do so. When Helix brought Tepe's parents to the island as leverage, Graham finally let go of his blind ignorance, and called in the Archer Foundation to shut Helix down.

Today, Graham and Tepe have remained professional, though their bond transcends their work for the Foundation.

Low-Level Elias Graham

Chamber: The African Alliance
Department: Home Office (0)
Class: Faceman
Level: 2

Strength:	10	**Dexterity:**	10
Constitution:	10	**Intelligence:**	14
Wisdom:	18	**Charisma:**	14
Vitality:	16	**Wounds:**	10

Defense: 11 (+1 class, +0 Dex)
Initiative Bonus: +6 (+2 class, +0 Dex, +4 Improved Initiative)
Speed: 30

Fort: +4 **Ref:** +0 **Will:** +6

Skills: Bluff +6, Craft (Model Buildings) +3, Cultures +9, Diplomacy +7, Disguise +4, Driver +2, Gather Information +6, Innuendo +6, Knowledge (African History) +5, Knowledge (Politics) +5, Languages +9, Perform (Public Speaking) +4, Read Lips +6, Sense Motive +6

Feats: Great Fortitude, Improved Initiative

Attacks

.40 backup pistol	+1 ranged (1d12)

Gear: Encrypted laptop

Common Gadgets: Sub-cochlear implant, danger unit (ear implant), safety field cufflinks

Mid-Level Elias Graham

Chamber: The African Alliance
Department: Home Office (0)
Class: Faceman
Level: 9

Strength:	10	**Dexterity:**	10
Constitution:	10	**Intelligence:**	14
Wisdom:	18	**Charisma:**	16
Vitality:	54	**Wounds:**	10

Defense: 15 (+5 class, +0 Dex)
Initiative Bonus: +11 (+7 class, +0 Dex, +4 Improved Initiative)
Speed: 30

Fort: +6 **Ref:** +3 **Will:** +8

Skills: Bluff +12, Craft (Model Buildings) +6, Cultures +16, Diplomacy +14, Disguise +12, Driver +8, Gather Information +12, Innuendo +12, Knowledge (African History) +10, Knowledge (Politics) +10, Languages +16, Perform (Public Speaking) +10, Read Lips +10, Sense Motive +10

Feats: Field Operative, Great Fortitude, Improved Initiative, Quick Use (Diplomacy), Weapon Focus (.40 pistol)

ATTACKS

.40 backup pistol +7 ranged (1d12)

Gear: Encrypted laptop

Common Gadgets: Sub-cochlear implant, danger unit (ear implant), safety field cufflinks

HIGH-LEVEL ELIAS GRAHAM

Chamber: The African Alliance
Department: Home Office (0)
Class: Faceman
Level: 16

Strength:	11	**Dexterity:**	11
Constitution:	10	**Intelligence:**	14
Wisdom:	18	**Charisma:**	16
Vitality:	93	**Wounds:**	10

Defense: 20 (+10 class, +0 Dex)
Initiative Bonus: +17 (+13 class, +0 Dex, +4 Improved Initiative)
Speed: 30

Fort: +9 **Ref:** +5 **Will:** +11

Skills: Bluff +16, Craft (Model Buildings) +9, Cultures +22, Diplomacy +20, Disguise +18, Driver +10, Gather Information +16, Innuendo +15, Knowledge (African History) +14, Knowledge (Politics) +12, Languages +23, Perform (Public Speaking) +14, Read Lips +12, Sense Motive +13

Feats: Combat Instincts, Confident Charge, Field Operative, Great Fortitude, Improved Initiative, Quick Use (Diplomacy), Weapon Focus (.40 pistol)

ATTACKS

.40 backup pistol +13 ranged (1d12)

Gear: Encrypted laptop

Common Gadgets: Sub-cochlear implant, danger unit (ear implant), safety field cufflinks

THE COMPANY

Si vis pacem para bellum.
"If you want peace, prepare for war."

—Vegetius, Roman military author

During the Cold War, the United States relied upon the CIA's covert operations arm to project force when the direct use of the U.S. military would have led to war. But the fact that the CIA is primarily an intelligence-gathering tool makes it a poor substitute for a true army.

The Company, the American Chamber of Archer's protectorate, merges the information resources of the United States' intelligence agencies with the military might of the nation's armed forces. A hybrid of last-strike brute force and classic Cold War espionage techniques, the Company would be poised as the world's foremost spy powerhouse, but the scandals that have rocked this partially-corrupt agency haunt it to this day.

THE COMPANY'S MISSION

The Archer Foundation calls upon the Company when it needs fast (and often dirty) results, typically of a military or paramilitary nature. The Company is Archer's enforcement arm, operating worldwide whenever the Foundation needs military force. It differs from Room 39's Ultracorps in its tactics and intent; the latter usually operate early during operations, before the need for outright violence becomes necessary and precision results are crucial. Company operations, on the other hand, are more often than not quite loud, with a lot of collateral fallout.

The Company is rarely used in well-populated areas, nor is it called in when prisoners, technology, or locations must be captured. Subtle missions of this nature are the purview of other Chambers. Company operatives often to assist with such missions, however.

Company intelligence operations are generally restricted to deep insertion campaigns, well within enemy territory.

Function

Not all Company men are soldiers. Every army requires a skilled and well-informed support staff of spies, strategists, technicians, correspondents, and suppliers. For this reason, the American Chamber has developed as an operational cell of its own (though one with a far sharper focus than Archer's cells in other regions).

As a unit, the Company specializes in much the same activities as the United States, though they apply such tactics far more ruthlessly. Company agents are masters of economic espionage, using hard (paper) and soft (electronic) currency to fund their operations, manipulate world events, and sway or topple enemy front organizations and personnel. They utilize political warfare to influence opinion in target regions, or undermine their enemy's reputations.

Regardless of their standing with the Foundation, the Company is still perhaps the strongest of the Chambers, having burrowed into modern America's intelligence community at its roots. As a result, the Company has access to invaluable resources and connections, as well as the political reputation of the world's last remaining superpower.

All of this adds up to a powerful collection of information, military strength, and influence that Archer calls upon when it needs "the big guns." But this overt strength comes with a dangerous price – the greatest potential to pierce the Cloak and reveal the Foundation and its mission. Because of this, the Company is always kept at arm's length from the heart of the Conspiracy, and two or more layers of personnel, political misdirection, and outright lies are maintained between the two.

Common Company Operations

The Company almost always receives clear and concise mission parameters, with triply redundant backup plans, both to maximize its military regimen and due to the fallacious perception that the Chamber's "jarhead simpletons" are unable to think for themselves. When the Company receives few instructions, the mission usually involves simple goals, such as sterilizing an enemy base or occupied region.

Company operatives often work as the muscle of field teams including agents from other Chambers. Specialists with field gear – particularly cutting-edge military hardware available only to U.S. armed forces – enter the fray when only their talents can solve the problem at hand. And many times, Company agents are merely collected with hardware redistributed to Archer operatives in the field.

Internally, the Company works a little differently. It endorses unorthodox problem-solving tactics and trains its operatives to understand the political and social ramifications of their actions (both in the long and short term). Company agents follow the simple understanding of the Special Forces – regardless of what outsiders think of them, they understand and accept the responsibility of their positions, keep a level head, and get the job done.

With all this in mind, the Company performs many common operations for the Foundation. The bulk are included here, along with how they apply in the *Shadowforce Archer* setting.

Combat Search and Rescue (CSAR): When agents, allies, specialists, or contacts are trapped in a hostile area, Company teams might covertly enter the area, seek out the targets, and extract them. The level of acceptable casualties (on both sides) changes from one mission to the next, but the intent is always the same – bring the targets home alive. In the *Shadowforce Archer* setting, this type of mission takes place after another mission has failed and the operatives have been taken prisoner, or during one of the many minor conflicts that erupt in Africa, the Middle East, or Europe.

Counter-Proliferation: Company operatives are frequently called when there is imminent danger from a weapon of mass destruction (nuclear, chemical, biological, or bacteriological). Such situations are always critical and time-sensitive.

The "Fix": The "Fix" is a term used by certain soldiers and underworld figures, meaning "compromise, blackmail, and misdirection." When operatives are called upon to fix someone, they are being ordered to ruin them – financially, socially, politically, or even emotionally. This type of work requires a detached mindset which many agents lack.

The Archer Foundation often uses this tactic against enemies who are in a position of power (particularly if they are also well known), and when direct action is not an option. A classic example of the Fix is the case of Madame Izichi, of Izichi Industries, whose stranglehold of the Pacific Rim arms trade was almost as dangerous as the small third world nation she planned to buy with the profits – until Company representatives revealed her plans to the Yakuza and the Triads. Within days, the situation dissolved into an easily manipulated (and contained) street war between the rival gun-lords.

Foreign Relations: Like the CIA, the Company often contacts, organizes, and trains outside militias, foreign militaries, and guerrilla groups. It is uniquely prepared for this mission, since the Company maintains many agent cells in hot spots around the world that can be called upon at a moment's notice.

"The Front Door": When diplomacy and subversion fail, it's time for action. The Company excels at quick raids and direct frontal assaults, cleaving enemy forces in half and cutting them off from their chain of command, communication lines, and supply depots. This type of mission also includes less honorable endeavors (kidnapping and assassination) when the need for them arises.

Archer rarely uses this option unless facing a militarily-superior foe which cannot be defeated through any other means. Front Door operations are generally conducted by non-Archer ops.

Intelligence Operations (a.k.a. "Hostile Recon"): Most of the time, true intelligence gathering missions go to other Chambers (according to their individual specialties), but sometimes the required data is heavily guarded or the odds in an area are stacked against stealth teams. In this case, the Company goes in to retrieve the intel by force. This type of mission also includes operations intended to disrupt or destroy enemy intelligence-gathering facilities, and also the fine art of diversions.

"Lifers": Company operatives are kept on a short leash, rarely allowed to operate outside strictly-observed protocols. But some agents have proven themselves worthy of reduced supervision – the right to travel where and when they feel they can make a difference (until they are activated, of course). These agents are called "lifers."

The Company's premier field operative John Hunter *(see page 81)* and his team are lifers, as are many of the Chamber's most trusted long-term agents. Lifers must frequently contact the Hub or a Chamber satellite *(see pages 75),* and are forbidden to conduct Front Door operations without approval. When activated (usually without warning, through a designated code word or signal), they must immediately make contact with their handler to receive their mission objectives.

Most lifers carry a good deal of "personal" equipment with them in the field, including sidearms, communication gear, and the ocassional PsiTech gadget. When sent on a mission, their contact or a local specialist hands out additional items.

Peace Operations: Company operatives often assist with operations promoting peace. This type of mission is most likely to draw non-combatant Company operatives into the field. Traditional agents are also brought along – as security, or as a "backup plan" if peace talks fail.

Agent Expectations

Players who enjoy aggressive agents will likely find the Company appealing. The average agent of this Chamber is physically rugged and scrappy, used to being in the eye of the storm. Career military men, soldiers of fortune, and gritty mercenaries all work well as part of this Chamber.

But there is also another side to the Company – the planners and analysts, intelligence agents and vehicle specialists, all of whom have a role out in the field which is just as crucial as that of the "junkyard dogs." The Company employs a tremendous number of civilians (mainly academics), whose function it is to support the rest of the team during missions.

Regardless of team position, however, all Company agents share certain characteristics. All are physically fit, capable of surviving in the wilderness and hostile territory. All are free of debilitating conditions, such as reduced vision, nerve disorders, and the like (or they hide their problem well). All have one or more fields of expertise (demolitions, close assault, or SCUBA, for example). All have nerves of steel and the will to endure even the most uncomfortable conditions.

The Company is highly task-oriented, funneling resources and personnel through specific channels into specific projects toward a specific goal. Like the CIA, it is strictly compartmentalized, with each section of the Chamber dedicated to a closely defined job. Once a mission begins, nothing and no one may stand in the way of the objective, and there is rarely room for negotiation or reconsideration.

Company agents are well-trained, well-equipped, and have access to many resources that other Chambers don't, including superior intel and technology (including PsiTech).

One last thing. Company agents don't volunteer; the Chamber hand-picks them for their talents. Agents of the Company should be designed accordingly.

Company Tactical Data

The Company relies heavily upon the tactical, technological, and informational superiority of the United States as its weapons in the struggle against global threats. In particular, it relies upon the U.S. militaries, which already have everything they need – doctors and hospitals, lawyers and courts, teachers and schools, mechanics, secret agents, police, infantry, and pilots, just to scratch the surface. They have chains of command and career ladders – a built-in structure for the Chamber to adopt. Finally, if needed, the Company is fully self-sufficient, which is an incredible help when organizing and executing covert missions.

Company PsiTech

As one would expect, the Company devotes most of its technological development to creating tools of war. Yet war requires a great many tools to succeed, not all of which are designed exclusively to harm. Company operatives frequently rely upon PsiTech stealth technology to approach and evade enemy forces without detection. They also utilize gadgets to help them traverse difficult terrain.

Chamber Organization

Despite its constant operations and dozens of one-shot missions, the Company's structure remains perfectly simple. Most core personnel and resources are pooled within three U.S. organizations – the Central Intelligence Agency (CIA), Defense Intelligence Agency (DIA), and National Security Agency (NSA), with the Department of Defense (DoD) and National Security Council acting as an umbrella over the whole affair.

The "Hub"

The Hub is the center of the Company web, where all its important decisions are made. Not a physical office so much as an informal, undocumented band of administrators, military leaders, paper-pushers, and bureaucrats, this rogue agency within the U.S. government and military takes its cues from the Foundation home office in Australia. The Hub is responsible for identifying potential threats within the Company's shadow communities, and assigning and directing mission teams to take care of them. It secretly siphons resources from the U.S. government, using bogus project names, forged expense reports, and a variety of other means, funneling them to Company agents as needed.

Most Hub personnel and resources belong to the CIA's four Directorates, and are "borrowed" without the U.S. government's knowledge when necessary. They forge personnel rosters to look like U.S. agents loyal to the Conspiracy are on vacation while in the field, and place numerous resources "on loan" for Company agents' use.

Most personnel and resources are stolen from the Directorate for Administration, the heart of the Archer Conspiracy's American Chamber. Over eighty percent of the Company's missions are filtered through the Directorate of Administration, and agents cultivated in the Directorate are responsible for funding, organizing, and commanding agents of the entire Chamber.

Historically, the Hub drew heavily upon the power of the CIA's Director of Central Intelligence (DCI), who – by virtue of the National Security Act of 1947 – had control of not only his own agency, but most other U.S. intelligence agencies as well. But when the scandals of the 1960s and '70s brought so much attention to the DCI's high-profile position, the Company withdrew deep into the CIA's operational Directorate and laid low until the time was right to climb back to the top.

That time has not yet come.

Today, Hub operatives are gathered in most departments of the U.S. government, grouped together in small cells of 3 to 12 agents, dedicated to tightly defined jobs or goals. When a cell is compromised, they are immediately "burned" (cut off from all other cells), and a backup cell trained to perform the same function is activated.

For example, Cell B10 is in charge of selecting new field agents. It scours the thousands of government, military, industrial, and civilian applications that the CIA review each year, and passes along the few dozen they think might have something to offer. This is B10's only function; it does absolutely nothing else for the Company. Should it ever be discovered or infiltrated, Cell B11 – whose efforts mirror those of B10, even though they never see each other – is ready to pick up where B10 left off.

The CIA has many valuable traits to offer the Company. Within the halls of its Langley, Virginia headquarters and beyond, practically everything is "need to know" only, allowing the Company to work largely without interference. Also, the "Agency" (as the CIA is often called) breaks down into geographic divisions which rely heavily upon intel from foreign agencies (in what are called "liaison relationships"), providing a ready avenue for communication with Archer's other Chambers.

Chamber "Satellites"

The bulk of non-CIA Company operatives work in one of two satellite agencies – the Defense Intelligence Agency (DIA) or the National Security Agency (NSA), each of which offers a number of important benefits. Being the collection center for all military intelligence, the DIA provides the Company with much of its tactical data, as well as connections with the armies of other nations. NSA – beyond further solidifying the Company's internal security – provides technical and technological support, as well as secure communications *(see below)*.

Company agents in each of these satellites are organized just as those in the CIA (broken into cells with redundant backups, all with specific parameters). For the purposes of communication, there is no difference between agents of the Hub and its satellites; the division exists merely because operatives cannot easily transfer between agencies of the U.S. government.

Once the National Security Council (NSC) was considered a Hub satellite, but since the death of Secretary of Defense Joseph Broch in 1998, there has been no Company representative among them. The Foundation hopes to rectify this following the elections of 2004, when their plans for Col. Alan Deitrich reach fruition *(see page 84)*.

Field Operations

Company field operatives receive orders from the Hub or one of its foreign liaisons, which are usually quite detailed and almost always coded with a private NSA cipher known to the receiving cell. The CIA maintains operations headquarters (called *stations*) in each major nation, usually located at the U.S. Embassy in the nation's capital city, but the Company rarely filters information through them. Most stations are relatively small and it is very hard to get anything through without drawing attention to it.

Field operatives usually work missions in small teams of 3–5 agents, supported when necessary by specialists with specific talents *(see page 266 of the Spycraft Espionage Handbook for more about specialists).* They perform their missions as quickly and efficiently as possible, then pull out of the area and contact the Hub through a pre-arranged channel or contrivance to receive their next op. Agents are only authorized to contact a local station if there is an immediate and significant threat (for instance, a weapon of mass destruction primed to attack a major populated city).

Communications

The final aspect of Company organization holds everything else together – its communications network. This takes the form of a tremendous volume of data, covertly transferred back and forth within existing U.S. channels. The vast majority of these are coded messages buried within otherwise innocuous reports which – after agents decipher them – are funneled to the "Pit," the CIA's enormous shredding and document destruction center at Langley.

Some messages, however, are too pressing for usual channels. These go through the National Intelligence Tasking Center as coded sections of National Intelligence Topics (NITs), which are distributed quickly and directly to the Company's Control and all relevant operatives.

Company Resources

The Company has a great many facilities at its disposal, some of which involve official U.S. endeavors they have reshaped to the cause, and others which are purely their own.

Training Facilities

Company operatives are trained in a wide variety of espionage and warfare techniques at several specialized locations around the U.S. and the world. But all Company operatives begin their training elsewhere – usually in the U.S. armed forces or intelligence community. They are recruited only when Company handlers know that they can handle the Chamber's rigorous mission.

Standard operating procedure for training Chamber operatives is to use existing training facilities and "hide in plain sight." In fact, there is only one Company-only base in the world – the Kennel *(see page 77)* – where trainees learn advanced military techniques.

The following is a short list of Company training facilities in the United States.

The Farm (codenamed ISOLATION): The CIA term for its secret training facility spread across several thousand acres of woodland territory outside Williamsburg,

Virginia. Otherwise known as Camp Peary, the Farm is the CIA's foremost hotspot for tutoring saboteurs, infiltrators, and master spies.

The Joint Military Intelligence College: This DIA facility at Bolling Air Force Base in Washington, D.C. is an open university which offers Bachelors' and Masters' degrees in espionage. Many new recruits come here to learn basic tradecraft (the tools and techniques of spying).

The Kennel: One of the Archer company's two super-spy schools, this Butte, Montana military compound runs candidates through the company's personalized version of Boot Camp: twelve grueling weeks of special forces, weapons, survival, and counterespionage training. All physical adepts take special courses here to learn the applications and limits of their talents.

The National Cryptologic School: NSA operates this branch of operations in a seven-story tower of the FANX (Friendship Annex) complex immediately outside the Baltimore-Washington (Friendship) International Airport, where students attend basic, advanced, and Ph.D.-level signals intelligence, cryptographic, and analytic courses.

Other facilities exist for specialized training, many of them temporary or mobile. For example, agents learn cryptography, languages, and cultural skills at the Presidio (San Francisco, California). Jungle survival is taught in places like Panama, and skiing, climbing, and winter survival training takes place at locations like the illustrious 10th Mountain at Fort Drum, New York.

Operation UNDERWORLD

In 1942, the FBI coordinated with the U.S. Mafia to protect the eastern seaboard from potential Nazi incursions. When the Allies landed in Italy later in the war, this relationship extended into Europe. The operation publicly disbanded following the Axis defeat, but the Company secretly maintained it, recruiting from American-based crime families and organizations (including, during the scandalous 1960s, the Black Panthers) to manage many of its domestic operations.

Operation UNDERWORLD has been radically successful, resulting in perhaps the strongest homefront of any Chamber in the world. Street gangs provide a perfect context for counterespionage, being both accepted and well-connected coast-to-coast. In fact, Fade's criminal empire in Europe is rumored to use the same principles in its infrastructure.

Recently, however, UNDERWORLD has found itself in direct competition with the International Mafia, Yakuza, and a new Russian mob founded by renegade Confederacy operatives *(see page 80 for more about the Inner Circle and its "Crazy Ivans")*, all of whom are suddenly encroaching on U.S. territory with incredible zeal. This situation now borders on an all-out street war in every major city of the United States – one which the Company is ill-prepared to deal with.

The Defense Intelligence Network (DIN)

The incredible wealth of information available to the U.S. intelligence community is rivaled only by the speed with which it is transmitted. One resource the Company frequently relies upon – the Defense Intelligence Network – embodies this creed. An encrypted, closed-circuit telecast to invite-only viewers around the world (including many Company operatives), the DIN broadcasts aerial and satellite images, audio reports, sit-reps, critical news, and other items of national interest. The Company often taps into this CNN-like service for updates, or to share coded messages between agents in the field.

Overwatch

At one time, world intelligence agencies relied upon inaccurate satellite photos which had to be recovered from jettisoned capsules after re-entry. Later orbital technology advanced to the level where images could be beamed directly back to Earth as soon as they were taken, allowing fast response to important world events. Now, the Archer Foundation has taken the next step.

Project OVERWATCH is a global surveillance system coordinating existing satellites (some abandoned by their parent nations) through a core orbital platform launched by an independent contractor (the Omnium Corporation) in 1984. The system is among the most advanced early warning and reconnaissance tools in the world, utilizing state-of-the-art technologies to remotely immerse commanders in situations happening hundreds or thousands of miles away.

The Company operates OVERWATCH mainly because its parent organizations are already trained and equipped to use the technology, but the information gleaned using the system is transmitted worldwide to Controls and agents for use during Foundation ops.

Covert Action Teams

Finally, there are the combatants of the Company, the men (and recently women) who wage the secret war on the front lines...

Airborne Rangers (U.S. Army): Generally, Rangers are expected to support U.S. infantry, working in huge formations, but the Company recruits them for their secondary purpose as small long-range recon teams. Ranger training focuses on leadership, physical and stress training, recon, mountaineering, and navigation in harsh terrain.

Delta Force (U.S. Army): First Special Forces Operational Detachment – Delta (1st SFOD-Delta) is a mission-tailored combat unit, trained to be combat-ready in under four hours. Delta Force training focuses on firearms use, first aid, vehicle maintenance, and close combat techniques. Since the early 1990s, Delta Force has included women in its ranks, conducted covert intelligence raids, and worked indirectly with the DIA.

Force Recon (U.S. Marines): Force Recon scouts landing sites for the U.S. Marines and performs periodic long-range recon missions. Their regimen is similar to that of the Airborne Rangers, though more focused on amphibious and harsh-environment training.

Special Forces (U.S. Army): The parent branch for Delta Force, Special Forces is called in for long-term operations. Unlike the other groups listed here, Special Forces bring their own support equipment, and transport heavy ordnance with them on their missions. Special Forces training includes psychological conditioning, stress-combat techniques, and specialized technical skills. All Special Forces recruits learn a foreign language.

SEALs (U.S. Navy): SEAL troops usually operate from a Navy task force, which provides their logistic support, and perform quick recon, underwater operations, and assassination. SEAL training focuses on SCUBA, demolitions, and physical conditioning.

The Sons of Valhalla

One of the most unusual resources the Company has at its disposal (and one they don't tell the Archer Foundation about) are the Sons of Valhalla. This biker gang – part of the infamous "Hell's Angels" – actually serves as a seasoned mission team mainly composed of soldiers and wheelmen. The Sons of Valhalla grew up together, voluntarily toured together in Vietnam (when they were recruited into the Conspiracy through resident CIA contacts), and now ride together as a mobile agent cell working throughout the continental U.S.

The Game in the U.S.A.

U.S. espionage has always been associated primarily with the Central Intelligence Agency *(see below)*, but the American syndicate of spies is in truth much larger and far more complicated.

U.S. Intelligence Agencies

The following agencies have been infiltrated by the Archer Foundation or are involved in the Company's current plotlines. Additional agencies are forthcoming in the *Company* sourcebook.

Central Intelligence Agency (CIA): The United States' peacetime intelligence and covert action arm was formed by the 1947 National Security Act, which also founded the Department of Defense and the National Security Council. Today, the CIA's mandate includes countering the proliferation of weapons of mass destruction, drug trafficking, international organized crime, and industrial (economic) espionage. The Director of Central Intelligence (DCI) is head of the CIA, and reports to the National Security Council, which oversees high-risk covert operations.

The CIA consists of several Directorates, each with a broad function. The Directorate for Operations collects foreign intelligence and conducts counter-inteligence outside the U.S. The Directorate for Intelligence analyzes gathered data and produces reports. The Directorate for Administration handles personnel and physical security. The Directorate for Science and Technology includes many offices: the Office of Technical Services develops espionage techniques and trains operatives in how to use them; the Office of SIGINT assists the National Security Agency (NSA) with signals intelligence; the National Photographic Interpretation Center studies aerial and satellite recon; and the Foreign Broadcast Information Service (FBIS) monitors world television and radio, producing transcripts.

The CIA operates without disclosing its official titles, salaries, budget, or contracts, and it can award permanent residency to aliens and their families (such as defectors and foreign agents).

Defense Intelligence Agency (DIA): Part of the Department of Defense (DoD), the DIA acts as a centralized hub for collecting and disseminating all U.S. military intelligence. It also oversees subordinate organizations and provides intelligence to UN peacekeeping forces, terrorist task teams, and law enforcement agencies working against drug traffickers.

The DIA often dispatches U.S. ambassadors and attachés on foreign diplomatic missions (during which they covertly gather military intelligence about the governments they visit). These representatives enjoy diplomatic immunity, enforced by the U.S. government.

While the DIA is an established U.S. agency, the U.S. government frequently overlooks it, coming under fire as a duplication of other intelligence organizations and relying upon information from other agencies to operate.

The DIA answers to the Secretary of Defense, the Joint Chiefs of Staff, the CIA's Director of Central Intelligence, United and Specified Commands, and other authorized agencies.

DIA headquarters is located at the Pentagon. More than sixty percent of its personnel are civilians.

Federal Bureau of Investigation (FBI): The Federal Bureau of Investigation is the U.S. government's chief domestic investigative and policing cell. Agents of the FBI counter foreign incursions on U.S. soil, including covert intelligence gathering, terrorism, organized crime, sabotage, public corruption, civil rights violations, and abduction of U.S. citizens.

The FBI has the authority to arrest suspects of international and domestic crime on U.S. soil, and has been responsible for the capture of many foreign spies and saboteurs including Aldrich Ames and the Walker Spy Ring.

These days, the FBI's primary focus is on terrorism and the profiling and capture of serial killers (through their Psychological Crimes Division).

National Security Agency (NSA): NSA (convention demands that the agency be referred to as "NSA," not "the NSA") provides comprehensive information security to the United States. Within this broad mission, NSA is authorized to intercept and catalog any foreign communication, with only a few restrictions (one specifying they replace American citizens' names with the term "U.S. citizen" on all transcripts).

NSA regularly taps telephone lines, intercepts radio, radar, and missile guidance signals as well as foreign space traffic, and provides dedicated communications gear and protocols for U.S. operatives working overseas. It also operates and maintains most U.S. government computer systems.

NSA also creates secure codes and ciphers for the U.S., while cracking those of other nations. The elite technicians of NSA's Central Security Service (CSS) and its Special Collection Service (SCS) operate under a shroud of secrecy, eavesdropping on intelligence targets in hostile territories.

Finally, NSA frequently plans operations conducted by other agencies. It was behind the U-2 spy plane missions of the 1960s. If desired, it could even orchestrate its own.

NSA has gained a reputation as a snoop's paradise, alternately referred to as the "Puzzle Palace," "No Such Agency," and "Never Say Anything." Its enormous budget (estimated at over 4 billion dollars a year) and the intense demands of working with it (operatives must seek permission to marry foreigners and visit only agency-approved doctors and dentists) contribute to this view.

Playing the Great Game

"A wise man I trust once said, 'So long as his eyes remain clear, the patriot will always serve the greater good.'"

– Col. Alan Deitrich

Mission Management: Somewhat paradoxically, the Conspiracy's most violent arm is rather squeamish when it comes to information extraction. The typical Company field agent prefers a "clean kill" to any operation requiring treachery or deceit. Given growing economic and social ties between East and West, the Company now redirects most operations that might "taint" the Chamber's reputation to the PAC.

Damage Control: The betrayal of Dennis Gray was a devastating blow to the Company's already stained reputation. Worse, and known only to the Company's new Control and a handful of key Hub directors, Dennis Gray requested a complete catalogue of Company assets before he went to ground, asking that only one physical copy be made. That file is now missing.

Dirty Little Secrets: The Company have never been very good at keeping secrets, as their beleaguered history shows. The benefit, of course, is that there is nothing for anyone to dig up about them. Company agents often take this to an extreme, wearing their indiscretions on their sleeves, defying the other Chambers to embarrass them. No one has ever managed to.

Leverage: Four years ago, Company agent John Hunter headed up a team of operatives who raided a South American base presumably belonging to the Hand of Glory. They met little resistance, securing the area with ease. The complex proved to be a storing ground of sorts, a stockpile of captured war treasures collectively worth several hundred thousand dollars but independently unimpressive. Knowing that they couldn't return the relics to their rightful owners all at once without arousing suspicion, the Company shipped the lot back to the United States and stored it in an unused

Virginia bunker. They planned to trickle the items back into the public slowly, one or two at a time, with appropriated personnel. Hunter unexpectedly volunteered to take control of the operation. As a somewhat more worldly operative of the Conspiracy, well-schooled in the shadow history, knew the truth – that the Company had stumbled onto a collection of minor mystic relics. Rather than funnel them into the hands of their previous owners (many of whom had been dead for years), Hunter set up an elegant underground courier service, sending the relics to the Guardians of the Whispering Knife. The relics were carried one or two at a time, by low-status agents who could move under the Conspiracy's radar, and delivered into the hands of Guardian liaisons in foreign Chamber offices or elsewhere in the world. The Guardian's liaison to the Company was never informed, for fear that his proximity to Deitrich might jeopardize the operation, but the Guardians responded. Several months ago, after more than twenty of the relics were slipped safely into the Middle East, a detachment of Guardian agents arrived at the Company's doorstep, as a "show of support" for the Company as it rebuilds following the Shop break. This arrangement has shocked many in the Conspiracy, who view the Guardians as too trustworthy to consort with the disreputable U.S. Chamber. Aside from ensuring that Hunter's clandestine salvage operation continues, these Guardians have greatly boosted the Company's foundering standing with the other Chambers, offering it unexpected leverage during yet another shaky period of its history.

Assets: With his claws dug deeply into the largest military-industrial complex in the world, Col. Deitrich found it relatively easy to set aside a little something special for all those "worst case scenarios" his analysts rant about – a medium-yield fission warhead. Sequestered in a presumably abandoned missile silo and lost in the recent political shuffle under the codename ACE OF SPADES, this insurance policy makes the Company - and more specifically, Col. Deitrich himself – the world's only covert nuclear power. Dietrich knows that using the device is tantamount to professional (and quite possibly personal) suicide, but if the fate of the Earth falls into the hands of a madman, he'll be ready to press the button.

Current Plotlines

The Company is currently embroiled in several major plotlines of the *Shadowforce Archer* setting, three of which are listed below. Any would make an excellent hook for a Mission or Serial. Many will be developed as part of the official *Shadowforce Archer* storyline.

Operation BONFIRE (Code: Black): The Shop used many of the Foundation's resources to prepare for their betrayal. This has left a foul taste in the mouths of the Company "Old Boys," who want nothing short of brutal justice against Archer's former R&D department. The Archer Foundation has since launched Operation HAYSTACK, to look for the renegade mentalists and those who were left behind to hinder Chamber operations. Its careful approach grates on the Old Boys, however, who have secretly launched their own search for the Shop (codenamed BONFIRE), utilizing force and intimidation.

In particular, the Old Boys are looking for ex-NSA agent Dennis Gray, the Company's former Control, who spearheaded the Shop's American activities – and vanished with them when they broke away. Prior to his departure, Gray was one of the most respected Controls in Company history, making his betrayal all the more bitter.

Operation FALLOUT (Code: Black): The Foundation has always suspected that, if the Cloak were ever actually pierced, the Company would be responsible. Their worries may finally have come home to roost. In 2000, a CIA "ferret search" (surprise internal inspection) yielded discrepancies in old National Intelligence Estimates (NIEs), long since swept under the carpet by the American Chamber. Dorien Spencer, the inspector who found the inconsistencies, is currently lobbying to resurrect the 1970s campaign to disclose CIA malpractice, and access the legendary "Family Jewels" document which compiled all of the CIA's Cold War missteps. The Company, which has so far remained undetected, is scrambling to keep the file closed.

The "Crazy Ivans" (Code: Red): Recent reports from UNDERWORLD agents indicate a striking increase in gang violence across the nation, linked primarily to the incursions of a Russian mob cell known as the "Crazy Ivans." The Company has long known of the Russians – even protecting them from Confederacy hitmen sent to eliminate them when they would not return home – but now that it appears they are peddling a distilled version of the Russian physical adept serum as a street-drug called "Rocket," the time for a final confrontation fast approaches.

The Company Genre

The American Chamber is a place of maverick, uncontrolled action, where gutsy acts of bravado outweigh the subtleties of classic espionage. Military spy tactics are the name of the game here. The loud nature of the average Company unit may make them difficult to include in some Serials. Players should consult the Game Control before generating a Company agent.

Archtypes: Action Man, G.I. Joe, Hitman (the comic book character), Kraven the Hunter, Jesse Custer and the Saint of Killers from *Preacher,* Max Steele, Nick Fury and S.H.I.E.L.D., Punisher, Rambo, the Unknown Soldier (the comic book character), Wolverine, and any big-budget action movie star (Bronson, Schwarzenegger, Stallone, Willis, etc.).

Inspirations

The following is an incomplete list of suggested viewing, reading, and listening for players of this agency, and the Game Control.

Books: *The Dogs of War* by Frederick Forsyth, *Firestarter* by Stephen King, *Merc* (comic book), *G.I. Joe* (comics – original version and recent revival, not the 90s variant), *The 'Nam* (comic book), *Preacher* (comic book), *The Unknown Soldier (*comic book), anything by Jack Higgins *(The Eagle Has Landed, Night of the Fox, On Dangerous Ground),* anything by W.E.B. Griffin (*The Corps* series, *Brotherhood of War* series).

Movies: *All the President's Men, Black Hawk Down,* the *Die Hard* movies, *Firestarter, Ice Station Zebra, The Professional* (a.k.a. *Leon*), *Missing in Action, Navy Seals, Peacemaker,* both *Predator* movies, *Proof of Life,* the *Rambo* movies (especially the second one), *Red Dawn, Saving Private Ryan, U-571,* anything by Don Simpson and Jerry Bruckheimer *(Armageddon, The Rock, Con Air),* anything by James Cameron (*True Lies*).

TV Shows: *The A-Team, Action Man, The Agency, Airwolf, Black Sheep Squadron, Combat, G.I. Joe, Max Steele, Soldier of Fortune, Inc., Tour of Duty, The West Wing.*

Music: *Aliens* score, the *Apocalypse Now* soundtrack, *Conan the Barbarian* score, *Gladiator* score, *The Professional* score, *The Siege* score, *Starship Troopers* score, *Terminator 2* score, heavy classical music (especially Wagner).

Computer and Console Games: *Medal of Honor: Allied Assault, Soldier: Metal Gear Solid* and its sequel, the *Twisted Metal* driving series.

Hunter, John D.

Codename: ORION
Archer Identity Number: 09-991607-539
Nationality: United States of America
Gender: Male **Handedness:** Right
Height: 6 ft. 1 in. **Weight:** 205 lbs.
Eyes: Hazel **Hair:** Long, Dirty Blonde
Psion Class: Non-latent
Place of Birth: Bethesda, Maryland, USA
Date of Birth: 1968.01.23
Distinguishing Characteristics: Three dogtags (one his father's)

BACKGROUND

The Company's premier field team is headed up by a second-generation Navy SEAL culled from the Farm, where his father trained new cadets until his suicide in 1996. John Hunter was personally recruited into the Company by Col. Alan Deitrich *(see page 84)*, though recent events have placed tremendous strain on their relationship.

Hunter believes in the Archer Foundation's mission, but sees the Company crumbling under the weight of four generations of old school hardliners who want to use it as a private army, stamping out evil without regard for innocents caught in the crossfire. He still remembers his father's only explanation for leaving the Chamber: "I can't tell where the enemy stops and we start any more," and, though he could not understand then, he is beginning to now.

John Hunter is one of many Archer agents classified as "fragile" (that is, wavering in their dedication to the cause), but he is not yet broken, and still has much to offer. Rugged, industrious, and adventuresome, John is perfect for difficult missions in unusual terrain (though some argue that his affinity for peril stems from a desire to meet his maker). Hunter also has the uncanny ability to fit in anywhere. Once, after dispatching four enemy divers off the coast of Russia, he dragged himself onto shore, stripped off his wetsuit, splashed vodka on his face, and stepped into an elegant party with no one the wiser.

LOW-LEVEL JOHN HUNTER

Chamber: The Company
Department: Military Ops (2)
Class: Pointman/Soldier
Level: 3/3

Strength:	16	**Dexterity:**	16
Constitution:	16	**Intelligence:**	12
Wisdom:	12	**Charisma:**	11
Vitality:	67	**Wounds:**	16

Defense: 15 (+2 class, +3 Dex)
Initiative Bonus: +7 (+4 class, +3 Dex)
Speed: 30

Fort: +11 **Ref:** +7 **Will:** +5

Skills: Balance +8, Climb +7, Demolitions +7, Driver +9, First Aid +5, Intimidate +5, Jump +7, Profession (Military) +6, Spot +7, Survival +5, Swim +7, Tumble +9

Feats: Martial Arts, Point Blank Shot, Precise Shot, Punching Basics, Snap Shot, Surge of Speed

ATTACKS

7.62×51mm assault rifle	+8 ranged (2d10)
H&K MP5 SMG (9mm)	+8 ranged (1d10)
Survival knife	+8 melee (1d6+3)

Gear: Hollow-point ammunition

Common Gadgets: Sub-cochlear implant, "snake suit" (all options), endorphin patches (3)

MID-LEVEL JOHN HUNTER

Chamber: The Company
Department: Military Ops (2)
Class: Pointman/Soldier
Level: 6/7

Strength:	16	**Dexterity:**	16
Constitution:	16	**Intelligence:**	12
Wisdom:	12	**Charisma:**	13
Vitality:	136	**Wounds:**	16

Defense: 18 (+5 class, +3 Dex)
Initiative Bonus: +11 (+8 class, +3 Dex)
Speed: 30

Fort: +14 **Ref:** +10 **Will:** +8

Skills: Balance +11, Climb +11, Demolitions +10, Driver +14, First Aid +8, Intimidate +8, Jump +12, Profession (Military) +9, Spot +10, Survival +8, Swim +10, Tumble +12

Feats: Far Shot, Lay Down Fire, Martial Arts, Point Blank Shot, Precise Shot, Punching Basics, Sharp-Shooting, Snap Shot, Surge of Speed, Weapon Focus (7.62 rifle)

ATTACKS

7.62×51mm assault rifle	+14 ranged (2d10)
H&K MP5 SMG (9mm)	+14 ranged (1d10)
Survival knife	+14 melee (1d6+3)

Gear: Hollow-point ammunition

Common Gadgets: Sub-cochlear implant, "snake suit" (all options), endorphin patches (3)

HIGH-LEVEL JOHN HUNTER

Chamber: The Company
Department: Military Ops (2)
Class: Pointman/Soldier
Level: 10/9

Strength:	16	**Dexterity:**	16
Constitution:	16	**Intelligence:**	12
Wisdom:	12	**Charisma:**	14
Vitality:	195	**Wounds:**	16

Defense: 21 (+8 class, +3 Dex)
Initiative Bonus: +14 (+11 class, +3 Dex)
Speed: 30

Fort: +17 **Ref:** +12 **Will:** +11

Skills: Balance +12, Bluff +6, Bureaucracy +6, Climb +12, Demolitions +12, Driver +18, First Aid +12, Intimidate +10, Jump +12, Profession (Military) +11, Sense Motive + 6, Spot +12, Survival +10, Swim +12, Tumble +14

Feats: Controlled Burst, Coordinate Fire, Far Shot, Lay Down Fire, Martial Arts, Point Blank Shot, Precise Shot, Punching Basics, Punching Mastery, Rapid Shot, Sharp-Shooting, Snap Shot, Surge of Speed, Weapon Focus (7.62 rifle), Weapon Specialization (7.62 rifle)

Attacks

7.62×51mm assault rifle	+19 ranged (2d10)
H&K MP5 SMG (9mm)	+19 ranged (1d10)
Survival knife	+19 melee (1d6+3)

Gear: Hollow-point ammunition

Common Gadgets: Sub-cochlear implant, "snake suit" (all options), endorphin patches (3)

Hendricks, Molly

Codename: CLIO
Aliases: None
Archer Identity Number: 21-773910-513
Nationality: United States of America
Gender: Male **Handedness:** Left
Height: 5 ft. 9 in. **Weight:** 145 lbs.
Eyes: Black **Hair:** Cropped, red
Psion Class: Non-latent
Place of Birth: New York, New York, USA
Date of Birth: 1979.03.12
Distinguishing Characteristics: None

Background

The youngest member of John Hunter's field team is Molly Hendricks, a stunning, vivacious civilian operative who calls herself a "progressive explorer." Brought into the Company for her sharp mind and prodigal skill with close combat weapons (particularly archaic ones), Molly is the only child of billionaire jet-setters who indulged her every whim. She spent many years bouncing from one idle passion to another before she struck her true calling: archaeology.

Molly spent the next three years poring over every historical text she could get her hands on and traveling to dig sites all across the world. Her parents offered to fund a college education in the subject, but she refused, claiming that formal learning took too long ("It's more posturing than pondering," she would say). When it became apparent that Molly would not abandon her new hobby, her parents offered to fund an organization dedicated to the enterprise, which is now widely considered one of the foremost efforts into uncovering the past.

Molly was recruited by the Company as part of Hunter's team when they were sent into South America to stop a deranged mastermind from resurrecting an army of fallen Aztec warriors. Her many languages, cultural knowledge, and unexpected combat prowess all came together to unexpectedly assist the mission, and she has been working with Hunter ever since.

Low-Level Molly Hendricks

Chamber: The Company
Department: Military Ops (2)
Class: Fixer
Level: 1

Strength:	12	**Dexterity:**	13
Constitution:	12	**Intelligence:**	16
Wisdom:	12	**Charisma:**	11
Vitality:	9	**Wounds:**	12

Defense: 12 (+1 class, +1 Dex)
Initiative Bonus: +1 (+0 class, +1 Dex)
Speed: 30

Fort: +2 **Ref:** +3 **Will:** +1

Skills: Appraise +5, Balance +4, Climb +3, Cultures +5, Demolitions +3, Gather Information +3, Jump +2, Knowledge (Archaeology) +9, Languages +6, Listen +3, Move Silently +3, Profession (Digger) +6, Search +8, Spot +3, Tumble +5

Feats: Filthy Rich, Sidestep

Attacks

.357 Magnum pistol	+1 ranged (2d4+1)
Survival knife	+1 melee (1d6+1
Satchel charge (thrown)	+1 ranged (5d6/lb.)

Gear: Flash goggles, climbing kit

Common Gadgets: Sub-cochlear implant

MID-LEVEL MOLLY HENDRICKS

Chamber: The Company
Department: Military Ops (2)
Class: Fixer
Level: 8

Strength:	12	**Dexterity:**	13
Constitution:	12	**Intelligence:**	17
Wisdom:	13	**Charisma:**	11
Vitality:	48	**Wounds:**	12

Defense: 17 (+6 class, +1 Dex)
Initiative Bonus: +4 (+3 class, +1 Dex)
Speed: 30

Fort: +5 **Ref:** +7 **Will:** +3

Skills: Appraise +10, Balance +9, Climb +8, Cultures +10, Demolitions +8, Gather Information +8, Jump +6, Knowledge (Archaeology) +14, Languages +11, Listen +8, Move Silently +8, Profession (Digger) +11, Search +14, Spot +8, Tumble +10

Feats: Filthy Rich, Improved Weapon Focus (Survival Knife), Sidestep, Weapon Focus (Survival Knife)

ATTACKS

.357 Magnum pistol	+7 ranged (2d4+1)
Survival knife	+1 melee (1d6+1)
Satchel charge (thrown)	+7 ranged (6d6/lb.)

Gear: Flash goggles, climbing kit

Common Gadgets: Sub-cochlear implant

HIGH-LEVEL MOLLY HENDRICKS

Chamber: The Company
Department: Military Ops (2)
Class: Fixer
Level: 15

Strength:	12	**Dexterity:**	14
Constitution:	12	**Intelligence:**	17
Wisdom:	13	**Charisma:**	11
Vitality:	87	**Wounds:**	12

Defense: 24 (+12 class, +2 Dex)
Initiative Bonus: +12 (+6 class, +2 Dex, +4 Improved Initiative)
Speed: 30

Fort: +8 **Ref:** +11 **Will:** +6

Skills: Appraise +17, Balance +12, Climb +12, Cultures +12, Demolitions +12, Gather Information +12, Jump +12, Knowledge (Archaeology) +21, Languages +16, Listen +12, Move Silently +11, Profession (Digger) +18, Ride +6, Search +20, Spot +13, Tumble +15

Feats: Expertise, Filthy Rich, Improved Initiative, Improved Weapon Focus (Survival Knife), Sidestep, Weapon Focus (Survival Knife), Weapon Master (Survival Knife)

ATTACKS

.357 Magnum pistol	+13 ranged (2d4+1)
Survival knife	+14 melee (1d6+1)
Satchel charge (thrown)	+12 ranged (6d6/lb.)

Gear: Flash goggles, climbing kit

Common Gadgets: Sub-cochlear implant, Wild Card Gadget

DEITRICH, COL. ALAN J.

Codename: NAPALM
Aliases: None known
Archer Identity Number: 05-112954-331
Nationality: United States of America
Gender: Male **Handedness:** Right
Height: 6 ft. 0 in. **Weight:** 190 lbs.
Eyes: Black **Hair:** Salt and pepper
Psion Class: Non-latent
Place of Birth: Miami, Florida, USA
Date of Birth: 1951.12.08
Distinguishing Characteristics: Severe chemical burns on left arm, torso, and neck

BACKGROUND

The current Company Control walks a fine line between the young idealists of his unit and their jaded elders. While he remains civil and restrained with those who toe the Company line, he has been known to erupt violently at those who fail to work with the team. Most Chamber agents see Deitrich as a mixed blessing; he's an obviously competent soldier, having risen through the ranks of the Marine Corps during Vietnam, but he's also a career spook who joined the CIA under shrouded circumstances during his last tour overseas.

Deitrich was discharged from the military after suffering extensive injuries during a carpet bombing operation (ironically involving weapons contracted from his own family's business, Southern Chemical Trust), but retained his position with the CIA following the war, tutoring operatives in the nuts and bolts of spying at the Farm, the Joint Military Intelligence College, and elsewhere. During this time, he took many leaves of absence, presumably to treat a condition stemming from his injuries, but rumor holds that he was actually running clandestine operations for the CIA (and later, the Company) throughout Asia and the Middle East.

Today, Deitrich remains well-liked within the U.S. political arena, and has aspirations to become Secretary of Defense in 2004.

LOW-LEVEL VERSION

Chamber: The Company
Department: Military Ops (2)
Class: Soldier
Level: 2

Strength:	16	**Dexterity:**	12
Constitution:	14	**Intelligence:**	10
Wisdom:	12	**Charisma:**	13
Vitality:	23	**Wounds:**	14

Defense: 12 (+1 class, +1 Dex)
Initiative Bonus: +3 (+2 class, +1 Dex)
Speed: 30

Fort: +5 **Ref:** +3 **Will:** +1

Skills: Climb +4, Demolitions +2, Profession (Military) +2, Survival +2, Tumble +3

Feats: Ambidexterity, Two Weapon Fighting, Weapon Focus (.45 pistol)

ATTACKS

.45 service pistols (2)	+4	1d10+2

Gear: Military dress uniform, medals

MID-LEVEL VERSION

Chamber: The Company
Department: Military Ops (2)
Class: Soldier/Snoop
Level: 5/4

Strength:	16	**Dexterity:**	13
Constitution:	14	**Intelligence:**	10
Wisdom:	12	**Charisma:**	14
Vitality:	88	**Wounds:**	14

Defense: 16 (+5 class, +1 Dex)
Initiative Bonus: +7 (+6 class, +1 Dex)
Speed: 30

Fort: +7 **Ref:** +6 **Will:** +4

Skills: Bluff +8, Bureaucracy +5, Climb +5, Cryptography +5, Cultures +4, Demolitions +5, Diplomacy +5, Gather Information +5, Innuendo +4, Intimidate +6, Knowledge (Company Secrets) +5, Knowledge (Archer Secrets) +4, Languages +5, Move Silently +6, Profession (Military) +6, Profession (Politics) +4, Surveillance +7, Survival +5, Tumble +5

Feats: Ambidexterity, Combat Instincts, Confident Charge, Mobility, Persuasion, Police Training, Two Weapon Fighting, Weapon Focus (.45 pistol)

ATTACKS

.45 service pistols (2)	+9	1d10+2

Gear: Military dress uniform, medals

HIGH-LEVEL VERSION

Chamber: The Company
Department: Military Ops (2)
Class: Soldier/Snoop
Level: 8/8

Strength:	16	**Dexterity:**	13
Constitution:	14	**Intelligence:**	10
Wisdom:	13	**Charisma:**	15
Vitality:	126	**Wounds:**	14

Defense: 20 (+9 class, +1 Dex)
Initiative Bonus: +12 (+11 class, +1 Dex)
Speed: 30

Fort: +10 **Ref:** +9 **Will:** +7

Skills: Bluff +12, Bureaucracy +11, Climb +7, Cryptography +9, Cultures +7, Demolitions +7, Diplomacy +10, Gather Information +7, Innuendo +6, Intimidate +8, Knowledge (Company Secrets) +7, Knowledge (Archer Secrets) +4, Languages +5, Move Silently +6, Profession (Military) +8, Profession (Politics) +5, Surveillance +11, Survival +7, Tumble +5

Feats: Advanced Skill Mastery (Persuasive), Ambidexterity, Combat Instincts, Confident Charge, Improved Two-Weapon Fighting, Mobility, Persuasive, Police Training, Sidestep, Two Weapon Fighting, Weapon Focus (.45 pistol)

ATTACKS

.45 service pistols (2)	+14	1d10+2

Gear: Military dress uniform, medals

The European Commonwealth

Fiat justitia ruat coelum.
"Let justice be done, though the heavens fall."

– Latin proverb

Europe exists on two distinctly different levels. Skyscrapers of gleaming steel and mirrored glass rocket toward the heavens at the center of cities hundreds or thousands of years old, blending old world romance with the technological marvels of today. Famous exotic spy capitals like Prague, Marseilles, Berlin, and Bruxelles – though updated through the years – retain the same sentiment as during the chaos of the early 20th Century, the revolutions of the 17th, and before.

Against this backdrop the action of the European Commonwealth unfolds. A political powerhouse with connections and influence in every nation on the continent, the Commonwealth stands ready to bring Europe into the 21st Century, kicking and screaming if necessary.

The Commonwealth Mission

Europe maintains a precarious balance between the ethics of justice and peace. These ethics are not mutually exclusive, but they are far from mutually supportive. Archer has charged the Commonwealth with safeguarding Europe – with acting as a dual observation and enforcement arm, dedicated to the ideals of continental and global peace (usually, but not always, in that order). Yet ultimately Europe's power brokers are in practice more concerned with meting out justice – *eliminating* threats rather than *countering* them.

This ruthless mentality pervades the Conspiracy in Europe, though it manifests quite differently according to those involved. Both of Europe's Controls – Stefan Bartolomei and Fade *(see pages 96 and 98, respectively)* – have their own agendas as well.

Function

Archer's decision to assign two Controls to Europe has allowed the Chamber to spread its specialties quite far and still maintain a high degree of skill in all their efforts. On the one hand, agents working for or with the Gemeinschafft Consortium are well-versed in the ways and means of the world political arena, and how to bend or break them if necessary. They are consummate masters of the spoken word, the legal writ, and the distribution and use of power. Gemeinschafft – the high priests of globalization – have long since elevated conspiracy to a high art form.

On the other hand, the criminal minions of Archer's very own mastermind, "Fade," are a motley collection of grifters, burglars, sting artists, corrupt government officials, smugglers, and organized crime families. Fade's extralegal subordinates operate under a loose set of rules designed to hone them into a razor-sharp scalpel for the Conspiracy, ready to carve out threats at a moment's notice. In exchange, Fade and his legions are allowed to rule the European underworld, forming an invisible nation that is rapidly growing into a world power.

An unusual aspect of the Commonwealth's activities is that they generally take place in the open, without the many layers of deceit that other Chambers demand. More than half the Commonwealth's regular operatives are also public figures. Many of the European Consortium's most important functions for the Archer Foundation, such as countering the dangers of global surveillance programs like the multi-national ECHELON network and U.S. Carnivore system, are handled either in a court of law or through well-publicized criminal actions. Secret actions do take place, but they are not the norm in Europe.

Commonwealth Missions

The Commonwealth performs a great many tasks for the Foundation, many of which the other Chambers are unable (or unwilling) to perform themselves. For this reason, Commonwealth missions frequently take their agents into foreign territories.

Conspiracy: European political figures have always had a very real fear of conspiracy. This fear often extends into the realm of espionage, where agents spy on one another out of routine as much as for specific purposes. The Commonwealth not only condones this behavior, but feeds it, utilizing the skepticism and trepidation of the public to control it.

Conspiracy is not merely a tool in Europe; it is a lifestyle. Commonwealth agents learn to suspect contrivance at all times, and to use the same tactics against their enemies. Nearly every Commonwealth mission either alludes to conspiracy or actively creates it.

Blackmail, Disinformation, Propaganda, and Slander: The Commonwealth sometimes employs less savory methods in its duties, including the manipulation of information to alter the public's opinion or force someone's hand. New ideas are constantly introduced and old ones quashed or spun in different directions according to a script only the Chamber's innermost circle knows. The Gemeinschafft Consortium dedicates two hundred personnel to detecting when media tampering, rumor control, and outright lies are needed, and countless more (many of whom are placed solely for this purpose) to spread the word of the day. Most Commonwealth missions include a spin the Chamber wishes to place on fallout from the operation.

Counterintelligence: The Commonwealth recognizes that its loose, public organization and questionable methods leave it open to attack, and dedicates a great many resources to countering that eventuality. Security, while no more effective than in other shadow communities around the world, is much greater here. Internet, phone, and physical mail communications are regularly monitored. Commonwealth Agents must frequently track down and plug "leaks in the system," or intercept and terminate enemy spies.

Infiltration: The Commonwealth's two halves both excel at infiltration missions. Agents of Fade's organization handle the physical entry while Gemeinschafft focuses on keeping prying eyes (both electronic and physical) away from the field team during the operation. This cooperation has proved highly successful during several high-profile missions – including a spectacular raid on the Omnium offices just last year – and the Archer Foundation now calls upon the Commonwealth first when it needs a covert insertion team.

Legal Manipulation: Conglomerates don't become as large and powerful as Gemeinschafft without a crack legal team at the ramparts, fending off hostile takeovers, government intervention, and private-sector complaints. The Consortium employs hundreds of attorneys and wields incredible courtroom power. While most field agents do not find themselves reciting closing arguments, they may end up working with (or for) the Praetoriat *(see page 93)*, which secretly acts as judge, jury, and executioner across the beleaguered continent.

Mediation: The European Commonwealth has kept dozens of nations at relative peace for over fifty years. This is largely due to the efforts of its carefully selected cadre of mediators, which it assigns to political negotiations, treaty summits, and other international gatherings. Occasionally these mediators (who are usually trained field operatives or civilian specialists) receive additional clandestine parameters, but most often they are simply included in the proceedings as neutral advisors or observers. Commonwealth Agents often find themselves on this type of mission, protecting someone on this type of mission, or performing some other function to support the endeavor.

Political Machinations: Just as Gemeinschafft employs a legal department to help control the creation and interpretation of laws by European nations, it also keeps a division of political analysts – society samplers who secretly infiltrate enemy parties and offices – to provide inside data about them, as well as speech writers, campaign organizers, and media specialists to focus the continent's political eyes where they want them. But this is only the beginning; unlike the world of law, which is run almost solely by attorneys, the world of politics is greatly influenced by public opinion and key influential figures, including pop-culture icons. A good number of these icons are Commonwealth plants, agents working to shift public opinion and change votes. Political machination operations can also be much more sinister, including blackmail, kidnapping, and terrorism (all of which the Commonwealth has conducted without Archer sanction).

Recruitment: Perhaps more than any other Chamber, the European Commonwealth is responsible for recruiting potential agents into the Conspiracy. With many of its operatives regularly traveling around the world as part of EU delegations, business partnerships, concert tours, and public appearance circuits, the Commonwealth embodies the global spy community Archer is constantly building.

Sabotage and Theft: The Gemeinschafft Consortium regularly engages in illegal activities to support its projects, but it rarely involves itself personally in such matters. More often than not, such dangerous work is left to Fade's people *(see page 89)*. Many sabotage and theft operations are thinly-veiled industrial espionage, but the Foundation integrates Fade's agents into mission teams when their services are required.

Seduction: Psychological manipulation is part of most espionage operations, but many agents of the Commonwealth specialize in it, seducing or otherwise coercing the uninitiated into helping them. Agents of

Gemeinschafft's Ninth Division (Operation SERAPH) are recruited exclusively based on their physical and personal charms, and trained in the fine arts of seduction, entrapment, and manipulation. These men and women (referred to as "Angels" in the field) spend long periods of time deep in enemy territory or sent with mission teams when villains or their henchmen have a confirmed weakness for the opposite sex.

Surveillance: With so much of Europe's espionage activity conducted out in the open, surveillance often involves little more than leasing an office with a strategically placed window. Most European spy circles cluster in a few insular communities, where everyone knows everyone else, gossip is the language of choice, and interpreting events becomes far more important than noticing them.

Agent Expectations

The European Commonwealth offers players a wide variety of options, perhaps more so than any other Chamber. From classic Cold War spy masters to edgy modern provocateurs to glamorous cinematic operatives, all the standards are employed here. But the Commonwealth also offers several options unavailable or improbable elsewhere, such as the celebrity spy (using the world of movie- and music-making as a cover for Foundation business), the media and information mogul (operating with intelligence gleaned from a thousand split-second updates), and the political machinator (wielding policy rather than a pistol).

Commonwealth operatives are the undisputed masters of subversion and spin doctoring, responsible for the Foundation's most complex machinations. They are also the Foundation's leaders in the criminal underworld.

Tactical Data

The rules of the Game are different in Europe. Trust and honor are long-forgotten concepts, replaced by guile and unchecked ambition. Battles are won more often with words than with bullets; lies, threats, promises of scandal and ruin... all of these are common tactics used by Commonwealth agents and their enemies. Nowhere is the Game elevated to a higher level; nowhere is strategy more crucial to success.

Specialists see much more use in Europe than in most other areas. Middle men, money launderers, couriers, informants, and the like are essential links in the system here, regularly called upon during operations and pitted against Archer's finest throughout the streets and alleys of Paris and Rome. All the major players in the espionage drama have organized networks of supporting specialists, and rely on them heavily to play the Game effectively.

The Game is ever-evolving in Europe. The players constantly ignore, break, and rewrite the rules, fostering the region's atmosphere of lawlessness.

Commonwealth PsiTech

A number of gadgets included in Archer's standard field package have come out of Europe. Specifically, they've come out of the Gemeinschafft Consortium's private research and development office, which has assumed the somewhat arrogant nickname "The Foundry." Operating behind its front company, Icon Entertainment – an upscale gadget house catering to wealthy yuppies – the Foundry's global mail-order business distributes PsiTech, loosely disguised as objects of a similar theme.

For instance, certain popular high-end pocket computers include email and global positioning/roadside assistance. A special model (not listed on the Icon website or in its catalog) includes an electronic ciphering and satellite upload system for Archer agents, which is commonly used to safely communicate from the field.

The Foundry is also responsible for the Foundation's signature sub-cochlear implant *(see page 206)* and palm-print gun security device *(see page 212)*.

Chamber Organization

The Commonwealth's diversity requires a diverse structure. Beyond having two disparate Controls, Europe's Archer Foundation agents are also divided into several camps, each with its own goals and ideals.

The European Union

The European Union is comprised of fifteen countries – Austria, Belgium, Denmark, Finland, France, Germany, Greece, Ireland, Italy, Luxembourg, The Netherlands, Portugal, Spain, Sweden, and the United Kingdom of Great Britain and Northern Ireland – which have banded together to create mutually beneficial laws, markets, and social systems, and to provide security for their citizens. Originally founded in 1951 with only six countries, the European Union has become a formidable world power, and is now poised to have a tremendous impact on all levels of government and society.

The European Union basically consists of five institutions – the European Parliament (representing the public), the European Council (representing government), the European Commission (upholding the interests of the Union), the Court of Justice, and the Court of Auditors – which are in turn supported by other departments.

The Union's primary thrusts at the moment are its expansion into southern and eastern Europe, and the establishment of unified trade goals and practices.

The Archer Foundation has ardently (if quietly) supported the Union since its inception, using its European Commonwealth arm to defend the Union when necessary. In exchange, the Union frequently offers its growing political clout to endorse less questionable policies posed by Archer and the Commonwealth, and periodically helps to cover some of Archer's operations when they grow beyond the local intelligence agencies' ability to contain. The Foundation's presence within departments of the Union is light; no part of the Union has more than a few operatives.

Headquarters

Unlike other Chambers, the European Commonwealth has no stable headquarters. Instead, agents in Europe rely entirely on dead-drops, encrypted email, listservs, chat boards, pre-arranged signals, and anonymous meetings. A common practice involves waiting at a designated place with a license plate combination (often not in the order seen on the plate); when the vehicle shows up, the agent gets in and is taken to a secure location where mission parameters or updates can be conveyed.

The Commonwealth announces emergencies by one of several TV or radio stations. Agents must tune in to certain stations for at least five minutes once every hour, three hours, six hours, or twelve hours, per their assignment. The method in which emergency warnings are conveyed depends on the format. Talk shows might use code words; music programming might include coded messages in the tempos or words of songs; TV news programs might include images with hidden meaning or use code phrases that prompt a given response from field agents; and agents often use the Archer cipher system built into cell-phones to interpret information. Methods change frequently to avoid detection or compromise.

One unique method of transmitting information in Europe is the use of commercial blimps with huge digital display screens mounted on their sides. Code words, images, and even minute-to-minute updates and orders run across the screen for agents below, usually scripted by command personnel posing as the blimp's crew. This mobile operations headquarters is especially useful during operations in densely populated areas, and during important events (such as political rallies, sports events, and the like).

The Gemeinschafft Consortium

The Gemeinschafft Consortium has adapted well to the rapid advancements of the last century, growing into one of the business giants of the new millennium. Like its peers, the Consortium includes many smaller organizations, most of which have still more subsidiaries. Gemeinschafft is involved with companies from many different industries, but focuses on military defense, transportation, shipping, and electronic development.

Some of the most prominent Gemeinschafft's subsidiaries are GlobalTech, responsible for information technologies contracted by governments and businesses; Equinox Motors, whose vehicle designs have been widely purchased by world militaries and movie companies, and include the wildly popular Sagittarius design seen in Katt Wilde's string of adventure films *(see page 212)*; and Utopia Designs, the parent company of Icon Entertainment and E•Topics, a computer software engineering firm.

The Consortium also supports several high-profile charities, including a medical research foundation ("Galen's Ward," at the forefront of Archer's human genome research) and a variety of Third World support agencies.

Gemeinschafft operates as a legitimate business, and the Conspiracy has no influence on most of its endeavors. In general, the Consortium only involves the Foundation in one of its interests if no less invasive option is available, and then only for a limited time. Most often, the Consortium's contribution to Archer's effort takes the form of legal assistance, business and political leverage, and equipment.

The Gemeinschafft Consortium employs a custodial "security service" to guard its sites and protect its personnel. Most of these men and women were recruited from French Special Forces units, such as the DGSE's Action Service and Ile Choc, following their dismissal.

"Fade"

It is unknown how long the criminal genius known as Fade has operated in Europe, or where he originates from. He surfaced for the first time in the early 1950s, convincing many disorganized youth camps and street gangs to rally under his banner. Fade's methods are unconventional, but unquestionably effective. Acting as a modern-day Fagin, he directs thousands of unrecognized youth hostels across Europe, providing food, shelter, and family to tens of thousands of the disenfranchised, forgotten, and neglected.

Since Raymond Archer brought him into the fold in 1957, Fade has used his wards as a private army, one which can operate without arousing suspicion and which has access to many unique skills and backgrounds. Fade's hostels communicate with one another through graffiti (another effective, if infuriating, practice), and are most often called upon by the Foundation for infiltration, sabotage, and theft missions.

COMMONWEALTH RESOURCES

The European Commonwealth's source agencies in German and French intelligence provide the Chamber with many valuable resources. The DGSE, for instance, has an annual budget in excess of 200 million francs, and the DCRG's open relationship with the Foundation provides access to their files (unparalleled in France, and perhaps in Europe) in exchange for paramilitary and espionage support.

LEGAL COUNSEL

As mentioned, one of Gemeinschafft's chief contributions to the Conspiracy is their legion of lawyers. These attorneys keep agents out of jail, and if that mission fails, defend them in court. They also prosecute cases against Archer's enemies, jailing them or hobbling their efforts.

The majority of the Consortium's lawyers are presently wrapped up with their Union interests, and in the well-publicized court case against Salvador Vega *(see "The Praetoriat," page 93)*.

OPERATION SERAPH

Gemeinschafft's Ninth Division began as a military spy ring under the direction of East German Cold War strategist Madeline Raine. Conceived as a covert infiltration program, SERAPH assigned women to military, government, and intelligence officials, whom they would seduce for state secrets. SERAPH operatives operated extensively in West Germany (particularly in Berlin), and often lived with their marks for months or years at a time.

After the Soviet Union collapsed, SERAPH was absorbed by the Consortium (who had known of the operation for many years) and its Angels became available to the Commonwealth. Today both male and female agents are trained by SERAPH, and long-term operations are far less common.

THE GAME IN EUROPE

Of all Europe's intelligence organizations, those of France and Germany are most closely connected to the Archer Conspiracy. Through their European Controls and contacts, the Foundation regularly pits these groups against one another to prevent cooperative discovery of their efforts, and to circumvent the established checks and balances systems when planning and executing missions. Unfortunately, this fosters a greater sense of paranoia than in any of the other shadow communities, making Europe the most volatile intelligence community in the world.

EUROPEAN INTELLIGENCE AGENCIES

The European Commonwealth is most deeply entrenched in France's General Directorate for External Security (DGSE) and Germany's Federal Intelligence Service (BND), though in practice these organizations provide little more than personnel and funding. Planning and many supporting efforts are handled by the invisible minions of the Gemeinschafft Consortium and Fade's criminal underworld.

France: General Directorate for External Security (DGSE): Though plagued by a reputation for ruthlessness through its early years, the *Direction Générale de la Sécurité Extérieure* has settled into a comfortable niche. It now specializes in the fields of industrial and electronic espionage, especially with regards to commercial enterprise. This focus blends well with the mentality of the European Commonwealth.

The DGSE is officially in charge of counter-espionage efforts outside France, and the collection of supporting data. Unofficially, it maintains close ties with French businesses and has been known to conduct domestic surveillance in violation of its charter. It is strong both at home and abroad, with economic, political, and technological contacts all over the world, and maintains civilian operatives (called "honorable correspondents") in high-profile diplomatic and business positions.

One of the DGSE's most illustrious resources was the covert operations arm known as the Action Service (presumably disbanded after the 1985 destruction of the Greenpeace ship *Rainbow Warrior*). Many Action Service personnel released following the embarrassing failures of the 1980s and 1990s were recruited by the Commonwealth, as part of the Gemeinschafft Consortium's security service *(see page 89)*.

France: Directorate for Surveillance of the Territory (DST): The *Direction de la Surveillance du Territoire* was founded in 1944, and expanded during the 1982 French intelligence reorganization to better accommodate its mission of counterintelligence inside French borders. The DST is better-funded and much more widely respected than the DGSE, though it suffered some of the fallout from their counterparts over the years. This, coupled with their similar objectives, has frequently sparked confrontation between the two agencies.

France: Central Directorate of General Information (DCRG): Founded in 1941, the *Direction Centrale Renseignements Généraux* works to monitor groups and individuals whose activities may affect France, and inform the French government about them. The DCRG is perfectly structured to help the European Commonwealth, consisting of small teams of specialists within focused fields of study, and having access to dedicated research and analysis support divisions. But the Commonwealth rarely relies upon the DCRG, primarily because its files and personnel are available to other agencies, leaving the Chamber open to attack.

Germany: Federal Intelligence Service (BND): The Archer Foundation's German interests include the *Bundesnachrichtendienst,* which recently expanded its operations from a Soviet focus to a worldwide view. The BND constantly monitors worldwide communications (telephone, radio, fax, and telex), and it has operatives in every corner of the globe, posing as embassy staffers, who regularly report back to the German government (and, through discreet channels, controllers of the European Commonwealth). In turn, the Commonwealth intercepts pertinent information before it becomes public, acting on it or erasing it if necessary. The BND has no law enforcement powers, relying on German police services – or, in some instances, the Commonwealth – to physically counter potential threats.

Playing the Great Game: Fade

"I trust that world will protect itself from cowards, from madmen, and even from me."

– Fade

Mission Management: Fade's organization is hindered by the integrity of Europe's shadow community. With questionable backgrounds and motives, these "old world" spies are poorly suited for public tasks or diplomacy. Fade shuffles such assignments off to Gemeinschafft whenever possible, or to the African Alliance when necessary. Fade's agents willingly work with agents of all the Chambers, though they are most ardent when working with operatives of the Foundation – partly because of Two's open support of Fade since Raymond Archer's retirement, but mostly because so many Foundation operatives are telepaths, capable of exposing their checkered pasts.

Damage Control: Fade has been one of the most rabid proponents of anti-Shop initiatives, acting with unbridled fury. There is talk that he takes the Shop's betrayal personally, and some worry that he might take the war to bring the renegades to justice too far.

Dirty Little Secrets: It's no secret among Fade's private army that he is trained in the mystic arts, though to what extent remains a mystery. Fade refuses to speak of his training, or reveal any of it to his pupils (a point of contention with many of them). Indeed, he refuses to deal with mystics at all, shunning them completely and excommunicating any of his people who take an interest in the mystic world. The latest exile claims that Fade flew into a rage after he asked about a symbol that he'd seen several times during his private lessons – a wavy figure in the shape of a curved dagger.

Leverage: Fade offers two distinct advantages to those under his wing – though one remains a promise until and unless "disaster strikes." First, Fade is seemingly able to access INTERPOL's criminal records at will, adjusting or erasing records as needed. He has on several occasions saved his pupils from lengthy prison sentences with this technique. The source of his access is as yet unknown. Second, Fade promises that if the worst should ever come to pass – "you'll know what I mean when it happens" – arrangements have been made for all his minions to go to someplace called Sanctuary. Fade claims that only those gifted with physical adept abilities will be able to enter the safe haven, and that all others must follow them, but he assures all that they will be taken care of – "even as the rest of the world collapses."

Assets: Fade has a secret, one that dates back to the beginning of the 20th century. Through his black market connections he has come into possession of a large supply of serum for activating the physical adept gene. While the raw serum has the same drawbacks that caused the Foundation to ban its use in the 1950s, Fade has been able to combine it with newer techniques to identify latent adepts, and selectively activate only those who can withstand the genetic transformation. This has allowed to Fade to secretly build up a cadre of enhanced agents, whom he has carefully filtered back into the ranks of his criminal organization.

Playing the Great Game: Gemeinschafft Consortium

"Among conspirators, trust is the economy, and favors are the coin."

– Stefan Bartolomei

Mission Management: Possibly because of its long history of traditional espionage, the Gemeinschafft Consortium is especially reluctant to recruit and develop psionic spies. Stefan has made it clear that the Archer Foundation is and should remain the Conspiracy's premier psionic wing, and that he wants nothing to do with such research. When focused on their own area of expertise (manipulations of all sorts) Commonwealth teams often look to the African Alliance – their energy (and often naivete) make them excellent partners for complex and daring schemes.

Damage Control: The Consortium's meager PsiTech research was conducted under the strictest of security. Consequently, the Shop's departure had the least effect in Europe, where very few personnel turned and practically no physical damage was suffered. Having survived the break largely unscathed, Stefan Bartolomei found it easy to down play the Shop's actions, even championing them once or twice in private meetings (a position he has since recanted in the face of Shop-sponsored terrorism).

Dirty Little Secrets: Unbeknownst to anyone outside the Consortium's halls of inner power, Gemeinschafft has long upheld a right of passage agreement with P.E.R.I.L., allowing the enemy Russian spies to move freely throughout Europe in exchange for the same courtesy in Russia. Over the last twenty years, this arrangement has greatly profited both parties, each of whose operations are firmly rooted in the other's territories. Recently, however, Fade's organization has noticed P.E.R.I.L. operatives moving through Europe, and has set up an impromptu embargo. The fighting has already begun, and it's anyone's guess how long it can go on without someone discovering the Consortium's double-dealings.

Leverage: As might be expected, the Gemeinschafft Consortium's leverage is global in scope. The surprise might lie in the fact that it was provided to them by the Conspiracy itself. In 1950, when the Pact was established, each Chamber was charged with maintaining a part of the Conspiracy's support structure. The Consortium acted as the Conspiracy's court, maintaining the by-laws originally set up for all the Chambers, and ratifying new ones. The only Chamber immune to their judgments was the Guardians, who govern and adjudicate themselves. The Consortium is by and large fair with this power, but they do periodically use it to absolve a cherished agent who has strayed from the Conspiracy line, or support a by-law that will benefit them over the other Chambers.

Assets: Stefan Bartolomei is the sole heir of a long tradition of espionage and domination, and those loyal to him – by choice or not – number in the thousands. He is also heir to the fortunes of countless generations of crime, corruption, and greed, making him the single richest man on Earth. Though he would never admit it, Stefan could easily drop the hammer on anyone at any time, calling upon his vast fortune to ruin anyone, up to and including any leader of the free world – or Two himself.

CURRENT PLOTLINES

Europe currently finds itself in a precarious position, as enemies loom on all sides. The Archer Foundation asks whether the sudden surge of threats in the area is due to the increasing strain each Control's private agenda has on the Chamber; leaders of the Commonwealth claim it is just a sign of the times.

Gemini (Code: Black): In 1999, a dangerous new threat emerged in Luxembourg: a villain known as Gemini. Cursed with the power to shift forms and steal new ones (along with memories and skills) by virtue of a powerful mystic artifact called Quetzalcoatl's Thorn *(see page 234)*, Gemini has vowed to topple the Gemeinschafft Consortium and its allies as retribution for the death of his brother.

This is not the first time that the Commonwealth has encountered Gemini. They once knew him as Thomas Fellows, an Archer Pawn *(see page 53 for more about Pawns)* who, with his twin brother James, volunteered for a top secret Foundation study. Both were latent psions, but only Thomas was surgically triggered. The process granted him uncharted sensitivity to mystic items of all kinds, but like Helix's tragic experiments in the early 1970s, fueled his power by sapping others – in this case, his brother, James. Thomas was unable to control the reaction, and as he grew in power, he watched James slowly wither away.

After James' death, the tests continued, largely to see whether Thomas constituted a threat to anyone else, but also to determine the extent of his psion ability (which was unique at the time). One study placed him in a 100-room mansion with a single hidden artifact: Quetzalcoatl's Thorn. When told to recover the item, he did so in record time (43 seconds, including the climb up two flights of stairs), but he failed to emerge. The researchers went in after him, accompanied by two guards. All were brutally slaughtered, and Thomas vanished, not to be seen again until 1999.

Gemini is unhinged, homicidal, and totally dedicated to destroying the Commonwealth and the Foundation. The reasons for his disappearance and his current intentions are unknown. Gemini is currently the focus of a worldwide Foundation manhunt.

The Praetoriat (Code: Red): For several years, Europe has been plagued by a vigilante justice group which calls itself the Praetoriat. Countless murders, kidnappings, and terrorist acts have been attributed to the group, who use a finely crafted inch-high silver carving of a Roman praetor (their namesake) as a calling card. The number and identities of Praetoriat leaders has always been a mystery, but the recent arrest of Salvador Vega, a hitman believed to be in their employ, may change this. Currently in negotiations to name his Praetoriat contacts in exchange for a reduced sentence, Vega may be the key to bringing down this criminal ring.

The Commonwealth Genre

The genre of the European Commonwealth is, like the Chamber that fashions it, double-edged. Half the organization focuses on identifying potential threats and eliminating them using political and legal means, contributing to an atmosphere of taut thriller action guided by unseen masters. The other half is the face for Europe, an eclectic crew of diplomats, celebrities, thieves, and street-level criminals who promote the glamorous life of professional spies and whose retribution is well-known. This latter half brings to Europe a sense of paranoia and fear: the knowledge that no street corner is safe, no home secure.

Archetypes: Burke from *Aliens*, Black Widow, Tyrell from *Blade Runner,* Sydney Savage from *Danger Girl,* Daredevil, Elektra, Gambit, Lynch from *Gen 13,* Kingpin, Punisher, Jason Wynn from *Spawn,* Dillinger from *Tron,* any of the characters from *Star Chamber* or *Pitch Black.*

Inspirations

The following is a short list of inspirations for both sides of the Commonwealth. Game Controls and players looking for ideas and general Chamber atmosphere should start here.

Books: *Daredevil, Punisher, Vigilante* (all comic books).

Movies: *The Assignment, Codename: Dancer, Entrapment, The Firm, Following, The Game, House of Games, M, Memento, Mission: Impossible 1, The Pelican Brief, The Real McCoy, The Score, The Spanish Prisoner, The Star Chamber, Thief, The Thomas Crown Affair, To Catch a Thief, The Usual Suspects, Wall Street.*

TV Shows: *The Equalizer, Highlander: The Raven, It Takes a Thief, Mission: Impossible, Noble House* (mini-series), *Remington Steele, The Saint* (both series), *Thieves.*

Music: *Alien 3* score, *Dark City* soundtrack, *La Femme Nikita* score, *Shadowrun* score (by Orion Design Studio), *The Usual Suspects* score; trance is typically evocative of the European Commonwealth.

Computer and Console Games: *The Driver* series, *Hitman, Syndicate* and *Syndicate Wars, Thief.*

Wilde, Katherine "Katt"

Codename: CIRCE
Aliases: Wildcat
Archer Identity Number: 02-981-439882
Nationality: Unknown (presumed European)
Gender: Female **Handedness:** Right
Height: 5 ft. 7 in. **Weight:** 130 lbs.
Eyes: Green **Hair:** Red
Psion Class: Non-latent
Place of Birth: Unknown
Date of Birth: Unknown (mid- to late-20s)
Distinguishing Characteristics: Belly-button ring, "Euro-flash" style

Background

Easily the most public Archer agent, Katherine Wilde is sleek, sexy, and dangerous – more than any man can handle, but everything all of them want. She uses these traits to her advantage, flaunting her charms as a world-famous celebrity and seducing thousands with her in-your-face style. This is what makes her so formidable – Katt is a spectacle of seduction; every move, word, and glance is engineered to make you fall in love...

Katt is a celebrity icon, blurring the line between entertainment mediums. Her latest album, "Hearts on Fire," recently went triple-platinum, the fourth installment of her action-adventure movie series, *Catwalk,* is due out in the summer of 2003; and rumors persist that a biography of her life is in production for a prominent cable network. Sharp, witty, and personable, Katt handles her own promotion, and carefully controls her public image.

Privately, Katt spies for the Foundation, using her position to travel the world and her skills as a cat burglar, acrobat, and escape artist to silently infiltrate enemy installations.

But there are some things even "Wildcat" can't control. Her origins, for instance, are a complete mystery. Taken in by Fade after she tried to pick his pocket on the streets of Milan, she has spent the last twenty years searching for her parents.

LOW-LEVEL KATHERINE WILDE

Chamber: The European Commonwealth
Department: Power Brokerage (1)
Class: Faceman
Level: 5

Strength:	12	**Dexterity:**	16
Constitution:	13	**Intelligence:**	15
Wisdom:	11	**Charisma:**	19
Vitality:	37	**Wounds:**	13

Defense: 16 (+3 class, +3 Dex)
Initiative Bonus: +7 (+4 class, +3 Dex)
Speed: 30

Fort: +4 **Ref:** +4 **Will:** +3

Skills: Balance +6, Bluff +6, Climb +6, Craft (Songwriting) +6, Diplomacy +6, Disguise +6, Driver +4, Innuendo +4, Intimidate +6, Jump +4, Move Silently +4, Open Lock +6, Perform +11, Profession (Celebrity) +6, Read Lips +5, Search +5, Sleight of Hand +5, Spot +5, Tumble +6

Feats: Acrobatic, The Look, Martial Arts

ATTACKS

Stiletto knife	+4 melee (1d6+1)
.40 backup pistol	+6 ranged (1d12)

Gear: Per assignment

Common Gadgets: Sub-cochlear implant, Icon ProStar 7 (all options), cell phone slip-away unit

MID-LEVEL KATHERINE WILDE

Chamber: The European Commonwealth
Department: Power Brokerage (1)
Class: Faceman/Cat Burglar
Level: 10/2

Strength:	12	**Dexterity:**	17
Constitution:	13	**Intelligence:**	15
Wisdom:	11	**Charisma:**	19
Vitality:	81	**Wounds:**	13

Defense: 21 (+8 class, +3 Dex)
Initiative Bonus: +12 (+9 class, +3 Dex)
Speed: 30

Fort: +6 **Ref:** +9 **Will:** +5

Skills: Balance +12, Bluff +11, Climb +10, Craft (Songwriting) +7, Diplomacy +15, Disguise +10, Driver +5, Innuendo +5, Intimidate +9, Jump +5, Move Silently +7, Open Lock +10, Perform +15, Profession (Celebrity) +10, Read Lips +7, Search +7, Sleight of Hand +7, Spot +5, Tumble +10

Feats: Acrobatic, Combat Instincts, Kicking Basics, The Look, Martial Arts, Master Fence

ATTACKS

Stiletto knife	+9 melee (1d6+1)
.40 backup pistol	+11 ranged (1d12)

Gear: Per assignment

Common Gadgets: Sub-cochlear implant, Icon ProStar 7 (all options), cell phone slip-away unit

HIGH-LEVEL KATHERINE WILDE

Chamber: The European Commonwealth
Department: Power Brokerage (1)
Class: Faceman/Cat Burglar
Level: 10/8

Strength:	12	**Dexterity:**	17
Constitution:	13	**Intelligence:**	15
Wisdom:	11	**Charisma:**	20
Vitality:	114	**Wounds:**	13

Defense: 25 (+12 class, +3 Dex)
Initiative Bonus: +16 (+13 class, +3 Dex)
Speed: 30

Fort: +8 **Ref:** +12 **Will:** +7

Skills: Balance +16, Bluff +16, Climb +14, Craft (Songwriting) +10, Diplomacy +14, Disguise +11, Driver +8, Innuendo +6, Intimidate +10, Jump +12, Move Silently +10, Open Lock +14, Perform +18, Profession (Celebrity) +15, Read Lips +8, Search +10, Sleight of Hand +10, Spot +10, Tumble +15

Feats: Acrobatic, Breakfall, Combat Instincts, Fast Pick, Fast Swipe, Kicking Basics, Kicking Mastery, The Look, Martial Arts, Master Fence, Traceless

ATTACKS

Stiletto knife	+12 melee (1d6+1)
.40 backup pistol	+14 ranged (1d12)

Gear: Per assignment

Common Gadgets: Sub-cochlear implant, Icon ProStar 7 (all options), cell phone slip-away unit

KINCAID, ASHLEY

Codename: OUBLIETTE
Aliases: "Brooke," "Dot," "H21," "Sage"
Archer Identity Number: 71-089231-008
Nationality: Greek
Gender: Female **Handedness:** Right
Height: 5 ft. 7 in. **Weight:** 125 lbs.
Eyes: Black **Hair:** Raven black
Psion Class: Physical Adept (Grade B)
Place of Birth: Athens, Greece
Date of Birth: 1973.07.09
Distinguishing Characteristics: None

BACKGROUND

Ashley Kincaid has many names, but she is most often called "Oubliette." As an agent of Operation SERAPH, Oubliette's assignments usually involve seduction, a mission for which she is uniquely suited. Gorgeous and enticing, she can wrap any man around her finger, insinuate herself into his life, and seize his innermost secrets. Only after the target is left high and dry, his heart broken and his mind reeling, does he realize what's happened.

Oubliette perhaps relishes her position too much. Others call her "H21," the German codename for Mata Hari, due to her effectiveness and zeal. Some even say that Oubliette is addicted to romance, and worry that her entanglements may one day be her undoing. Her record with the Conspiracy is thus far spotless, however, which keeps such concerns to a minimum... for now.

When not on assignment, Oubliette "lives the scene," working the European club circuit like a seasoned pro. Countless shattered lovers trail behind her, a single white rose left behind on their pillows after her unexpected departure. On occasion, she fills in as one of Katt Wilde's backup dancers – usually when they are sent on a mission together.

Oubliette loves to use Memory Flesh *(see page 211)* when in the field, taking on traits her targets' profiles claim they are vulnerable to.

LOW-LEVEL ASHLEY KINCAID

Chamber: The European Commonwealth
Department: Power Brokerage (1)
Class: Faceman/Telepath
Level: 2/1

Strength:	13	**Dexterity:**	16
Constitution:	10	**Intelligence:**	12
Wisdom:	10	**Charisma:**	18
Vitality:	21	**Wounds:**	10

Defense: 14 (+1 class, +3 Dex)
Initiative Bonus: +6 (+3 class, +3 Dex)
Speed: 30

Fort: +2 **Ref:** +5 **Will:** +3

Skills: Bluff +7, Cultures +6, Diplomacy +8, Disguise +8, Gather Information +5, Innuendo +5, Intimidate +8, Languages +4, Perform +7, Profession (Celebrity) +4, Read Lips +4, Search +5, Sense Motive +5, Sleight of Hand +4, Spot +4

Feats: ESP Basics, Intuitive Basics, The Look, Mimic

Psion Skills: Empathy +10, Telempathy +6

ATTACKS

Stiletto knife	+2 melee (1d6+1)

Gear: Per assignment

Common Gadgets: Sub-cochlear implant, memory flesh (at least two or three at a time)

MID-LEVEL ASHLEY KINCAID

Chamber: The European Commonwealth
Department: Power Brokerage (1)
Class: Faceman/Telepath
Level: 6/4

Strength:	13	**Dexterity:**	16
Constitution:	10	**Intelligence:**	12
Wisdom:	10	**Charisma:**	20
Vitality:	60	**Wounds:**	10

Defense: 19 (+6 class, +3 Dex)
Initiative Bonus: +11 (+8 class, +3 Dex)
Speed: 30

Fort: +4 **Ref:** +9 **Will:** +5

Skills: Bluff +11, Cultures +8, Diplomacy +10, Disguise +12, Gather Information +7, Innuendo +8, Languages +5, Perform +11, Profession (Celebrity) +6, Read Lips +5, Search +5, Sense Motive +6, Sleight of Hand +5, Spot +5.

Feats: Feats: Advanced Skill Mastery (Mimic), ESP Basics, Imprint Basics, Intuitive Basics, The Look, Mimic

Psion Skills: Empathy +18, Dominion +12, Telempathy +13

ATTACKS

Stiletto knife	+7 melee (1d6+1)

Gear: Per assignment

Common Gadgets: Sub-cochlear implant, memory flesh (at least two or three at a time)

High-Level Ashley Kincaid

Chamber: The European Commonwealth
Department: Power Brokerage (1)
Class: Faceman/Telepath
Level: 10/7

Strength:	13	**Dexterity:**	16
Constitution:	10	**Intelligence:**	12
Wisdom:	10	**Charisma:**	22
Vitality:	93	**Wounds:**	10

Defense: 22 (+9 class, +3 Dex)
Initiative Bonus: +17 (+14 class, +3 Dex)
Speed: 30

Fort: +7 **Ref:** +11 **Will:** +9

Skills: Bluff +16, Cultures +10, Diplomacy +14, Disguise +14, Gather Information +10, Innuendo +10, Languages +6, Perform +14, Profession (Celebrity) +8, Read Lips +5, Search +8, Sense Motive +8, Sleight of Hand +5, Spot +6

Feats: Advanced Skill Mastery (Mimic), Advanced Skill Mastery (Persuasive), Combat Instincts, ESP Basics, Imprint Basics, Intuitive Basics, Intuitive Mastery, The Look, Mimic

Psion Skills: Empathy +26, Dominion +19, Telempathy +20

Attacks

Stiletto knife +11 melee (1d6+1)

Gear: Per assignment

Common Gadgets: Sub-cochlear implant, memory flesh (at least two or three at a time)

Bartolomei, Stefan

Codename: MENTOR
Aliases: "Regent"
Archer Identity Number: 19-716553-091
Nationality: French
Gender: Male **Handedness:** Left
Height: 5 ft. 11 in. **Weight:** 165 lbs.
Eyes: Dark blue **Hair:** Black, cropped
Psion Class: Telepath (Grade A)
Place of Birth: Orléans, France
Date of Birth: 1959.09.11
Distinguishing Characteristics: Rubs fingers together (like a "rolling fist") when thinking

Background

Most of the rumors about the Gemeinschafft Consortium are true. The group has been around for over a hundred years, and has roots in the noble families of ancient Europe. Gemeinschafft's CEO is called Regent, and is considered to be sitting in for the Consortium's founder, Bruno Vangeli, who is exalted by all, even so many years after his death. Each Regent is named by his predecessor, and takes a vow to uphold a long list of complicated rules and by-laws governing the operation of the business partnership.

Stefan Bartolomei is the latest Regent, named unexpectedly by his predecessor, the last of the Gemeinschafft line. Prior to taking over the Consortium, Bartolomei worked with the DGSE's paramilitary Action Service unit, and earned a reputation as the man to see about the European intelligence scene. His appointment as Regent of the Consortium caused much turmoil, and resulted in many resignations from those who assumed he had bribed or blackmailed his way into the position. Many more remained, plotting to remove him at the first opportunity – by force, if necessary.

Regardless of his reputation, Bartolomei has been a positive influence on the Consortium. His long history in Europe and no-nonsense demeanor have kept the organization on the top of Europe's espionage Game for over a decade.

Low-Level Stefan Bartolomei

Chamber: The European Commonwealth
Department: Power Brokerage (1)
Class: Snoop
Level: 5

Strength:	12	**Dexterity:**	12
Constitution:	13	**Intelligence:**	14
Wisdom:	12	**Charisma:**	10
Vitality:	31	**Wounds:**	13

Defense: 15 (+4 class, +1 Dex)
Initiative Bonus: +4 (+3 class, +1 Dex)
Speed: 30

Fort: +2 **Ref:** +4 **Will:** +4

Skills: Bureaucracy +5, Computers +5, Concentration +4, Cryptography +6, Cultures +4, Demolitions +4, Diplomacy +4, Driver +4, Gather Information +8, Innuendo +4, Knowledge (Gemeinschafft Secrets) +8, Languages +2, Listen +4, Mechanics +4, Move Silently +4, Profession (Military) +4, Read Lips +8, Search +5, Sense Motive +8, Spot +4, Surveillance +8

Feats: Field Operative, Filthy Rich, Point Blank Shot

ATTACKS

7.62×39mm semi-automatic rifle +3 ranged (2d8)

Gear: Per assignment

Common Gadgets: None

MID-LEVEL STEFAN BARTOLOMEI

Chamber: The European Commonwealth
Department: Power Brokerage (1)
Class: Snoop
Level: 12

Strength:	14	**Dexterity:**	12
Constitution:	13	**Intelligence:**	14
Wisdom:	12	**Charisma:**	10
Vitality:	70	**Wounds:**	13

Defense: 21 (+10 class, +1 Dex)
Initiative Bonus: +8 (+7 class, +1 Dex)
Speed: 30

Fort: +5 **Ref:** +7 **Will:** +7

Skills: Bureaucracy +12, Computers +7, Concentration +6, Cryptography +12, Cultures +6, Demolitions +9, Diplomacy +5, Driver +6, Gather Information +12, Innuendo +8, Knowledge (Gemeinschafft Secrets) +15, Languages +6, Listen +6, Mechanics +8, Move Silently +6, Profession (Military) +6, Read Lips +14, Search +7, Sense Motive +10, Spot +6, Surveillance +10

Feats: Extreme Range, Far Shot, Field Operative, Filthy Rich, Five Star Service, Point Blank Shot

ATTACKS

7.62×39mm semi-automatic rifle +7 ranged (2d8)

Gear: Per assignment

Common Gadgets: None

HIGH-LEVEL STEFAN BARTOLOMEI

Chamber: The European Commonwealth
Department: Power Brokerage (1)
Class: Snoop
Level: 18

Strength:	14	**Dexterity:**	12
Constitution:	14	**Intelligence:**	14
Wisdom:	12	**Charisma:**	10
Vitality:	121	**Wounds:**	13

Defense: 25 (+14 class, +1 Dex)
Initiative Bonus: +12 (+11 class, +1 Dex)
Speed: 30

Fort: +8 **Ref:** +9 **Will:** +9

Skills: Bureaucracy +16, Computers +10, Concentration +6, Cryptography +16, Cultures +8, Demolitions +10, Diplomacy +8, Driver +6, Gather Information +16, Innuendo +10, Knowledge (Gemeinschafft Secrets) +21, Languages +8, Listen +8, Mechanics +10, Move Silently +10, Profession (Military) +6, Read Lips +18, Search +10, Sense Motive +16, Spot +10, Surveillance +14

Feats: Extreme Range, Far Shot, Field Operative, Filthy Rich, Five Star Service, Increased Precision, Point Blank Shot, Precise Shot

ATTACKS

7.62×39mm semi-automatic rifle +10 ranged (2d8)

Gear: Per assignment

Common Gadgets: None

"FADE"

Codename: None
Aliases: None
Archer Identity Number: 08-973692-081
Nationality: Unknown
Gender: Male **Handedness:** Right
Height: 6 ft. 1 in. **Weight:** 185 lbs.
Eyes: Unknown **Hair:** Unknown
Psion Class: Physical Adept (Grade unknown)
Place of Birth: Unknown
Date of Birth: Unknown
Distinguishing Characteristics: None

BACKGROUND

Only a handful of people have ever seen Fade face-to-face. Raymond Archer may have been the first when he brought the enigmatic cult leader into the Foundation's Pact in 1957, though he never repeated what he saw. Fade communicates with everyone except his closest operatives (whom he treats like a small family) from the shadows, away from prying eyes. Those who have seen up him close claim that his face is impossible to make out, as if it's constantly shifting, warping as a reaction to the light.

Fade apparently has the best interests of the Foundation (and the world) at heart, not only building a formidable group uniquely equipped to handle many of the the dangers of the modern world, but also intervening personally during times of crisis. In 1975 he joined the strike team sent to the "Eden" island base; with a small cadre of his followers, he infiltrated the stronghold's lowest levels – even penetrating the highest level of the death maze known as the Labyrinth – and was the first to face Helix directly.

Fade is a physical adept of uncharted strength and remarkable discipline. Capable of startling feats of dexterity and speed and master of several martial arts, Fade has never been known to lose a fight, let alone be caught. During his early days operating without Archer's sanction, he was hunted by many organizations on both sides of the law. His ability to vanish into his surroundings without a trace earned him his name.

LOW-LEVEL "FADE"

Chamber: The European Commonwealth
Department: Unknown
Class: Physical Adept
Level: 7

Strength:	20 *	**Dexterity:**	20 *
Constitution:	18 *	**Intelligence:**	18 *
Wisdom:	16 *	**Charisma:**	12 *

* estimated, based on occasional sightings; may be exaggerated (or grossly under-gauged)

Vitality: 71 **Wounds:** 18

Defense: 19 (+4 class, +5 Dex)
Initiative Bonus: +9 (+4 class, +5 Dex)
Speed: 30

Fort: +9 **Ref:** +7 **Will:** +8

Skills: Balance +11, Bluff +10, Climb +11, Computers +10, Concentration +10, Cryptography +8, Demolitions +9, Diplomacy +10, Disguise +15, Driver +10, Electronics +9, Escape Artist +12, Gather Information +10, Hide +13, Innuendo +12,

Intimidate +12, Jump +13, Knowledge (Archer Secrets) +14, Knowledge (European Secrets) +14, Languages +10, Listen +10, Move Silently +15, Occult +8, Open Lock +10, Pilot +10, Profession (Crusader) +14, Ride +10, Search +10, Sense Motive +10, Spot +10, Surveillance +10, Tumble +15

Feats: Adrenal Basics, Adrenal Mastery, Blind Fight, Combat Instincts, Weapon Focus (Scimitar), Sidestep

Psion Skills: Deadly Hands +14, Energy Burst +14, Flesh Armor +13, Speed Control +14

ATTACKS

Scimitar	+9 melee (1d12+5)

Gear and Gadgets: Unknown

MID-LEVEL "FADE"

Chamber: The European Commonwealth
Department: Unknown
Class: Physical Adept
Level: 14

Strength:	20 *	**Dexterity:**	20 *
Constitution:	18 *	**Intelligence:**	18 *
Wisdom:	16 *	**Charisma:**	14 *

* estimated, based on occasional sightings; may be exaggerated (or grossly under-gauged)

Vitality: 125 **Wounds:** 18

Defense: 23 (+8 class, +5 Dex)
Initiative Bonus: +13 (+8 class, +5 Dex)
Speed: 30

Fort: +13 **Ref:** +9 **Will:** +12

Skills: Balance +13, Bluff +10, Climb +13, Computers +12, Concentration +11, Cryptography +8, Demolitions +9, Diplomacy +12, Disguise +15, Driver +10, Electronics +9, Escape Artist +12, Gather Information +14, Hide +13, Innuendo +15, Intimidate +12, Jump +18, Knowledge (Archer Secrets) +20, Knowledge (European Secrets) +20, Languages +11, Listen +10, Move Silently +22, Occult +8, Open Lock +12, Pilot +10, Profession (Crusader) +20, Ride +10, Search +10, Sense Motive +11, Spot +11, Surveillance +11, Tumble +17

Feats: Adrenal Basics, Adrenal Mastery, Ambidextrous, Blind Fight, Combat Instincts, Mobility, Weapon Focus (Scimitar), Improved Weapon Focus (Scimitar), Sidestep, Swift Strike

Psion Skills: Deadly Hands +18, Energy Burst +18, Flesh Armor +17, Speed Control +18

ATTACKS

Scimitar	+13 melee (1d12+7)

Gear and Gadgets: Unknown

HIGH-LEVEL "FADE"

Chamber: The European Commonwealth
Department: Unknown
Class: Physical Adept
Level: 20

Strength:	20 *	**Dexterity:**	20 *
Constitution:	18 *	**Intelligence:**	18 *
Wisdom:	17 *	**Charisma:**	15 *

* estimated, based on occasional sightings; may be exaggerated (or grossly under-gauged)

Vitality: 195 **Wounds:** 18

Defense: 27 (+12 class, +5 Dex)
Initiative Bonus: +17 (+12 class, +5 Dex)
Speed: 30

Fort: +16 **Ref:** +11 **Will:** +15

Skills: Balance +15, Bluff +12, Climb +15, Computers +14, Concentration +13, Cryptography +8, Demolitions +9, Diplomacy +12, Disguise +17, Driver +12, Electronics +9, Escape Artist +15, Gather Information +17, Hide +15, Innuendo +18, Intimidate +12, Jump +20, Knowledge (Archer Secrets) +19, Knowledge (European Secrets) +24, Languages +13, Listen +10, Move Silently +25, Occult +8, Open Lock +15, Pilot +10, Profession (Crusader) +23, Ride +10, Search +12, Sense Motive +13, Spot +13, Surveillance +13, Tumble +20

Feats: Adrenal Basics, Adrenal Mastery, Ambidextrous, Blind Fight, Blindsight 5' Radius, Combat Instincts, Mobility, Weapon Focus (Scimitar), Improved Weapon Focus (Scimitar), Sidestep, Swift Strike, Surge of Speed, Weapon Master (Scimitar)

Psion Skills: Deadly Hands +20, Energy Burst +20, Flesh Armor +19, Speed Control +20

ATTACKS

Scimitar	+17 melee (1d12+8)

Gear and Gadgets: Unknown

The Guardians of the Whispering Knife

"For though we live in the world, we do not wage war as the world does. The weapons we fight with are not the weapons of the world. On the contrary, they have divine power..."

—2 Corinthians 10:3-4

The Guardians of the Whispering Knife are the eldest of the Foundation's Chambers, rooted in a secret mystic history revealed to no one outside their order – not even Raymond Archer, the man who brought them into the Conspiracy. They trace their origins to antiquity, having served pharaohs and kings as mystics, soldiers, advisors, and assassins. They wield powers only an intimate connection with the occult world can provide, and they have knowledge of modern supernatural enemies before the Foundation encounters them. No one is sure where the Guardians acquire their knowledge, or what the source of their mystic power is, but everyone in the Foundation recognizes the need for their guidance in an age where myth and legend bubble to the surface with deadly results.

The Guardians' Mission

When Raymond Archer gathered members of the world's intelligence community in 1950, he made sure the Guardians were represented. When he first met their enigmatic emissary, Umbra, a world of incredible mystic power opened up to him – an ancient earth whose cultures were responsible for the psion powers he'd gained, the mystic forces the Guardians still wielded, and many horrors yet to be unleashed.

Archer knew that the Guardians were the only ones prepared to face many of the less conventional challenges facing the delicate new world balance. He also knew from Umbra's guarded responses to his pressing questions that the order would not simply hand over their secrets to a fledgling and unproven protectorate.

So he struck a deal. He brought the Guardians into the fold as advisors, and established a Guardian liaison in each of the other Chambers who could watch for mystical threats – threats which only they could defeat.

The Guardians were only too happy to comply. Their ancient mission, as related to the Conspiracy's founders, was one of intelligence gathering and collection – primarily concerning strange and mystic events around the world. Over the centuries, they have taken an interest in politics and war as well, and hint at involvement in many world struggles, both within and outside the Middle East.

The Archer Foundation's charter offered the Guardians a perfect opportunity to expand the scope of their operations. No longer would they be restricted to unstable partnerships with single world leaders. Now they could focus their attention on the entire world, using the extensive resources of what they expected to be a powerful and wide-reaching organization.

The Guardians trusted Raymond Archer to make good on his promise to establish a global administration, and ensured that his dream was largely unfettered by the sudden and unexpected rise in supernatural and cult-like activity since 1950. In return, they have received a ground-floor invitation to the greatest espionage conspiracy of all time.

Function

The Guardians possess insight unavailable to anyone else in the Conspiracy, and are regularly called into mission briefings when anything unusual (read: not readily explainable) occurs. Guardians frequently accompany agents into the field for such missions as well *(see Common Guardian Missions, next page)*.

Most Guardians are mystics, and nearly all focus their weapons training on the use of blades (both thrown and hand-held). Both of these skills play a significant role in the Guardians' religion. They keep details about their faith well-shielded (none speak of it to outsiders), but the results of their focused regimen speak for themselves. Guardians are some of the finest knife- and sword-fighters in the world, and their powerful mystics are capable of healing others, glimpsing the future, and sensing evil.

The Guardians' mystic abilities work effectively on traditional missions as well, and their peculiar ability to sense the realm of the dead – called *shadespeaking* – also plays a regular role in today's operations, especially murder investigations. *See page 216 for more information about this ability, as well as the shade-speaker prestige class.*

In addition to their mystic and occult expertise, the Guardians share many skills with other Chambers of the Conspiracy that come in handy while in the field. They are remarkable infiltrators, able to bypass and ignore modern security systems. Guardians are also well-versed in survival skills, having operated in the worst terrain on earth before and after joining the Foundation. The Guardian's ancient enemies – occult sorcerors, power-mad cults, and irresponsible archaeologists – tend to congregate in uncivilized areas, and sites of mystic power only appear in cities when the cities are built over them.

Finally, the Guardians specialize in a talent they rarely indulge in – assassination. Dating back to their early history, they have tempered their murderous techniques with a strict social code. The Guardians never kill by request (they rarely kill for any reason other than necessity), and often refuse to assassinate certain targets because they are "not deserving of death." How the Guardians discern whose life should and should not end is a mystery, but the Foundation has learned to accept their decisions. In practice, those whom the Guardians spare always turn out to be useful allies, or possessing qualities that enrich and aid the world.

Like most of their history, the Guardians refuse to talk about their martial talents and uncanny sense of character, saying only that they are remnants of "another age, when we were young and acted rashly."

Common Guardian Missions

As discussed above, Guardians accompany Foundation agents on any mission involving the occult, or the supernatural, or any other aspect of the mystic world. The liaisons from each office only occasionally venture out into the field, usually working as controlling advisors who request aid from the Guardians' secret headquarters in the Middle East when it's needed.

When a Guardian is required, the Foundation – who prefer to associate with known quantitites – usually requests one whom it has worked with before. This has resulted in only a small number of Guardians working with Foundation teams, all of whom are known throughout the Conspiracy, as well as in certain pockets of the world's shadow communities, though rarely for what they really are.

Guardians can and frequently travel anywhere at anytime, to work with any Foundation team. This versatility is an incredible asset to the Foundation, whose work rarely follows predictable patterns. Some Guardians prefer to work with certain Chambers or agent teams, and the Order usually honors their wishes. After all, there are plenty of Guardians willing to venture out into the world and take part in the Foundation's grand and exciting mission; if a few settle down into a regular team, no one will mind.

Special Note: This arrangement makes it extraordinarily easy for Game Controls to accomodate Guardian agents in regular field teams.

Guardians are always a part of any operation in North Africa or the Middle East. The arrangement was a promise from Raymond Archer himself, and so far no one has dared break it.

Agent Expectations

The Guardians of the Whispering Knife are perfect for players who relish mysterious men of action. They are Archer's one link to the realm of the supernatural, with unique mystic abilities and ritual magic at their disposal. They are enigmatic and strange yet also extremely adaptable – full of roleplaying opportunities.

The Guardians allow players to portray agents who are different from those found in most traditional action-adventure and espionage stories – agents frequently reserved for momentary forays into an unseen world. With the Guardians in the mix from the beginning, the world of the supernatural becomes accessible.

The Guardians act as a living force from the ancient past taking an active role in the events of the present. They are steeped in arcane tradition, belief, and power that was old when the great pyramids of Egypt first towered toward the heavens. They have seen and aided the rise of civilizations and the fall of Empires, a calm center in the sandstorm of history. Though timeless, they are by no means complacent.

The average Guardian is a deeply spiritual person, guided by the beliefs of his ancestors. He knows the true nature of life and death and embraces both with equal passion. This means that, though he might find satisfaction in dispatching an evil soul, he also finds joy in the laughter of a child or the embrace of a friend. Every Guardians remembers that they serve the entire world, and that their actions are vital in keeping it safe. They may be mysterious, but the Guardians are still very human.

Because the Guardians are acutely aware of their role in the grand scheme of things, they act extremely well as team players. They are remarkably efficient and strive to inspire the same level of excellence in those around them. Almost any team can benefit from the inclusion of a Guardian, whether acting as infiltrator, interpreter, advisor, or assassin. The only limit to a Guardian's potential is the imagination of the player behind him.

Tactical Data

The Guardians of the Whispering Knife meet their objectives today in the same fashion as they always have; swiftly, precisely, and with mortal accuracy. They perfected their tactics over generations, honed to a razor-fine edge that can cleave an enemy to shreds – or cut him off from all support, vulnerable to the Foundation or another Chamber.

The defining element of Guardian methods is patience. They are eternally vigilant, watchful for the optimum moment their action will be most effective.

Until that instant, they study and plot, weighing dozens of options and possible scenarios, and prepare. Little surprises a Guardian of the Whispering Knife.

A Guardian in action is as focused as his weapons. His body becomes another tool at his disposal, unfettered by fear, anger, or pain. Ultimately, the Guardian's physical self – his shell – is viewed as just another channel for inner strength. Emotions and worldly concerns all fall away when it is time to act.

While most Guardians are adept with modern weapons, most prefer "ageless weapons," claiming that knives, swords, and bows are spiritually pure. Of course, a Guardian Soldier won't refuse to use a sniper rifle if it is best suited for the situation, but when killing at range, most prefer their unique *nas ruh* ("soul blade") throwing knives *(see below)*. Many Guardians also apply new technology to traditional weapons (knives with micro-polymer blades, ceramic compound bows, and so on).

Nas Ruh Blades

The "soul blades" carried by most Guardians are weighted and balanced throwing knives with remarkable precision and few chances for error.

Damage	Error	Threat	Range	Wgt
1d4+1	1	19-20	20 ft.	1 lb.

Nas ruh blades cost 1 budget point each, and have no actual cost (as they cannot be bought on the open market). A Guardian agent may only requisition up to his agent level in *nas ruh* blades for any mission.

Guardian Artifacts

The Guardians are not without their own brand of special weapons – mystic relics they have protected for millennia. Chief among these ancient artifacts are their *nas ruh* throwing knives and the shadespeakers' *washaif* blades, both presumably created in the spiritual world the Guardians protect.

An item more commonly used in the field is the *'irif* ring, a band of onyx engraved with archaic symbols that glow with a pale white light when the ring is worn. The image of a golden dagger – the Whispering Knife – lies inside the stone of each *'irif* ring. Light reflected through the stone offers the illusion of a thin line of blood trailing down the edge of its blade, pooling into a drop at the tip.

Guardian legend holds that each *'irif* ring holds the essence of a djinn, which offers a sense of the ancient. When a Guardian wears one, he joins with the wearers of all other *'irif* rings. Direct communication is not possible, but each wearer has an acute awareness of the others' presence. The Guardians use the rings most often to coordinate and synchronize deadly assaults upon their enemies. At one time the Guardians had over one hundred of these artifacts. Through the ages, most have been lost or destroyed. Only two dozen remain in use.

For 'irif statistics, see the gadget section on page 210.

Chamber Organization

The Guardians' society remains a secret – even from the Archer Foundation. They have their own culture, talents, and allies, which they often use to warn the Foundation of potential crises and supernatural threats. Little is known of the ancestral home of the Guardians, save that it lies somewhere within the Middle East, and that it dates back centuries, if not millennia. Nearly all contact with the Guardians takes place through the liaisons assigned to each Chamber and the agents who are called in to assist with specific missions.

When Guardian liaisons leave their posts – through choice, old age, or death – the Order takes every effort to ensure that their replacement blends into their new post. Oddly, agents of the Foundation have observed that replacement liaisons somehow know everything their predecessor did – sometimes including information they have no earthly business possessing. The Foundation never made an effort to learn how this is possible – they understand that the Guardians would simply refuse to answer.

Social Data

In an effort to better blend in with other cultures, Guardian field operatives practice the mannerisms and cultural eccentricities of the world's largest communities. Guardians also wear clothing appropriate for their destination from the moment they leave their homeland.

During operations that demand anonymity – particularly missions involving assassination or infiltration – Guardians don a ritual outfit *(the jâmid)*. Bunched to conceal one's gender as well as identity, the jâmid has been cherished among the Guardians' society for millennia.

Devout gnostics, the Guardians' religious beliefs and practices permeate every level of their lives. Prayers and rites commonly include intense meditation and physical dedication, involving elaborate exercises with knives against a backdrop of burning incense, chants, and evocative music.

Extremely private with spiritual matters, Guardians practice alone at designated times and under controlled circumstances. On occasion, however, they perform complex communal rituals which produce results best described as magical. The most common reason for these rituals is to counteract harmful spiritual tampering (usually by groups like the Hand of Glory – *see page 246*). In times of crisis, however, the Guardians perform these ceremonies for their own benefit, giving themselves an extra edge on the eve of battle.

The Guardians also practice many social rituals, some of which have been witnessed when liaisons practice them. One such ritual is referred to as weapon painting, and bonds a Guardian with his chosen armament. During this ritual, the Guardian makes a careful slice along his chest and allows his blood to drop along the weapon's blade. Tradition holds that this must be done so that the weapon may not harm its owner, having already tasted his essence. Weapon painting occurs around a large fire during a new moon, and participants are expected to display their new weapons and mastery of them before and after the ceremony.

Another ritual has no formal name but plays a critically important role in the Guardians' culture. Immediately after a Guardian dies, any other Guardians remain on hand to help his soul make the transition to the next world. They hold constant vigil to fend off dangerous spirits and elements. Guardians do not mourn a departed spirit, since they have personal knowledge of the afterlife. What has been seen of their funerals is festive, with much music and dancing.

The Guardians cremate the bodies of their brethren on a giant pyre. After the pyre burns out, they collect the ashes in an urn and entrust it to family or a devoted friend. Guardians have been known to go to great lengths to return a fallen friend's body – Guardian or not – to their people.

Guardian Resources

The Guardians' relationship with the Archer Conspiracy affords them many resources and luxuries they would otherwise not have access to, from new sources of information about the espionage world (which often includes information about the spiritiual world) to remarkable advancements in modern science and technology. But the Guardians were not the only ones to benefit from this alliance – the Foundation now has access to thousands of years of mystic experience, an army of melee weapons experts, and a couple of special resources they never expected.

Shadespeakers

Guardian society is strictly ordered, broken into many castes and sects. The Archer Foundation is only aware of some of these groups – primarily those from which they draw liaisons are. One caste that caught the Foundation off guard are the shadespeakers, Guardians who can sense and sometimes speak with the dead. Shadespeakers are religious in appearance, but most certainly mystic in nature. Their lives are ritualistic observances of those with whom they have communicated, each a close friend or respected enemy.

Many shadespeakers serve as assassins. The Guardians feel that none lead the irredeemable to their final spiritual dwelling better than they. Shadespeakers also prove incredibly helpful during missions and investigations involving bodies, as they can often gain information from the deceased's spirit that is unavailable from its body.

For more information about shadespeakers (and a mystic prestige class dedicated to them), see page 216.

The Voice

The speed with which liaisons communicate with their homeland (and the woman known as Aurora, who passes as their cultural Control) is staggering. In times of crisis, liaisons have been known to receive answers from Aurora or her subordinates in minutes, seemingly without any phone call or email exchange. The Foundation only recently discovered the reasons for this, during a mission in which Aurora was captured and held hostage by the Assassins *(see page 110)*. Word of her abduction reached the Guardian liaison at the Foundation before one of the last surviving members of the mission team called into the home office. Guardians arrived on the scene and eliminated the Assassin cell before a strike team a mere half hour away reached the site.

The Foundation assumed that the Guardians who saved Aurora were in fact shadowing the envoy when she was taken, but a second Archer agent trapped in the cell with her reported that she spoke into the air, apparently with both the liaison and the strike team that freed them.

It is unknown whether this ability is limited to Aurora, or if all Guardian leaders had it throughout their history.

Training

Unlike other shadow communities, the Guardians don't have specialized institutes with drill instructors and textbook routines to memorize. Every day is a trial for them, and the greatest reward is survival.

Individual Guardians sometimes pair off, passing along their skills. For example, a Guardian who spent time within the Shin Bet General Security Service might share his knowledge of Israeli counter-intelligence techniques, while a Guardian who has never left his people might tutor the finer points of weaponsmithing. The bonds formed between these teachers and students are close, and considered sacrosanct by the Guardians' community.

Guardians spend a portion of every day meditating, visualizing their weaknesses and the methods by which they might eliminate them. In essence, they perceive themselves as spiritual knives, whose blades can always be sharpened and polished. True completion comes only as the Guardian's spirit finally leaves his physical body, returning to the forge of the universe.

Sparring: Combat training is an integral part of Guardian life. One of their favorite pastimes is sparring, during which two or more Guardians gather in a large circle, pitting their weapons and minds against one another in a flurry of blades, blows, and bravado. Though minor injuries are common, no Guardian ever spars with the intention of harming his opponent. In fact, sparring partners are often the best of friends, and there is even a distinct style of sparring that couples enjoy during courtship, known as the sharpness of the heart. The hint of danger often provides a romantic rush.

The Crucible of God: When a Guardian is ready to test his skills against the devices of his ancestors, he makes a pilgrimage into the desolate wilderness and wanders the acrid wastes alone, without food or water. Following signs only he can see, he is drawn to a remote area and undergoes what a mystic challenge the Guardians refer to as The Crucible of God.

The Crucible reportedly pits the Guardian against an infinite number of physical and mental obstacle courses, each designed to usher the Guardian to a new level of proficiency. Those who survive say they could not consciously choose their tests. The tests chose them.

Most Guardians make this journey only a few times in their lives. Those who offer their skills to the Archer Foundation, however, have been known to test themselves annually, perpetually striving to refine their abilities for the good of the world.

The Crucible can happen anywhere and at anytime, though it has never been known to interrupt a mission or other important Fondation business.

Transformation: When a Guardian is ready to make a crucial transition in his life (i.e. a player decides he wants to multi-class), he enters a deep trance. His breathing and heart rate all but cease and, without careful examination, he appears dead. But like a caterpillar in a cocoon, he mentally redistributes his energy, preparing himself for the new challenge. When he recovers from his trance (which rarely lasts longer than 48 hours), he feels refreshed and ready to experience the world anew.

The Game in the Middle East

Agencies in Northern Africa and the Middle East play the Game by their own rules. Subtlety rarely works here; many people consider acts of violence and terrorism not only viable political tactics but – more often than not – Divine will.

This is a land in constant conflict, one which has been divided by religious beliefs for hundreds of years. Enemies appear within and without, and most governments devote incredible resources to monitoring their own citizens. The outside world, as a rule, comes as an afterthought.

Intelligence Agencies

The following are just a few of the prominent agencies in the region. Additional agencies and the plots that surround them will be detailed in the *Guardians of the Whispering Knife* sourcebook.

Saudi Arabia: General Directorate of Investigation (GDI): The GDI is the Ministry of the Interior's security service and, like the rest of the Saudi government, works in accordance with the *Shari'a* (Islamic law). The GDI focuses its intelligence-gathering services primarily upon its own citizens, sharing information with *Mutawwa'*, the Saudi religious police. The GDI also monitors potentially corrupting foreign influences, especially of the relgious variety. Saudi Arabia is a strictly Islamic nation and does not tolerate other religions. Anyone arrested by the GDI remains isolated during the initial phase of the investigation, which can last for months. Even afterward, prisoners are only allowed limited interaction with lawyers and family. Punishments meted out by the GDI are frequently severe, to serve as an example to others.

Jordan: General Intelligence Department (GID): The GID was established in 1964 to protect the internal and external security of the Kingdom of Jordan. The GID Director is appointed by royal decree, based on a decision made by the Counsel of Ministers. Officers are also appointed by a royal decree that comes from a recommendation by the Director General.

The GID's mandate is to counteract terrorism and physical sabotage at home. It also works against "intellectual sabotage and attempts to infiltrate the Jordanian society." Finally, a new directorate was founded in 1996 that gives the GID authority to counter the traffic of contraband. The Jordanian Prime Minister can also assign the GID duties as long as he specifies them in writing.

Egypt: General Intelligence Agency (GIA): Considered ineffectual by the outside world, Egypt's intelligence agency is still a force to be reckoned with on its own turf. Since its reorganization by the German master spy General Reinhard Gehlen, the GIA has built a reputation for relentlessness within Egypt's own borders.

At times throughout its history, the GIA has operated without government authority. Today, it still functions separately from the Egyptian military, but its actions are closely monitored.

The GIA's specialty is audio surveillance.

Iran: Ministry of Intelligence and Security (VEVAK): The government of Iran believes that Muslims the world over comprise a single community known as the Ummah, which must be directed by one holy regime. With their successful revolution in 1979, Iranian leaders declared themselves the head of that regime, sentinels for all members of the Islamic faith. They are absolutely dedicated to liberating the Ummah from corrupting influence, and willing to use any means – up to and including terrorism – to achieve that goal. VEVAK provides intelligence for such brutal operations.

VEVAK has carried out terrorist actions on its own, often focusing on dissidents within its own territory. It has also trained extremist Islamic military forces around the globe, including segments of the Bosnian army.

To secure themselves in foreign lands, VEVAK agents commonly operate out of Iranian consulate offices and embassies, often disguised as diplomats (which provides them diplomatic immunity).

Israel: Mossad–Institute for Intelligence and Special Tasks: In 1951, the Central Institute for Coordination and Central Institute for Intelligence and Security merged into Mossad, the first line of defense against Israel's enemies. Since then, Mossad has been Israel's foremost covert action, counter-terrorism, and intelligence gathering group. Headquartered in Tel Aviv, Mossad is divided into eight departments, though details about its internal organization are sketchy.

Some Mossad departments are infamous, such as the Special Operations Division (Metsada), responsible for psychological warfare, sabotage, and assassination. Others are less overt; the Collections Department performs espionage operations abroad under diplomatic or unofficial cover, and the Political Action and Liaison Department distribute information between allied foreign intelligence services.

The identity of Mossad's Director has traditionally been a state secret. But in 1996, the Government announced the appointment of Major General Danny Yatom to the post, flying in the face of tradition.

Israel: Shin Bet General Security Service (GSS): Israel's internal security and counter-intelligence organization is commonly believed to have three operational departments.

The Protective Security Department guards government buildings and embassies, scientific installations, important parts of industry, and the national airline, El Al.

The Arab Affairs Department fields anti-terrorist agents and develops terrorist profiles. This division combats the military arm of Hamas, the Islamic Resistance Movement.

Finally, the Non-Arab Affairs Department uncovers foreign intelligence operatives, especially those of former Soviet bloc nations.

All foreigners who travel to Israel face potential scrutiny from the GSS, whose continued use of "special measures" during interrogations has prompted investigations to make sure they do not violate the Geneva Convention.

A Note on Language

The Guardians speak a dialect of Arabic that contains several archaic terms. Other Arabic speakers easily understand them, but notice that the accent is a bit peculiar (a close analogy is the difference between English spoken by the British and English spoken by the Irish). With practice, however, Guardians can adjust their accent to mimic those of other regions.

On occasion, agents of the Foundation have also heard the Guardians speak to each other in another tongue – one unlike any language in the world – and they utilize a sign language as well. The Guardians closely protect both of these tongues. They refuse to use them in the presence of others unless they absolutely must speak privately, and then keep their sentences short enough to prevent the witnesses from reconstructing their words.

Mechanics: Any Guardian agent can mask his original accent with a Languages (DC 10) skill check. Further, Guardian agents may take skill ranks in their native tongue *(hakika)*, which allows them to communicate both verbally and non-verbally.

PLAYING THE GREAT GAME

"Trust in the wisdom of the Ancients, though their nightmares now walk among us."

– Aurora

Mission Management: The Guardians have always considered their secrecy to be their greatest shield. To maintain it they have been known to flatly decline Foundation directives involving large scale or highly public actions, even within their own shadow community. These operations tend to fall to the African Alliance more often than not. The Guardians largely try to handle their own affairs internally, but their longstanding relationship with Room 39 (dating back to before World War II – *see page 38*) make the British Chamber their leading choice when they must turn to outside help.

The Legend of the Whispering Knife

The name of the Guardians' Chamber derives from their secret society's Arabic title – *Harasa b'al-Skeen al-Hamsa*. This is the name Conrad Archer came to know them by, and it has remained ever since. But its significance was not understood until 1944, during Operation: GODSMASHER *(see page 38)*.

During the mission to prevent the Nazi mystic exploration of the island of Crete, the Guardian attaché Umbra wielded a weapon of unprecedented power – an ancient dagger with a golden blade, reportedly responsible for leading the Room 39 mission team to Eva's inner sanctum.

The dagger, called *Hiss* in the Guardians' native tongue, was unable to save Umbra from Eva's clutches. When Conrad and Raymond Archer arrived for the final battle against her, they found Umbra's body upon a large stone altar, murdered with a single blow to the chest. Hiss was nowhere to be found.

Since that day, the Guardians have refused to speak of the weapon, saying only that it is a relic of their ancient beginnings, and a religious heirloom of fantastic significance. When Archer expressed concern that the blade might have been lost at Crete, or worse, stolen by Eva Kraus, the Guardians laid it to rest, saying that "Hiss cannot be taken from us. It is our history, and our future."

Agents debriefed about Operation: GODSMASHER marveled at Hiss, citing it as the reason for Room 39's success on the island. They also spoke of the dagger with a certain degree of unease, remembering not only its incredible ferocity, but the voices whispering on the wind whenever it shed blood – whispered voices twisted in agony...

Damage Control: As discussed on page 207, the latest generation of Guardians includes precious few latent shadespeakers, yet more than a few latent psions have been identified. Ten years ago, the Guardians took the unprecedented step of allowing several geneticists to come live with them, to help nurture their fledgling psions and determine how they came to be. With the Shop's defection, these men and women vanished – along with the subjects of their research. Enraged, the Guardian elders have sent out dozens of operatives to scour the world for the traitors and bring their kidnapped children home. Today, the Guardians are closer to the Conspiracy than ever before, and their agents – much needed in this time of crisis – are far more commonly seen. But the price for this mixed blessing is high, and may yet be paid in blood.

Dirty Little Secrets: The Guardians' most closely guarded secret is their vision of what could have been. Charged with protecting the world from the very threats it now faces (the eruption of psion latency, the emergence of mystic power, and the social and political events they caused), the Guardians have to wonder how much better it might have been like if they had succeeded.

Leverage: Agents of all Chambers arrive when summoned, but Guardians are known for arriving when they are needed - often when word of trouble has yet to spread beyond the contact Chamber. This uncanny knack for being in the right place at the right time has earned them a solid reputation as the "friends" of the Conspiracy, eager to support all others however they are able. Many Guardian relationships – and the liaisons they maintain with every Chamber – have earned them several remarkable pieces of leverage that they could use against their peers, if they chose to. But as history has proven time and again, the Guardians are an honorable people, and unwilling to take advantage of such situations – unless they absolutely have to.

Assets: The rest of the Conspiracy (and parts of the world's shadow communities) are well aware of the Guardians shadespeakers – rare operatives who can seemingly speak with the dead. What they are as yet unaware of, however, is that certain of these operatives continue to serve the Guardians even after death. These ghosts prowl the middle realms, a place mystics call "The Fringe" *(see the upcomming Archer Foundation Chamber book for more)*. Their unmatched stealth and immortal strength makes them the perfect spies, and the ultimate saboteurs.

CURRENT PLOTLINES

The Guardians of the Whispering Knife have an active role in several major plots of the *Shadowforce Archer* setting. Three such plotlines appear here, to give the Game Control hooks for his own serial. Many of these and several more will be developed and expanded upon as part of the official *Shadowforce Archer* storyline.

A Cult Following (Code: Black): Many religions predicted the end of the world at the dawn of the new millennium, gathering dedicated followers and indoctrinating them into their sects. When the calendar changed without incident, most of these assemblages disbanded. One group, the Flowers of Anubis, did not. The Flowers still believe that the world is about to end, and are doing everything in their power to guarantee it. Their members have robbed museums and historical sites, stealing artifacts and arcane knowledge to fund and fuel their enterprise. Now they are producing a specialized chemical agent to spark off a fiery storm throughout Earth's atmosphere, wiping the world clean once and for all. The Guardians are racing against time to stop them.

Evolve or Die (Code: Yellow): Helix's scientific tampering with psion powers apparently created a startling effect among the Guardians. Since the early 1980s, far fewer latent shadespeakers have been born. Concurrently, a number of children have been identified as latent physical adepts, mentalists, and telepaths, traits their people have exhibited only rarely before.

Members of this new generation have had a noticeably difficult time deciphering the ancient methods and morals of their people, and the traditionally spiritual Guardians must now consider science as a solution to the problem. Some theorize this was another facet of Helix's devious plan all along.

Macedonia Rising (No Code Yet Assigned): On August 31, 2001, precious artifacts from the tomb of ancient Macedonian Queen Euridice were stolen under mysterious circumstances. Authorities found no sign of forced entry at the site (near the northern Greek village of Vergina) which is fenced and guarded around the clock. The area is not accessible to tourists.

The artifacts, including three marble female figurines and three statues of sphinxes approximately seven inches tall, were hacked off Euridice's ornate throne. Because the figures were photographed, well documented, and internationally known, the Culture Minister immediately excluded the possibility they might turn up on the art smuggling market.

He was right.

The figures were stolen by Vasil Acevska, a security guard who worked at the tomb for fifteen years. Acevska discovered a crumbling scroll in a bombed-out cave that depicted not only the figurines, but also their true purpose. Queen Euridice once used them in a powerful ritual shortly after the birth of her son, Philip. The ritual channeled the powers of the gods of war and wisdom into the infant, instilling him with a great destiny — building a united Macedonian kingdom and leading it to the most powerful position in the Mediterranean world. Philip did both of these things and in turn, fathered one of the most famous conquerors in history, Alexander the Great. The power of Euridice's magic carried from one generation to the next.

Acevska scoured the world for the right child to re-create the ritual for, and has finally found him: Ljubcho Taneva, the son of the militant nationalist Filip Taneva, who has amassed a small but devoted following. The elder Taneva is infamous for his hateful tirades against the country's minority populations (especially ethnic Albanians) and its southern neighbor, Greece. Acevska plans to approach Taneva with his knowledge of the occult, hoping the father will allow his son to be part of the ritual. If the man refuses, Acevska plans to kidnap the boy and perform the ritual anyway.

Acevska is convinced the child will return Macedonia to its historical glory, leading an army to crush its old foes. He further hopes that Ljubcho will have a son one day who will go on to conquer the world, continuing what Alexander the Great failed to finish.

Making A Killing (Code: Red): Several times in the last century, lone assassins have changed the course of history. Lee Harvey Oswald, Sirhan Sirhan, James Earl Ray, and Yigal Amir all presumably worked alone, and yet most appeared vacuous when apprehended. Another, little known, fact about them is that each bore a distinctive tattoo over their left breast — a dark wavy dagger that seemed to play tricks on the eyes, almost hovering over their skin. Even more remarkable, these tattoos vanished within hours of the assassins' capture, shortly before the attackers seemingly lost all memory of their vicious actions. (Only rarely have these incidents have ever made it into public record, and then they were hushed up rather quickly, either by nervous superiors or the Guardians.)

As with many unexplained coincidences in the *Shadowforce Archer* setting, the reasons for these events is linked to the invisible world inhabited by the Archer Foundation, and the Guardians of the Whispering Knife. In 1078, a mystic named Hassan-I Sabbah departed from the Ismailis faction of Islam, forming a cult that would become known as Assassins. In his mountain fortress of Alamut, Sabbah drugged his followers and programmed them as mindless killers, deploying them to take out social leaders in public spectacles. Each of these programmed killers bore the same strange tattoo as their modern counterparts.

The Assassins began as the antithesis of everything the Guardians believe in, and over the last several hundred years have become one of their most hated enemies. The Guardians only know them by their sign — the *sabah beden* (literally in the Guardian tongue, "ghost body") — which appears in their presence, elusive yet never hidden, always giving them away. The sign manifests on the physical bodies of their dominated killers but never on the bodies of Assassins themselves. Instead it appears near the true Assassins as "part of the scenery" (a crack in a wall, a shadow in a mirror, a wisp of smoke). Some say it trails the Assassins like a curse. Others say that's precisely what it is...

Disciplines of the Blade

The Guardians of the Whispering Knife take great pride in their moral rectitude. They see their weapons as metaphors for the virtues they embrace, the challenges they face, and the world they live in. Collectively, these adages are known as the *Disciplines of the Blade*. Below are the ten most common, and their meanings.

- *To be of use, a blade must keep its edge.* A Guardian must constantly refine and test his skills.
- *A blade is not a bow.* A Guardian must suffer no delusions, being honest with himself with others. He should expect the same in return.
- *A blade is to be held securely in its sheath.* A Guardian must be in command over his passions, never losing self-control.
- *After a blade strikes, it cannot undo its injury.* A Guardian must clearly see what is right and wrong in all situations, and take responsibility for the course he chooses to follow.
- *Every blade has to be forged.* A Guardian must be patient in his life, for everything that is to be eventually will be.
- *The most dangerous blade is the one that is hidden.* A Guardian must be vigilant in every situation.
- *A blade that is not respected will cut the hand that wields it.* A Guardian must give proper regard to those around him, and demand the same from those close to him.
- *To avoid tarnish, a blade has to be polished.* A Guardian must love his family, friends, and people to remain strong.
- *Even the strongest blade can be shattered.* A Guardian must be humble in his affairs, never falling victim to overconfidence.
- *A blade is a reflection of its creator.* A Guardian must honor the purity of his immortal soul and remember the divine power that crafted it.

The Guardians have learned to watch for this sign, and use it as a warning that enemies are near. Unfortunately, the sign doesn't particularly reveal the identity of the Assassin(s) – only that they are present. It is for this reason that many Assassins dwell only in well populated areas, and travel as part of larger groups, where they can hunt the Guardians on equal footing.

Today, most Assassins live peacefully in Iran, Syria, and India, content to spend their time away from death. But there remain secret cabals of their number dedicated to spreading seeds of chaos and destruction across the world, coordinating assassinations that threaten to shatter the security we currently enjoy. To make matters worse, their techniques have been adopted by some of the most powerful governments and organizations in the world – including many of Archer's foes.

The Guardians Genre

Exotic. Mystic. Arcane. Mysterious. Deadly. These are defining terms for the Guardians of the Whispering Knife. Undisputed masters of melee combat and wielders of ancient mystic power, the Guardians are lethal warriors transplanted from another time. They give a magical twist to classic espionage.

Archetypes: Ardeth Bay and the Magi (from the recent *Mummy* movies), Snake Eyes (from *G.I. Joe*), Elektra (from the *Daredevil* comics), Qui-Gon Jinn and Mace Windu (from *The Phantom Menace*), Captain Benjamin L. Willard (from *Apocalypse Now*), Ghost Dog (from *Ghost Dog: The Way of the Samurai*)

Inspirations

The following is an incomplete list of suggested viewing, reading, and listening for Guardians players and the Game Control, when they require inspiration for the group.

Books: *Assassin!: The Bloody History of Political Murder* by Paul Elliot, *Batman* (comic book), *The Bible, Elektra: Assassin* by Frank Miller, *Encyclopedia of Death and the Afterlife* by James R. Lewis, *Hellboy* (comic book), *The Kabbalah, The List of 7* and *The 6 Messiahs* by Mark Frost, *Living Races of the Sahara Desert* by Briggs, *The Mummy or Ramses the Damned* by Anne Rice, *Papyrus of Ani* (The Egyptian Book of the Dead), *The Quar'an, Seven Pillars of Wisdom: A Triumph* by T.E. Lawrence, *The Talmud, The Torah, The Templars and the Assassins: The Militia of Heaven* by James Wasserman; anything by Dean Koontz *(Dark Rivers of the Heart, Phantoms, Servants of Twilight),* anything by Brian Lumley (especially *Necroscope* and the *Dream cycle*), anything by Thomas E. Monteleone (*Blood of the Lamb, The Reckoning, the Borderlands* anthologies).

Movies: *Arabesque, Fallen, Indiana Jones and the Last Crusade, King Solomon's Mines, Lawrence of Arabia, Lost Souls, The Mummy, The Mummy Returns, Raiders of the Lost Ark, Sixth Sense, Stir of Echoes, Tomb Raider.*

TV Shows: *Angel, Brimstone, Buffy the Vampire Slayer, Friday the 13th: The Series, In Search Of..., Kolchak: the Night Stalker, Neverwhere, Night Visions, The Others, Outer Limits* (both versions), *Psi-Factor, Relic Hunter, Twilight Zone* (both versions), *Ultraviolet, X-Files.*

Music: *Africa North: A Rough Guide to North African Music, Desert Poems* by Stephan Micus, *Flying Carpet* by Claude Challe, *Gedida* by Natacha Atlas, *The Hunter, the Hunted* by Alex Cremers, *Lawrence of Arabia* soundtrack, *The Mummy* score, *The Mummy Returns* score, *Sif Saffa: New Music From The Middle East, The 13th Warrior* score, anything by Ofra Haza.

Computer and Console Games: *Alone in the Dark* series, *Gabriel Knight* series, *Nocturne.*

MIDNIGHT

Codename: NEMESIS
Archer Identity Number: 67-403886-773
Nationality: North African (Egyptian)
Gender: Male **Handedness:** Both
Height: 6 ft. 0 in. **Weight:** 175 lbs.
Eyes: Black **Hair:** Raven Black
Psion Class: Physical Adept (Grade A)
Place of Birth: Alexandria, Egypt
Date of Birth: Unknown
Distinguishing Characteristics: Always wears his jâmid and uses a voice filter

BACKGROUND

A strict professional, Midnight is a ruthless, remorseless killing machine who believes compassion and sentiment have no place in the cutthroat world of secret agents. He is lethal in hand-to-hand and ranged combat, specializing in "naked kill" techniques and the use of throwing knives and archery.

The Foundation targeted Midnight for liquidation in 1993 following a series of brutal political slayings across northern Africa. However, the Guardian sent to eliminate him – an empath named Mina – felt only turmoil and pain beneath his intensity. She captured him instead, a task only possible with her ability to amplify his distracting emotions, and returned him to the Center, where he was studied by Chamber psions.

They soon determined that "Midnight" was merely a role the prisoner had been conditioned to play. He was no more responsible for his actions than a mastermind's minion. The Guardians tried to break his programming, with little success (mainly limited to flashes of his former life). They also tried to determine who had twisted him so completely, again in vain.

With few other recourses (save killing him and being done with it) the Guardians accepted Midnight into their ranks, and spent the last eight years training him to kill for the right reasons. Someday, they hope to break down the wall in his head, and return him home.

LOW-LEVEL MIDNIGHT

Chamber: The Guardians
Department: Urban Assault (4)
Class: Soldier
Level: 7

Strength:	16	**Dexterity:**	16
Constitution:	12	**Intelligence:**	10
Wisdom:	12	**Charisma:**	8
Vitality:	58	**Wounds:**	12

Defense: 16 (+3 class, +3 Dex)
Initiative Bonus: +9 (+6 class, +3 Dex)
Speed: 30

Fort: +6 **Ref:** +7 **Will:** +3

Skills: Balance +7, Climb +7, Intimidate +3, Jump +7, Profession (Assassin) +7, Spot +7, Survival +7, Tumble +7, Use Rope +4

Feats: Blind Fight, Lightning Draw, Marksman, Point Blank Shot, Precise Shot, Quick Draw, Rapid Shot, Snap Shot

ATTACKS

Throwing knife	+10 ranged (1d4+3)
Composite Bow	+10 ranged (1d6+3)
7.62×45mm assault rifle	+10 ranged (2d8+2)

Gear: *jâmid* *(see page 102)*

Common Gadgets: Voice disguiser (external)

MID-LEVEL MIDNIGHT

Chamber: The Guardians
Department: Urban Assault (4)
Class: Soldier/Physical Adept
Level: 7/7

Strength:	16	**Dexterity:**	16
Constitution:	13	**Intelligence:**	10
Wisdom:	12	**Charisma:**	10
Vitality:	105	**Wounds:**	13

Defense: 20 (+7 class, +3 Dex)
Initiative Bonus: +13 (+10 class, +3 Dex)
Speed: 30

Fort: +11 **Ref:** +9 **Will:** +10

Skills: Balance +9, Climb +9, Intimidate +7, Jump +9, Occult +9, Profession (Assassin) +11, Spot +9, Survival +9, Tumble +9, Use Rope +4

Feats: Blind Fight, Lightning Draw, Marksman, Point Blank Shot, Precise Shot, Quick Draw, Rapid Shot, Sensory Basics, Sensory Mastery, Snap Shot, Untraceable Power (Combat Sense), Untraceable Power (Extra Spectral Sight)

Psion Skills: Combat Sense +10, Extra Spectral Sight +9

Attacks

Throwing knife	+13 ranged (1d4+3)
Composite bow	+13 ranged (1d6+3)
7.62×45mm assault rifle	+13 ranged (2d8+2)

Gear: *jâmid* *(see page 102)*

Common Gadgets: Voice disguiser (external)

High-Level Midnight

Chamber: The Guardians
Department: Urban Assault (4)
Class: Soldier/Physical Adept
Level: 10/10

Strength:	16	**Dexterity:**	16
Constitution:	14	**Intelligence:**	10
Wisdom:	12	**Charisma:**	11
Vitality:	166	**Wounds:**	14

Defense: 23 (+10 class, +3 Dex)
Initiative Bonus: +17 (+14 class, +3 Dex)
Speed: 30

Fort: +16 **Ref:** +11 **Will:** +11

Skills: Balance +10, Climb +10, Intimidate +10, Jump +10, Occult +10, Profession (Assassin) +15, Spot +10, Survival +10, Tumble +10, Use Rope +8

Feats: Blind Fight, Controlled Burst, Controlled Strafe, Hail of Bullets, Lightning Draw, Marksman, Point Blank Shot, Precise Shot, Quick Draw, Rapid Shot, Sensory Basics, Sensory Mastery, Snap Shot, Stamina Battery, Untraceable Power (Combat Sense), Untraceable Power (Extra Spectral Sight)

Psion Skills: Combat Sense +16, Extra Spectral Sight +15

Attacks

Throwing knife	+18 ranged (1d4+3)
Composite bow	+18 ranged (1d6+3)
7.62×45mm assault rifle	+18 ranged (2d8+2)

Gear: *jâmid* *(see page 102)*

Common Gadgets: Voice disguiser (external)

Aurora

Codename: SPECTRUM
Aliases: None
Archer Identity Number: 01-006011-004
Nationality: Saudi Arabian
Gender: Female **Handedness:** Right
Height: 5 ft. 2 in. **Weight:** 120 lbs.
Eyes: Pale Brown **Hair:** White
Psion Class: Latent Physical Adept
Place of Birth: Syrian Desert, Saudi Arabia
Date of Birth: 1940.05.23
Distinguishing Characteristics: Waist-length hair worn in loose braids

Background

Aurora is the daughter of Umbra, who was the first Guardian to contact Room 39 and Conrad Archer *(see page 38)*, and she is the last surviving member of their sect. She has been the Guardians' cultural and spiritual Center for more than forty years, and is cherished by all.

Wise beyond her years, Aurora has seen more things in her lifetime than most people would dare dream, embracing triumphs and tragedies with the same tranquil grace. She understands the dual enigmas of life and death, but realizes that words cannot truly express a solution. She has dedicated her life to embodying the truths she discovered, her every word and action a lesson for her "children," the Guardians.

Aurora is still amazingly spry and quite active in the Chamber's home territory. She retains much of her youthful energy and martial prowess, which – combined with her considerable psion power – is more than a match for any foolish challenger.

Since her abduction by and escape from the Assassins four years ago, Aurora has become far more interested in matters outside the Guardians' homeland. Rumor contends that she is searching for something – or someone.

LOW-LEVEL AURORA

Chamber: The Guardians
Department: Basement
Class: Pointman
Level: 2

Strength:	14	**Dexterity:**	12
Constitution:	14	**Intelligence:**	12
Wisdom:	18	**Charisma:**	12
Vitality:	20	**Wounds:**	14

Defense: 12 (+1 class, +1 Dex)
Initiative Bonus: +2 (+1 class, +1 Dex)
Speed: 30

Fort: +4 **Ref:** +3 **Will:** +8

Skills: Bluff +4, Bureaucracy +6, Cryptography +4, Diplomacy +6, Disguise +4, Driver +2, First Aid +6, Handle Animal +5, Knowledge (Guardians) +6, Knowledge (Occult World) +6, Languages +4, Listen +5, Sense Motive +6

Feats: Quick Healer, Scholarly

ATTACKS

Scimitar	+3 melee (1d12+2)
Throwing knife	+2 melee (1d4+2)

Gear: None

Common Gadgets: *jâmid (see page 102* with built-in disguise enhancer modification, *'irif* ring *(see page 210)*, anti-psi safety field (disguised as right earring), bug detector (external unit)

MID-LEVEL AURORA

Chamber: The Guardians
Department: Basement
Class: Pointman
Level: 9

Strength:	14	**Dexterity:**	12
Constitution:	14	**Intelligence:**	12
Wisdom:	20	**Charisma:**	12
Vitality:	72	**Wounds:**	14

Defense: 15 (+4 class, +1 Dex)
Initiative Bonus: +5 (+4 class, +1 Dex)
Speed: 30

Fort: +6 **Ref:** +5 **Will:** +14

Skills: Bluff +6, Bureaucracy +10, Cryptography +6, Diplomacy +10, Disguise +7, Driver +5, First Aid +8, Handle Animal +9, Knowledge (Guardians) +13, Knowledge (Occult World) +13, Languages +7, Listen +7, Sense Motive +12

Feats: Blind-Fight, Cleave, Power Attack, Quick Healer, Scholarly

ATTACKS

Scimitar	+8 melee (1d12+2)
Throwing knife	+7 melee (1d4+2)

Gear: None

Common Gadgets: *jâmid (see page 102)* with built-in disguise enhancer modification, *'irif* ring *(see page 210)*, anti-psi safety field (disguised as right earring), bug detector (external unit)

HIGH-LEVEL AURORA

Chamber: The Guardians
Department: Basement
Class: Pointman
Level: 16

Strength:	14	**Dexterity:**	13
Constitution:	14	**Intelligence:**	12
Wisdom:	20	**Charisma:**	13
Vitality:	125	**Wounds:**	14

Defense: 17 (+6 class, +1 Dex)
Initiative Bonus: +7 (+6 class, +1 Dex)
Speed: 30

Fort: +9 **Ref:** +8 **Will:** +20

Skills: Bluff +8, Bureaucracy +16, Cryptography +8, Diplomacy +19, Disguise +9, Driver +5, First Aid +11, Handle Animal +11, Knowledge (Guardians) +20, Knowledge (Occult World) +20, Languages +9, Listen +9, Sense Motive +17

Feats: Blind-Fight, Cleave, Combat Instincts, Great Cleave, Power Attack, Quick Healer, Scholarly

ATTACKS

Scimitar	+14 melee (1d12+2)
Throwing knife	+13 melee (1d4+2)

Gear: None
Common Gadgets: *jâmid (see page 102)* with built-in disguise enhancer modification, *'irif* ring *(see page 210)*, anti-psi safety field (disguised as right earring), bug detector (external unit)

The Pan-Asian Collective

"One who knows, does not speak."

—Lao Tzu, Tao Te Ching

From 1936 to 1945, the Kempei Tai, a covert Japanese secret police organized under the military, was the most feared organization in the Far East. With nearly limitless authority and a sadistic commander, the Kempei Tai conducted counterespionage missions and rooted out traitors within Japan and its occupied territories. It performed this task with brutal efficiency, arresting, imprisoning, and executing thousands of alleged enemies of the state. Though overzealous, xenophobic, and racist, the Kempei Tai was one of the most successful counterespionage agencies during the Second World War.

When the Archer Pact formed in 1950, it grouped the whole of Southeast Asia into a single Chamber charged with policing its own people. The early agents of the Pan-Asian Collective turned to the Kempei Tai as their model for such an intelligence organization. Though not nearly as brutal or xenophobic as its ancestor, the PAC's roots lie firmly in Kempei Tai tactics – laced with a healthy dose of the training Conrad Archer received from Wong Fei-Hung, of course *(see page 26)*.

The Collective Mission

While initially tasked with policing its own people and ensuring that the conflicts of the region didn't boil over into large-scale war, the PAC has evolved into something a little different. It began its operations by infiltrating and spying on its own governments. PAC agents became so good at this that the Chamber's mission expanded to include general information-gathering and deep cover infiltration.

Today, the Pan-Asian Collective is the foremost intelligence-gathering Chamber in the conspiracy. It has hundreds of agents planted in organizations and governments worldwide, and its steady supply of information is unmatched.

Function

The fractious nature of the Far East causes many problems for the PAC. None of the nations in the area trusts any other, and old rivalries and memories of crimes both real and imagined linger. Thus, the Chamber finds it difficult to get its member nations to cooperate. It must therefore work outside the individual countries and their respective intelligence agencies to achieve its aims.

As mentioned, the PAC's primary mission is information collection. It uses deep cover agents, black marketeers, government officials, and even criminals to glean the data that it feeds back to Archer. Early on, though, Collective controllers discovered that information wasn't enough. If they wanted not only to know about conflicts but prevent them, another talent was required: political and psychological manipulation. Hence, the PAC have become masters at breaking psyches, brainwashing, misdirection, subterfuge, and outright lies.

Common Collective Missions

Many PAC operatives are deep cover agents operating by themselves in hostile territory. Most receive a mission objective and a loose set of parameters within which to conduct it. After that, they are on their own. How they accomplish their objectives is not half as important as getting the job done.

This loose structure raises some concerns about rogue agents and unacceptable operating techniques, but so far the Collective has been embroiled in very few embarrassing incidents. Control relies on the Chamber's rigorous training and the near-fanatical dedication of his agents to ensure no lingering fallout during their missions. Still, critics claim that it is only a matter of time before something goes disastrously wrong.

Collective agents perform numerous functions in the field. Owing to its large-scale infiltration and intelligence-gathering operations, the Chamber fields a disproportionate number of facemen, with snoops, fixers, and pointmen coming in a close second.

Infiltration (Deep Cover Assignments): This job is the bread and butter of the PAC, which specializes in putting moles inside organizations – friendly and hostile – with orders to ferret out and report information. Many of these assignments are long-term. The agent insinuates himself into the target and spends years informing Archer of its activities. During such operations, PAC telepaths might literally rip secrets from the minds of their targets.

Agents of the Collective most often receive short infiltration assignments, such as getting inside an enemy base or group as an advance scouting or sabotage team. This is not always a glamorous job, but can often be quite dangerous. Compromised moles often find themselves cut off from help, with only their wits to aid in escape.

Political Manipulation (Psych Jobs): This type of mission is also dangerous, and often dirty. The objective is to manipulate a group or government to take a certain course of action, frequently with the ultimate goal of toppling it. PAC agents seduce, encourage, or otherwise coerce key officials into doing what the mission planners want. Common examples include encouraging someone to push for a crackdown on a certain terrorist group, open diplomatic relations with a foreign power, or betray their employer. These missions have been dubbed "psych jobs" by some Archer agents, owing to the frequent use of psychological manipulation on the target. Telepaths excel on such missions.

Theft: Agents of the Pan-Asian Collective make excellent thieves due to their uncanny ability to move unseen and infiltrate enemy organizations. While most missions focus on stealing information or secrets, the Collective also steals technology, and it has been known to run defection and rescue operations as well. Equipment theft generally necessitates additional support staff, as such operations typically involve a much greater risk.

The PAC also handles defections (more often than not into its own ranks). Such operations involve at least one agent in contact with the defector. Whether this agent is responsible for physically escorting the defector back to the home office or merely for planning his escape depends on the mission.

Finally, PAC agents often coordinate with those in other Chambers to perform recon during rescue operations. With the Collective's vast international network of spies, it is occasionally in a position to offer an inside man for the job. The Collective rarely does this, since it compromises the mole's cover, but it does happen.

Sabotage: While the Pan-Asian Collective rarely engages in Cold Missions *(see Room 39, page 124)*, it does conduct other forms of sabotage. Chamber agents have destroyed key information or research, willfully provided false information to foil an operation, and destroyed enemy facilities outright by detonation, arson, or informing the local authorities. Typically, one or more deep cover agents gather information prior to a sabotage mission, but on occasion agents are sent in to learn what the enemy is up to and then destroy their scheme.

Assassination: Though this type of mission most often falls to the Guardians of the Whispering Knife, the PAC can stomach the worst operations when it deems them necessary. While some involve either a deep cover agent or an insertion team murdering a target, the Chamber prefers quiet missions when possible. It either arranges to have the target disappear or makes his death look like an accident. In such cases, the assassin is usually a mole within the enemy organization. The Collective usually has backup plans in place if something goes wrong, but all PAC assassins know that the consequence of failure may be death.

Smuggling: With its basis in criminal organizations and other secret societies *(see page 26)*, the PAC engages in some smuggling. Many operations simply serve as fronts for more important smuggling jobs, and many more involve counter-smuggling missions. Usually, the Collective plants an agent in a smuggling ring to gather information and track shipments. If it determines that the target is too dangerous, it either sabotages the operation or calls in a strike team against it. Otherwise, it embezzles some of the profits to feed its own operations. This type of mission is another point of contention with other members of the Archer Conspiracy, but the information gained on the black market has been instrumental in many important coups for the Foundation, including the smooth handover of Hong Kong from Britain to China in 1997.

"Peace" Operations: Generally speaking, the Pan-Asian Collective is suspicious of Westerners in its midst, but it does provide specialized martial arts training for other Archer agents when needed.

AGENT EXPECTATIONS

Asianphiles and players who enjoy classic Cold War infiltration missions, psychological intrigue, and over-the-top martial arts action should find the Pan-Asian Collective to their liking. The average agent of this

Chamber combines mental acuity and manipulative skills with martial prowess. PAC agents are in almost constant danger and must walk a knife's edge, balancing cautious restraint with deadly blizzards of unarmed combat.

Agents of the Pan-Asian Collective must be of sound body, mind, and spirit at all times. The Asian philosophy of balance in all things dictates that when an agent neglects one of the pillars of being, the whole person suffers. Since its agents live in continual peril, they must be in top shape at every moment. The mind must be alert and focused so that the agent's mission can be carried out with the greatest degree of success. His or her spirit must be strong so that dedication never falters and fear or desperation cannot cause harm. And the body must be fit so if the agent must defend himself or herself, triumph is assured.

In keeping with this ethic, the Collective spends a great deal of time training its agents, perhaps more than any other Chamber. With its mission of infiltration, the PAC places a premium on moving undetected. Stealth training occurs, but the Chamber is more interested in its agents moving around in plain sight without being seen. All PAC agents learn the art of disguise and operating in public. Facemen in particular must learn to assume other identities flawlessly. They spend years developing disguises and never go into the field until they can fool their closest friends and relatives.

Additionally, because agents often must operate alone in perilous situations, the Collective demands that they be able to defend themselves. Help is not always forthcoming, so all PAC operatives learn to fight and win on their own. They go through a rigorous martial arts regimen, turning their bodies into finely tuned killing machines. With the Agency's extensive research into the application of psion powers, many agents have also developed the superhuman kung fu abilities of movies and anime.

While many agents from the Collective are facemen, every mission needs technical support from fixers and snoops. A good wheelman often means the difference between escape and capture, and the versatile skills of a pointman are required to plan and execute a complex Psych Job. Players should not feel restricted to any one class, regardless of the initial mission type.

Despite that, the ability to work alone remains a key trait in many Collective agents. While they cooperate within the faction and as part of multi-Chamber teams, PAC agents are often lone operatives deep behind enemy lines. The Chamber has an extensive network designed to aid such agents, but those who spend a few years in the field learn to rely only on themselves.

Tactical Data

The Pan-Asian Collective approaches all missions using a three-tiered philosophy based on the Asian concept of balance. Body, Mind, and Spirit are all key to the successful completion of an operation. These are known as the **Three Treasures** and used to effectively execute a mission.

First, the mind, or *shen,* evaluates the situation. The agent or planner gathers intelligence, assesses the enemy's strengths and weaknesses, and plans for his moves in accordance with that knowledge, usually tailoring his own strengths and weaknesses to counter those of his opponent.

Next, the agent employs *chi,* or the spirit. The agent focuses his own chi while looking to upset the chi of his opponent. Internal discord leads to failure, and the PAC agent looks to exploit this. He or she stirs the pot and attempts to create minor chaos in the enemy camp, making it ripe for toppling.

Finally, the agent acts, employing *jing,* or physical wellness. With his shen, the agent observed, looking for weakness. With his chi, he sowed the seeds of discord, creating an opening. Now, the agent strikes at that opening – that weakness – with jing, the raw power of his physical being.

All PAC operatives learn this approach, and it applies to all missions. It doesn't matter if the goal is theft, assassination, manipulation, or simply observation. The agent examines the situation to find a weakness, softens that Achilles heel by upsetting the balance of the enemy, and then strikes to exploit the hole he has created.

The Teachings of Wong Fei-Hung

Born in 1847, the martial arts prodigy Wong Fei-Hung has become a legend the world over. His exploits as a Cantonese physician who fought against the invading Manchu emperors of the Chi'ing Dynasty have been documented in film, books, and by word of mouth for almost a century. He was trained in many martial arts, but specialized in the Hung Gar style, and several personal disciplines he created, including the tiger-crane form of Hung Gar and a combination known as the "nine special fists."

Fei-Hung reportedly died in 1924, though the Foundation knows that he was alive and abroad as late as 1941, when he encountered a severely wounded Conrad Archer in the South Pacific. He saved the psion from a brush with death (too late to avert disaster unfortunately, as the Japanese attack plans Archer was carrying never reached Pearl Harbor in time), and soon became fast friends with the aging healer.

Wong Fei-Hung traveled with Conrad Archer for a time, and some stories say he was there during the final conflict against Avery Schillingsfield in 1944. Regardless, his influence on the Archer family (and the Conspiracy they created) is obvious – most Pan-Asian Collective martial arts begin with Fei-Hung's teachings. Indeed, the world's foremost experts in the old master's many styles rank among PAC's warrior elite.

A final rumor spirits through the PAC occasionally – one that only the most wild-eyed believe. Some say that Conrad Archer repaid Fei-Hung with the greatest gift he had to offer – a sample of the physical adept serum.

Collective PsiTech

Most PsiTech employed by the Collective is geared towards infiltration.

One of the Collective's most useful tools is a Disguise Enhancer, which they usually incorporate into a piece of clothing such as a jacket or shirt. This device projects images into a subject's brain to fool his senses. It must be preprogrammed for a particular appearance, but unlike Memory Flesh and Chameleon Suits *(see page 205)*, there is virtually no limit to the alteration; a petite Japanese woman can appear to be a huge Russian man if necessary. The device also assists in the perception of sound, making the agent's voice suit his appearance. No actual physical change occurs; the operative looks just as he usually does. But those who see him *believe* they are seeing someone else. The agent must be careful around security cameras, since these devices have no brains in which to implant false information.

With the Shop's break and sabotage of Archer PsiTech, some of this equipment has begun to randomly fail without warning, often at inopportune moments. Fortunately, most deep cover agents using Disguise Enhancers are immune to this sabotage, as they haven't been back to HQ in years.

Another common device is known as a "Void." These handy gadgets are typically placed inside jackets or other clothing and allow the user to store weapons, tools, and other objects that would normally be too large to conceal. They wrap around the object in question, meshing them into the person's appearance as flawlessly as possible (eliminating the bulge caused by a hidden sword, for example). Obviously, the Void only works on objects which can logically be carried by an agent in the first place; the Void cannot help with furniture, for instance, or vehicles. Shop sabotage of these items has been insidious; hidden objects are often destroyed by a contact acid (which may also seriously injure the agent once activated).

Chamber Organization

Despite its foundation in the Kempei Tai, the PAC has a distinctively Chinese flavor. Several Kempei Tai spymasters were brought over to China in the early 1950s, but their role remained largely advisory. They helped found the Chamber's basic organization, but they did not simply pick up where they left off at the end of World War II.

The Chamber tried vainly to gain the cooperation of the governments which they were tasked with policing, but Korea was already at war with the U.S. and Ho Chi Minh was causing the French no end of trouble in Vietnam. Japan was officially demilitarized, and the Chinese were engaged in rebuilding after the Japanese occupation. While the PAC was able to infiltrate the fledgling Chinese security agencies, getting inside other nations proved more difficult.

At this point, the founders decided to rely on another means of controlling their constituency: organized crime. Old Kempei Tai contacts provided inroads into the Yakuza in Japan, and many Chinese officials turned to the Triads, who began to emerge as major criminal powers in the Far East. It took a decade, but by 1960 the Collective had agents throughout all the major crime families and moles within CELD and the New China News Agency, and it used these unconventional sources to gain information.

As a result, the modern PAC is more accurately a sophisticated Triad family than an intelligence agency. Regional commanders, referred to as *Dai Lo* (literally "big brother"), report directly to the the Collective in Beijing. Dai Los are each in charge of many agents, whom they protect from the dangers the Archer Foundation faces. While every agent recognizes that he could be cut loose if things go badly, operatives have the right to expect their Dai Lo to make every effort to prevent this from happening. In return, their loyalty is unwavering, their service perfect.

The arrangement is unusual in that it creates a hierarchy similar to that of other Chambers, but it breeds more personal loyalty than organizational devotion.

The Philosophy of the Five Animals

Another aspect of Chinese culture incorporated into the Chamber is the Philosophy of the Five Animals. The Shaolin Monks revered many animals, but five represented the highest ideals of their doctrine and were incorporated into their kung fu. These animals are the Dragon, the Snake, the Tiger, the Leopard, and the Crane. Each represents a key idea from Shaolin philosophy that has been adapted into the structure of the Pan-Asian Collective.

The Dragon is a majestic creature in Chinese folklore, and its swerving movements promote the positive flow of shen, keeping a person mentally fresh and alert. Kung fu artists using Dragon techniques do not block or run away from their opponents, but swerve around these attacks to counterstrike.

The Snake is similar to the Dragon, but smaller and less majestic. Sometimes referred to as an "earthly dragon," its primary essence lies in its softness. Snake specialists absorb their opponents' blows and redirect them, focusing them into new attacks. The movements of the Snake promote the development and flow of chi, benefiting spiritual health.

The Tiger's essence is its raw power, power located in the bones. It is primal strength, matter in its finest state. This internal force develops a person's jing, keeping him or her physically fit. Tiger practitioners strike their opponents with raw power and ferocity.

Just as the Snake is similar to the Dragon, the Leopard is related to the Tiger, but the Leopard's power lies in its muscles. Its primary essence is speed; where the Tiger uses raw power to overcome its opponents, the Leopard relies on quick movements to drive that force home.

Finally, the Crane is elegant and quiescent. It is a patient, graceful bird that can support all of its weight on a single leg for hours. When it takes flight, it becomes the very definition of grace. Crane kung fu masters use elegant and graceful strikes upon their opponents, and the animal teaches focus for inner peace and quietude.

In this way, the Five Animals offer the kung fu artist a philosophy both for fighting and for excellence in life. The first three animals – Dragon, Snake, and Tiger – represent the Three Treasures discussed on page 114 while the Leopard teaches speed and the Crane grace. With this in mind, the Collective has divided itself into five divisions representing the Five Animals.

The Dragon division organizes and plans. The PAC's Control is part of the Dragon, as is his senior staff. This division oversees all that the Chamber does and coordinates the activities of each Dai Lo.

The Snake is charged with counterintelligence and repairing damage to the organization. This division seeks out and eliminates those who would harm the Chamber. It also makes recommendations to fill empty positions, handles promotions, and is responsible for the overall health of the organization.

Tiger division is responsible for the Collective's use of force. When a mission involves strike teams, assassination, or violence of any kind, the agents of Tiger division carry it out.

To carry out espionage missions effectively requires reliable information and speedy delivery of equipment to the field. The Leopard handles most intelligence-gathering and PsiTech research; it moves swiftly to support all other divisions in their operations.

Finally, Crane division is responsible for the quiescence of the Collective. An espionage agency that operates overtly, especially one that is part of a secret society like the Archer Conspiracy, is ineffective. It becomes exposed and confounded at every turn. Hence, the operatives of the Crane ensure that the Pan-Asian Collective remains hidden from the world at large. Crane agents often work closely with those of the the Dragon to ensure discretion.

Agents rarely work for a single division. These divisions are a superstructure for the Chamber, and agents commonly receive mission directives from more than one. For instance, the agents' Dai Lo may say "these orders come from Tiger division," or some such.

Field Operations

Most operatives in the field are assigned a handler who coordinates their activities. This person is usually their Dai Lo, who reports to the division commander in charge of the mission. The division commanders then coordinate efforts between operations and the Dragon.

The most important person in this chain of command is the Dai Lo since he serves as the hub of all information, handing it down to agents and collecting it for Control. The Dai Lo is also responsible for the safety of all the agents under him. When something goes wrong on a mission, he must swiftly inform his superiors and mobilize his resources to assist the agent. While it may be impossible to rescue a trapped agent, the Dai Lo usually exhausts every possible option trying to save the stranded operative. Only when all reasonable attempts have failed will he declare the agent lost.

Agents in the field can sometimes employ the resources of the CELD *(see page 118)*, the New China News Agency, or another intelligence group to complete their missions. With the reams of bureaucratic red tape involved and the general lack of funds, however, this is rare. Despite its effective infiltration of most Eastern governments, tight resources limit what the PAC can bring to bear in support of its agents.

The PAC's Triad allies, on the other hand, have access to vast territories and moles within key government agencies, and can easily smuggle information, equipment, weapons, and personnel into hostile territory. Triad smugglers handle the transportation and off-loading of supplies, while Collective agents avert the police or military.

Communications

Communications in the field are handled in a similar fashion. With the great number of deep cover agents infiltrating important government agencies, phone contact is difficult at best, and unsecure in the extreme. The PAC instead relies heavily upon dead drops, coded messages, and face-to-face meetings during field operations.

Fortunately, because most moles make use of Disguise Enhancers, this is not as risky as it sounds. Operatives can assume the identity of one person when undercover and meet with their handlers as someone else, thereby reducing suspicion. Often, PAC agents use multiple Disguise Enhancers to maintain different identities, allowing them to pose as several different people at once. One disguise is the mole, another meets the handlers, and still another receives instructions. Handlers with Disguise Enhancers can contribute further to the subterfuge.

When things go wrong, every agent has an emergency code that he can phone into their handler, alerting them that the mission has been compromised. Such calls are quickly forwarded up the chain of command for instructions.

Collective Resources

Despite the lack of standard intelligence agencies it can bring to bear, PAC has access to numerous and varied resources.

Training Facilities

One of the benefits that the Collective has received through its infiltration of the CELD is training facilities. The Chinese intelligence agency has two that the chamber uses regularly.

The first is its basic training school at CELD headquarters in Beijing. Sequestered within the Forbidden City, this school trains agents in the fine arts of infiltrating foreign governments, seeking out potential traitors, and manipulating the media. All PAC agents, except for those recruited directly from the CELD, go through this training program. The Dragon considers this training a key component of its operational strategies, and keeps numerous moles in the program to ensure access to it.

CELD also maintains a training facility in Lhasa, Tibet. This school focuses on training Chinese agents working on the Western and Southern frontiers of the People's Republic, but the PAC has made it into something more. Top Secret classes that require special clearance (i.e. you have worked for the Collective) prepare agents to work with the Triads and the Yakuza, focusing on the nuts and bolts of smuggling operations, and offer expanded kung fu and weapons training.

Applying the Three Treasures to a Mission

Here's an example of how the Collective approaches a mission from the perspective of the Three Treasures (see Tactical Data), illustrating a simple information-gathering mission where the agent has been directed to bug a diplomat's office.

Shen: the Mind

Posing as a janitor, the agent learns the routines and protocols of the diplomat's office. She observes the personalities of the diplomat, his staff, and the security personnel, searching for weaknesses she can exploit. During her observations, she notices that the diplomat has an eye for beautiful women. She also notices that the staff is a little lazy and likes to leave the office early on Friday. Security is tight and professional, though, with changes occurring frequently.

Chi: the Spirit

Through one of her contacts, the agent arranges to have exotic escorts visit the diplomat. She arranges these visits regularly on late Friday afternoons, and ensures that these trysts take the diplomat away from the office. She also establishes a camaraderie with key staff members, always extolling the virtues of leaving a little early on Friday – after all, they work hard enough during the rest of the week, don't they? Finally, she sabotages the elevator to the diplomat's office so that it gets stuck periodically, causing security to expect the problem occasionally.

Jing: the Body

One Friday when the weather is particularly nice, the agent strikes. She makes certain the diplomat leaves the office for his regular rendezvous (a rendezvous she arranged, with a specialist she hand-picked). Once again, she encourages the staff to leave early – this time with offers of a social gathering off-site. Finally, she arranges for the elevator to stick while the current guard's replacement is on the way up. She then disguises herself as a guard and relieves the current soldier, encouraging him to take the stairs. "Who knows how long it will take to get it fixed?" she asks.

Once free and clear, she plants the bug in the office undetected. Then the elevator problem is solved, and the actual duty officer arrives. He relieves her, and she slips out of the building without anyone realizing what has happened.

This is a simplified example, but it demonstrates how the Pan-Asian Collective likes to operate when it can: evaluate, weaken, and strike.

In addition to co-opting these formal facilities, the PAC maintains several bases throughout the region where agents can hone their craft. An elite karate dojo in Okinawa (the White Crane School of Karate) actually serves as a Collective front designed to train operatives in martial arts. Chan-Ngo, a technology firm in Saigon, specializes in PsiTech development and training. A secret base hidden within the bowels of the temple on Elephanta Island in Bombay focuses on advanced infiltration and political manipulation techniques.

The Lung Triad

The Lung Triad, headquartered in Hong Kong, is one of the largest, most powerful crime families in the Far East. It has holdings in Kuala Lumpur, Taipei, and Manila, and its influence extends throughout the Pacific Rim. It is also one of the Collective's principal allied smuggling operations.

The Lungs specialize in gunrunning, which makes them extremely effective in transferring equipment to PAC spies across Southeast Asia. Since 1956, the Lungs have served as the principal source of equipment for PAC agents during deep cover assignments, and they often provide support when a military strike is required.

Few Lung soldiers are aware of the Collective, but the majority of their leaders regularly communicate with PAC Dai Lo, and can provide periodic assistance to Chamber agents in areas where they have active cells – assuming the agents can reach them, of course.

In addition to general help, the Lungs help fill the Collective's coffers. Getting materials and information in and out of hotspots often requires payoffs. In exchange for protection from the local governments (membership in a Triad is punishable by death in China) and support for important deals, the PAC gets 20% of the gross profit of all Lung activities. This arrangement has led to the Collective kicking a few doors open for their Triad cohorts, providing them new business (and giving the rest of the Archer alliance another behavior to frown upon).

The Lungs remain independent of the Collective, but the relationship has become so incestuous over the past 30 years that it is now difficult to distinguish the two. Officially, the Pan-Asian Collective disdains the sale of illicit drugs, and shuts down outfits that it feels are destabilizing an area. But unofficially it is content to profit from these activities to help keep its own operations alive.

Tokajiro Musashi

Tokajiro-sama runs one of the most influential Yakuza families in Tokyo. His operations are not nearly as expansive or as profitable as those of the Lung Triad, but he remains the Collective's most powerful ally in Japan. Unlike the Lungs, he doesn't run weapons. He occasionally brokers information, but works mainly to grease the wheels in his home territory. The influential Tokajiro can set appointments and meetings with a whisper and a handful of cash to the right people.

Agents who require access to diplomats, key officials, or secure buildings can usually get them by appealing to Tokajiro. The agent must request an audience, outlining the mission objectives and, in general terms, what assistance is needed. Tokajiro runs these audiences like a samurai lord listening to his vassals, and he must feel as though he has been given the proper amount of face before he will agree to help.

In general, Tokajiro's a pain to deal with, and most agents of the Collective hate to involve him in an operation. But for access to secrets in Japan and Okinawa – particularly when dealing with the local criminal underworld – there is no better resource.

The Game in Asia

Intelligence services along the Pacific Rim have long been known as much for spying on their own people as for external security. Their primary intelligence targets are, in order, Russia, India, Vietnam, and the United States.

Far East Intelligence Agencies

Because there are so many intelligence agencies operating in the region (some of them working from very small countries), it is impossible to give even a short overview of the Asian spy world. We have therefore elected to cover only the agencies of which the Collective makes the greatest use, or is most involved.

China: Central External Liaison Department (CELD): The Central External Liaison Department is one of the primary foreign intelligence agencies for the People's Republic of China. It works principally to collect, index, and evaluate public intelligence sources around the world. It maintains an up-to-date catalogue of all government officials worldwide, and monitors the movements of known foreign operatives. It also performs most of China's espionage and counter-espionage.

CELD works closely with the Chinese Communist Party, and has officers stationed at every Chinese Communist Embassy and consulate. It has an internal department called the Central Control of Intelligence (CCI) that directs its activities. Unfortunately, CELD is hamstrung by rigid control from the Communist Party, which likes to keep a close eye on its citizens, particularly those who deal in espionage. All operations must go up through the Central Control of Intelligence and then to the party.

This condition is particularly debilitating for the Archer Conspiracy, as CCI is just as apt to stumble onto their operations as those of legitimate moles or traitors. The Asian habit of spying on friendly organizations to ensure loyalty makes things even more difficult.

Regardless, CELD is an effective espionage agency. It has compromised numerous U.S. officials in the past ten years and, with China's vast land area and thinly-veiled imperial designs on countries such as Taiwan and Tibet, its agents extend their influence over a wide stretch of Southeast Asia.

China: Ministry of State Security (MSS): The Ministry of State Security, a complex agency focused on foreign data collection and analysis, dominates the Chinese intelligence arena. Headquartered in Beijing, the MSS spies not only on China and its neighbors but also the rest of the world, paying close attention to the U.S. (in particular California's Silicon Valley).

The MSS is modeled roughly after the KGB, with eleven Bureaus and a Foreign Affairs division. It offers foreign nationals diplomatic support and travel expenses to turn on their countries, and for coordinating Chinese operatives who work abroad, especially on their return from foreign operations.

China: New China News Agency: Many Chinese journalists are, in fact, spies. With their broad base of international contacts and access to information, these individuals can provide the government with valuable intelligence. Many of them also engage in active espionage operations in addition to gathering information. Journalists in the United States often seek out government officials that can be turned (or at least bribed).

Playing the Great Game

"Trust is a thing both earned and granted. Lacking one or the other, the principle collapses. I fear that trust has long since gone missing between the Chambers, not earned or granted, but merely forgotten."

– Tien-kai Tsong

Mission Management: The Pan-Asian Collective once relied heavily on the tough and versatile agents of the Russian Confederacy, forming one of the tightest bonds of the Conspiracy. But this relationship has cast a terrible shadow over the East now that the bulk of the Russian Chamber has become a rogue power, and the PAC finds itself increasingly estranged from the rest of the Conspiracy. Most often, PAC agents must face their missions alone, without assistance unless they can count on a personal relationship to outweigh the bias against their superiors. PAC agents continue to rebuild what was once a very strong reputation among the shadow communities of the world.

Damage Control: The Shop's explosive departure was a terrible blow to Collective's self-confidence. Once the self-appointed watchdogs of the Conspiracy, the PAC must now deal with not one but two massive insurrections within their own sphere of influence. While Control and his closest associates strive to rebuild the Collective's relationship with the home office, many agents are rebuilding the Chamber's "face," hoping they can put some of the bad blood behind them, and start fresh. So far, success has been elusive.

Dirty Little Secrets: In the early 1960s, an industrious PAC Control, Chien-po Ming, struck upon the poorly-conceived plan to "test" his Chamber by pitching outside mercenaries at it. He privately set up a secret operations arm of the Pan-Asian Collective – the Toad Division – and laundered money to them through a Dai Lo loyal only to him (and the profit to be made from the mercenary attacks). The mercenaries, hired from the ranks of Company expatriates following the Korean and early Vietnam conflicts, eagerly leapt at the chance to ply their trade in familiar territory, and an enemy was born. Over the last forty years, this band of mercenaries – whom the PAC believes to be a terrorist cell called Chrysanthemum Dawn – have periodically drawn the PAC into sight and intentionally clashed with them. Each time they strike a PAC target or PAC-protected target, then vanish. Today, over 20 years since the mastermind of this scheme died of a heart attack, the attacks continue, and the mercenaries continue to be paid out of the PAC coffers, all without the knowledge of a single PAC operative.

Leverage: The Pan-Asian Collective has much leverage on many organizations, but their greatest source of information recently has been a volunteer Dragon operative named "Tam." A personable man by nature, Tam is programmed with a subliminal instruction to relay the most critical information he sees and hears each month back to the Dragon. Once they knew he was ready, the Dragon sent Tam on a global test tour of the Chambers, asking nothing of the other Chambers and waiting to see which one would catch Tam first. As it happens, none of the other Chambers noticed him as he glided through their security, ignorantly reporting back to the Dragon with new information each month. The Dragon's test of the other Chambers' security had been a complete success (or failure, depending on how you look at it). Then, three months ago, Tam vanished while visiting Gemeinschafft's home office in Europe. The Dragon assumed that their mole was finally discovered, and gave high marks to the Consortium, moving on to other projects – until they received another message from Tam. This time, he reported from a remote base in Norway. From his scattered notes, the Dragon deciphered that Tam had somehow been captured by the Hand of Glory *(see page 246)*, who assumed he was a VIP of the Conspiracy. Tam's personality was gone, replaced by a new, more violent lieutenant serving the Hand, but the subliminal programming continued to work. For the last three weeks, the Dragon have been collecting data about the Hand of Glory, Tam's location, and his work with the criminal organization.

Assets: With his agents buried in each of the other chambers, Tien-kai Tsong sometimes sees the Conspiracy in a clearer light than its masters in the Foundation, and what he sees is a structure creeping towards collapse. He has also had the privilege of examining the original training scrolls penned by Wong Fei-Hung and has made a startling discovery: not only did Fei-Hung survive and continue to write a decade or longer after history records his death, but he writes of Conrad Archer... after the assault on Helix's stronghold! Tsong now seeks to unearth the truth behind Archer's final years in the hopes that such knowledge may help reunify the organization that is his legacy.

CURRENT PLOTLINES

The Pan-Asian Collective has several operations going at the moment, all of which make excellent hooks for a campaign. Here are two key examples:

Operation: BODY DOUBLE (Code: Yellow): At the signing of the Archer Pact, it was obvious that the European and American spymasters of the West did not understand the politics or the culture of the Asian nations. Nor did they appear to trust their Eastern allies. Wars in Korea and then Vietnam during the Conspiracy's early years did little to help this cultural impasse.

After organizing and perfecting its infiltration techniques, the Collective set out to make certain it would have nothing to fear from its Western allies. Instituting Operation: BODY DOUBLE, the PAC slowly placed moles within the other Archer Chambers, starting small, but steadily gaining ground. Today, the Collective has a deep cover agent near the operations centers of nearly every other Chamber in the Conspiracy – all but the mysterious Guardians of the Whispering Knife. These agents secretly spy on the other Chambers and report back to the Collective as often as they can (as infrequently as once a year, or less).

The Snake division conceived of this operation was as a means of protecting the Collective; it is now a joint venture between the Snake and the Crane. All information goes to the Dragon for coordination with other units. Since the Shop's betrayal, this mission has become a high priority, so that the PAC can act pre-emptively if something similar happens with another Chamber.

Operation: BODY DOUBLE suffered a serious setback from the Shop's actions. Weeks before the Research and Development department went rogue, controllers within BODY DOUBLE started receiving strange communiqués from its team in the Shop, but they were unable to interpret the messages. When the secession occurred, this wing of BODY DOUBLE went dark. Control now believes that these messages were warnings, but that the agents sending them were already compromised and unable to relate the situation clearly without revealing BODY DOUBLE to the traitors.

Everybody associated with BODY DOUBLE has vanished or gone to ground since the Shop broke away from Archer. No attempts to reestablish contact with the cell have succeeded, and Control must now admit that all agents involved were lost. Some fear, though, that at least one of these operatives sided with the Shop's twisted goals and betrayed the rest of the team. The truth is not likely to appear until the missing operatives do.

Operation: BODY DOUBLE has since attempted to track down the renegade Shop agents, but thus far, all such attempts have met with failure.

Dr. Fu and the Lung Triad (Code: Red): Recently, a secret faction within the Lung Triad has begun supplying arms and other supplies to Dr. Fu, an old nemesis of the Pan-Asian Collective *(see page 240)*. This faction – headed by Tommy Lung, an ambitious nephew of the Triad's current Dai Lo, Lung Chiu Lee – is well aware that the Collective views Dr. Fu as a serious threat to stability in the region, but it also sees a business opportunity. Fu pays well for their connections, and is reportedly establishing a campaign to ignite new revolution in China.

If this double-cross became common knowledge among the world's intelligence communities, it could rock the Chamber to its very foundation, costing it face with the rest of the Conspiracy and crippling its ability to communicate with its undercover agents. Worse, if the plot is not uncovered, Dr. Fu may succeed with his latest plot, sparking open conflict and destabilizing all of Southeast Asia.

Several teams of Collective operatives, supported by loyal Lung specialists, have recently been dispatched to deal with the problem.

THE COLLECTIVE GENRE

The genre of the PAC involves over-the-top anime-style martial arts action married with political and psychological intrigue. It evokes the best Cantonese melodramas and wire fu flicks. Things are quiet, staid, and moody... until the action starts. Then things get out of control in a hurry. If you've seen Jackie Chan, Jet Li, Bruce Lee, Michelle Yeoh, or your favorite anime character do it, the PAC can do it, too.

Archetypes: *Battle Angel Alia,* Bruce Lee, Ethan Hunt from *Mission: Impossible 2,* Jackie Chan, Jet Li, Michelle Yeoh, and everyone from *Aeon Flux, Akira, Golgo 13: the Professional, The Matrix,* and *Spyboy* (the comic book).

INSPIRATIONS

Here's a list of sources that GCs and players looking for inspiration may want to explore.

Books: *Crying Freeman* (comic), *Dark Minds* (comic), *No Honor* (comic), *Spyboy* (comic), William Gibson's "Cyberpunk" book series *(Neuromancer, Count Zero, Mona Lisa Overdrive, Burning Chrome).*

Movies: *Agent Akia* (anime), *Akira* (anime), *Appleseed* (anime), *Battle Angel* (anime), *Black Rain* (the Ridley Scott film), *Bubblegum Crisis* (anime), *Charlie's Angels* (the film), *Crouching Tiger, Hidden Dragon* (for the intrigue and the wire fu), *Crying Freeman* (anime and live action film), *Deep Cover, Dirty Pair* (anime), *Face/Off, Fist of Legend, Ghost in the Shell* (anime), *Golgo 13: the Professional* (anime), Jackie Chan's *First Strike,* Jackie Chan's *Who am I?, The Long Kiss Goodnight, Manchurian Candidate, The Matrix, Mission: Impossible 2, My Father is a Hero* (a.k.a. Jet Li's *The Enforcer*), *Organized Crime and Triad Bureau, The 6th Day, Supercop, Total Recall,* and all things John Woo, Jackie Chan, Jet Li, and Michelle Yeoh.

TV Shows: *Aeon Flux, Jackie Chan Adventures.*

Music: *Akira* score, *Blade Runner* soundtrack (any version), *Robotech* soundtrack (especially the Perfect Collection), *Rush.*

DAREKA

Codename: ECHO
Aliases: Chi Ling, Madame Xin
Archer Identity Number: 08-671093-663
Nationality: Half American, half Vietnamese
Gender: Female **Handedness:** Right
Height: 5 ft. 7 in. **Weight:** 130 lbs.
Eyes: Black **Hair:** Black
Psion Class: Physical Adept (Grade A)
Place of Birth: Hong Kong, China
Date of Birth: 1972.08.01
Distinguishing Characteristics: All white eyes (no pupil) when psion abilities are active

BACKGROUND

Dareka has been a ward of the Foundation her entire life, the only survivor of a plane crash that claimed her entire family. The Conspiracy is the only life she has ever known, making her a perfect candidate for Operation POLTERGEIST.

Conceived by Archer's Bishops *(see page 53),* POLTERGEIST trains and equips advanced infiltration operatives, agents who can go anywhere, anytime, without detection. Dareka has been the project's greatest achievement. Trained in the historic Kempei Tai methods of impersonation, she can spend months or even years with an assumed name, and assumed friends.

Dareka's skills are augmented by strong physical adept abilities and a prototype bodysuit which, among its many wondrous uses, can completely shield her from sight. She also carries several weapons designed exclusively for her, including her trademark polycarbonate sai.

Over the years, Dareka has worked miracles in her field, revealing enemy organizations with devastating efficiency. But her most recent mission – to track a new threat encroaching on Archer's territory from Asia – has somehow gone horribly wrong. On the eve of identifying the new threat, Dareka stopped reporting in to the Collective. Her superiors fear that she may have finally slipped into a role for good – or worse, that she has somehow been turned against them.

LOW-LEVEL DAREKA

Chamber: The Pan-Asian Collective
Department: Wetworks (6)
Class: Fixer
Level: 6

Strength:	14	**Dexterity:**	17
Constitution:	12	**Intelligence:**	12
Wisdom:	10	**Charisma:**	10
Vitality:	37	**Wounds:**	12

Defense: 8 (+5 class, +3 Dex)
Initiative Bonus: +7 (+2 dept., +2 class, +3 Dex)
Speed: 30

Fort: +4 **Ref:** +10 **Will:** +2

Skills: Balance +8, Bluff +5, Climb +7, Demolitions +5, Driver +8, Electronics +6, Escape Artist +7, Hide +7, Jump +8, Intimidate +8, Listen +7, Move Silently +5, Open Lock +8, Profession (Assassin) +8, Search +8

Feats: Dodging Basics, Flawless Identity, Martial Arts, Throwing Basics

ATTACKS

Polycarbonate sai	+6 melee (1d6+2)

Common Gadgets: Advanced Chameleon Suit. This suit renders its wearer invisible *(see page 171 of the Spycraft Espionage Handbook)* which gives her total concealment. Its internal power supply lasts for up to three hours without requiring a recharge (which takes 30 minutes).

MID-LEVEL DAREKA

Chamber: The Pan-Asian Collective
Department: Wetworks (6)
Class: Fixer/Physical Adept
Level: 6/8

Strength:	14	**Dexterity:**	18
Constitution:	12	**Intelligence:**	13
Wisdom:	10	**Charisma:**	11
Vitality:	98	**Wounds:**	12

Defense: 24 (+10 class, +4 Dex)
Initiative Bonus: +15 (+4 dept., +7 class, +4 Dex)
Speed: 30

Fort: +10 **Ref:** +11 **Will:** +8

Skills: Balance +16, Bluff +5, Climb +14, Demolitions +8, Driver +9, Electronics +6, Escape Artist +11, Hide +14, Jump +17, Intimidate +10, Listen +7, Move Silently +16, Open Lock +14, Profession (Assassin) +12, Search +8

Feats: Dodging Basics, Dodging Mastery, Five Style Adept, Flawless Identity, Holding Basics, Kicking Basics, Martial Arts, Punching Basics, Throwing Basics

ATTACKS

Polycarbonate sai +10 melee (1d6+2)

Common Gadgets: Advanced Chameleon Suit. This suit renders its wearer invisible *(see page 171 of the Spycraft Espionage Handbook)* which gives her total concealment. Its internal power supply lasts for up to three hours without requiring a recharge (which takes 30 minutes).

HIGH-LEVEL DAREKA

Chamber: The Pan-Asian Collective
Department: Wetworks (6)
Class: Fixer/Physical Adept
Level: 10/10

Strength:	15	**Dexterity:**	20
Constitution:	12	**Intelligence:**	13
Wisdom:	10	**Charisma:**	11
Vitality:	135	**Wounds:**	12

Defense: 29 (+14 class, +5 Dex)
Initiative Bonus: +19 (+4 dept., +10 class, +5 Dex)
Speed: 30

Fort: +13 **Ref:** +15 **Will:** +11

Skills: Balance +20, Bluff +10, Climb +18, Demolitions +10, Driver +10, Electronics +10, Escape Artist +15, Hide +20, Jump +20, Intimidate +12, Listen +12, Move Silently +20, Open Lock +18, Profession (Assassin) +18, Search +10

Feats: Dodging Basics, Dodging Mastery, Five Style Adept, Flawless Identity, Holding Basics, Holding Mastery, Kicking Basics, Martial Arts, Punching Basics, Punching Mastery, Throwing Basics, Throwing Mastery

ATTACKS

Polycarbonate sai +14 melee (1d6+2)

Common Gadgets: Advanced Chameleon Suit. This suit renders its wearer invisible *(see page 171 of the Spycraft Espionage Handbook)* which gives her total concealment. Its internal power supply lasts for up to three hours without requiring a recharge (which takes 30 minutes).

TSONG, TIEN-KAI

Codename: HAN
Aliases: The Black Dragon
Archer Identity Number: 03-546598-772
Nationality: Chinese
Gender: Male **Handedness:** Right
Height: 5 ft. 9 in. **Weight:** 175 lbs.
Eyes: Brown **Hair:** Graying black
Psion Class: Non-latent
Place of Birth: Nanking, China
Date of Birth: 1948.03.17
Distinguishing Characteristics: Never smiles, deep age lines

BACKGROUND

Tien-Kai Tsong was a top planner (and PAC mole) in the MSS before he became active Control of the Chamber seven years ago. Often called the Black Dragon due to the many black ops missions he oversaw for the MSS, Tien-Kai's ruthlessness and fortitude are legendary; he will track an enemy to the farthest ends of the Earth. His commanding presence and edgy, grim demeanor lead some to believe that the stress of his position with the Conspiracy may be consuming him.

In truth, however, all of this is something of a front. Tsong, whose schoolboy days at Hunan Normal University were tarnished by bullies and merely average grades, forged his way into a post at the MSS with a manufactured reputation and not a little guile. These traits also brought him to the attention of the PAC. It recruited him while he was still with the MSS, to become first an informant, then a mole, and ultimately an agent and full-fledged Control.

The Black Dragon is a cautious man who approaches every situation with care and consideration. He does not shrink from violence, but firmly believes in Archer's mission of peace, and dedicated to building bridges whenever possible. Archer recognizes this practical idealism as the PAC's best hope for integrating with the other Chambers.

LOW-LEVEL TIEN-KAI TSONG

Chamber: The Pan-Asian Collective
Department: Wetworks (6)
Class: Snoop
Level: 4

Strength:	14	**Dexterity:**	12
Constitution:	14	**Intelligence:**	14
Wisdom:	11	**Charisma:**	16
Vitality:	43	**Wounds:**	14

Defense: 14 (+3 class, +1 Dex)
Initiative Bonus: +6 (+3 dept., +2 class, +1 Dex)
Speed: 30

Fort: +3 **Ref:** +3 **Will:** +2

Skills: Bureaucracy +8, Computers +8, Concentration +7, Cryptography +6, Diplomacy +5, Disguise +6, Driver +6, Electronics +7, Gather Information +7, Hide +6, Knowledge (Archer Secrets) +6, Knowledge (Collective Secrets) +7, Listen +5, Move Silently +6, Read Lips +5, Search +6, Sense Motive +5, Spot +5, Surveillance +5

Feats: Alertness, Martial Arts, Track

ATTACKS

Tiger claws +4 melee (1d3+4)

Gear: Laptop with secure satellite uplink to Overwatch *(see page 125 of the Spycraft Espionage Handbook).*

Common Gadgets: None

MID-LEVEL TIEN-KAI TSONG

Chamber: The Pan-Asian Collective
Department: Wetworks (6)
Class: Snoop
Level: 11

Strength:	14	**Dexterity:**	13
Constitution:	15	**Intelligence:**	14
Wisdom:	11	**Charisma:**	16
Vitality:	75	**Wounds:**	15

Defense: 20 (+9 class, +1 Dex)
Initiative Bonus: +12 (+4 dept., +7 class, +1 Dex)
Speed: 30

Fort: +5 **Ref:** +6 **Will:** +9

Skills: Bureaucracy +10, Computers +10, Concentration +13, Cryptography +12, Diplomacy +10, Disguise +11, Driver +6, Electronics +7, Gather Information +13, Hide +5, Knowledge (Archer Secrets) +11, Knowledge (Collective Secrets) +13, Listen +10, Move Silently +6, Read Lips +9, Search +10, Sense Motive +10, Spot +10, Surveillance +10

Feats: Advanced Skill Mastery (Alertness), Alertness, Martial Arts, Track, Zen Focus

ATTACKS

Tiger claws +7 melee (1d3+4)

Gear: Laptop with secure satellite uplink to Overwatch *(see page 125 of the Spycraft Espionage Handbook).*

Common Gadgets: None

HIGH-LEVEL TIEN-KAI TSONG

Chamber: The Pan-Asian Collective
Department: Wetworks (6)
Class: Snoop
Level: 18

Strength:	14	**Dexterity:**	13
Constitution:	15	**Intelligence:**	14
Wisdom:	13	**Charisma:**	16
Vitality:	121	**Wounds:**	15

Defense: 25 (+14 class, +1 Dex)
Initiative Bonus: +16 (+4 dept., +11 class, +1 Dex)
Speed: 30

Fort: +8 **Ref:** +9 **Will:** +9

Skills: Bureaucracy +15, Computers +14, Concentration +20, Cryptography +12, Diplomacy +16, Disguise +18, Driver +6, Electronics +9, Gather Information +20, Hide +5, Knowledge (Archer Secrets) +11, Knowledge (Collective Secrets) +20, Listen +16, Move Silently +6, Read Lips +9, Search +12, Sense Motive +16, Spot +14, Surveillance +17

Feats: Advanced Skill Mastery (Alertness), Alertness, Blind-Fight, Blindsight 5' Radius, Martial Arts, Track, Zen Focus, Zen Mastery

ATTACKS

Tiger claws +11 melee (1d3+4)

Gear: Laptop with secure satellite uplink to Overwatch *(see page 125 of the Spycraft Espionage Handbook).*

Common Gadgets: None

Room 39

"A fool sees not the same tree that a wise man sees."

– William Blake, *The Marriage of Heaven and Hell*

During World War I, a crack team of British code-breakers operating out of Room 40 in the Old Admiralty Building in Whitehall deciphered German messages and fed them to Allied units throughout Europe. Their greatest triumph came when they intercepted and deciphered a German communiqué to Mexico (the infamous Zimmerman Telegram), offering the country a bounty if it went to war with the U.S. Many consider this revelation the factor that brought the U.S. into the war, tipping the balance in favor of the Allies.

Had anyone known what was happening next door in Room 39, though, history might have been different. Here Conrad Archer researched the power of physical adepts. Room 39 was one of the founding chambers of the Archer Conspiracy in 1950, and it continues to this day as a key faction in the secret war.

Room 39's Mission

With its prevalence in the development of physical adepts and PsiTech weaponry, Room 39 is called upon to solve urban problems quietly. Its philosophy is precise and perfect execution of such delicate field missions as hostage rescues, anti-terrorist actions, and counterinsurgency. Room 39 focuses on careful analysis of all available information, thoughtful planning and preparation, and proper execution to make sure nothing goes awry during its ops.

For this reason, Room 39 most often works in densely populated areas and for high-profile missions. When things go wrong and people start asking questions, Room 39's agents move in, handle the situation, and get out before anyone realizes what has happened. In the Information Age, when global news agencies can report on events before intelligence communities learn of them, this Chamber's quick and precise tactics are vital for controlling media exposure.

Function

Room 39 likes to think of itself as a well-oiled machine, and information keeps the machine running. A mission without proper intel often goes disastrously wrong without warning. Thus, Archer's British Chamber employs a large group of cryptographers, spies, hackers, and intelligence analysts who acquire and study data. These planners seek out every scrap of information and use it to plot contingencies for every possible variable their mission teams might encounter.

As a unit, Room 39 specializes in intelligence analysis and special operations missions. As indicated above, the chamber employs hundreds of analysts who examine all the intelligence the agency gathers. While it collects information on its own, Room 39 relies heavily on the other chambers to provide it with much of the intelligence it examines. This allows the agency to focus on analysis instead of collection. In turn, Room 39 disseminates its findings to the other Chambers, tailoring them to best suit the needs of each.

Information most immediately useful to Room 39 (or which pertains to a mission they are assigned) goes to its own special ops team, Ultracorps *(see page 126)*. These operatives, largely recruited from MI6 and SAS, spearhead many of the Agency's field operations. They are called in for hostage rescue missions, when a high-profile terrorist organization must be countered, and to quietly take out political organizations that Archer deems an immediate threat, though this last function more frequently falls to the Company. Basically, when Archer wants dirty work done, it calls the Company. When it has a special ops mission that requires finesse and precision (such as rescuing a diplomat from terrorists), it relies on Room 39.

Common Room 39 Missions

Room 39 agents always have clear and concise mission goals. Their objectives frequently come with detailed flowcharts of if-then statements designed to account for as many variables as the mission planners can think of. The purpose of this design is less to keep agents from screwing things up than to accommodate "the Book," Room 39's endless list of mission protocols.

Room 39 field agents are expected to commit all contingency plans to memory. This can be a drawback, particularly when dealing with one or more moles, who have access to the same information. Most often, however, this meticulous design becomes one of the Chamber's greatest strengths, clearly defining where they can be of the most use.

Despite this wealth of planning, Room 39 operatives are encouraged to think for themselves. They are frequently sent on training missions, some of which purposely go horribly wrong so the agents have the opportunity to think on their toes. The big difference between most Chamber operatives and those of Room 39 is the fact that the latter have set routines for every suspected risk, challenge, or upset, which are called upon before branching out into unusual responses. While agents from other Chambers sometimes see Room 39 agents as stuffy slaves to the rules, they are a welcome addition when planning and precision are needed.

Combat Search and Rescue (CSAR): Room 39 specializes in extracting hostages, information, and technology from hostile forces. With Archer's number of acceptable losses always low, Room 39 often works to minimize friendly losses. When hostages must be rescued without innocent casualties and information recovered without the enemy realizing it's gone, the highly-trained operatives of Ultracorps are Archer's first choice.

Frequently, CSAR missions are initiated after another mission team scouts an area or gathers information on the targets. Room 39 then goes in to finish the job. Alternately, CSAR ops may begin when negotiations have failed.

Counter-Terrorism: Counter-terrorism usually has simple goals: kill the terrorists. Again, the Foundation draws the line between Room 39 and the Company according to where the terrorist activity is taking place. Room 39 works when terrorist activity occurs in densely populated or high profile areas (inside the city of Tokyo, for example), while the Company handles enemies rooted in less public areas (like the African jungle or one of the poles).

Counterinsurgency: These missions are similar to counter-terrorism, with one exception: they serve as pre-emptive strikes. A counter-terrorist mission reacts to a terrorist attack; counterinsurgency missions take out rogue cells before they can act. Room 39 handles these missions in densely populated or high-profile areas.

Intelligence Gathering: For the most part, Room 39 spends its time analyzing information, not gathering it. Sometimes, however, the Foundation feels the British Chamber is best suited for obtaining the information directly. Such field operations usually involve agents of the Broken Seal *(see page 126)* hacking into systems that cannot be accessed remotely.

For these missions Room 39 generally provides a fixer and possibly a pointman as support for a faceman from another Chamber. Such teams slip into the location and directly copy the files in question off the computer, attach a device designed to acquire them, or send them to an external receptacle such as a secure web site.

Sabotage (Cold Missions): Knowledge is power in the Information Age, and stealing or corrupting information can be as useful as counterinsurgency or direct assault. To thwart dangerous organizations, Archer sometimes orders Room 39 to destroy their information, effectively rendering them impotent.

Nicknamed Cold Missions for the euphemism "giving the enemy computer a cold," sabotage missions also involve agents breaking into enemy databases, but in this case, the object is to plant a virus that corrupts or destroys one or more files. Most of these viruses erase only the target files without corrupting others, then delete themselves from the system, wiping any trace of the crime. Larger scale viruses are sometimes engineered to destroy working prototypes of devices criminal organizations use to threaten the world.

"Peace" Operations: Room 39 also trains other intelligence and special ops teams in hostage rescue, counterinsurgency, and anti-terrorist action through its agents in SAS.

AGENT EXPECTATIONS

Players who enjoy obsessively precise agents, expert crisis-management personnel, and gadget-wielding strike team members may find Room 39 ideal for their needs. Average agents of this chamber are knowledgeable, strict, and regimented. They face danger with an unflappable exterior; though they may be afraid on the inside, their training provides them with the confidence to face nearly any plight with aplomb.

Room 39 agents have extraordinary access to information. The Chamber analyzes most of the Conspiracy's intelligence, and, while it does feed this analysis in part to individual Chambers, most of its handlers have the intel at their fingertips.

With this in mind, Room 39 archetypes are not confined solely to cool, collected soldiers. There is plenty of room for more cerebral counterparts: the men and women who access information, carefully weigh it, and use it as a weapon. Hackers, gadgeteers, and mechanics all make excellent character types for agents of Room 39. Many of these Agents carry laptops or gadget-building tools instead of pistols, but they are just as welcome during missions requiring technological support.

Room 39 takes a holistic view of every mission. Their ultimate goal is always foremost in its agents' minds, but unlike other chambers, they place an equal amount of importance on how they conduct the operation. Room 39 never approaches a mission in a cavalier manner; it acts with precision and certainty. It knows that failure to follow procedure jeopardizes not only the success of the operation, but also the lives of agents, and those they are charged with protecting.

Players should keep this in mind when considering this Chamber. Order is as important as success – at least, until "the Book" fails to cover a situation. Then it's up to the ingenuity of the agents at hand.

Tactical Data

Room 39 relies upon three basic tools to wage the war against global threats. First is its vast wealth of information, updated daily. Second is the weaponry available from the U.K. government. Room 39 has agents in every branch of the military, and access to weapons, supplies, and even vehicles when necessary. All of these acquisitions are neatly disguised as various military and intelligence operations.

Finally, Room 39 uses the World Wide Web. The Internet is a tremendous font of information, and the chamber has dozens of watchers dedicated solely to surfing in search of information that can be of use to Archer. The hackers of the Broken Seal also stretch their tendrils out into the 'net, penetrating databases, downloading information from secure sites, and sending viruses to enemy computers.

Room 39 PsiTech

Most of the PsiTech this Chamber uses is geared for field operations, and much of that has been tainted by the Shop. Enhanced weapons, safecrackers, anti-security devices, and special assault vehicles were standard tools of Room 39's trade, but with the Shop's sabotage, their agents now employ PsiTech with a certain degree of reticence. The chamber has begun adding "What to Do If Your PsiTech Fails in the Field" courses to its training regimen, and has attempted to adopt PsiTech malfunctions into the variables for its operational planning. However, the insidious nature of some residual sabotage continues to defy much of their careful planning.

Room 39 has begun experimenting with new kinds of PsiTech in the last few years. With the seemingly limitless potential of the Internet, it is particularly interested in harnessing psionic applications.

Chamber Organization

Room 39 keeps its base of operations at the Omnium Corporation's World Headquarters in London. Omnium is an "Applied Technologies" corporation specializing in business systems, routers, telecommunications software, and military applications. It bids on government contracts in the U.K., has satellite divisions in the U.S. and France, and owns a large percentage of the phone lines and routers in the U.K and Europe. It is also the principal front for Room 39.

Omnium was set up after the war, when Room 39 moved out of the old Admiralty Building. While Omnium does have legitimate divisions that perform the public company's work, most of its internal operations are actually given over to Room 39's mission. Room 39's Control, Sarah Singleton *(see page 135),* also acts as Omnium CEO, and must keep both the Chamber and the Omnium facade running smoothly. Under her direction, Omnium has grown into one of the most successful front companies in the Conspiracy, pulling in a tidy profit from its leased router lines and many multi-national contracts.

Within Omnium, Room 39 is divided into two distinct sub-units. Each plays a key role in carrying out the Chamber's mission.

Ultracorps

This division represents the core of what Room 39 is and what its principal focus used to be, employing the Chamber's deadly field operatives. Ultracorps recruits its field agents principally from SAS, but it also oversees spies in Five, MI6, and Special Branch. Most of the core planning and management of Room 39 takes place in the Ultracorps division, which handles agent training, coordinates with other Chambers, and is largely responsible for maintaining the Cloak.

When Room 39 must perform special ops, Ultracorps is most often assigned the task of planning and carrying them out. Hostage rescues, anti-terrorist actions, and counterinsurgency strikes are all the province of Ultracorps, as is Room 39's slavish devotion to regulations and protocol; the unparalleled success of the missions it plans is a source of pride for its controllers. Until recently, Ultracorps *was* Room 39, and it remains synonymous with the chamber's reputation and style to this day.

The Broken Seal

In 1992, Room 39 saw itself being pulled in several different directions at once. It recognized the need for special forces worldwide and wanted to focus on training and using its traditional operatives for special operations. But it also saw a need to develop contingencies for the proliferation of computer and Internet users, and the threat they posed to world security. It therefore decided to reorganize, forming Ultracorps to focus on special operations. The majority of its funding and focus went in this direction. Then it created a second division tasked with its other traditional mission of intelligence analysis, along with studying the burgeoning threat of computer hackers. This division was named the Broken Seal.

For the first five years of its existence, the Broken Seal labored in relative obscurity. By 1997, though, the division employed an army of computer experts to deal with dangers caused by the Internet explosion. Slowly, the Broken Seal took on more and more resources, staging a sort of internal power struggle within the Agency. In 2000, Sarah Singleton, a Gen X hacker and a graduate of the Broken Seal program, became Omnium CEO and Room 39 Control. Since taking over, she has given her former division even more focus and responsibility.

The Broken Seal handles electronic warfare. It develops computer technology designed to defeat the toughest security measures and penetrate the most guarded databases, and devises viruses used to cripple Archer's enemies. The Broken Seal has also created its own brand of operatives: hackers who provide cutting-edge technological support for other agents in the field.

In addition, the Broken Seal now develops PsiTech designed to enable its psions to directly interface with computer technology. In time, Room 39 hopes to create a new generation of wired spies capable of infiltrating anything connected to a phone line, cable, or satellite uplink.

Aside from the funding and organizational revolution, the division has also unintentionally engineered a cultural shift in Room 39. Many Broken Seal operatives are twenty- and thirtysomething rebels plugged into pop culture, counterculture ideals, and the Digital Age. They paint a stark contrast to the stodgy, traditional, regimental operatives of the past, and while they receive the same training as their older counterparts, their methods are very different.

As computer specialists, Broken Seal agents tend to think in terms of flowcharts, which is compatible with Room 39's traditional approach, but their attitude is both puzzling and disturbing to their elder counterparts. One thing is certain, though. Room 39's mission depends a great deal on the work they do and, while the traditionalists may find them distasteful, they can't fault their usefulness.

Field Operations

Room 39's agents in the field are supported by the chamber's moles in other branches of British Intelligence. MI6 maintains Station Houses throughout the world designed to give assistance to agents abroad. Only a small percentage of these Station Houses are loyal to Archer, and they must be contacted in code to ensure security, but the Station Managers (many of whom are not even aware they are assisting someone other than MI6) can be life-saving in a crunch.

MI6 divides the world into sections, each designated with a letter:

Section A	Africa
Section B	South & Central America
Section C	China
Section D	India
Section F	France
Section G	Eastern Europe & Germany
Section I	Spain and Portugal
Section J	Japan and Korea
Section M	The Middle East
Section N	North America
Section O	Scandinavian Countries
Section R	Italy and Switzerland
Section S	Russia and the former Soviet Union
Section V	Southeast Asia
Section Y	The Balkans

Station Houses appear in major cities within each sector, designated with the same letter prefaced by the word, "Station." For example, the Moscow Station House is designated Station S. In many cases, there may be more than one Station House per Section; auxiliary Stations are designated by the country in which the Station House is located (a Station House in Saigon would be Station V, Vietnam), or a -2 for the second Station in a country (a Station House in St. Petersburg would be Station S-2).

Support within the U.K. is a little trickier. While Room 39 does have agents within MI5 and Scotland Yard, Five's investigation into Archer's existence causes problems for the agency when it needs to operate on its own turf. Until further notice, all assistance from moles within domestic intelligence forces has been suspended, and operations that require the use of traditional spies on British soil are temporarily being farmed out to other Chambers.

Special ops are a different story. Ultracorps recruits heavily from within SAS, and Room 39 has many agents there. Most domestic support for such missions therefore comes from SAS.

Communications

With its electronic communications expertise, Room 39 keeps its agents informed with up-to-the-minute data, and closely monitors their movements. Agents frequently receive last-second mission updates.

However, the network is not as foolproof as it once was. Room 39 once developed a special cipher (code-named FUNNEL) with which it encoded messages between Control and agents. Not only were the messages electronically encrypted, but the text itself had to be deciphered to make sense. Recently this system suffered two significant setbacks.

First, the Shop's break with Archer left the Broken Seal unsure of the code's integrity. Control requested a new cipher (both a textual filter and an encryption program), but work has not yet been completed. Until the new code is functional, agents must reduce communications with the home office, and have the authority to act on their own when necessary.

Second, MI5 has intercepted several e-mail communiqués from field agents *(for more about this, see opposite)*. Though the domestics have not yet cracked FUNNEL, preliminary analysis has led them to believe that there may be a foreign spy ring operating on British soil. This near-breach of the Cloak has made Room 39 doubly cautious about communicating in the field.

So far as Room 39 knows, none of its Station Manager moles within MI6 have been compromised, and operations continue in the field as usual. They remain extremely wary, however, and are monitoring the situation closely.

Room 39 Resources

Entrenched as it is within the British intelligence community, Room 39 has a wide variety of resources at its disposal.

Training Facilities

Room 39 trains most of its agents through the intelligence agencies it has infiltrated. Operatives from MI6, MI5, Scotland Yard, and SAS all receive the bulk of their training within their individual service branches prior to recruitment. Ultracorps provides additional training at the famous Bradbury Lines SAS base in Hereford.

With the growing number of hackers and other non-traditional agents cropping up in the Broken Seal, Room 39 has instituted additional courses on electronic warfare, hacking, programming, and related skills at its Omnium headquarters. Prospective field agents, particularly those from Ultracorps, take a series of basic classes and then choose electives. Broken Seal agents are offered advanced instruction on cryptography, intelligence analysis, and computer applications.

The Omnium Corporation

For the high-tech spy, Omnium makes the ultimate front company. It is independently profitable; the leases of its routers and phone lines bring in hundreds of millions of pounds annually, and its defense contracts with foreign governments net billions more. It also develops commercial software for a wide variety of applications. All of these resources not only earn revenue, but are available to agents in the field when needed.

Moreover, Omnium's defense contracts grant it access to much Top Secret military information. The intelligence in question is rarely extraordinary, but the access it grants the Chamber makes it much easier for its agents to hack into secure government databases.

Finally, the Omnium Corporation provides an excellent cover. Chamber operatives often pose as Omnium salespeople, executives, and technicians when they travel undercover or enter restricted areas (though Room 39 has reduced its use of the Omnium cover since the Shop's betrayal).

Operation: DOPPELGANGER

After the secrets of PsiTech were captured in 1975 and the Shop was founded, most development in that field was theirs alone. Some of Room 39's planners correctly determined that a redundant program would increase project security, and instituted Operation DOPPELGANGER, the British Chamber's own PsiTech development office. Since the Shop's departure, DOPPELGANGER has proven incredibly helpful, providing a number of clean devices and arranging to test what the Shop left behind.

The Game in the U.K.

Included here are notes about British intelligence and the agencies that collect it.

U.K. Intelligence Agencies

Great Britain's intelligence community is divided into several major organizations. While most people associate MI6 with British Intelligence, it is only one facet of the U.K.'s spy network.

The Secret Intelligence Service (MI6): The Secret Intelligence Service, also known as MI6 (Military Intelligence Department 6) is roughly equivalent to the American CIA; it operates worldwide and conducts British spy operations on foreign soil. It heads undercover investigations, spies on foreign powers, steals secrets, facilitates defections, and (rarely) engages in assassination. Much of the agency's work during the Cold War centered on Berlin and the Soviet Union, but MI6 has operatives, stations, and safe houses all over the world.

The head of MI6 is known simply as "C," after Mansfield Cumming, the organizer and first head of MI6 in 1911 who went by that initial *(for more about Mansfield Cumming and early Room 39 operations, see Chapter 1)*. Ian Fleming's "M" is a veiled reference to the moniker.

MI6 operates largely without the interference of watchdog committees that plague the CIA. It answers only to the Prime Minister's cabinet, and all documents and information pertaining to its operations are classified Top Secret under the Official Secrets Act. As far as the public is concerned, MI6 is a national secret.

Prior to the 1980's, most MI6 operatives came from upper-crust British colleges and wealthy or titled families, leading critics to defame the organization as an old boys' club (the same argument leveled against the CIA in the 1960s and 1970s). But in the last twenty years, MI6 has yielded to pressure to recruit from a wider base of candidates.

MI5 (Military Intelligence Department 5): Aside from its central headquarters in London, the Secret Intelligence Service has no authority to operate within Great Britain. That directive falls to MI5, Britain's counter-espionage department. MI5 (sometimes called simply "Five" for short) is similar in some respects to the American FBI. Five acts to prevent foreign spying on British soil, and it analyzes information, watches suspected spies, and uncovers spy rings. Essentially, it must prevent other nations from doing to Great Britain what MI6 does to them. Five also handles counter-insurgency investigations, and to that end its agents track suspected Irish nationalists in an attempt to prevent terrorism, weapon smuggling, and other illegal activities.

Unfortunately, an ugly rivalry exists between Five and MI6. While the two agencies cooperate, both feel that the other is stepping on their toes. MI6 would happily take over Five's duties, feeling that their two missions are intertwined. Five, on the other hand, believes that MI6 frequently encroaches on its territory and wishes that its sister agency would stick to its own business.

Special Branch, Scotland Yard: Unlike the American FBI, Five has no authority to make arrests. For this, it turns to the first of Britain's satellite agencies, the Special Branch of Scotland Yard. Scotland Yard is a police force, not an intelligence agency, but its Special Branch works closely with Five to arrest proven spies. Basically, Five locates and exposes enemy agents working within Great Britain, and then turns this information over to Special Branch to make arrests. Both agencies have been extremely effective at rooting out and destroying foreign spy operations within the U.K.

Special Air Services (SAS): The Special Air Services (SAS) branch of the Royal Air Force (RAF) is a second satellite unit that deals with terrorist threats both within Great Britain and on foreign soil. This unit engages in military and hostage rescue missions, the most spectacular of which was the rescue of hostages at the Iranian Embassy in London in 1982 (after one of the hostages was killed by terrorists, SAS forces attacked the embassy, killing five of six terrorists, rescuing all of the remaining hostages, and losing no SAS men).

SAS is an elite group of special ops soldiers, and considered one of the best forces of its type in the world.

PLAYING THE GREAT GAME

"I trust numbers. They never lie to you."

– Sarah Singleton

Mission Management: Though tied together by history, language, and trade, Sarah Singleton has gone out of her way in recent months to pass operations on to Col. Dietrich's outfit in the United States. Anything that isn't tightly within the purview of the Broken Seal or Ultracorps has been offered to the Company. She claims that it is an effort to give the American Chamber additional chances to rebuild their credibility. Other controls speculate the Sarah is simply trying to free up her resources (and minimize her exposure) to deal with her own problems *(see Damage Control, below)*. Room 39's most trusted allies within the Conspiracy are certainly the Guardians, whom many of their operatives view as "good luck charms."

Damage Control: Consisting of the Conspiracy's undisputed masters of the computer age, Room 39's Broken Seal seems to have attracted more than its fair share of abuse from the Shop. While the hallmark destruction of labs and gadgetry is much the same as experienced by other high-tech chambers, the Shop seems to have devoted extra effort to exposing the Seal to the world. This cardinal sin of espionage has raised questions as to why this Chamber – and only this Chamber – was subject to such attacks...

Dirty Little Secrets: Since well before the founding of the Archer Conspiracy, Room 39 has kept files – thousands of files – dedicated to its enemies, its allies, and everyone else. Room 39 systematically calculates every permutation of every best- and worst-case scenario involving any of them, and everything in-between. When they're done, they store the files away, locked safely out of sight where they can cause no damage. These inquiries continue to this day, and these collected files contain all the dirty little secrets Room 39 ever slid under the proverbial rug – all in one place.

Leverage: When the 1950 Archer Pact was signed, Room 39 became the couriers of the Conspiracy, a duty they had gained much experience with during WWII. At first by foot and telegraph and later by phone, electronics, and satellites, Room 39 has always delivered messages between Chambers. This privileged position offers them unique leverage over every other part of the Conspiracy, though it is leverage they never use, taking their role in Archer's plan very seriously.

Assets: With the Archer Foundation's increasing secrecy concerning psion development, Sarah has decided to keep her own psion research close to home. Room 39's focus on the fledgling discipline of electrokinesis has begun to yield fruit – Broken Seal researchers have combined the principles of information theory with their psionic training, producing several new prodigies, who seem to think in machine code and whose outrageous code-breaking skills are unparalleled.

CURRENT PLOTLINES

Room 39 is engaged in several plots at the moment, any of which would make an excellent hook for an ongoing campaign.

Operation: SMOKESCREEN (Code: Red): Room 39's biggest problem at the moment is not the fact that the Shop has broken away or that power-mad occultists seek to bring about a new Reich. The trouble comes from its own backyard. MI5 is on to them.

In 1996, the Security Service Act brought several of Room 39's civilian activities to light, and drew Five's scrutiny. The Joint Intelligence Committee was brought into the matter, doubly threatening the covers the Chamber put in place. Room 39 scrambled to deflect MI5's investigations, even attempting to turn the blame back on the domestics. Unfortunately, the MI5 agents received public interest immunity to protect Military Intelligence from outside scrutiny, and the situation was left unresolved.

Then, almost concurrently with the Shop's break, Five intercepted several e-mails from Room 39 field agents. After only two weeks, they broke the FUNNEL encryption program and began work on the text cipher. (Today, Room 39 believes that the Shop coordinated this discovery, though they have little evidence to back up that assumption.)

MI5's renewed interest in the British Chamber is cause for much concern. The fact that the emails were headed for an Omnium sub-station is even worse; now the domestics are directing their efforts to determining the nature and interests of the corporation. Three of its employees – two of whom were actually Room 39 operatives – have been arrested, questioned, and released. (Both operatives have been placed on inactive duty until the situation stabilizes.)

Room 39's effort to dodge MI5 is codenamed SMOKESCREEN, and entails complex distraction plans and the implantation of several moles into the enemy organization. So far, only one of the Room 39 moles has made it onto MI5's operations team (nicknamed "The Spycatchers," after Richard Hollis' book of the same name). The agent (codenamed Witful) currently strives to slow MI5's textual decryption or destroy the samples, so far with little success.

Room 39 is painfully aware of MI5's skill at uncovering spy rings, and Five refuses to give up the investigation. Every time they appear to hit a dead end, someone (probably the Shop) feeds them another clue.

The noose draws tighter by the week, and the Chamber may need to take radical action to bring the crisis to a halt.

Operation: GREENBACK (Code: Yellow): Despite Omnium's earning power for Room 39, it runs a very high-tech operation that requires a lot of funding. Moreover, telecommunications is an extremely competitive industry requiring millions of pounds in research alone. Hence, in addition to the spying and intelligence analysis, Room 39 is engaged in corporate espionage.

A secret division of Broken Seal hackers regularly steals secrets and, on occasion, illegally transfers funds from foreign corporations. With the changing landscape of the European Economy and the dominance of the European Commonwealth Chamber on the continent, Omnium is feeling the pressure to remain competitive. It has thus far used these secrets to secure better government contracts, fund its own activities, and sabotage the research and development work of competing firms. In fact, Operation: GREENBACK was instrumental in sinking the proposed merger between Sprint and MCI/Worldcom.

The Archer Foundation knows nothing about this operation, and if it did there would be hell to pay at the top levels of Room 39. It operates contrary to the cooperative goals of the Archer Pact. At present, Sarah Singleton is unaware of Operation: GREENBACK, but some within the program believe that she would approve if she discovered it.

The Room 39 Genre

The best description for the Room 39 genre is "techno-thriller." All the classic elements of suspense and espionage are there, but there is an emphasis on technology and applied military science. Broken Seal operatives are plugged-in technophiles who use the latest gadgets to aid their Ultracorps brethren in the field. Field agents are generally split between perfectly-trained soldiers and cyberpunk-style hackers who use computers and electronic equipment as their weapons of choice.

Archetypes: Jack Bauer (Kiefer Sutherland from *24)*, Impossible Mission Force, Net Force, Rainbow Six, Sherlock Holmes, Sid Vicious with a laptop.

Inspirations

Players and Game Controls interested in Room 39 are invited to look up these inspirations for the Chamber.

Books: Anything by Tom Clancy *(Red Storm Rising, Rainbow Six, Without Remorse), Snow Crash* by Neal Stephenson, the Sherlock Holmes novels.

Movies: *Aliens, Clear and Present Danger, Hackers, The Lawnmower Man* (the original, preferably with the 44 minutes of excised footage restored), *Patriot Games, Sneakers.*

TV Shows: *24, UC Undercover.*

Music: British industrial and techno-rave, any score incorporating military cadence (*Aliens, Starship Troopers,* etc.).

Computer and Console Games: *Deus Ex, Rainbow Six* (the definitive counterterrorism squad game series).

Savage, Emily

Codename: ATHENA
Aliases: None
Archer Identity Number: 99-012018-716
Nationality: English (Naturalized)
Gender: Female **Handedness:** Right
Height: 5 ft. 5 in. **Weight:** 125 lbs.
Eyes: Green **Hair:** Ash-blonde
Psion Class: Non-latent
Place of Birth: Vancouver, British Columbia
Date of Birth: 1980.05.15
Distinguishing Characteristics: Red streak through hair, signature goggles

Background

The daughter of Lord Reginald Savage (now known to be the nefarious "Argus" – *see page 153*), one of Archer's most accomplished Cold War agents, Emily showed all the signs of following in her father's footsteps. But her mother, an ex-KGB sleeper stationed in Canada, cloistered Emily, telling her that her father died years before.

During her formative years, Emily blossomed as an incredible athlete and a rabid information junkie. She remained informed about world events even while on Olympic tour, when she took the silver in gymnastics.

Then the bomb came, or rather the bullet. Emily's mother was found dead in their Vancouver beach house, the victim of an apparent suicide. No note was left, nor any explanation – only the revelation shortly thereafter that her father was still alive, and that he belonged to a globe-spanning organization dedicated to safeguarding the precarious peace of the 20th Century. Emily joined her father in London, and soon after became an agent of Room 39. Today she is considered one of the foremost investigators in the world, her keen senses bringing more than one mission to a successful close.

Emily displays a prodigal gift with gadgets, constructing several even though she is classified "non-latent" as a psion. Her signature goggles are her own design.

LOW-LEVEL VERSION

Chamber: Room 39 (Broken Seal)
Department: Computer Espionage (3)
Class: Snoop
Level: 1

Strength:	12	**Dexterity:**	17
Constitution:	11	**Intelligence:**	17
Wisdom:	18	**Charisma:**	14
Vitality:	8	**Wounds:**	11

Defense: 14 (+1 class, +3 Dex)
Initiative Bonus: +4 (+1 class, +3 Dex)
Speed: 30

Fort: +0 **Ref:** +4 **Will:** +5

Skills: Balance +5, Bureaucracy +5, Climb +5, Computers +9, Cryptography +9, Cultures +7, Electronics +7, First Aid +4, Gather Information +9, Hide +6, Hobby (Web Surfing) +8, Jump +5, Knowledge (Internet) +7, Languages +5, Listen +5, Move Silently +5, Search +5, Spot +6, Tumble +7

Feats: Mathematical Genius, Signature Gadget ("Savage" Forearm Console) *(See below.)*

ATTACKS

Walther PPK (9mm backup pistol) +3 1d10

Gear: Laptop computer (+5 rating), electronics kit, disguise kit, Swiss army knife

Common Gadgets: Cell phone, plus the following:

Gadget Goggles: These goggles have night and infrared sight and contain numerous gadgets, including a camera, an interface for most electronic devices, and a H.U.D. display linked to a special gun sight.

Mechanics: Emily ignores concealment bonuses from darkness when attacking, and receives a +2 bonus to attack rolls with any firearm which has the special linked gun sight attached.

"Savage" Forearm Console: This pair of armbands has all the abilities of an Icon ProStar 7. The console also boasts a chemical analysis center as well as a powerful computer.

Mechanics: As the Icon ProStar 7. In addition, the console can determine the chemical composition of any known substance collected with its attached sampling wand. Finally, the console's computer has a power rating of +5.

MID-LEVEL VERSION

Chamber: Room 39 (Broken Seal)
Department: Computer Espionage (3)
Class: Snoop
Level: 8

Strength:	12	**Dexterity:**	17
Constitution:	11	**Intelligence:**	17
Wisdom:	19	**Charisma:**	15
Vitality:	43	**Wounds:**	11

Defense: 19 (+6 class, +3 Dex)
Initiative Bonus: +8 (+5 class, +3 Dex)
Speed: 30

Fort: +2 **Ref:** +7 **Will:** +8

Skills: Balance +13, Bureaucracy +7, Climb +12, Computers +15, Cryptography +10, Cultures +10, Electronics +14, First Aid +6, Gather Information +11, Hide +8, Hobby (Web Surfing) +10, Jump +10, Knowledge (Internet) +9, Languages +8, Listen +9, Move Silently +7, Search +11, Spot +12, Tumble +14

Feats: Acrobatic, Alertness, Mathematical Genius, Signature Gadget ("Savage" Forearm Console)

ATTACKS

Walther PPK (9mm backup pistol) +7 1d10

Gear: Laptop computer (+5 rating), electronics kit, disguise kit, swiss army knife

Common Gadgets: Cell phone, plus the following:

Gadget Goggles: As low-level version above, except they have been upgraded to a +4 bonus to attack.

"Savage" Forearm Console: As low-level version, except they have been upgraded to a +8 power rating.

HIGH-LEVEL VERSION

Chamber: Room 39 (Broken Seal)
Department: Computer Espionage (3)
Class: Snoop
Level: 15

Strength:	12	**Dexterity:**	18
Constitution:	11	**Intelligence:**	17
Wisdom:	19	**Charisma:**	15
Vitality:	71	**Wounds:**	11

Defense: 25 (+12 class, +3 Dex)
Initiative Bonus: +12 (+9 class, +3 Dex)
Speed: 30

Fort: +5 **Ref:** +11 **Will:** +11

Skills: Balance +13, Bureaucracy +7, Climb +15, Computers +22, Cryptography +17, Cultures +10, Electronics +21, First Aid +6, Gather Information +18, Hide +8, Hobby (Web Surfing) +15, Jump +15, Knowledge (Internet) +14, Languages +8, Listen +18, Move Silently +10, Search +20, Spot +21, Tumble +21

Feats: Acrobatic, Advanced Skill Mastery (Alertness), Alertness, Extra R&D Support, Grand Skill Mastery (Alertness), Mathematical Genius, Signature Gadget ("Savage" Forearm Console)

Attacks

Walther PPK (9mm backup pistol)	+11	1d10

Gear: Laptop computer (+5 rating), electronics kit, disguise kit, swiss army knife

Common Gadgets: Cell phone, plus the following:

Gadget Goggles: As low-level version above, except they have been upgraded to a +6 bonus to attack.

"Savage" Forearm Console: As low-level version above, except they have been upgraded to a +10 power rating.

Combes, Alistair

Codename: CRACKERJACK
Aliases: Alvin Corsair; Marc McKinley
Archer Identity Number: 57-492653-290
Nationality: Scottish
Gender: Male **Handedness:** Right
Height: 6 in. 1 in. **Weight:** 225 lbs.
Eyes: Brown **Hair:** Blonde
Psion Class: Physical Adept (Grade B)
Place of Birth: Edinburgh, Scotland
Date of Birth: 1960.06.21
Distinguishing Characteristics: Scar along left jawline

Background

Crackerjack is one of the top operatives in Ultracorps. A consummate field agent, he embodies everything for which Room 39 stands: dedication, discipline, and precision. Combes joined the Royal Army at the age of 18 and moved into SAS only two years later. His idealism was simple and pure. He did everything for

Queen and Country. When his psionic abilities manifested three years later, a Room 39 mole recruited him.

Within months, Alistair was operating in Berlin, Istanbul, and other Cold War hotspots, working with covert strike teams to preserve the balance of power. He earned his codename through dogged perseverance and a flawless record. No team he has ever been assigned to has failed their mission.

Alistair is getting older now. He's entered his forties, and he's beginning to think that the Game may have passed him by. The world is changing, and he sometimes feels that he has become a bit of a relic. Still, as a Cold War kid trained to see threats everywhere, he recognizes the need for vigilance.

Though he still carries out missions in the field, Alistair now spends much of his time training the next generation of Room 39 superspies. He is typically only called in when the situation requires his refined skill – and his flawless reputation.

Low-Level Version

Chamber: Room 39 (Ultracorps)
Department: Urban Assault (4)
Class: Soldier/Physical Adept
Level: 4/3

Strength:	14	**Dexterity:**	15
Constitution:	16	**Intelligence:**	13
Wisdom:	14	**Charisma:**	10
Vitality:	69	**Wounds:**	16

Defense: 16 (+4 class, +2 Dex)
Initiative Bonus: +7 (+5 class, +2 Dex)
Speed: 30

Fort: +10 **Ref:** +5 **Will:** +6

Skills: Balance +6, Climb +6, Demolitions +8, Driver +6, First Aid +6, Hide +5, Intimidate +4, Jump +6, Knowledge (Urban Tactics) +6, Profession (Spy Trainer) +5, Spot +7, Tumble +6, Use Rope +6

Feats: Adrenal Basics, Metabolic Basics, Point Blank Shot, Precise Shot, Rapid Shot, Sensory Basics, Stamina Battery

Psion Skills: Combat Sense +4, Control Metabolism +5, Energy Burst +5, Invigorate +5, Psionic Purge +5, Psionic Sensing +4

Attacks

5.56×45mm assault rifle	+7	2d8+2

Gear: Riot vest and shield, hard helmet

Mid-Level Version

Chamber: Room 39 (Ultracorps)
Department: Urban Assault (4)
Class: Soldier/Physical Adept
Level: 9/5

Strength:	15	**Dexterity:**	15
Constitution:	16	**Intelligence:**	13
Wisdom:	14	**Charisma:**	11
Vitality:	122	**Wounds:**	16

Defense: 19 (+7 class, +2 Dex)
Initiative Bonus: +12 (+10 class, +2 Dex)
Speed: 30

Fort: +13 **Ref:** +7 **Will:** +10

Skills: Balance +6, Climb +7, Demolitions +11, Driver +6, First Aid +7, Hide +5, Intimidate +4, Jump +6, Knowledge (Urban Tactics) +12, Profession (Spy Trainer) +7, Sense Motive +4, Spot +11, Tumble +6, Use Rope +6

Feats: Adrenal Basics, Adrenal Mastery, Marksman, Metabolic Basics, Metabolic Mastery, Overcharge Power, Point Blank Shot, Precise Shot, Rapid Shot, Sharp-Shooting, Sensory Basics, Sensory Mastery, Stamina Battery

Psion Skills: Combat Sense +6, Control Metabolism +7, Energy Burst +7, Invigorate +7, Psionic Purge +8, Psionic Sensing +7

Attacks

5.56×45mm assault rifle	+13	2d8+2

Gear: Riot vest and shield, hard helmet

High-Level Version

Chamber: Room 39 (Ultracorps)
Department: Urban Assault (4)
Class: Soldier/Physical Adept/Counter-Terrorist
Level: 9/5/6

Strength:	16	**Dexterity:**	16
Constitution:	16	**Intelligence:**	13
Wisdom:	14	**Charisma:**	11
Vitality:	185	**Wounds:**	16

Defense: 21 (+9 class, +2 Dex)
Initiative Bonus: +17 (+15 class, +2 Dex)
Speed: 30

Fort: +16 **Ref:** +11 **Will:** +12

Skills: Balance +10, Climb +10, Demolitions +11, Driver +10, First Aid +11, Hide +8, Intimidate +6, Jump +8, Knowledge (Urban Tactics) +16, Profession (Spy Trainer) +11, Sense Motive +4, Spot +15, Tumble +12, Use Rope +6

Feats: Adrenal Basics, Adrenal Mastery, Controlled Burst, Coordinate Fire, Hail of Bullets, Lay Down Fire, Marksman, Metabolic Basics, Metabolic Mastery, Overcharge Power, Point Blank Shot, Precise Shot, Rapid Shot, Sensory Basics, Sensory Mastery, Sharp-Shooting, Stamina Battery

Psion Skills: Combat Sense +6, Control Metabolism +7, Energy Burst +7, Invigorate +7, Psionic Purge +8, Psionic Sensing +7

ATTACKS

5.56×45mm assault rifle	+20	2d8+2

Gear: Riot vest and shield, hard helmet

SINGLETON, SARAH

Codename: STILETTO
Aliases: Ginger Starr, The Silver Queen
Archer Identity Number: 57-990423-316
Nationality: English
Gender: Female **Handedness:** Right
Height: 5 ft. 6 in. **Weight:** 135 lbs.
Eyes: Green **Hair:** Strawberry Blonde
Psion Class: Non-latent
Place of Birth: Kent, England
Date of Birth: 1964.08.07
Distinguishing Characteristics: Kinky, strawberry blonde hair, usually worn up in a bun; light freckles

BACKGROUND

Room 39's Control attended Westfield College at the University of London where she earned her degree in European History. She was recruited into MI6 as an intelligence analyst in 1986, and in 1989 oversaw the upgrade of many of the agency's antiquated records into computer files. During the process, she grew into an incredible programmer – and a leading resource on British intelligence.

Sarah helped to found the Broken Seal in 1992, where she learned advanced programming techniques from some of the finest hackers in the world. Though by no means their peer, Sarah's vision nonetheless guided the blooming division to the forefront of Archer's global information network.

In 2000, Sarah was promoted to the head of Room 39, the youngest Control in Archer's history. She has utilized her influence to secure even more funding for the Broken Seal, which she sees as the Foundation's source of digital spies in the 21st Century.

Sarah is quiet and efficient. She runs her Chamber like a cabinet, with teams of advisors to oversee all the operations and report back to her. She is attentive and decisive, but only after she has all the facts. When she offers it, her word is final.

LOW-LEVEL VERSION

Chamber: Room 39 (Broken Seal)
Department: Home Office (0)
Class: Pointman
Level: 7

Strength:	12	**Dexterity:**	14
Constitution:	10	**Intelligence:**	17
Wisdom:	17	**Charisma:**	14
Vitality:	43	**Wounds:**	11

Defense: 5 (+3 class, +2 Dex)
Initiative Bonus: +9 (+3 class, +2 Dex, +4 Improved Initative)
Speed: 30

Fort: +4 **Ref:** +6 **Will:** +8

Skills: Bureaucracy +13, Computers +15, Concentration +10, Cryptography +12, Diplomacy +10, Driver +8, Electronics +12, Gather Information +10, Innuendo +8, Intimidate +6, Knowledge (History) +8, Knowledge (Room 39 Secrets) +13, Knowledge (Archer Secrets) +6, Read Lips +6, Sense Motive +8

Feats: Expertise, Field Operative, Improved Initiative, Mathematical Genius

ATTACKS

.45 target pistol	+7	1d10+2
Taser	+7	1d8

Gear: Laptop computer (+4 rating)

Common Gadgets: Void suit (to conceal gun when she is on the street)

MID-LEVEL VERSION

Chamber: Room 39 (Broken Seal)
Department: Home Office (0)
Class: Pointman
Level: 14

Strength:	12	**Dexterity:**	14
Constitution:	11	**Intelligence:**	17
Wisdom:	17	**Charisma:**	15

Vitality: 82 **Wounds:** 11

Defense: 18 (+6 class, +2 Dex)
Initiative Bonus: +12 (+6 class, +2 Dex, +4 Improved Initative)
Speed: 30

Fort: +6 **Ref:** +10 **Will:** +12

Skills: Bureaucracy +19, Computers +21, Concentration +16, Cryptography +17, Diplomacy +16, Driver +8, Electronics +17, Gather Information +14, Innuendo +12, Intimidate +8, Knowledge (History) +12, Knowledge (Room 39 Secrets) +20, Knowledge (Archer Secrets) +8, Read Lips +8, Sense Motive +12

Feats: Expertise, Field Operative, Improved Disarm, Improved Initiative, Lightning Reflexes, Mathematical Genius

ATTACKS

.45 target pistol	+12	1d10+2
Taser	+12	1d8

Gear: Laptop computer (+4 rating)

Common Gadgets: Void suit (to conceal gun when she is on the street)

High-Level Version

Chamber: Room 39 (Broken Seal)
Department: Home Office (0)
Class: Pointman/Hacker
Level: 14/6

Strength:	12	**Dexterity:**	14
Constitution:	12	**Intelligence:**	17
Wisdom:	17	**Charisma:**	15

Vitality: 129 **Wounds:** 12

Defense: 22 (+10 class, +2 Dex)
Initiative Bonus: +16 (+10 class, +2 Dex, +4 Improved Initative)
Speed: 30

Fort: +10 **Ref:** +14 **Will:** +18

Skills: Bureaucracy +25, Computers +28, Concentration +20, Cryptography +24, Diplomacy +20, Driver +10, Electronics +23, Gather Information +16, Innuendo +13, Intimidate +10, Knowledge (History) +15, Knowledge (Room 39 Secrets) +26, Knowledge (Archer Secrets) +12, Read Lips +10, Sense Motive +12

Feats: Expertise, Career Operative, Field Operative, Improved Disarm, Improved Initiative, Iron Will, Lightning Reflexes, Mathematical Genius

ATTACKS

.45 target pistol	+15	1d10+2
Taser	+15	1d8

Gear: Laptop computer (+4 rating)

Common Gadgets: Void suit (to conceal gun when she is on the street)

The Russian Confederacy

"I cannot forecast to you the action of Russia. It is a riddle wrapped in a mystery inside an enigma."

—Winston Churchill

The Cold War effectively ended in December, 1991, with the fall of the USSR. The Soviets' collapse also brought to a close the long twilight campaign of the illustrious KGB, whose efforts had plagued the intelligence agencies of Europe, Britain, and the U.S. for five decades. The KGB did not go quietly into the night, nor did it perish with dignity. Rioting crowds attacked its offices at 2 Dzerzhinsky Square, and even high-ranking KGB officers sold their stories to the press and to foreign governments. Following the Soviet Union's collapse, the KGB was just a hollow memory, tainted by bitter revelations and sensitive secrets laid bare to the world.

In November, 1991, the Archer Foundation made tentative contact with the Russian Confederacy, which had largely weathered the storm without support from the home office. Archer expected to find an effort already in place to guide the beleaguered nation through the dark autumn into a glorious new spring.

They could not have been more wrong.

The Confederacy Mission

In 1950, the Archer caucus determined that the Soviet Union was too dangerous a threat to be left alone. Unlike other shadow communities, the spies of Russia were secretly divided into two camps – those Archer trusted, and everyone else. Archer's finest safeguarded the world by fighting the Cold War inside Russia, countering the many elements of the nation perceived as a menace to the rest of the world. Unfortunately, the fact that most of the battles of the Cold War were fought away from Russia led Archer to believe that things in that region were "in hand."

In truth, however, Russia has been festering from within for a very long time. The real threat is a corrupt group of ranking intelligence officers, military commandants, and organized crime families called P.E.R.I.L. (the Project for Expansion, Retribution, Iniquity, and Lies) who initially used the lingering turmoil in Russia as a cover for their operations, sacrificing lesser threats to remain unnoticed by the Foundation. This tactic had the twofold effect of keeping Archer at bay and making them believe that progress was being made in Russia, and that there was nothing to worry about in the region. All the while, P.E.R.I.L. slowly eliminated or turned Archer's moles, gradually seizing the entire shadow community for themselves.

The Foundation discovered P.E.R.I.L. after the fall of the Soviet Union, when many of the organization's operations came to light *(see page 42)*. Chamber Control Davros Oleksandre openly joined their ranks shortly thereafter (though most believe that he worked for them for some time prior), taking most of the Chamber with him and declaring Russia free of the Foundation's influence and the by-laws of the Archer Pact, a safe haven for any seeking asylum from the world protectorate.

Over the last ten years, P.E.R.I.L. has increased its influence even further, expanding into the United States, Europe, and Asia and subverting more and more of Russia's splintered government against the Foundation.

Now faced with a private Cold War, this time against an insidious, patient criminal organization with interests all over the world, the Archer Foundation's mission in Russia relies on infiltration, sabotage, and grass-roots subversion. The agents of Archer's Russian Chamber – the Confederacy – are charged with liberating the region from dominant criminal control, cleaning house as it were, and toppling the demented regime of their former leader Oleksandre. Confederacy spies face this challenge with a glad heart, refusing to let the glory of their proud nation die, and certain that the strength of their convictions will lead them to victory.

Function

At home, the efforts of the Russian Confederacy most closely resemble guerrilla warfare. Operatives generally work alone or in small teams, and all answer directly to superior Archer field agents rather than a Chamber Control. Individual Confederacy operatives develop skills and equipment pools according to their needs, and establish private spy networks to suit their personal endeavors. In essence, each Confederacy agent team becomes an agency unto itself, supported only indirectly by the Archer Foundation.

Day to day, Confederacy agents live and operate inside the system created by P.E.R.I.L. and the many other criminal elements in the area, and they have adopted similar tactics. With both sides alternately attacking, terrorizing, and double-crossing each other, the conflict in the Russian arena is akin to a gang war,

with all the associated trappings. Invisible borders divide territories only sensed by the public, marking the boundaries for epic battles featuring brazen politicos, renegade generals and their private armies, and chemically enhanced psion soldiers.

Common Confederacy Missions

In their campaign to liberate Russia from P.E.R.I.L., agents of the Confederacy engage in many activities, all of them geared for revolution.

Counter-Espionage: Usually, counter-espionage takes the form of spies defending their homeland from external threats, but in Russia the tables have turned. Operatives of the local Archer Chamber perform counter-espionage against an occupying force in their own territory. On the one hand, their job is easier – the enemy is clear and easy to find; Foundation agents do not need to spend months searching for leads. But by the same token, they are the minority now, parasites feeding off of the same intelligence community they wish to overthrow. They do not have the resources of a government at their disposal, only their own wits and reflexes.

Covert Operations ("Night Strikes"): Most Confederacy operations involve clandestine raids against P.E.R.I.L. installations, kidnappings, wire-tapping, or similar acts of rebellion. Whether under cover of darkness or between patches of broad daylight, Confederacy agents specialize in physically frustrating the enemy. Night strikes are usually quiet – they enter, get the job done, and leave with the enemy none the wiser – but they also occasionally end with explosive action. Once again, agents of the Confederacy are prepared for either.

Rescue: P.E.R.I.L. is not above capturing, ransoming, or killing allies of the Confederacy to keep them at bay. They consider the Russian people little more than tools with which to manipulate their enemies. In both cases, Archer operatives are called in to rescue hostages.

Smuggling: Keeping the revolution equipped and funded are vital concerns to the Confederacy. Not only must they smuggle materials in and out of Russia for their own benefit, they must also support the many civilian and specialist cells they rely upon for aid. Even after ten years, the Confederacy's transport avenues are still not completely secure from the heavily-guarded and highly territorial smuggling rings P.E.R.I.L. and their criminal syndicates have fashioned.

"Sting" Operations: Taking a lesson from their KGB predecessors, agents of the Russian Confederacy are calculating and observant, prepared to spring on their opponents while reserving action until the precise moment for maximum effect. These practices match well with one of their most frequent operations – luring enemy agents into complex traps. These mind games place the enemy off guard before an important operation, or trick them into helping the cause.

"Wetworks": Russians coined the term "wetworks" to mean assassination, after the act of wetting the ground with blood. The KGB referred to execution as "demoting maximally." The Russian people have long been familiar with the act of murder, and their intelligence community is that much closer to it. Archer and its agents prefer not to cross that line, but Russia is a dangerous, volatile place. Confederacy operatives rely on killing as a last resort, but have a variety of options when the time comes.

Agent Expectations

Players who enjoy the Great Game at its purest, stripped down to the basics, find the Russian Confederacy appealing. Cut off from their chain of command and the support of their organization, Archer operatives in Russia rely only on their own wits and raw talent to overcome incredible odds. Danger lurks in every shadow, and there are no safe moments for agents to let their guard down.

However, the Chamber also appeals to players who want to bust the spy stereotype wide open, spinning it off in wild, unexpected, and frequently over-the-top directions. By virtue of biological, chemical, and psion research, the Russian Confederacy falls prey to (and periodically calls upon) all manner of incredible combatants, from telekinetics capable of flipping vehicles through the air to monstrous creatures only scarcely resembling their human origins.

This broad range of agent and enemy options leaves Russia open for many different serials, but also means that Confederacy agents should be prepared for anything. Russian operatives tend to be versatile, capable of shifting from one problem to the next quickly and fluidly. They are also highly intelligent and well versed in the ways of classic and modern espionage. They are careful, and while often plodding, starkly efficient. Russian agents enjoy the Game, playing as much for the thrill of the hunt as the satisfaction of victory.

Tactical Data

The war in Russia is fought between small Archer teams and the looming spy conglomerate P.E.R.I.L. Battles between these forces tend to be fast and furious, pitched life-and-death struggles for meager goals. Archer's heroes utilize hit-and-run tactics to chip away at P.E.R.I.L.'s defenses, carefully orchestrating the downfall of its outermost offices, but they are fighting an uphill battle. P.E.R.I.L.'s spy networks have been in place for decades, with informants everywhere, and they have the strength of nearly the entire Russian government on their side.

CONFEDERACY PSITECH

Regardless of its size and complexity, the Russian combine has relatively little technology at its disposal. Weapons, vehicles, computers, and scientific equipment are all outdated by fifteen years or more. This is one of the few things the Confederacy has in its favor right now – Archer provides them with vastly superior equipment than the average agent of P.E.R.I.L. or the corrupt Russian government, and plenty of money to buy their way through the system.

They do face one significant technological threat, however – the chemical monsters and biological aberrations created by Project PROMETHEUS *(see page 141)*.

CHAMBER ORGANIZATION

Agent teams working for the Foundation make their own organization in Russia, forging homes and lives for themselves as needed. Each team's story is different, subject to the needs of their mission and the dangers of the area they live in. Instead of focusing on them in this section, however, we will focus on the organization of their enemies, the operatives of P.E.R.I.L.

"The Aquarium" (Khodynke Airfield, Moscow)

P.E.R.I.L.'s headquarters (and the residence of the traitorous Chamber Control Davros Oleksandre) lies along the Khoroshevskiy Highway in the Khodynke suburb of Moscow in a nine-story building nicknamed the "Aquarium." The Russians also call this place *steklyashka* ("piece of glass") because most of its exterior surface is composed of windows. Some agents of the Russian Confederacy call it "the looking glass," the portal between the mundane world of espionage and Archer's secret world behind the scenes. To go "through the looking glass" is to enter that world.

Officially, the Aquarium is the headquarters for the GRU, the first and most effective agency compromised by the Archer Foundation. But with the near-complete corruption of the original Confederacy task forces, the Aquarium has become the center of P.E.R.I.L. operations in Russia. Davros Oleksandre is a ranking member of the GRU, and conducts the symphony which P.E.R.I.L. performs from his office on the seventh floor, overlooking the complex's incinerator and the airfield proper. Messages filter to him through diplomatic parcels or intelligence reports, and orders return to the field via trusted lieutenants and code buried in mundane transmissions.

Khodynke Airfield holds deep-rooted secrets, much like the Pentagon or Camp Peary in the United States. Members of all Russia's intelligence agencies work or visit there regularly, and everyone is watching everyone else for something they can use to their advantage. During the fall of the Soviet Union, this place became a flurry of activity, and remains so to this day, though in a subdued fashion. There is no place more inherently dangerous than the Aquarium.

Residencies

In World War II, the Soviets placed their handlers (who were called "residents") in nations adjacent to the area compromised by the spies they controlled (their "residencies"). This practice protected the handlers and the agents simultaneously, and kept the enemy off balance. In most cases, the Russians relied on foreign nationals capable of remotely coordinating complex networks to fill the role. This was the case with Leopold Trepper, who controlled the Red Orchestra spy network in Germany from his home in Bruxelles. It was also the case with Sandor Rado, whose residency (the "Lucy Spy Ring") spied on Germany but was controlled from Switzerland.

The practice of keeping residencies continues today, though roughly half of them (all operating within the territories of the former Soviet Union) are controlled by Russian patriots. Misdirection still plays a large part in the program, as all residencies irregularly shuffle between handlers, many of whom are not in the same region as the networks. This process has been particularly frustrating for agents of the Confederacy operating in Russia, who face a constantly revolving chain of command that is nearly impossible to track.

Training (Spy Schools)

Russia has always placed great emphasis on education, and its spies are no exception. The nation holds dozens of remote training camps, universities, military academies, and field simulations geared to bring a young Russian spy into the world of modern espionage. Many of these schools were once open to agents (and sometimes even civilians) of other nations, and attracted the finest pupils in the world.

P.E.R.I.L. expects perfection from its agents, and generally won't approach new candidates until they show promise with more or more specialities. Of course, this is a dangerous tactic, as many elder students have already been hardened in their ways, and find the criminal organization's methods unappealing.

CONFEDERACY RESOURCES

The Confederacy developed a number of special projects and espionage resources during the Cold War. Unfortunately, all have fallen into the hands of P.E.R.I.L. at this point, and are now used against agents of Archer's Chamber.

THE RED MARKET

Everything is bought and sold in Russia – weapons, secrets, technology, even people. The long-standing underworld market throughout the former Soviet Union (called the "Red Market" by natives, who remember the massacre in 1992 during a confrontation between agents of the Russian Confederacy and P.E.R.I.L.) is one of the many reasons that the Archer Foundation was reluctant to accept the area into its charter in 1950. The criminal organizations in Russia go back hundreds of years; the Foundation was justifiably concerned that advanced technologies and knowledge would eventually fall into the wrong hands.

They were right. Based on the ideas and information originally gained from the Archer Pact, P.E.R.I.L. has built the foundation of a world-spanning empire the likes of which has not been seen since the European de Medici and Hapsburg families. Today, the Red Market offers everything for sale. It can acquire military secrets the day after they are transmitted from foreign territories; it can have a small fleet of Russian destroyers, or even a nuclear submarine, ready at any port in Eurasia for the right price; it can smuggle anything, anywhere, anytime; and perhaps most impressive of all, it can provide private armies culled from the underfunded and undermanned prison system or military penitentiaries throughout Russia.

Agents of the Russian Confederacy rely on the Red Market just as often as their enemies do, bartering for equipment and supplies needed during operations (usually for inflated prices).

PROJECT SUPERLUMINAL

Prior to 1950, most nations developed psions by distilling samples of the original Minoan formula down to serums which they injected into their agents. While of varying potencies, these serums all had one thing in common – all of the injected agents (dubbed "serum soldiers") died a year or two after they acquired their powers.

In 1950, the Archer Pact provided all Chambers with the means to develop relatively low-risk psions, using methodical gene therapy and a lifelong regimen of focus exercises. The Pact forbade further use of psion serums, a stipulation which the Russian Confederacy ignored, privately refining its physical adept serums with Operation SUPERLUMINAL. When the mentalist and telepath formulæ were recovered from Eden in 1975 and made available through the Chamber network, the Russians created serums from them as well.

Russia's illicit psion research – first conducted by the Confederacy and later by P.E.R.I.L. – has always focused on increasing the strength of psions, never on reducing the risk involved in the process. Today, Operation SUPERLUMINAL has "perfected" two additional versions of the original psion serum, creating a whole new power scale:

- **Goliath:** The original psion serum is used by rank-and-file subjects in anticipation of large-scale or important P.E.R.I.L. operations. Agents enhanced with it die of system shock (a brain aneurysm, heart attack, etc.) in 11–16 months.
- **Cronus:** The first SUPERLUMINAL discovery, "Cronus" is far stronger than Goliath, but reduces the agent's life-span to under one year. P.E.R.I.L. uses Cronus for critical short-term operations.
- **Hyperion:** The foremost SUPERLUMINAL development, Hyperion taps the innermost latent potential, turning psion soldiers into one-man armies, but only for a short time. Hyperion-boosted agents often die in as little as three months.

Rules for SUPERLUMINAL's discoveries can be found on page 209.

Project PROMETHEUS

PROMETHEUS began as a bio-warfare weapons project to create a short-term "burst" virus that could be secretly injected into an enemy who would return to his base and infect others. The virus – originally codenamed AGAMEMNON – was supposed to incubate within the first victim for a period ranging from twelve to eighteen hours, after which it would become violently contagious. At the climax of its lifespan, the virus would kill its first victim, followed shortly by all other infected parties.

It was a lofty goal, and not a little morbid, but by the time that AGAMEMNON was initiated in 1983, P.E.R.I.L. had already spread its tendrils quite deep. Not above using engineered bio-toxins to meet their twisted ends, P.E.R.I.L. prepared to field test the virus on a persistent thorn in its side – a unit of soldiers called the Phantom Brigade, led by the legendary commander Nikolai Petrovich *(see page 144)*. What happened next was anything but expected.

Two days after quietly inoculating a Brigade Pointman on a busy Leningrad street, PE.R.I.L. inexplicably lost contact with the city's residency. When agents converged on the area, they encountered a band of hulking creatures, capable of tearing through walls and withstanding point-blank rifle fire. Worse, these engines of destruction wore remnants of Phantom Brigade uniforms and worked together, using traditional Russian military tactics. Nikolai's troops had survived AGAMEMNON, and they had *evolved* from it.

P.E.R.I.L. never took Leningrad (now called St. Petersburg) back from the Phantom Brigade, which set up the city as a base for Foundation penetrations into the rest of Russia. P.E.R.I.L. never pefected AGAMEMNON in its intended form, and instead turned it into Project PROMETHEUS, a research division which builds chemical monsters for its criminal cause.

Since 1983, the war in Russia has changed. Both sides in the semi-covert battle for Russia are constantly testing more and more radical options and variations of SUPERLUMINAL and PROMETHEUS, trying to out-muscle one another and leaving a wide trail of destruction in their wake. Villages vanish overnight, replaced by smoldering ruins and trails of witnesses babbling incoherent nonsense. If there is a new age for the war to save the world, Russia has already moved into it.

The Game in Russia

Contrary to the "thug in a poorly-fitting suit" motif of American cinema, Russian spies are clever and industrious, recognized in the world's intelligence community for long-term planning, stealth, and guile. During the Cold War, they specialized in the slow, meticulous cultivation of foreign spies, a reputation that persists today. Effective and well-timed use of seduction, blackmail, and psychological manipulation are hallmarks of the Russian spy syndicate.

Russian Intelligence Agencies

Until the fall of the Iron Curtain, the Russian intelligence system was evenly divided between the legendary KGB and the ruthless GRU, who maintained a fierce rivalry until the bitter end. These two organizations clashed operationally and ideologically, making for a difficult and often violent espionage landscape. This all changed in 1991, when sweeping changes transformed the Russian spy community, including the dismantling of the KGB.

Still, despite attempts to level the playing field and smooth relations between Russian spies, conflicts and turmoil are still common. The following sections detail some of the most influential agencies in Russia at the moment, with an eye toward their use in the *Shadowforce Archer* setting.

Chief Intelligence Directorate of the General Staff (GRU): The largest surviving remnant of Russia's Cold War spy operations is the GRU *(Glavnoye Razvedyvatelnoye Upravalenie)*, who created the *Chasti Spetsial'nogo Naznacheniya* ("Spetsnaz") troops of the Red Army, stole atomic secrets from both the Germans and the U.S, and operated the famous Lucy Spy Ring and the European "Red Orchestra." The GRU was Russia's first external intelligence agency, and formed many military intelligence agencies which are still in operation.

The GRU focuses on the collection and analysis of military intelligence, but its specialty is the dissemination of scientific data, including technological, biological, and military capabilities of enemy nations. With no internal policing force, the GRU lacks the ability to use blunt force the way it once did.

Today, the GRU serves as Russia's principal spy organ, its foreign operations the country's eyes and ears. Having largely remained outside the fallout of the changes the nation has endured, without allegiance or obligation to any of the myriad political factions rising out of the ashes of the Cold War, the GRU remains the most efficient, professional intelligence entity in Russia.

Federal Agency for Government Communications and Information (FAPSI): FAPSI is Russia's equivalent of the NSA *(see page 79)*, though with fewer restrictions placed on their operatives and a much more prevalent public presence. Founded in 1994, FAPSI is responsible for most communications security in Russia, and monitors most mail and computer, phone, and radio traffic that passes through the nation. It also handles cryptographic security, completing the parallel with NSA.

FAPSI's mission is loosely defined, allowing it to justify almost any activity, including the interception and invasion of financial and security transactions, and monitoring Internet use by private citizens. Some rumors hold that FAPSI has made progress compromising the banks and businesses of other nations in its effort to protect Russia's interests.

FAPSI has many resources at its disposal, including a private high-frequency satellite network, SIGINT (signals intelligence) facilities all around the world, and several commercial enterprises (including radio bands it leases to corporations and a host of email networks, banks, and government installations).

Foreign Intelligence Service (SVR): Like FAPSI, the SVR has taken over some of the KGB's responsibilities following the fall of the Iron Curtain; specifically, it collects political, economic, scientific, technical, and ecological intelligence (formerly the purview of the KGB's First Directorate). In practice, this means that the SVR steals business and technical intelligence to aid Russian businesses, controls a great number of foreign moles, and conducts covert operations as necessary to fulfill its charter.

Federal Security Service (FSB): The lion's share of Russia's intelligence budget goes to the FSB, which handles counter-intelligence within the nation and policing its military forces. The FSB also tracks Russia's nuclear stockpile and counters the rampant illicit trafficking of weapons through the Federation. Toward these ends, the FSB has devoted an entire department – Directorate "T" – to the training and field assignment of counterterrorism teams.

Unlike FAPSI, the FSB has limited powers on Russian soil. It cannot tap phone lines, break and enter, or tamper with mail without court permission.

Ministry of Internal Affairs (MVD): The tide of corruption presently seeping across Russia is countered by the Ministry for Internal Affairs (MVD), the Federation's national police. The MVD maintains departments for all aspects of crime-fighting – investigation, apprehension, and imprisonment. They manage penitentiaries and labor camps and supervise paroled prisoners, and their uniformed men and women bring miscreants to justice and fight riots, drug traffic, and the *Organyzatia* (Russian mob).

PLAYING THE GREAT GAME

"I trust that this dawn will be as cold as the last... yet my coat is thick and I have a heavy flask."

– Nikolai Petrovich

Mission Management: In light of its pitched conflict with P.E.R.I.L., the Russian Chamber is highly reluctant to engage in any operation outside of Russia unless it directly impacts the enemy's assets or there's a clear and present danger to the entire world. This leaves the Russians' long-time allies in the PAC to pick up the pieces throughout the region. On the home front, the Confederacy is turning more and more to their counterparts in Company for assistance against what is proving a superior military foe. The Confederacy's surviving elements have found American funding and willingness to partake in semi-covert strikes an enormous help in the war to retake the Motherland. Once again, history makes for strange bedfellows.

Damage Control: The Russian chamber was already in such a shambles when the Shop broke with Archer that one might think there was little more harm that could be done. Not true. The Confederacy's independent cells rely heavily upon the technological edge and extra personnel provided by the Conspiracy. Without them, Archer's finest on the Russian front line find themselves stretched incredibly thin, with the promise that conditions will only get worse as the months drag on.

Dirty Little Secrets: The Russian Confederacy has long since let go of secrets from the outside world. Their only secrets are kept from P.E.R.I.L. now.

Leverage: Before P.E.R.I.L. became a concern, the Confederacy infiltrated most major world governments (not making contact in nations where Archer already had influence), as well as civilian and industrial sectors. Many of these foreign cells remain loyal to the Confederacy today, and while some have returned to the Motherland to fight their new oppressors, others remain overseas to develop support for the Conspiracy, and their war at home. Still more remain on call to assist the Archer Foundation in times of need.

Assets: Nearly all of the Confederacy's assets now belong to P.E.R.I.L. – all but the dogged determination of the Chamber's seasoned operatives.

CURRENT PLOTLINES

Most plotlines in Russia revolve around the conflict between P.E.R.I.L. and the Confederacy; this section begins there.

P.E.R.I.L. (Code: Black): The Project for Expansion, Retribution, Iniquity, and Lies began in the Stalinist purges of the GRU and NKVD during the 1930s. P.E.R.I.L. was the brainchild of Lavrenty Pavlovich Beria, a twisted and ambitious lieutenant of Josef Stalin from 1938 until his death in 1953. Beria headed the NKVD during the final purges, and eventually came to control the Soviet Union's intelligence and security organs, making him one of the most powerful men in Russia when the nation entered the Second World War.

Lavrenty Beria was a despicable man whose public deviance and ruthlessness were a pale glimmer of his grand plan for the Motherland. Drawing upon the few military and intelligence commanders he trusted (i.e. those whom he had blackmailed or intimidated), Beria laid the groundwork for a shadow government in Russia, a silent echo of the Politburo ready to step in as the current cabinet slowly died off, resigned, or "vanished."

Josef Stalin worried that Beria had grown too strong, and arranged to discredit him in January of 1953. But Beria had prepared for retaliation from all quarters, even from Stalin, and left the Russian Premier mysteriously dead on the floor of his study, apparently the victim of a stroke. The true cause of Stalin's death is still unknown.

Beria's luck ran out in December 1953, when he was cornered and shot in the basement of the Moscow Military District Headquarters building, his body torched with gasoline. But his horrid legacy survived. His shadow government reemerged, and gained new allies throughout the 1950s. With the Foundation's involvement in the area, it became necessary to expand its influence among the people of the nation. The dark conspiracy contacted leaders of the *Organyzatia* crime syndicate, and the current form of P.E.R.I.L. began to take shape.

P.E.R.I.L. has been very careful in its seizure of Russia, and is now firmly entrenched on every level of society and government. Many claim that they engineered the fall of the Soviet Union in preparation for going public themselves, or instituting a puppet regime they could control without the trappings of the old ways. Regardless, they have now achieved everything that Beria set out to do; with only a few exceptions (most notably the Phantom Brigade in St. Petersburg and pockets of Confederacy resistance throughout the nation), they *are* Russia.

SMERSH (Code: Red): Smersh, Josef Stalin's infamous "killer elite," was publicly one of the greatest threats to Lavrenty Beria. Privately, however, it was one of his greatest assets. Beria helped to found the group, whose official name was *Smert' shpionam* (or "death to spies"). At first part of the NKVD, Smersh was firmly in Beria's camp, and he prepared it for Stalin. By the time the Premier assumed personal control of the organization in 1943, it was completely in Beria's palm, and remained there until his death, when the group's allegiance transferred to his shadow government.

Smersh officially disbanded in 1946, though its services were retained by the shadow government and it was reinstated after the formation of P.E.R.I.L. Today, Smersh acts as P.E.R.I.L's shock troops, conducting paramilitary raids against Confederacy burrows and enforcing the criminal organization's whims.

Operation BLUE ZEPHYR (Code: Red): Between glasnost in the late 1980s and the collapse of the Soviet Union, the western world has seen a rapid influx of Russian immigrants. Some of these immigrants were in truth P.E.R.I.L. operatives, sent to establish a foothold in the U.S. and European underworlds. By 1995, the Company knew of the Russian Mafia presence in their territory (the "Crazy Ivans"), as well as a pipeline between the Motherland and the west coast of the U.S., but Archer Control considered the problem beneath the attention of the American Chamber.

In 1997, the Ivans again made their presence known, when agents of the Russian Confederacy arrived in Los Angeles, San Francisco, Chicago, and Miami to bring their comrades home, dead or alive. The Company intercepted three of these attempts, but failed to safeguard the Russians operating out of Miami, who were gunned down near their homes. A formal Archer inquiry discovered that the hitmen were actually agents of P.E.R.I.L., sent to eliminate competition in the U.S.

But even this was a ruse. P.E.R.I.L. had sent the hitmen to undermine Company suspicion of their earlier plants. With the Crazy Ivans now considered an isolated community unconnected to P.E.R.I.L., the real work could begin. For the last four years, the Ivans have been slowly making inroads all across the nation, solidifying their control and preparing for a prolonged siege once the Company discovers them.

Last year, P.E.R.I.L. smuggled a special cargo into the United States – Dr. Aleksei Jenkho, a mentalist of no small talent, specializing in chemistry. P.E.R.I.L considered Jenkho a key factor in their plot to seize control of the American underworld. He brought with him a distilled version of the Hyperion physical adept serum (NR2k/m), which soon filtered onto the streets under the name "Rocket."

Rocket has since taken the U.S. drug scene by storm, replacing X as the rave favorite, and leaving tens of thousands hopelessly addicted. Rocket is also used by Ivan-controlled gangs who are waging street wars with the Italian mafia, the Yakuza, and other foreign underworld competitors. This conflict is reaching a fever pitch, throwing the ill-prepared Company off-guard while raking in millions for P.E.R.I.L.

The Novelist (Code: Yellow): The Millennium brought with it many incredible developments, including the Foundation's revelation that there is a leak in their system. A privately published semi-fictional novel entitled *My Life as a Secret Agent* (released in January 2000) depicts in excruciating detail many Archer protocols, challenges, and agents. Though authored anonymously, it is clear to the Foundation that someone in their organization is releasing vital secrets to the outside world.

Many of the most sensitive details originate in Russia, where the Foundation has directed its attention so far. Whether the leak comes from the Confederacy, P.E.R.I.L., or both, remains to be seen.

The Confederacy Genre

The Russian Confederacy's genre features stark contrasts in a shadowy world of bleak nihilism. There are heroes in the Confederacy's story, but they must often take the role of "antihero," forced to make hard choices and suffer incredible sacrifices to get the job done. Stories are bittersweet here, and the legacy of corruption and gloom linger as a dark cloud over the entire region. But these facets of the Russian Confederacy also make for one of the strongest roleplaying experiences in Shadowforce Archer; with the odds stacked so high against agents and so much history to overcome, their victories are likely to be all that much more fulfilling.

Archetypes: Angel from the TV series *Angel,* Decker from *Blade Runner,* Cable, Carl Stargher (the powerful villain) from *The Cell,* Major Maxim and Natalia Kassle from *Danger Girl,* Ramius from *The Hunt for Red October,* Remo Williams from the movie *Remo Williams: the Adventure Begins,* the villains from *Dick Tracy* and *The Rocketeer.*

Inspirations

When seeking inspiration for the Russian Confederacy, look to the classic espionage epics set in World War II (or, for that matter, any classic Cold War intrigue piece), and juxtapose it with elements of the following mainstream resources.

Books: *100 Bullets, Concrete, Gangland, Red Tide, Sam and Twitch, Sin City, Spawn, Strike Force: Morituri, Suicide Squad* (first 30 issues of original volume), and *The Tenth* (all comic books), anything by James Bryon Huggins (*Cain, Hunter, Leviathan*).

Movies: *Alphaville, Carrie 2: The Rage, Crimson Tide, Dark City, Dick Tracy, DOA* (both versions), the *Godfather* movies, *The Hunt for Red October, Jin-Roh: The Wolf Brigade* (OAV), *The Lady From Shanghai, The Maltese Falcon, North by Northwest, Notorious, Reds, Rocketeer, Rocky IV, Scarface, Spawn, The Third Man, The Untouchables, Vertigo.*

TV Shows: *Amerika* (mini-series), *Batman: The Animated Series and Batman Beyond, The Burning Zone, The Untouchables.*

Music: *Crimson Tide* score, *Dead Can Dance, The Hunt for Red October* score, gothic and industrial.

Petrovich, Nikolai

Codename: THESEUS
Aliases: None
Archer Identity Number: 89-349012-659
Nationality: Russian
Gender: Male **Handedness:** Right
Height: 6 ft. 3 in. **Weight:** 200 lbs.
Eyes: Black **Hair:** Black, thinning
Psion Class: Non-latent
Place of Birth: Irkutsk, Russia
Date of Birth: 1951.09.07
Distinguishing Characteristics: Signature symbol on epaulettes (Phantom Brigade emblem), signature weapon (Tula-Tokarev 1930 with hammer and sickle on palm grip)

Background

A career military man and Communist hardliner, Nikolai Petrovich has always been there for Mother Russia, even when she wasn't there for him. His fierce devotion to the state earned him several important posts over the years, including a several-year stint with the KGB during the height of the Cold War. But none of his assignments have brought him more pride than command of the Phantom Brigade, the Red Army's foremost stealth unit.

Nikolai was only recently recruited into the Archer Conspiracy, as part of the effort to reclaim Russia from the clutches of P.E.R.I.L. His service record speaks for itself, but his ardent distaste for change and resolute political views kept him off the short list for many years. Today, however, these traits are welcomed in the Russian Confederacy as signs of loyalty to the past, and dedication to return Russia to its former glory.

Nikolai's long-standing personal hatred of P.E.R.I.L. and virtual control of the rebel city of St. Petersburg make the him the perfect candidate to spearhead Archer's operations in Russia. The help of his Phantom Brigade, who have been chemically transformed into some of the most fearsome warriors on the face of the Earth, is no small boon for the Foundation, either.

LOW-LEVEL VERSION

Chamber: The Russian Confederacy
Department: Black Ops (5)
Class: Soldier
Level: 1

Strength:	16	**Dexterity:**	12
Constitution:	18	**Intelligence:**	14
Wisdom:	10	**Charisma:**	9
Vitality:	16	**Wounds:**	22

Defense: 11 (+0 class, +1 Dex)
Initiative Bonus: +2 (+1 class, +1 Dex)
Speed: 30

Fort: +8 **Ref:** +2 **Will:** +2

Skills: Climb +3, Demolitions +2, Driver +2, Intimidate +3, Jump +3, Spot +2, Tumble +2

Feats: Great Fortitude, Iron Will, Toughness

ATTACKS

Tula Tokarev (9mm service pistol)	+2	1d10

MID-LEVEL VERSION

Chamber: The Russian Confederacy
Department: Black Ops (5)
Class: Soldier
Level: 8

Strength:	16	**Dexterity:**	12
Constitution:	20	**Intelligence:**	14
Wisdom:	10	**Charisma:**	9
Vitality:	99	**Wounds:**	22

Defense: 14 (+3 class, +1 Dex)
Initiative Bonus: +7 (+6 class, +1 Dex)
Speed: 30

Fort: +13 **Ref:** +5 **Will:** +4

Skills: Balance +6, Bureaucracy +5, Climb +5, Demolitions +7, Driver +5, First Aid +5, Intimidate +10, Jump +5, Profession (Military) +7, Spot +2, Survival +5, Tumble +5

Feats: Cleave, Great Fortitude, Iron Will, Point Blank Shot, Power Attack, Precise Shot, Toughness, Weapon Focus (Dress sword)

ATTACKS

Tula Tokarev (9mm service pistol)	+9	1d10
Dress sword *	+12	1d8+6

** Error with a roll of 1-3, instead of 1-2*

Gear: NBC suit (at Leningrad base), Russian military jeep (stolen after he left service)

Common Gadgets: Palmprint identifier on 9mm (Mark II "Backfire" Edition with tracking modification)

HIGH-LEVEL VERSION

Chamber: The Russian Confederacy
Department: Black Ops (5)
Class: Soldier
Level: 15

Strength:	17	**Dexterity:**	12
Constitution:	20	**Intelligence:**	14
Wisdom:	10	**Charisma:**	10
Vitality:	173	**Wounds:**	24

Defense: 17 (+6 class, +1 Dex)
Initiative Bonus: +13 (+12 class, +1 Dex)
Speed: 30

Fort: +16 **Ref:** +8 **Will:** +7

Skills: Balance +8, Bureaucracy +9, Climb +7, Demolitions +14, Driver +8, First Aid +5, Intimidate +18, Jump +7, Profession (Military) +12, Spot +6, Survival +9, Tumble +9

Feats: Cleave, Cleaving Charge, Endurance, Great Cleave, Great Fortitude, Improved Weapon Focus (sword), Iron Will, Lay Down Fire, Point Blank Shot, Power Attack, Precise Shot, Toughness (2x), Weapon Focus (sword), Weapon Master (sword)

ATTACKS

Tula Tokarev (9mm service pistol)	+16	1d10
Dress sword *	+20	1d8+6

** Error with a roll of 1-3, instead of 1-2*

Gear: NBC suit (at Leningrad base), Russian military jeep (stolen after he left service)

Common Gadgets: Palmprint identifier on 9mm (Mark II "Backfire" Edition with tracking modification)

STAZLAUS, URI

Codename: CHARON
Aliases: The "Bogeyman"
Archer Identity Number: 43-817437-099
Nationality: Russian
Gender: Male **Handedness:** Left
Height: 5 ft. 10 in. **Weight:** 140 lbs.
Eyes: Steel-gray **Hair:** Black
Chemical Enhancement: Grade A
Place of Birth: Vilnius, Lithuania
Date of Birth: 1964.03.12
Distinguishing Characteristics: None (until he transforms — *see below*)

Background

Uri Stazlaus plays a very dangerous game. Publicly Nikolai Petrovich's right-hand man (and frequently a lieutenant of the Phantom Brigade when Nikolai is abroad), he is actually a double agent working for P.E.R.I.L. A loyal Communist like Nikolai, Uri believes that his boss's mission of state liberation is misguided, and that Mother Russia should rule the world. This sentiment made him quite vulnerable to the advances of Davros Oleksandre, who offered the soldier a place in the new order once Russia is dragged out of the ashes.

Uri is familiar with wearing two faces. When he was exposed to the AGAMEMNON virus, he did not automatically transform like his comrades, but instead gained the ability to shift between his human shape (which many claim is monstrous without the effects of the bio-agent) and that of a 8' tall albino predator called the "Bogeyman." Armed with lightning-fast reflexes and deadly natural weapons, the Bogeyman hunts spies in the outer ruins of Leningrad and the icy wastes of the Motherland, maintaining appearances until P.E.R.I.L. moves to take the city. When that time comes, Uri will be ready to turn on his old friends and assume his role in a new and more powerful Russia.

As yet, Nikolai is unaware of his lieutenant's betrayal, relying on his old friend like a brother.

Low-Level Version

Chamber: The Russian Confederacy
Department: Urban Assault (4)
Class: Soldier
Level: 6

Strength:	11	**Dexterity:**	14
Constitution:	10	**Intelligence:**	16
Wisdom:	9	**Charisma:**	9
Vitality:	45	**Wounds:**	10

Defense: 14 (+2 class, +2 Dex)
Initiative Bonus: +7 (+5 class, +2 Dex)
Size: Medium/Large
Speed: 30

Fort: +5 **Ref:** +5 **Will:** +1

Skills: Balance +10, Bluff +2, Climb +2, Demolitions +8, Driver +4, Intimidate +10, Jump +2, Spot +2, Survival +4, Tumble +5

Feats: Cleave, Darting Weapon, Expertise, Flashing Weapon, Point Blank Shot, Power Attack, Precise Shot

Attacks

9mm service pistol	+8	1d10
Survival knife	+7	1d6+2

Mid-Level Version

Chamber: The Russian Confederacy
Department: Urban Assault (4)
Class: Soldier
Level: 13

Strength:	11/19	**Dexterity:**	14
Constitution:	10	**Intelligence:**	16
Wisdom:	9	**Charisma:**	9
Vitality:	92	**Wounds:**	14

Defense: 17 (+5 class, +2 Dex)
Initiative Bonus: +12 (+10 class, +2 Dex)
Size: Medium/Large
Speed: 30

Fort: +8 **Ref:** +8 **Will:** +3

Skills: Balance +15, Bluff +7, Climb +7/+11, Demolitions +13, Driver +9, Intimidate +14, Jump +6/+10, Spot +7, Survival +9, Tumble +10

Feats: Assassin, Cleave, Cleaving Charge, Darting Weapon, Expertise, Flashing Weapon, Great Cleave, Master Assassin, Point Blank Shot, Power Attack, Precise Shot, Trail of Blood, Weapon Focus (Claw)

Charon Chem: This Chem looks and works just like a hybrid of Muscle and Endure, and requires a half action to activate. In monstrous form, Uri gains +8 STR and all the benefits of Endure. He can maintain the form for up to 10 hours, after which he must rest for a length of time equal to the time for which he was in monstrous form. The Charon Chem requires injections of a special variant Chem known only to Uri and his P.E.R.I.L. allies, which must be taken once every two weeks or he suffers all the drawbacks of both Muscle and Endure. Uri is the only known case of the Charon Chem.

ATTACKS

9mm service pistol	+15	1d10
(Claw) *	+18	1d4+6

** In monstrous form*

HIGH-LEVEL VERSION

Chamber: The Russian Confederacy
Department: Urban Assault (4)
Class: Soldier
Level: 19

Strength:	12/20	**Dexterity:**	14
Constitution:	10	**Intelligence:**	16
Wisdom:	9	**Charisma:**	9
Vitality:	129	**Wounds:**	14

Defense: 10 (+8 class, +2 Dex)
Initiative Bonus: +17 (+15 class, +2 Dex)
Size: Medium/Large
Speed: 30

Fort: +11 **Ref:** +10 **Will:** +5

Skills: Balance +20, Bluff +7, Climb +16/+20, Demolitions +13, Driver +14, Intimidate +21, Jump +16/+20, Spot +12, Survival +14, Tumble +15

Feats: Assassin, Cleave, Cleaving Charge, Darting Weapon, Expertise, Flashing Weapon, Great Cleave, Improved Weapon Focus (Claw), Master Assassin, Master Duelist, Point Blank Shot, Power Attack, Precise Shot, Rapid Shot, Trail of Blood, Ultimate Duelist, Weapon Focus (Claw), Weapon Master

Charon Chem: As mid-level version, above.

ATTACKS

9mm service pistol	+22	1d10
(Claw) *	+27	1d4+17

** In monstrous form*

OLEKSANDRE, DAVROS

MASTERMIND
Codename: TROPHONIUS
Aliases: Dimitri Denosov, Grigor Alshenko
Archer Identity Number: 88-091289-774
Nationality: Russian

Gender: Male	**Handedness:** Right
Height: 5'7"	**Weight:** 160 lbs.
Eyes: Black, icy	**Hair:** Black, clean-cut

Psion Class: Non-latent
Place of Birth: Leningrad, Russia
Date of Birth: 1955.08.06
Distinguishing Characteristics: Thick, distinctive Russian accent

BACKGROUND

In late 1982, Russian Chamber Control Andrea Komanich failed to report in. Inquiries revealed that she had suffered a fatal stroke, and that steps were being taken to replace her. Per established protocol, the Foundation demanded to review the new Control, a young military officer named Davros Oleksandre.

Oleksandre visited Australia for a month in the summer of 1982, and underwent extensive evaluation by the Lords. He was accompanied by Lelandra Marks, a P.E.R.I.L. operative and telepath of incredible power, boosted exponentially by Project SUPERLUMINAL *(see page 140)*. She protected him from Archer's interviewers and telepaths, guarding his many faithful years of service to the criminal organization.

After Oleksandre returned to Russia, he assumed control of the Chamber, as well as P.E.R.I.L., and prepared for what he believed was a period of great change. Contrary to most of the organization, he believed that the time would soon come when P.E.R.I.L. must reveal itself to Archer, and throw down the gauntlet in a new phase of the secret war. Privately, he has set things in place to wage that war, strengthening P.E.R.I.L.'s defenses and placing operatives to counter the Foundation's inevitable attack.

LOW-LEVEL VERSION

Chamber: The Russian Confederacy
Threat: P.E.R.I.L.
Department: Home Office (0)
Class: Wheelman
Level: 2

Strength:	14	**Dexterity:**	16
Constitution:	12	**Intelligence:**	14
Wisdom:	11	**Charisma:**	8
Vitality:	21	**Wounds:**	12

Defense: 14 (+1 class, +3 Dex)
Initiative Bonus: +4 (+1 class, +3 Dex)
Speed: 30

Fort: +1 **Ref:** +6 **Will:** +0

Skills: Balance +4, Boating +5, Bureaucracy +4, Demolitions +4, Disguise +2, Driver +11, Escape Artist +4, Intimidate +4, Mechanics +2, Open Lock +4, Perform (Public Speaking) +4, Pilot +5, Profession (Military) +4, Spot +4, Surveillance +4, Survival +4

Feats: Offensive Driving, Speed Demon

ATTACKS

.45 service pistol	+5	1d10+2

Gear: None

Common Gadgets: Radio tooth

MID-LEVEL VERSION

Chamber: The Russian Confederacy
Threat: P.E.R.I.L.
Department: Home Office (0)
Class: Wheelman
Level: 9

Strength:	14	**Dexterity:**	16
Constitution:	12	**Intelligence:**	14
Wisdom:	13	**Charisma:**	8
Vitality:	73	**Wounds:**	12

Defense: 18 (+5 class, +3 Dex)
Initiative Bonus: +8 (+5 class, +3 Dex)
Speed: 30

Fort: +4 **Ref:** +9 **Will:** +4

Skills: Balance +6, Boating +9, Bureaucracy +6, Demolitions +8, Disguise +5, Driver +18, Escape Artist +6, Intimidate +11, Mechanics +2, Open Lock +6, Perform (Public Speaking) +7, Pilot +9, Profession (Military) +10, Spot +6, Surveillance +8, Survival +8

Feats: Baby It, Demolition Derby, Firm Hand, Hold Together Baby, Oversteer, Offensive Driving, Relentless Pursuit, Speed Demon, Test Lap

ATTACKS

.45 service pistol	+12	1d10+2

Gear: None

Common Gadgets: Radio tooth

HIGH-LEVEL VERSION

Chamber: The Russian Confederacy
Threat: P.E.R.I.L.
Department: Home Office (0)
Class: Wheelman
Level: 16

Strength:	14	**Dexterity:**	16
Constitution:	12	**Intelligence:**	15
Wisdom:	13	**Charisma:**	9
Vitality:	119	**Wounds:**	12

Defense: 23 (+10 class, +3 Dex)
Initiative Bonus: +13 (+10 class, +3 Dex)
Speed: 30

Fort: +6 **Ref:** +13 **Will:** +6

Skills: Balance +6, Boating +16, Bureaucracy +11, Demolitions +10, Disguise +7, Driver +26, Escape Artist +6, Intimidate +18, Mechanics +2, Open Lock +6, Perform (Public Speaking) +12, Pilot +16, Profession (Military) +15, Spot +8, Surveillance +10, Survival +10

Feats: Advanced Skill Mastery (Speed Demon), Baby It, Defensive Driving, Demolition Derby, Firm Hand, Grand Skill Mastery (Speed Demon), Hold Together Baby, Instant Hotwire, Lane Dancer, Oversteer, Offensive Driving, Relentless Pursuit, Speed Demon, Test Lap

ATTACKS

.45 service pistol	+19	1d10+2

Gear: None

Common Gadgets: Radio tooth

"They're stronger than we give them credit for, you know. The rest of the world. That's what makes them so very dangerous."

– Tien-Kai Tsong, Pan-Asian Collective

THE OUTSIDE WORLD

Contested Regions

This section deals with two areas which only irregularly fall within any one Chamber's shadow community, and which are therefore hotbeds of espionage activity.

The Middle East

The Middle East the world recognizes today is a messy aftermath of 20th century colonialism. Its Mediterranean shores have fallen under the rule of a host of conquerors, both foreign and domestic, who built empires rather than countries. The Guardians of the Whispering Knife remember these centuries well. Tracing their lineage as far back as the Zealot dagger men who fought Roman occupation, the Guardians owe no fealty to any specific country or religion currently defining the face of the Middle East.

Unfortunately, the Middle East remains a fractured wall and not as wholly united as the media would have people believe. Thus the Guardians and all regional operatives must familiarize themselves with its 16 unique nations if they wish to operate with an informed mind.

Traveling

Movement between Middle Eastern countries is a tricky endeavor. Many local nations require visas in advance, and routinely turn travelers away. Exceptions include Bahrain, Israel, Jordan, Lebanon, and Turkey, all of which allow tourists to apply for visas upon landing. The same holds for British travelers visiting the United Arab Emirates (UAE). Both Kuwait and Qatar require someone to sponsor anyone seeking a visa, though most reputable hotels can provide this service. Iraq's borders are currently closed to visitors.

Ways around this problem include bribes and entering by ground from another Arab country. The latter solution is safest because many Middle Eastern countries allow for "transit" visas across their territory for travelers trying to reach another nation by car. Notable exceptions include Iraq and Iran, who mine each other's borders almost daily (average of 25 mines per square mile), and Israel. Most Middle Eastern nations refuse someone entry if their passport has an Israeli stamp inside. Egypt and Jordan are far more forgiving of this (on condition of a small "gift"), and smart agents carry passports with false pages that they can rip out in an emergency.

Hotspots

While terrorism and the Israel-Palestinian struggle are Middle Eastern buzzwords and dangerous darlings of the media, they are not the only concerns for groups like the Guardians. The following are "active case files" or issues that require constant protection/surveillance.

Dual Jurisdictions: There are currently two nations who fall into dual jurisdiction status: Egypt and Libya. While both clearly belong to Africa, and thus overlap with African Alliance territory, these two nations' involvement in Middle Eastern affairs places them under the Guardians' political mandate. This collision of jurisdictions has resulted in interpersonal clashes between both factions whenever Libya or Egypt volunteers to host the Pan-Arab Summits.

Oil: Oil is an economic nuclear bomb, and until recently, OPEC (the Organization of Petroleum Exporting Countries) has had its finger on the switch. Saudi Arabia's expansive oil fields provide many nations with their sole source of petroleum. With Russia opening up the Caspian Sea oil fields and undercutting the Organization with its price for crude, however, the OPEC juggernaut is slowly floundering. This has pitted the Guardians against the Russian Confederacy as of late.

Terrorism: Many Arab nations fear terrorism as greatly as the Western Hemisphere does, and not all terrorism is Arabic or Islamic. Middle-Eastern terrorism is often a herald of political dissatisfaction and a move against the ruling body. When the Ayatollah Khomeini overthrew the Shah in 1979, 300 radicals stormed the Grand Mosque in Mecca and took worshippers hostage. Over 250 people died in the 10 days it took to retake the mosque. Ever since, Saudi Arabia has feared a popular revolt from conservative factions. Turkey and Iraq regularly commit atrocities against the Kurds and Armenians, resulting in higher terrorist activity; meanwhile the Mujahedin Khalq Organization, a group operating in Iraq with 35% female membership, wishes to liberate Iran... not to mention the Palestinian liberation cells operating from Southern Lebanon or training camps in Syria, or the Israeli extremists who assassinated Prime Minister Rabin for seeking concessions with the Palestinians.

The Black Market

The Middle East's black market is growing steadily thanks to its proximity to former Soviet-run Azerbaijan, Armenia, and Turkmenistan. A steady supply of Russian-made weapons, helicopters, and tanks find their way into the Middle East through Iran and Iraq. Meanwhile Syria's military ruling body, the Ba'ath, relies on its old contacts within Soviet Russia, hiring specialists and mercenaries from the former Cold War power. There are also allegations that P.E.R.I.L. cells operate in the highest echelons of Syria's government thanks to the Russian advisors.

South America

When the signatory members of the Archer Pact first put pen to paper, South America was little more than an impoverished backwater, a place of such minute political and economic importance that the region never receive a position within the proposed chambers. Both the Archer Foundation and the Company kept an eye on the area, but they believed that no true menace to world stability could arise in the region. This belief was wrong.

The first radical shift in the region followed the close of World War II. Rumors surfaced that the Demagogue's elite inner circle, the Hand of Glory, escaped to secret Argentinean bases and that the Demagogue himself might have accompanied them. While no reputable agency of the day could confirm these rumors, their effect was electric. Hundreds, possibly thousands, of Nazis trickled into the region. Whether the Hand of Glory ever truly relocated there or not, it became a recruiting ground and hiding place for hundreds of sympathizers. This immediately brought the region to the Conspiracy's attention, but it was too late to establish the widespread penetration it enjoys elsewhere.

The situation deteriorated further as cocaine became a major export. Cartels rapidly arose to manage growth, processing and distribution of the drug. These financial juggernauts quickly acquired private armies and networks of informants spanning the globe. The influence of the cartels over local governments eroded the Foundation's efforts to gain control in the area, as powerful overlords bought and sold entire governments and assassination and terror became commonplace. The Company spearheaded an effort to destroy the cartels, but met with only limited success. Recently, the rogue elements of P.E.R.I.L. began funneling information and resources to the cartels.

The modern South American landscape is a collage of extremes: endless expanses of the Amazon Basin nestled against the unforgiving starkness of the Andes Mountains. Vast arid stretches lie only hours from the greatest rainforest in the world. The human landscape is just as diverse, with lavish mansions of the cartel overlords not far from some of the worst slums on Earth. High-tech industry has taken root in the same countries where old-fashioned cowboys still herd livestock from horseback. More than anywhere else, agents here risk injury and even death from the local wildlife – not to mention P.E.R.I.L. operatives in Brazil.

Travel

While South American roads are something of a local joke, river travel and air power make a sizable portion of the continent readily accessible. The physical obstacles and sheer size of the region are often more daunting than the legal hurdles. While traditional requirements for passports and visas remain in place, most areas are so rife with corruption that a few hundred dollars paves the way for all but a column of armored tanks. Paradoxically, high-class accommodations dot the larger cities as much of the region relies on the lucrative tourist trade. Outside of the major urban areas, hotels become almost non-existent, and agents may find themselves boarding with a local or more likely roughing it.

Hotspots

While the entire region is "out of control" by Archer standards, a number of different factors regularly top regional director's action item lists.

Dual Jurisdictions: The Foundation has a tendency to trip over its own feet in South America like nowhere else. The Company has long considered the region "North America's backyard," and take a downright proprietary attitude toward Foundation business in the region. Many speculate that past embarrassments have made them unusually touchy. The Archer Foundation and the PAC also have ties in the region. With massive immigration and investment by the Japanese, Pan-Asian operatives are common in the area. Finally, patriotic elements of Room 39 flooded the region during the Falkland Islands conflict and many of them put down roots after seeing the local level of disorder first-hand.

Cartels: With P.E.R.I.L.'s blessing, the local overlords have begun to strike against the Foundation directly in this region. This is the start of the Foundation's first true hot war, a fight they may not be prepared for. The Company continues to amp up the firepower, but the Foundation's sanctions make this slow-building fight an uphill battle.

Emeralds: South America has always been a major world supplier of emeralds, but with the Shop's defection, this production has taken on a sinister new light. Many of the Shop's newest gadgets contain minute flecks of emeralds in their circuitry. While the Foundation's best remaining mentalists struggle to untangle the principles behind these new devices, simple chemical analysis has conclusively proven that all the gems come from Ecuadorian mines, possibly as few as three. These enormous pits of black earth and heavy machinery rank amongst the most dangerous work environments imaginable (dozens of native workers die each year), and it would be a serious understatement to describe security as "tight."

The Eyes of Argus

ENEMY OF THE FOUNDATION

Founded in 2000, the Eyes of Argus have two primary missions. Their charter is to ferret out events linked to the Archer Conspiracy, and bring them to the public's attention. Privately, the Eyes are also interested in conspiracies and cover-ups in general, and they posted their theories on the Argus website prior to its unexpected shutdown.

Once, the Eyes relied on their audience to keep them safe; so long as it was more dangerous for Archer to eliminate them than to leave them be, the Eyes remained safe from direct retribution. Unfortunately, since their founder went into hiding *(see opposite)*, the site has apparently gone down, replaced with a page for a Foundation front company. Most of the Eyes have followed Argus; a few suffered worse fates.

Membership

With the Argus website down, the Foundation has turned its attention to the real problem – Argus himself – leaving the individual Eyes to their own devices. Most of them continue the effort privately, using the Foundation's search for Argus to gain new information about them, which they promptly pass along to their audience through discreet channels.

The original Eyes of Argus are:

Jonathan Black: Foreign Correspondent

After high school, Johnny grabbed a backpack and took a season off in Europe, always keeping meticulous notes. Six months later, a small overseas publisher offered to print excerpts from his journal and fund another six months of travel. Since then, he has written about several foreign countries, using the pen-name "Johnny B. Goode." His guides are useful, but hard to find.

Jonathan's travels placed him in a position to physically spy on many of the Eyes' targets. Unfortunately, he may have come too close to one of them – Sabine Albrecht *(an alias for Eva Kraus; see page 156)*. Johnny vanished shortly before Argus was revealed, and is still missing.

Augustus Gentry: Photo and Historical Analyst

A Professor of Germanic Religion and a practicing pagan Germanic priest, or Godhi, Augustus spends most of his time teaching classes in Norse Mythology or working on the many papers he publishes under his real name every year.

Gregory Kean: Webmaster

Gregory Kean ("Greg" to his friends) graduated from the University of Miami in 1996 with a BS in Computer Science after spending many hours in the Indy Lab. Until the Argus website went down, he lived in California and worked as a computer technician, devoting his spare time to the group's online concerns. Since then he has lost touch with them, returning to a (mostly) normal life.

Carl McGee: Reporter

Carl is a 20-year veteran reporter who might have had a future in real journalism if it weren't for his big mouth – and integrity. Until last year, Carl jumped from job to job, always hoping for a real gig with a real newspaper, but spent most of his time writing for various tabloids. Carl's work with the Eyes was perhaps broader than others', focusing not only on the Archer Conspiracy but many others as well. Carl continues to write, undaunted by the loss of the Argus website.

"Peregrine": Informant

Argus' "insider" with the U.S. Intelligence community, Peregrine provided the Eyes with information that otherwise would have been unavailable. Peregrine has followed Argus into hiding, hoping that the buffer he placed between himself and the other Eyes will be enough to keep him safe.

DAVID RUSSELL: FINANCIER

A prominent financier during the 1980s, David managed the Eyes' finances until the upset. He has since returned to his position with the high-profile online trading company NetGains. His loyalties, if he has decided them, remain his personal domain.

SAVAGE, LORD REGINALD

MASTERMIND
Aliases: Argus, The "Ghost"
Nationality: British
Gender: Male **Handedness:** Right
Height: 5 ft. 10 in. **Weight:** 160 lbs.
Eyes: Black **Hair:** Black, thinning
Psion Class: Non-latent
Place of Birth: Sussex, England
Date of Birth: 1939.01.06
Distinguishing Characteristics: Always wears black gloves, carries sword-cane

BACKGROUND

Argus has been a thorn in the Archer Foundation's side for many years. First appearing as the "Ghost," a lone computer terrorist wreaking havoc in the electronic records of Room 39's Broken Seal, Argus spent years searching for something in the Foundation's files. Last year, presumably after finding it, he founded the Eyes of Argus *(see opposite)*, a group of (mostly) uninvolved civilians, and charged them with bringing Archer's operations to light.

Then, through an anonymous tip, the Foundation discovered Argus' true identity: Lord Reginald Savage, formerly of Room 39 and a retired legend of the Cold War. This news came as a powerful blow to the Foundation, which had always placed Savage on a high pedestal. His attention to detail, blunt common sense, and industrious nature foiled the plots of countless criminal masterminds, and his eccentricities had never failed to amuse.

But to the Foundation, Savage was now the same as the villains he had helped to bring down. The information he'd sought for so long proved that the Foundation had used Cleaners to liquidate everyone affected by Helix's psion plague in 1975 – including his late wife, Katrina Danilova, a former agent of the Russian Confederacy. For her death, which he could not forgive, he will force the Foundation into the open to answer for their many "crimes against society," or die trying.

LOW-LEVEL VERSION

Threat: Eyes of Argus (formerly Room 39)
Department: Home Office (D-0), retired
Class: Pointman
Level: 3

Strength:	16	**Dexterity:**	12
Constitution:	14	**Intelligence:**	18
Wisdom:	18	**Charisma:**	10
Vitality:	27	**Wounds:**	14

Defense: 2 (+1 class, +1 Dex)
Initiative Bonus: +2 (+1 class, +1 Dex)
Speed: 30

Fort: +4 **Ref:** +3 **Will:** +7

Skills: Bluff +5, Computers +12, Concentration +7, Cultures +5, Driver +2, First Aid +10, Forgery +5, Knowledge (Archer Secrets) +12, Knowledge (Room 39 Secrets) +12, Occult +4, Open Lock +3, Search +6, Sense Motive +8

Feats: Mathematical Genius, Power Attack, Scholarly

ATTACKS

Sword cane	+5	1d6+3

Gear: Laptop computer (+4 rating)

Common Gadgets: None

MID-LEVEL VERSION

Threat: Eyes of Argus (formerly Room 39)
Department: Home Office (D-0), retired
Class: Pointman
Level: 10

Strength:	16	**Dexterity:**	12
Constitution:	14	**Intelligence:**	18
Wisdom:	20	**Charisma:**	10
Vitality:	80	**Wounds:**	14

Defense: 15 (+4 class, +1 Dex)
Initiative Bonus: +5 (+4 class, +1 Dex)
Speed: 30

Fort: +7 **Ref:** +6 **Will:** +12

Skills: Bluff +12, Computers +12, Concentration +14, Cultures +10, Driver +10, First Aid +14, Forgery +12, Knowledge (Archer Secrets) +15, Knowledge (Room 39 Secrets) +17, Occult +8, Open Lock +9, Search +10, Sense Motive +16

Feats: Cleave, Cleaving Charge, Mathematical Genius, Power Attack, Scholarly

Attacks

Sword cane	+10	1d6+3

Gear: Laptop computer (+4 rating)

Common Gadgets: None

High-Level Version

Threat: Eyes of Argus (formerly Room 39)
Department: Home Office (D-0), retired
Class: Pointman
Level: 17

Strength:	16	**Dexterity:**	12
Constitution:	14	**Intelligence:**	18
Wisdom:	20	**Charisma:**	10
Vitality:	132	**Wounds:**	14

Defense: 18 (+7 class, +1 Dex)
Initiative Bonus: +8 (+7 class, +1 Dex)
Speed: 30

Fort: +10 **Ref:** +9 **Will:** +15

Skills: Bluff +18, Computers +14, Concentration +23, Cultures +15, Driver +13, First Aid +18, Forgery +14, Knowledge (Archer Secrets) +22, Knowledge (Room 39 Secrets) +24, Occult +15, Open Lock +16, Search +14, Sense Motive +23

Feats: Cleave, Cleaving Charge, Great Cleave, Mathematical Genius, Power Attack, Scholarly, Trail of Blood

Attacks

Sword cane	+15	1d6+3

Gear: Laptop computer (+4 rating)

Common Gadgets: None

The Hand of Glory

ENEMY OF THE FOUNDATION

This calculating, ruthless organization rose from the ashes of the dismantled Third Reich. Though this group existed in many forms since then, it is known today as The Hand of Glory.

Goal

The Hand of Glory's ultimate goal is simple: global domination. To obtain its objective, the Hand causes chaos, destruction, and terror, usually in specific, strategic locations.

Bases

The Hand of Glory has bases and safe houses scattered all over the world. Its primary headquarters, however, lies in one of the most unforgiving environments on the planet: Antarctica. Located on the Ronne Ice Shelf, the site resembles an insignificant exploration outpost, exactly what its designers had in mind. In truth, however, it is a futuristic fortress, fitted with high-tech defenses, living and training quarters for hundreds of fanatical minions, a retractable airfield, and a submarine base beneath the ice.

Many Hand of Glory operations have focused on protecting the location of their headquarters, including the coercion of several world leaders, who later went on to ensure that the icy continent remain a world "free zone." This has largely allowed the organization to avoid public scrutiny.

Other notable locations used by the Hand of Glory include Lÿceanu Castle in the Carpathian Mountains (where Hand soldiers are typically trained), Zumwald Keep in Bavaria (where Hand recruits are often subjected to mind-control conditioning derived from the Demagogue's frozen body – *see page 46*) and De Oro Valley in Chile (where Hand scientists have set up several research facilities).

Organization

Eva Kraus *(see page 156)* lords over the Hand of Glory, and wields her authority with an iron fist. Eva created the Hand, and considers every base, every artifact, and every minion hers. She is not above punishing those who disobey her orders, nor using unsavory methods to do so.

The rest of the organization follows a loose structure. Directly under Kraus stand her loyal lieutenants. Politics among these twenty men and women are incredibly cut-throat, both figuratively and literally, each trying to one-up the others to gain influence and power. The four most successful (i.e. ruthless) use the dubious codenames Flashfire, Jackboot, Dozer, and Nova.

The lieutenants each command thousands of loyal minions, recruited from almost every nation and social class, who have come to see The Hand of Glory as an instrument to usher in a new age for humanity. The vast majority of these men and women have been ritually brainwashed, their memories and personalities wiped away and replaced with a template created by Eva's brutal telepaths. After the process, Hand of Glory minions are literally incapable of betraying the organization, let alone disobeying a command. If ordered to, they would readily die in battle (a purpose for which Eva or her lieutenants will happily direct them should they require a distraction). Minions work in squads of ten to twenty, depending on the needs of each operation.

Lastly come those individuals and organizations that serve the Hand of Glory without realizing it. Kraus has key agents pulling the strings of some of the world's most notorious militant groups, including the Neo-Nazis, Ku Klux Klan, Hamas, and many separatist militias.

Recruiting Methods

For a secret organization, the Hand of Glory is surprisingly well-staffed. Mercenaries, criminals, and thugs make up a significant part of the rank and file, kept in line through Kraus' personal charisma, the lure of power, and any number of other base motives. But the Hand needs average citizens as well and lures them in using many methods.

One of the most effective recruiting techniques is also one of the most subtle. Kraus witnessed firsthand the effectiveness of propaganda wielded by the Demagogue during the Second World War, and now uses similar tactics for her own purposes. Three of her lieutenants and dozens of her regular sycophants hold key positions in popular media, slipping subliminal messages into advertising and entertainment with equal ease.

Two of the most successful forays include:

Mind Over Matter

Called a pseudo-religion by many, Dr. J. Van Houston's series of self-help books and tapes have become a phenomenon over the past thirty-five years, helping people "unlock their ultimate potential and become fully actualized human beings." Those who follow Houston's advice and exercises unwittingly become more susceptible to various subliminal messages the Hand employs.

Zeta Omega Delta

A growing collegiate fraternity that has taken root in several prominent campuses in North America and Europe, Zeta Omega Delta holds its members to the higher standards. Only the best and brightest young men are admitted after a careful screening process; they favor impressionable minds from rich families. The loyalties and contacts forged among its members serve to shape and mold the future leaders of the Hand. Once a pledge joins, he stays a Zeta Man for life.

Funding

The Hand of Glory has been quite proficient in acquiring capital for its operations. It uses many illicit methods (arms and drug smuggling are two favorites), but also a surprising number of perfectly legal ventures. Just because these enterprises are legitimate, however, does not make them virtuous.

Banks, savings and loans, and credit card companies make great fronts for the Hand, allowing it to launder illegal money with ease. Investment and real-estate brokerages are also successful money makers, as are Johnson, Macbane, and Sato (a multi-national firm specializing in international law) and Grandeur Records (an aggressive music label known for both its diverse artists and popular boy bands).

A significant number of freight, shipping and trucking services around the world are at least partially owned by agents of the Hand, and carry steady traffic in materials, goods, and even troops. Attempts to infiltrate passenger services such as airlines, rail companies, and even cruise ships have met with only moderate success – partially due to the public nature of these services, but primarily because the Archer Foundation has already made significant progress with them.

The Hand has also made active use of various segments of industry, sometimes to its advantage and sometimes to its detriment *(see Green Lucifer and Mr. Gaunt, below)*. The most profitable and serviceable company is the international Iron Seed Corporation, which originated as a supplier of agricultural products but quickly branched out into other lucrative areas – including service contracts for the United States, Canada, Great Britain, Australia, Germany, and Israel. Funded by tax revenues, Iron Seed researches and produces everything from chemical agents for crops to environmentally friendly plastics. It really makes a profit, however, in secretly developing weapons for its government patrons. Of course, Iron Seed covertly keeps the technology for itself as well.

Artifacts and Rituals

Thanks to the secret source of Kraus' power *(see opposite)*, the Hand of Glory has a deep interest in mystic artifacts and knowledge of occult importance. Hand patrons routinely fund archaeological digs and anthropological expeditions, and Hand agents often infiltrate such expeditions, yielding the organization not only powerful relics but the educated minds that understand them. The Hand originally focused its efforts on items of Germanic and Norse myth, but now hunts for items and secrets of all cultures. The Guardians of the Whispering Knife have had several bloody confrontations with the Hand of Glory. Both sides of this quiet war have vowed to destroy the other.

Ritual magic plays an important role in Kraus' schemes. She takes great care in cultivating Hand members who have the belief and understanding necessary to fuel these arcane rites, who can release and control mystic energies unseen for centuries. The Guardians of the Whispering Knife are keenly aware of this influx of magical power and are doing their best to counter it.

Current Plotlines

The Hand of Glory is behind many of the troubles in the Shadowforce Archer setting. Here are two of the current plots it has a hand in.

The Green Lucifer

Dedicated to the ideals of chaos and terror, the Hand of Glory has a new tool at its disposal – a little device Hand scientists dubbed "The Green Lucifer." About the size of a pack of cigarettes, the Green Lucifer emits an ultrasonic frequency specifically designed to trigger human adrenal responses, effectively enhancing any emotion. With a radius of approximately thirty feet, the device has proven especially adept at triggering anger and hostilities. The Hand is preparing to use dozens of Green Lucifers at crowded events around the world, from sporting venues to concerts to political rallies, as part of a larger operation.

Mr. Gaunt

Not every Hand research project yields results like the Green Lucifer, much to the horror of scientists in De Oro valley. At a discreet Iron Seed facility, doctors experimented with enhancing and controlling the abilities of some of the world's most brutal criminals. A subject known only as "Mr. Gaunt" became too powerful for his masters to manipulate and escaped, leaving a trail of carnage behind him. Reports indicate that he has manifested stunning physical adept and telepath traits. Due to countless experimental procedures, his body operates at an astonishing metabolic rate and he appears impervious to pain.

Kraus, Eva

MASTERMIND
Aliases: Evelyn Schillingsfield, Eva Hitler
Nationality: British
Gender: Female **Handedness:** Right
Height: 5 ft. 11 in. **Weight:** 150 lbs.
Eyes: Blue **Hair:** White
Mystic Class: Grade A (and beyond)
Place of Birth: Bristol, England
Date of Birth: 1857.11.25
Distinguishing Characteristics: Mystic symbol appears on palm when Eva draws on the mystic powers of the entity within her

Background

The Archer Foundation's search for Eva Kraus, wife of the man who became Helix and the founder of the Hand of Glory, is codenamed Hecate. This is a top priority for all Chambers, with at least twenty agents assigned to it at any given time.

Eva was once known as Evelyn Schillingsfield, but she has not been human for decades. She was subsumed by a vicious entity considered ancient even by the elder Guardians of the Whispering Knife. This being uses her as a tool to return the world to the state it remembers from its birth: the Ice Age. Through this entity, Eva has received the wisdom of ages, incredible mystic power, and apparent immortality.

Yet she is still incomplete. Once, the entity within her had a companion which ruled by its side, a being of equal power but opposite temperament, a being of fiery wrath. Eva has spent the last hundred years searching for this twin, buried by their enemies thousands of years ago.

The Third Reich rose to power partly with her help, as she recovered the third Minoan psion formula and granted its power to the Demagogue, Adolf Hitler. But this was merely one step – at the end of World War II, Eva trapped the Demagogue in a block of ice, lingering between life and death, and used his powers of mind-control to dominate her minions, the mystically-enhanced shock-troops of the Hand of Glory.

(Eva is a criminal mastermind – see page 246 for details about her organization)

LOW-LEVEL VERSION

Threat: The Hand of Glory
Department: None
Class: Pointman
Level: 7

Strength:	12	**Dexterity:**	10
Constitution:	16	**Intelligence:**	16
Wisdom:	18	**Charisma:**	16
Vitality:	64	**Wounds:**	16

Defense: 13 (+3 class)
Initiative Bonus: +3 (+3 class)
Speed: 30

Fort: +7 **Ref:** +4 **Will:** +9

Skills: Bluff +10, Concentration +10, Cryptography +8, Cultures +12, Disguise +10, Escape Artist +10, Gather Information +10, Hide +10, Innuendo +10, Intimidate +10, Knowledge (The Ancients) +10, Knowledge (Occult and Mystic Artifacts) +10, Languages +11, Listen +10, Move Silently +10, Occult +11

Feats: Dodging Arts, Endurance, Kicking Arts, Martial Arts

ATTACKS

Lightning Bolt	Special	1d6/10 minions used

Gear: 100 bonded minions

MID-LEVEL VERSION

Threat: The Hand of Glory
Department: None
Class: Pointman
Level: 14

Strength:	12	**Dexterity:**	10
Constitution:	16	**Intelligence:**	16
Wisdom:	20	**Charisma:**	16
Vitality:	124	**Wounds:**	16

Defense: 16 (+6 class)
Initiative Bonus: +6 (+6 class)
Speed: 30

Fort: +9 **Ref:** +6 **Will:** +14

Skills: Bluff +11, Concentration +15, Cryptography +10, Cultures +20, Disguise +13, Escape Artist +12, Gather Information +15, Hide +10, Innuendo +12, Intimidate +14, Knowledge (The Ancients) +15, Knowledge (Occult and Mystic Artifacts) +15, Languages +18, Listen +16, Move Silently +15, Occult +18

Feats: Blind Fight, Dodging Arts, Dodging Mastery, Endurance, Kicking Arts, Martial Arts

ATTACKS

Lightning Bolt	Special	1d6/10 minions used

Gear: 500 bonded minions

HIGH-LEVEL VERSION

Threat: The Hand of Glory
Department: None
Class: Pointman
Level: 20

Strength:	12	**Dexterity:**	10
Constitution:	16	**Intelligence:**	16
Wisdom:	22	**Charisma:**	16
Vitality:	168	**Wounds:**	16

Defense: 18 (+8 class)
Initiative Bonus: +8 (+8 class)
Speed: 30

Fort: +12 **Ref:** +9 **Will:** +18

Skills: Bluff +13, Concentration +21, Cryptography +13, Cultures +28, Disguise +18, Escape Artist +12, Gather Information +18, Hide +10, Innuendo +24, Intimidate +25, Knowledge (The Ancients) +15, Knowledge (Occult and Mystic Artifacts) +21, Languages +24, Listen +16, Move Silently +15, Occult +25

Feats: Blind Fight, Blindsight 5' Radius, Dodging Arts, Dodging Mastery, Endurance, Kicking Arts, Kicking Mastery, Martial Arts

ATTACKS

Lightning Bolt	Special	1d6/10 minions used

Gear: 2,000 bonded minions

THE SHOP

ENEMY OF THE FOUNDATION

Nam et ipsa scientia potestas est.
"Knowledge itself is power."

–Francis Bacon

The newest threat to the Archer Foundation originates from within. The Shop – techno-wizards capable of breaking the boundaries of ordinary science by virtue of the mentalist psion formula, captured from Helix in 1975 – has seceded from Archer, breaking free and forming its own organization. In doing so, it has robbed the Foundation of one of its greatest strengths, the PsiTech with which it outwits its opponents.

But the Shop's break cuts much more deeply than the loss of PsiTech. Archer can no longer be sure of its own agents. The Shop belonged to the Conspiracy for over 25 years. It understands the system – and how to use it against the Foundation. Anyone might be an Archer plant. The threat is not merely limited to former (or current) Shop operatives.

GOAL

The Shop's reasons for breaking away are still unknown, though the Foundation is reasonably certain that the mentalists have a grand scheme of some kind, and that their betrayal was just the first step toward something much worse. Evidence of their plans dates back several years *(at least – see "One Step Ahead," opposite)*, and Shop activity since the break has been much more frequent and well-executed than the Foundation would expect from a reactive enemy.

Most Shop operations focus on medical and biomechanical research. Specifically, they have performed several raids on leading unaligned research facilities, capturing samples of dangerous toxins, experimental vaccines, and (perhaps most worrisome) nanotechnology. In every case, they have sterilized the site, leaving no evidence trail.

BASES

The Shop spent many years preparing to leave the Conspiracy, and by the time their plan went into action earlier this year, they already had several isolated headquarters prepared. Each is a fully operational scientific research station protected by rogue operatives (and new recruits) using weapons and vehicles stolen from Archer or improved since the break.

The most frustrating feature of Shop outposts, however, is that they are completely unconnected to the rest of the organization. Of the four bases that Archer operatives have discovered – outside Bangor, Maine (U.S.A.); in Mors, Denmark; near Khaskovo, Bulgaria; and along the coast northeast of Odessa in the former Soviet Union–none was even equipped to contact another base, let alone the organization's central headquarters.

Each Shop outpost has a specific purpose which it fulfills without direction or support. For instance, the directive of the Bangor installation was limited to developing a single piece of technology – the anti-psi grenade *(see page 204)*. The Mors base produced nothing but information, running an endless number of computerized spy-vs-spy simulations in a fractal-based virtual environment, many of which mirror recent Shop operations. The Bulgarian outpost's directive involved using gene-splicing to produce an aggressive aberrant cell, although Archer was unable to determine what, if any, use this cell had. Finally, the Odessa base – all nine acres of it – was devoted to building a piece of PsiTech three inches across, fully self-contained, with no apparent link to any other device and no evident function.

Based on these limited examples, the Foundation has come to the conclusion that there are at least two types of Shop bases at present. The first produces weapons and devices of obvious purpose, such as the anti-psi grenade (though how the organization distributes such items remains unknown), and the second focuses on parts of a larger program, most likely connected to the reason the Shop broke away.

ORGANIZATION

There must be a central office for the Shop, if with no other function than to send out the agent teams that Archer is contending with of late. Unfortunately, it appears that the most direct method of discovering this base's location – interviewing captured Shop operatives – is not an effective option *(see "One Step Ahead," opposite)*. Currently, the Foundation lacks even the most rudimentary information to deduce its internal organization, though there are two leading theories.

Some believe that everything the Foundation has seen about the Shop to date is a lie, a smokescreen built to keep Archer away from the true organization long enough for the Shop to achieve a certain level of strength or accomplish some sinister goal. In Archer's experience, this option is most plausible, though unappealing.

A minority theory holds that the Shop has only one important base, from which all active operations originate; everything else supports this one group. Given the years of planning that went into the Shop's rise as a criminal empire, most Archer strategists roundly reject this idea.

Regardless of its organization, the Shop employs several important lieutenants to plan and lead operations in the field. Archer has identified two prominent Shop agents:

- **Kryptos:** A Shop Pointman who delights in confusing Archer's operatives with complex personalized "games" designed to conceal his real intentions (or just annoy the opposition).
- **Strik-9:** One of the most deadly individuals in the world, Strik-9 is an inhumanly fast and agile genetic mutation whose blood has been converted into a lethal poison. Strik-9 employs a wide variety of blades which he coats with samples of his own blood, though he favors a pair which attach over his hands and extend six inches out from each finger, allowing him to swipe directly at enemies. The attachments prick each finger, draining just enough blood to automatically (and continually) coat each blade.

One Step Ahead...

Prior to its betrayal, the Shop employed most of the world's precogs (psions capable of limited future-sight). These men and women were remarkably handy, often receiving hunches about the proper devices to issue to agents who were about to go out into the field. Nearly all of these men and women went with the Shop, and now help the organization to stay one step ahead of the Foundation.

The Shop has also developed a foolproof method for protecting its agents' secrets. Should telepaths attempt to make contact with a Shop agent's mind, a surgically implanted device emits lethal feedback, usually killing both parties. The few who have survived this experience currently languish in a vegetative state, permanent patients of the Foundation's medical division. Archer's finest surgeons have attempted to physically remove the implants, though the attempt has always resulted in the death of the Shop operative.

Current Plotlines

The Foundation works constantly to decipher the logic behind the Shop's actions. Two activities under review at this time are:

Stockholm, Sweden

The Shop has begun tracking Foundation movements in northern Europe, feeding currency marked with a low-grade radioactive isotope into the hands of local Archer agents. Commonwealth spies recently discovered this operation when they found the isotope during a visit to a Confederacy Hot Suite (biocontainment facility). Archer has not yet tipped off the Shop, hoping to use the discovery to track the criminal organization.

Goose Bay, Newfoundland

After revealing Shop saboteurs at the Goose Bay military air base, a Company helicopter crew engaged them in a prolonged river chase. None of the Shop agents were captured, but the chase revealed a dangerous new invention at their disposal – a synthetic armor the Foundation calls Ballistic Flesh *(see page 210)*.

Gray, Dennis

MASTERMIND
Aliases: Dennis March, Jason Östberg
Nationality: United States of America
Gender: Male **Handedness:** Right
Height: 5 ft. 10 in. **Weight:** 150 lbs.
Eyes: Brown **Hair:** Gray
Psion Class: Mentalist
Place of Birth: San Francisco, U.S.A.
Date of Birth: 1960.07.02
Distinguishing Characteristics: Bushy eyebrows, square jaw

Background

Dennis Gray was practically born on the fast track to stardom in the U.S. intelligence community. Almost a year before graduating from UC Berkeley with a Master's in Computer Science, Gray was recruited into NSA, where he quickly made a name for himself and attracted the attention of the Archer Foundation. Two years later, after Archer decided that he was "Company material," Gray joined the Conspiracy as a specialist.

Gray became a Foundation agent during Operation GAINSBOROUGH in 1992, when he helped the Company flush out a Shop mole in NSA. Unknown to his fellow Archer agents, however, he was contacted by a second

Shop mole who offered him inside knowledge about his new employers and a lucrative and powerful position in their criminal organization if he betrayed Archer.

So began nine years of scheming. His rise to Chamber Control was a synthesis of charisma, careful planning, and treachery, which left a powerful Shop ally in a position very close to the Foundation's heart. Gray used this position to secretly administer the Shop's U.S. interests and prepare for their betrayal; by 2002, much of the Company was connected to the Shop, whose departure nearly destroyed the Chamber. Gray spared them, however, perhaps in search of a worthy opponent.

(Dennis is a criminal mastermind – see page 244 for details about his organization)

Low-Level Version

Threat: The Shop (formerly The Company)
Department: None
Class: Wheelman
Level: 2

Strength:	14	**Dexterity:**	16
Constitution:	13	**Intelligence:**	12
Wisdom:	13	**Charisma:**	12
Vitality:	18	**Wounds:**	13

Defense: 14 (+1 class, +3 Dex)
Initiative Bonus: +4 (+1 class, +3 Dex)
Speed: 30

Fort: +1 **Ref:** +6 **Will:** +1

Skills: Balance +4, Boating +6, Bureaucracy +2, Computers +2, Cryptography +2, Driver +6, Electronics +2, Intimidate +2, Mechanics +4, Pilot +6, Spot +2, Surveillance +2

Feats: Speed Demon, Surge of Speed

Attacks

7.62×39 SAW machinegun	+5	4d4
.45 service pistol	+5	1d10+2

Common Gadgets: Sagittarius (his personal favorite), ballistic flesh, anti-psi grenades (5)

Mid-Level Version

Threat: The Shop (formerly The Company)
Department: None
Class: Wheelman
Level: 9

Strength:	14	**Dexterity:**	17
Constitution:	14	**Intelligence:**	12
Wisdom:	13	**Charisma:**	12
Vitality:	72	**Wounds:**	14

Defense: 18 (+5 class, +3 Dex)
Initiative Bonus: +8 (+5 class, +3 Dex)
Speed: 30

Fort: +5 **Ref:** +9 **Will:** +4

Skills: Balance +5, Bluff +4, Boating +6, Bureaucracy +3, Computers +3, Cryptography +3, Demolitions +6, Disguise +5, Driver +8, Electronics +5, Intimidate +6, Mechanics +8, Open Lock +6, Pilot +8, Spot +6, Surveillance +6

Feats: Defensive Driving, Grease Monkey, In My Sights, Mobility, Offensive Driving, One Hand on the Wheel, Shot on the Run, Sidestep, Speed Demon, Surge of Speed

Attacks

7.62×39 SAW machinegun	+12	4d4
.45 service pistol	+12	1d10+2

Common Gadgets: Sagittarius (his personal favorite), ballistic flesh, anti-psi grenades (5)

High-Level Version

Threat: The Shop (formerly The Company)
Department: None
Class: Wheelman
Level: 16

Strength:	14	**Dexterity:**	17
Constitution:	14	**Intelligence:**	13
Wisdom:	13	**Charisma:**	13
Vitality:	125	**Wounds:**	14

Defense: 23 (+10 class, +3 Dex)
Initiative Bonus: +13 (+10 class, +3 Dex)
Speed: 30

Fort: +7 **Ref:** +13 **Will:** +6

Skills: Balance +10, Bluff +8, Boating +10, Bureaucracy +4, Computers +5, Cryptography +5, Demolitions +11, Disguise +16, Driver +15, Electronics +6, Intimidate +8, Mechanics +9, Open Lock +6, Pilot +10, Spot +6, Surveillance +7

Feats: Baby It, Defensive Driving, Diving Shot, Grease Monkey, Hold Together Baby, In My Sights, Lock it Down, Mobility, Offensive Driving, One Hand on the Wheel, Shot on the Run, Sidestep, Speed Demon, Surge of Speed

Attacks

7.62×39 SAW machinegun	+19	4d4
.45 service pistol	+19	1d10+2

Common Gadgets: Sagittarius (his personal favorite), ballistic flesh, anti-psi grenades (5)

"Now listen up, you international playboy maggots! In the real world, all your mind games, chemical strength, and parlor tricks won't save your worthless hides! Come Doomsday, all you have are your instincts, and two weeks with me."

– Nostrum, The Archer Foundation

NEW AGENT OPTIONS

Shadowforce Archer Agents: Step-by-Step

The standard process for creating an agent is described in Chapters 1-4 of the *Spycraft Espionage Handbook*. This section is supplementary to that material, and presents the differences between designing an agent for the Shadowforce Archer world setting, and designing one for a more generic setting.

Unchanged Steps

Steps 0 (checking with your GC and the other players), 1 (ability scores), 4 (assigning and adjusting your ability scores), 5 (recording department and class features), 6 (selecting skills), 8 (selecting backgrounds), 9 (recording derived values), 10 (requisitioning starting gear), and 11 (fleshing out your agent) are all unchanged.

1.5 Choose Chamber

Choose your agent's original Chamber (where he was recruited and trained) from the following list.

- African Alliance
- Archer Foundation
- Company
- European Commonwealth
- Guardians of the Whispering Knife
- Pan-Asian Collective
- Room 39
- Russian Confederacy

This added step has no mechanical effect on your agent (outside of opening up a few feat and gear choices). The Chambers are all equivalent in the basic *Shadowforce Archer* setting.

2. Choose Department

Each of the Foundation's Chambers has divisions equivalent to the departments presented in *Spycraft*. Thus, your agent may come from any department, regardless of his Chamber *(see next)*. Of course, some combinations (especially some of the established departments, such as the Power Brokerage, being chosen by a Guardian) may seem strange, but remember that the Foundation actively exchanges agents between Chambers to cross-pollinate skills and experience. Once again, consult your GC if you have any questions, and eliminate any combinations you're not comfortable with.

3. Choose Class

Your agent may be from any class presented in *Spycraft*. In addition, this book includes three new base classes.

- Mentalist
- Physical Adept
- Telepath

Each of these base classes is described in Chapter 5.

This book also presents five prestige classes – classes you must multiclass to enter, with certain prerequisites you must fulfill before you can take them.

- Cat Burglar
- Counter-terrorist
- Hacker
- Sniper

Each of these prestige classes is described later in this chapter.

The final prestige class – the shadespeaker – is only available to Guardians of the Whispering Knife. It is described in Chapter 6: The Mystic World.

7. Select Feats

In addition to the feats listed in the *Spycraft Espionage Handbook,* most agents may also choose from mystic feats *(see page 218),* and if you are a psion psion, physical, mentalist, or telepath feats *(see Chapter 5),* as appropriate.

Additional Agent Options

Shadowforce Archer presents a few more options, some of which are only available to agents of certain Chambers and backgrounds.

Chemical monsters: Russian Confederacy agents may, with GC approval, choose chems *(see page 172)* to augment their agent. Chems are dangerous and usually have a lasting effect on the agent and the game. We do not advise GCs to include them in early Shadowforce Archer games.

New gadgets: A host of new gadgets (called "PsiTech" in *Shadowforce Archer*) can be found on page 203.

Prestige Classes

Prestige classes represent specific strengths of the Archer Foundation, those agents who have specialized skills and abilities. Some prestige classes are story-specific, while others are advanced professions, specialties, or archtypes. Some prestige classes are obvious extensions of base classes (the hacker, for example, is an obvious extension of the snoop); others are entirely new concepts.

Within this book, we've included five prestige classes, with more to follow in each *Shadowforce Archer* supplement.

Game Control Alert

Prestige classes are always optional. Some may not meet the tone or power level the GC has set for his game, and so he may always choose not to include a prestige class in his game. Classes banned for agents should also be banned for NPCs.

Choosing a Prestige Class

A newly created (1st-level) agent may not choose a prestige class, as agents must meet certain requirements before multiclassing into them – often including a specified agent level and certain "in-game" conditions, such as actions that must have been performed or membership in exclusive organizations. Once an agent meets these requirements, however, he is free to multiclass into and out of these classes as if they were one of the six classes presented in the *Spycraft Espionage Handbook*.

All rules for multiclassing apply when choosing a prestige class. *(See page 34 of the Spycraft Espionage Handbook for more information about multiclassing.)*

Each of these prestige classes is described later in this chapter.

Losing Prerequisites

Should an agent gain levels in a prestige class, then somehow no longer meet the prerequisites (for example, when a Sniper enters old age, his Dexterity might fall below the prerequisite score), he loses all special abilities granted by that class. The agent still retains the base attack bonus, saves, initiative bonus, defense bonus, gadget points, and budget points granted by the class, as well as any skills and feats he may have acquired while a member of the class.

Prestige Classes and NPCs

These classes are not available solely to agents; anything the agents can do unto others, can also be done unto them. The GC should feel free to create henchmen, foils, masterminds, and other NPCs – friend or foe – with levels in a prestige class. Keep in mind, though, that prestige classes are a relative rarity. If the agents run into snipers every mission, the novelty will quickly wear thin. But when used sparingly, prestige classes can easily contribute to creating a memorable villain or NPC.

Prestige classes are also highly effective for defining the setting, personalizing it through its characters.

Prestige Class Core Abilities

In most ways, prestige classes operate the same as base classes – with one exception. You may gain the core ability of one prestige class in addition to the core ability of your base class. However, you only gain the core abilities of the first base class and the first prestige class you enter, no matter how many times you multiclass thereafter.

Cat Burglar

While fixers are usually well-suited for the trespassing needs of a field team, they are not always adequately prepared to break into impossibly high security facilities, and evade the authorities after completing the mission. Cat burglars excel at such assignments. Masters of stealth, breaking and entering, and second-story work, the cat burglars' connections to the criminal underworld – specifically in the area of fencing or tracing stolen goods – can be extremely useful, as can their formidable social skills.

Abilities: Cat burglars rely on a variety of Dexterity-based skills, so that is their most important ability. Intelligence plays a large role as well, to grant them the skill points for the wide array of skills at their disposal.

Vitality: 1d8 plus Constitution modifier per level

Requirements

To become a cat burglar, an agent must meet all of the following requirements.

Agent Level: 5+
Climb: 8 ranks
Open Lock: 8 ranks
Feats: Acrobatic, Master Fence

Class Skills

The cat burglar's class skills and key abilities are listed below:

Class Skill	Key Ability
Appraise	Int
Balance	Dex
Bluff	Cha
Boating	Dex
Climb	Str
Concentration	Wis
Craft	Int
Driver	Dex
Electronics	Int

Escape Artist	Dex
Hide	Dex
Hobby	Wis
Jump	Str
Knowledge	Int
Listen	Wis
Move Silently	Dex
Open Lock	Dex
Pilot	Dex
Profession	Wis
Search	Int
Sleight of Hand	Dex
Spot	Wis
Surveillance	Wis
Tumble	Dex
Use Rope	Dex

Skill Points at Each Level: 8 + Int modifier.

CLASS FEATURES

All of the following are class features of the cat burglar:

Class Feats: The cat burglar gains the following feats at 1st level.

Armor Proficiency (Light)
Weapon Group Proficiency (Melee)
Weapon Group Proficiency (Hurled)

Nimble: The agent gains a +1 Department bonus to all Dexterity skill checks. This is the cat burglar's core ability.

Case: The trick to defeating modern security is knowing exactly what you are facing, and what it can't see. Facilities have a security rating of 0 to 10 *(as explained in the Mastermind system on page 246 of the Spycraft Espionage Handbook)*. The agent may spend one hour moving around within line of sight of one or more buildings to "scout" the site, making a Surveillance check with a DC of 20 + the facility's security rating to learn the security rating of that facility.

At 5th level, the agent may spend 1 BP or $100 in field expenses to acquire plans and equipment to 'foil' building security, reducing the effective security rating of a facility he has already successfully cased by 1. He may do this a number of times per serial equal to his cat burglar class level.

At 9th level, the agent's expertise with circumventing security devices and patrols extends to the rest of his team during a covert penetration. As long as the cat burglar remains in verbal or visual contact with the rest of the team, the reduced security rating (from use of the foil ability) applies to his entire team. If any team members are not in contact with the cat burglar, they do not receive this benefit (though any other team members in contact with the cat burglar do).

Honor Among Thieves: The criminal underworld is a society unto itself, one that respects accomplishment as much as it shuns outsiders and newcomers. There is a fierce sense of fraternity amongst recognized "operators," all of whom thumb their noses at "The Man." Beginning at 2nd level, the disposition of other criminals improves by one grade when he introduces himself and offers his criminal "handle." This bonus is applied after the normal roll to improve an NPC's disposition.

At 7th level, the agent's reputation becomes so impressive that criminal's disposition increases by two grades. Keep in mind that allies and helpful NPCs expect to be treated with respect in return, and hope to get a piece of the action (usually a monetary reward) by making themselves of service to a criminal as skilled as the agent is reputed to be.

Bonus Feat: At 3rd level, the cat burglar receives a bonus covert or skill feat. He must still meet all prerequisites for this feat. He receives another bonus feat from these trees at 5th, 7th, and 9th level.

Go to Ground: By necessity as much as training, the cat burglar is an expert at evading pursuers – particularly the authorities. He knows all the secret

TABLE 4.1: THE CAT BURGLAR

Lvl	Base Att Bon	Fort Save	Ref Save	Will Save	Def Bon	Init Bon	Budg Pts	Gadg Pts	Special
1	+0	+0	+2	+0	+1	+1	3	0	Case (scout), *nimble*
2	+1	+0	+3	+0	+2	+1	6	1	Honor among thieves
3	+1	+1	+3	+1	+3	+2	9	2	Bonus feat
4	+2	+1	+4	+1	+3	+2	12	3	Go to ground (hiding), improvise tools
5	+2	+1	+4	+1	+4	+3	15	3	Bonus feat, case (foil)
6	+3	+2	+5	+2	+5	+4	18	4	"Do I want to know?"
7	+3	+2	+5	+2	+6	+4	21	5	Bonus feat, Honor among thieves
8	+4	+2	+6	+2	+6	+5	24	6	Go to ground (chases), sucker punch
9	+4	+3	+6	+3	+7	+5	27	6	Bonus feat, case (penetrate)
10	+5	+3	+7	+3	+8	+6	30	7	Impossible dodge

paths, underground clubs, and people who can help him escape – or how to find them. At 4th level, the agent may never completely fail a Hide or Move Silently check to evade a pursuer so long as he is able to break away from their line of sight at least once and does not roll an error. Further, when the agent rolls an error using Hide or Move Silently, the GC must spend an extra action die to activate a critical failure.

At 8th level, while in a chase as the prey, the agent may select finishing maneuvers as if his lead were 5 lengths higher than it really is.

Improvise Tools: Starting at 4th level, the cat burglar suffers no penalties to his Climb and Open Lock skill checks due to the lack of an appropriate kit (climbing, lockpicking, etc.).

"Do I Want to Know?": Cat burglars sometimes seem to come up with handy items... without a receipt. The agent may spend an hour to "acquire" any item costing less than $200. He may only do so a number of times per serial equal to his cat burglar class level. Multiple uses of this ability cannot be combined to acquire more expensive items. All such items are removed from play at the end of the serial (mission) – they probably find their way back onto that truck they fell off of. Maybe.

Sucker Punch: While the cat burglar shies away from combat, chance encounters with guards are unavoidable. In these cases, the burglar prefers to keep the fighting short and the legal consequences to a minimum. Starting at 8th level, when making an attack that causes subdual damage, the burglar does not have to spend an action die to convert a threat to a critical.

Impossible Dodge: There is one last thing a master thief absolutely detests – pain. At 10th level, when the cat burglar is struck by a critical hit, he may make a Reflex save with a DC equal to the damage of the attack. If the save succeeds, the critical is canceled and the damage is applied to his vitality instead.

Counter-Terrorist

One of the most dire threats to peace in the modern world are the terrorist organizations that target civilian property and lives. Fighting such a threat requires a different kind of soldier, trained for a different kind of battlefield.

While many nations maintain their own counter-terrorist task forces, the Archer Foundation would be remiss in its mission if it ignored such threats. Counter-terrorists often work with teams of agents to provide advice and expertise in situations where civilian lives are at risk.

Abilities: As with any soldier, the physical abilities – Strength, Dexterity, and Constitution – are important. However, as counter-terrorists often operate in urban environments, often with civilians confusing the situation, high Wisdom and Charisma scores are also important, sometimes even outweighing the more martial abilities.

Vitality: 1d10 plus Constitution modifier per level

Requirements

To become a counter-terrorist, an agent must meet all of the following requirements.

Base Attack Bonus: +5
Spot: 8 ranks
Sense Motive: 4 ranks
Feats: Precise Shot

Class Skills

The counter-terrorist class skills and key abilities are listed below:

Class Skill	Key Ability
Balance	Dex
Bluff	Cha
Climb	Str
Craft	Int
Demolitions	Int
Diplomacy	Cha
Driver	Dex
First Aid	Wis
Hobby	Wis

Intimidate	Str or Cha
Jump	Str
Knowledge	Int
Move Silently	Dex
Profession	Wis
Search	Int
Sense Motive	Wis
Spot	Wis
Surveillance	Wis
Swim	Str
Use Rope	Dex

Skill Points at Each Level: 6 + Int modifier.

Class Features

All of the following are class features of the counter-terrorist.

Class Feats: The counter-terrorist gains the following feats at 1st level.

Armor Proficiency (Light)
Armor Proficiency (Medium)
Armor Proficiency (Heavy)
Weapon Group Proficiency (Melee)
Weapon Group Proficiency (Handgun)
Weapon Group Proficiency (Rifle)
Weapon Group Proficiency (Tactical)

Quick-Thinking: The agent rolls two dice whenever he spends an action die to add to an initiative roll. Further, the agent may perform a regroup action while fighting defensively, gaining a +4 to his Defense that round. This is the counter-terrorist's core ability.

Special Tactics: The counter-terrorist is a highly trained operative dedicated to finding and neutralizing threats hiding in highly populated areas. This calls for careful observation and precise weapons control. At 1st level, the agent ignores penalties to his Listen, Search, and Spot rolls caused by the presence of crowds.

At 5th level, the agent may make attacks which cause normal damage, converting the damage into subdual damage, without suffering the –4 penalty to his attack roll.

Finally, at 9th level, the agent never completely fails a Listen, Search or Spot check while searching a person for hidden weapons, unless he rolls an error. Even when an error is rolled, the GC must spend an extra action die to activate a critical failure.

Precision Takedown: The counter-terrorist frequently works in cramped spaces (like airliners, crowded subways, and even inside homes) and may have to deal with enemies who use human shields. In response he learns to make shots under the worst of circumstances and with minimal visibility. All enemies with cover are considered to have 25% less cover against the agent's attacks.

At 7th level, the agent makes attacks as if his targets had 50% less cover.

Bonus Feat: At 3rd level, the counter-terrorist receives a bonus basic combat or covert feat. He must still meet all prerequisites for this feat. He receives another bonus feat from these trees at 5th level, 7th level, and 9th level.

Crowd Control: At 4th level, the counter-terrorist may keep civilians calm and safe in almost any situation. Once per session as a full action, he may improve the disposition of an entire crowd by 1 grade. This represents the counter-terrorist "controlling the crowd," preparing them to follow his orders. This action is usually followed closely by instructions for the civilians to go prone, or hide behind any available cover (requests which gain the benefit of the improved disposition modifiers).

At 8th level, the agent may improve a crowd's disposition by 2 grades.

Table 4.2: The Counter-Terrorist

Lvl	Base Att Bon	Fort Save	Ref Save	Will Save	Def Bon	Init Bon	Budg Pts	Gadg Pts	Special
1	+1	+1	+1	+0	+0	+1	3	0	*Quick-thinking*, special tactics (locate)
2	+2	+2	+2	+0	+1	+2	6	1	Precision takedown (–25% cover)
3	+3	+2	+2	+1	+1	+3	9	1	Bonus feat
4	+4	+2	+2	+1	+2	+3	12	2	Crowd control (1 level), safe attack
5	+5	+3	+3	+1	+2	+4	15	2	Bonus feat, special tactics (subdue)
6	+6	+3	+3	+2	+2	+5	18	3	Negotiator
7	+7	+4	+4	+2	+3	+6	21	3	Bonus Feat, precision takedown (–50% cover)
8	+8	+4	+4	+2	+3	+6	24	4	Crowd control (2 levels), tactical commander
9	+9	+4	+4	+3	+4	+7	27	4	Bonus Feat, special tactics (improved locate)
10	+10	+5	+5	+3	+4	+8	30	5	Moment of truth

This ability extends to non-stress situations as well, though the counter-terrorist may not use it to affect individuals or groups of less then 5 people.

All disposition effects are lost at the end of the scene.

Safe Attack: At 4th level, the counter-terrorist has become an expert at keeping innocent bystanders safe from harm. When the counter-terrorist rolls an error making an attack, the GC must spend an extra action die to cause him to hit an innocent bystander or fellow agent.

Negotiator: The counter-terrorist is a master of one-on-one negotiation. At 6th level, any time the counter-terrorist attempts to defuse a tense situation by negotiating, his calm words cause any opponent to treat him as if his disposition towards the agent was 1 grade better. This is in addition to a normal roll to influence the character's disposition, and is applied *before the influence roll* (making the opponent more receptive to traditional methods). This doesn't change the opponent's actual stance toward the agent, but does make the opponent more open to any deals the agent may offer.

Tactical Commander: At 8th level, once per session as a half action, the agent may coordinate combat activities with his entire team. All members of the team gain the benefits of the counter-terrorist's 4th level ability, Safe Attack, for the remainder of the combat.

Moment of Truth: There comes a time when negotiations have failed and only decisive action can prevent further tragedy. At 10th level, once per session, the agent may make one extra half action that absolutely comes before all other characters may act that round (if two counter-terrorists use this ability in the same round, the one with the higher initiative total goes first; if their initiative totals are also tied, the one with the highest initiative bonus goes first; if their initiative bonuses are tied, randomly determine who acts first). The agent gains a +5 surprise bonus to any roll required by the action. Further, the results of this action do not cause any other character to cease being flat-footed, even if attacked by the agent – the action is simply too fast and unexpected for them to react to at all.

HACKER

In the computer age, hackers are essential to the Archer Foundation's smooth operation. They are electronic wizards, versed in both breaching secure systems, and securing the Conspiracy's own systems against similar electronic attack.

Hackers are often deployed with teams whose missions revolve around government agencies and corporations – anyone with an extensive and secure computer network.

Abilities: Far and away the most important ability for a hacker is Intelligence, the key ability to many of a hacker's skills, including Computers and Cryptography. Since the hacker has an extensive skill list, a high Intelligence will provide the required skill points. Wisdom holds secondary importance; several of the hacker's skills depend upon it.

Vitality: 1d8 plus Constitution bonus per level

REQUIREMENTS

To become a hacker, an agent must meet all of the following requirements.

Agent Level: 5+
Computers: 8 ranks
Cryptography: 8 ranks
Feats: Mathematical Genius

CLASS SKILLS

The hacker's class skills and key abilities are listed below:

Class Skill	Key Ability
Appraise	Int
Bluff	Cha
Bureaucracy	Cha
Computers	Int
Concentration	Wis
Craft	Int
Cryptography	Int
Cultures	Wis
Diplomacy	Cha
Driver	Dex
Electronics	Int
Forgery	Int
Gather Information	Cha
Hobby	Wis
Innuendo	Wis
Knowledge	Int
Languages	Wis
Listen	Wis
Mechanics	Int
Profession	Wis
Search	Int
Sense Motive	Wis
Sleight of Hand	Dex
Spot	Wis
Surveillance	Wis

Skill Points at Each Level: 8 + Int modifier.

CLASS FEATURES

All of the following are class features of the hacker.

Class Feats: The hacker gains the following feats at 1st level.

Armor Proficiency (Light)
Weapon Group Proficiency (Handgun)

Custom-Built System: No true hacker would ever consent to using an off-the-shelf computer for any length of time. The hacker's personal, custom-built machine is considered to have a +2 computer rating when he uses it, above and beyond the computer's normal rating. If the hacker's custom-built computer is destroyed, it requires one week and either 2 BP or $1000 to modify the next computer he purchases or is issued to his own specifications. This is the hacker's core ability.

Hard-wired: Hackers must stay sharp to perform their electronic artistry, but some tasks call for endless repetition or patience in the face of glacial progress. The hacker faces these challenges with the same machine-like calm as his computer. He receives a +4 to all Concentration checks.

At 5th level, the hacker can go for a full (24-hour) day without food or sleep with no penalty to his Intelligence-based skills.

At 9th level, the agent may ignore any one penalty that would affect one of his Intelligence-based skills for one full (24 hour) day, including all ability damage to Intelligence from one source (such as poison, illness, or psionic attack). This stacks with previous bonuses from the hard-wired ability.

Synchronize: At 2nd level, the hacker can act as an electronic pointman, coordinating insertions into installations with computer-controlled security, so long as the building has a computerized security system that he has access to. The hacker may give one other agent a +2 bonus to all skill checks made to penetrate the computer-controlled security system. This bonus applies to all rolls made to hide from security cameras, open electronic locks, etc. In order to use this ability, the hacker must be logged into the installation's computer system, either over the Internet (if the installation's system is linked to the Internet), or on-site (by working on a dedicated terminal inside the building). This ability requires the hacker to access the secured system *(see the Computers skill)*. Working from a dedicated terminal inside the site doubles the bonus the hacker offers to his teammates (+4). Root account access triples the bonus (+6). This ability (and its bonuses) lasts as long as the hacker remains logged into the installation's system.

At 7th level, the hacker may use this ability twice per session, and may grant the bonus to his entire team.

Math Wiz: The hacker cranks code and crushes numbers like nobody else. It is more than just a job; it's an obsession. At 3rd level, the agent receives the Advanced Skill Mastery Feat for his Mathematical Genius Feat. At 5th level, he gains the Quick Use feat for the Computers skill. At 7th level, he receives the Grand Skill Mastery Feat for his Mathematical Genius Feat. Finally, at 9th level, he receives the Perfect Skill Mastery Feat for Mathematical Genius. The normal agent level requirements for these specific Advanced Skill Feats are waived for this agent (allowing the hacker to acquire them levels before any non-hacker could do so).

Lockout: Starting at 4th level, the hacker may attempt to cut one or more users off from a computer system. This ability is invasive and obvious (at least to the users booted from the system, who may physically alert other users to the hacker's activities). The hacker makes an opposed Computers check versus the target user. Success locks that user out of the system for a number of rounds equal to the difference between the rolls. A critical success locks the targeted user out for as long as the hacker is logged into the system.

At 8th level, the hacker's lockout roll may selectively deny access to any or all users other than himself. The hacker makes a Computers skill check against the target user with the highest Computers skill. Again, any targeted users are locked out for a number of rounds equal to the difference between the rolls, with a critical success locking the targeted users out as long as the hacker is logged into the system.

Either form of this ability may be used a number of times per session equal to the hacker's class level. This ability requires root access to the computer system in question *(see the Computers skill, page 44 of the Spycraft Espionage Handbook)*.

Sift: While a tremendously valuable tool for information-gathering, the Internet's sheer size makes each search a daunting task. At 4th level, the hacker learns how to best go about searching for specific information on the Internet. When the hacker makes a Gather Information check while using the Internet, he may never completely fail, even if he rolls an error. Further, the GC must spend an extra action die to activate a critical failure for such rolls.

Fingerprints: Every hacker has his own idiosyncrasies, electronic 'fingerprints' others can use to identify him. At 6th level, while examining another hacker's handiwork, a hacker can determine who cracked the system by making an Education check with a DC equal to 10 plus the target hacker's agent level. Success indicates the agent has identified the crack as the work of a hacker he either knows, or has heard of, and provides any relevant information the hacker knows about the culprit (such as the city he operates out of, the programs he uses, etc.) The Game Control is the ultimate arbiter of what the hacker knows about the target hacker.

Hacker Culture: While most hackers prefer to be seen as the "aloof technophile" or "one-man-hacking-army," many difficult hacks and traces require effective face-to-face networking with people. Tracing passwords or culprits off-line is often the only way to proceed. Fortunately, just mentioning their on-line "handle" to serious computer users often opens doors for the hacker. At 8th level, after the hacker makes the normal roll to influence the disposition of an NPC with a Computers skill of 8 or higher, the NPC's disposition toward the hacker improves by 1 grade.

Ghost in the Machine: At 10th level, the hacker may invade a computer system and perform actions inside without detection. The computer system's operation is never compromised so there is no way for other users and security programs to notice him (unless, of course, he blows his roll or locks one or more users out of the system). At any time, the hacker may make a Computers check (DC normal for breaking into the system – *see the Computers skill*). Success renders all his uses of the computer system invisible to other users for a number of rounds equal to the difference between his roll and the DC. A critical success renders all his uses of the system invisible to other users until he logs out.

This ability does not conceal uses of the computer system which have physical effects outside the system (such as shutting down computer-controlled security or powering the system down), or which directly affect other users (such as locking them out or adjusting their terminal settings).

Table 4.3: The Hacker

Lvl	Base Att Bon	Fort Save	Ref Save	Will Save	Def Bon	Init Bon	Budg Pts	Gadg Pts	Special
1	+0	+0	+1	+1	+1	+1	3	1	*Custom-built system*, hard-wired (concentrate)
2	+1	+0	+2	+2	+1	+1	6	2	Synchronize (solo)
3	+1	+1	+2	+2	+2	+2	9	3	Math wiz (advanced)
4	+2	+1	+2	+2	+2	+2	12	4	Lockout (single), sift
5	+2	+1	+3	+3	+3	+3	15	5	Hard-wired (all-nighter), math wiz (quick)
6	+3	+2	+3	+3	+4	+4	18	6	Fingerprints
7	+3	+2	+4	+4	+4	+4	21	7	Math wiz (grand), synchronize (team)
8	+4	+2	+4	+4	+5	+5	24	8	Hacker culture, lockout (all)
9	+4	+3	+4	+4	+5	+5	27	9	Hard-wired (persevere), math wiz (perfect)
10	+5	+3	+5	+5	+6	+6	30	10	Ghost in the machine

Sniper

In case of emergencies, the Foundation's Chambers each maintain a stable of operatives dedicated to black operations – a "dirty tricks squad," so to speak. While these agents sometimes operate alone, they are just as frequently used to supplement the abilities of a team.

The most common of these operatives (and the most feared) are snipers. Trained extensively in a variety of firearms, the sniper specializes in eliminating an opponent from great distances.

Abilities: Considering the sniper's reliance on stealth, Dexterity is without a doubt his most prized ability. This is particularly true since the sniper specializes in the use of long-range weaponry. Wisdom, with its emphasis on accurate perception and patience, is also key for the successful sniper.

Vitality: 1d10 plus Constitution bonus per level

Requirements

To become a sniper, an agent must meet all of the following requirements:

Agent Level: 5+
Dexterity: 13+
Hide: 6 ranks
Surveillance: 6 ranks
Feats: Far Shot, Marksman

Class Skills

The sniper's class skills and key abilities are listed below:

Class Skill	Key Ability
Balance	Dex
Bluff	Cha
Climb	Str
Concentration	Wis
Craft	Int
Disguise	Cha
Driver	Dex
Hide	Dex
Hobby	Wis
Intimidate	Str or Cha
Jump	Str
Move Silently	Dex
Open Lock	Dex
Profession	Wis
Search	Int
Sleight of Hand	Dex
Spot	Wis
Surveillance	Wis
Tumble	Dex
Use Rope	Dex

Skill Points at Each Level: 6 + Int modifier.

Class Features

All of the following are class features of the sniper.

Class Feats: The sniper gains the following feats at 1st level.

Armor Proficiency (Light)
Weapon Group Proficiency (Rifle)

Precise: At 1st level, whenever the sniper uses an action die to add to a firearms damage roll, he rolls two action dice instead of one. This is the sniper's core ability.

Reposition: It is essential for the sniper to move quickly from location to location between shots, to avoid the massive counterattacks his actions usually provoke. At 1st level, the sniper gains the Run feat. At 5th level, he gains the Mobility feat. At 9th level, he gains the Increased Speed feat.

Magic Touch: The sniper's accuracy with firearms is superior even to that of dedicated soldiers. At 2nd level, the sniper gains a +1 to his base attack bonus when using firearms. This bonus is included when determining if the sniper meets the prerequisites for any ranged combat feats. At 7th level, this bonus increase to +2.

Bonus Feat: At 3rd level, the sniper gains a bonus covert or ranged combat feat. He must still meet all prerequisites for this feat. He receives another bonus feat from these trees at 5th level, 7th, and 9th level.

Deadly Aim: At 4th level, if the target of one of the sniper's firearms attacks is within 1 range increment, the sniper adds an additional +1d6 damage to his damage roll. At 8th level, this bonus improves to +2d6 to targets within two range increments. Should the sniper have the Increased Precision feat, this ability's range is increased by one range increment.

One Shot: Starting at 4th level, the sniper's error range with all firearms attacks is reduced by one. If this reduces the error range to less than one, the error range remains at one, but the GC must spend an extra action die to activate a critical miss.

Surprise Shot: Starting at 6th level, the sniper's threat range with firearms attacks increases by 2 when he targets an opponent he has surprised, or who is currently denied his Dexterity bonus to Defense (such as when the target is caught flat-footed or immobilized).

Disappear: At 8th level, the sniper is an expert at concealing his firing position. Any character attempting to spot the sniper after he makes a ranged attack with a rifle must roll a Spot check opposed by the sniper's Hide check. The sniper's Hide check is modified by +1 per 100 feet of distance from which he fired. If the sniper's weapon is silenced or subsonic, the modifier is raised to +2.

Million Dollar Skill: The sniper's Proficiency with firearms seems almost mythical. At 10th level, as a full action, the sniper may take 10 while making a single firearms attack. This is considered a "natural 10" and is a threat if the sniper's threat range is 10-20 or better. This requires complete concentration, and the sniper loses all Dexterity and dodge bonuses to his Defense for the entire round. The sniper may still benefit from normal aiming and bracing actions taken the previous round.

Project Prometheus

The semi-covert war in Russia has taken a bizarre turn in the last twenty years, introducing new-generation warriors born from the twisted discoveries of the chemical age. Scarcely-human constructs which can only be described as "monsters" and "abominations" stalk the shadows, defying the laws of nature as they change the rules of the Great Game.

"Chemical monsters" are a reality in *Shadowforce Archer* – humans augmented beyond the limits of the flesh, gaining impossible strength, endurance, and physical abilities that overshadow all previous instances of genetic engineering. Some think chemical monsters are the next step in human evolution, others (commonly psions) see them as a forced aberration of the path.

Origin of the Species

The original AGAMEMNON virus *(see page 141)* was mutagenic in nature. It attached to a target's DNA and slowly merged with it until it triggered a violent metamorphosis. This was supposed to cause the DNA to effectively unravel, destroying the cohesion between the target's cells and reducing him to a fleshy mass of indistinct proteins.

But the virus unexpectedly triggered a completely different kind of change. Instead of degrading, the target's DNA reorganized, effectively recreating the target as an entirely new being: a monstrous mutation of the original.

Project PROMETHEUS has picked up where this accidental discovery left off. Using recombinant DNA techniques, PROMETHEUS engineers soldiers of devastating power, humans capable of taking Archer's war to the next level...

Table 4.4: The Sniper

Lvl	Base Att Bon	Fort Save	Ref Save	Will Save	Def Bon	Init Bon	Budg Pts	Gadg Pts	Special
1	+1	+0	+2	+0	+1	+1	1	0	*Precise*, reposition (Run)
2	+2	+0	+3	+0	+1	+2	2	1	Magic touch (+1)
3	+3	+1	+3	+1	+2	+3	3	2	Bonus feat
4	+4	+1	+4	+1	+2	+3	4	3	Deadly aim (1d6), one shot
5	+5	+1	+5	+1	+3	+4	5	3	Bonus feat, reposition (Mobility)
6	+6	+2	+5	+2	+4	+5	6	4	Surprise shot
7	+7	+2	+6	+2	+4	+6	7	5	Bonus feat, magic touch (+2)
8	+8	+2	+6	+2	+5	+6	8	6	Deadly aim (2d6), disappear
9	+9	+3	+7	+3	+5	+7	9	6	Bonus feat, reposition (Increased Speed)
10	+10	+3	+7	+3	+6	+8	10	7	Million dollar skill

Current Endeavors

PROMETHEUS research is focused in three directions at the moment.

Physical Augmentation

The majority of PROMETHEUS is devoted to refining the effects of the original AGAMEMNON virus. New and more powerful chemical monsters appear every day.

Technological Enhancement

P.E.R.I.L.'s research and development division has not limited itself to enhancements of the flesh; it has also delved into the potential of merging technology with its chemical monsters, devising armor, weapons, and even biological agents to wield on the field of battle. Through gyro-stabilization, unconventionally large weapons can be mounted on augmented soldiers, whose physical frames can withstand the added recoil. Armor is grafted directly onto their bodies, or woven into their skin to form a super-hard dermal layer that can withstand intense environmental shifts and limited heavy weapons fire. P.E.R.I.L. scientists are even devising "skins" allowing chemical monsters to endure the pressures of the ocean floor or the vacuum of deep space.

Hybrids

Certain labs are conducting research into splicing human DNA with that of various animals. Though the results have been only marginal thus far, the potential remains for creating natural (non-chemically enhanced) warriors of even greater power than their predecessors.

The Engineered

Only two groups have ready access to the AGAMEMNON virus at present, though rumors persist of a man calling himself "Othello" who brazenly offers samples on the Red Market *(see page 140)* for the price of ten million U.S. dollars.

P.E.R.I.L. (Pages 136, 242)

P.E.R.I.L. are responsible for most of the dirty research conducted in this field – and countless atrocities perpetuated along the way.

The Phantom Brigade (Page 141)

The Phantom Brigade have allied with the Archer Foundation to research the virus (under conditions significantly more humane than those maintained by P.E.R.I.L.). Thus, their discoveries become available to other Archer agents. The Archer Foundation condones this research as a necessary evil of the war in Russia – a horrible war that requires horrible measures to win.

Chemical Monster Rules

"Chems" are powerful treatments designed to alter an agent's body in a fundamental – and permanent – way. Agents interested in signing up for a chem treatment should be aware that it's a one-way trip. Most chem treatments, once begun, must continue for the rest of the agent's life.

Receiving a Chem Treatment

In order to survive a chem treatment, the agent must meet all listed requirements. In addition, he cannot have any psion levels – psions invariably suffer a fatal reaction to chem treatments. Once the treatment has been administered, the agent can never gain any psion levels. Finally, he must either belong to the Russian Confederacy or receive the Game Control's permission (usually with the caveat that he build the reason for the treatment into his background).

Agents may also receive chem treatments during play, as part of a storyline or other event (though the Game Control is warned not to force chems on his players without their permission – doing so constitutes a violation of trust).

Boosters

An agent who has received a chem treatment must receive regular chem "booster shots" or suffer the listed adverse effects. Kickstart is unique in that it causes no lingering addiction. There is currently no known treatment to cure an agent of a chem addiction.

Overdosing

Because chems are so powerful and unstable, it is an extremely bad idea to use more than one treatment. Should this happen, roll d%. If the roll is higher than the agent's Constitution, he immediately dies, dropping to –10 wound points.

Chem Treatments

This section describes the most common chem treatments, and the format for treatment listings.

Chemical Name

The chem treatment's name is followed by a general description of its appearance and purpose, and then the following information.

Boosters: How often the agent must receive booster treatments to avoid withdrawal symptoms.

Requirements: The requirements an agent must meet to take the chem treatment.

Benefits: The beneficial effects of the chem treatment.

Drawbacks: The detrimental effects of the chem treatment, including withdrawal symptoms.

Endure

Endure is a dark red fluid pumped into the agent's body in large quantities, completely replacing his blood. Although it superficially resembles blood, Endure is much more, allowing the agent to withstand greater damage – and even heal wounds before they become life-threatening. However, the Endure must be flushed out of the agent's body and replaced with a fresh dose every week (a process requiring 4 hours and the proper transfusion facilities to perform), or it causes permanent damage to his health.

Boosters: Weekly

Requirements: Con 15+

Benefits: The agent receives damage reduction 2/–, regains 2 vitality points at the end of every round, and is immune to critical hits. In addition, wound points heal at the rate of 1 per hour, instead of 1 per day. Finally, the agent does not have to make a saving throw in order to survive massive damage *(see page 178 of the Spycraft Espionage Handbook).*

Drawbacks: Every treatment the agent misses causes 2 points of permanent Constitution damage and the agent permanently loses the ability to spend action dice for any purpose. The agent can still earn the XP that comes with an awarded action die, but the dice themselves are useless to him.

Gill

Gill is a syrupy green solution that is administered in two doses, one behind each ear. This treatment is actually a retrovirus carrying carefully engineered DNA. The user grows an unobtrusive set of gills behind his ears, acquiring the ability to breathe water as well as air.

Boosters: Quarterly

Requirements: Con 11+

Benefits: The agent gains the ability to breathe water as well as air, and does not suffer from the drowning rules when immersed in water.

Drawbacks: An agent is incapable of speech while using his gills and for 1 minute afterward as the water is flushed from his system. In addition, an agent who fails to receive his booster shot on time loses the ability to breathe air as the injected DNA takes over his respiratory system. This means that he suffers from the drowning rules unless immersed in water. Fortunately, this side effect reverses itself once the proper booster has been injected.

Kickstart

Kickstart is a thick black emulsion injected directly into the heart of an agent who shows no signs of life. Kickstart contains a number of nanites suspended in carrier liquid. Once injected, the nanites repair and restart the heart, then travel through the rest of the body making additional repairs as they go, before finally deactivating, after which they are flushed from the agent's body through normal waste release. In this manner, the nanites can restore life to a dead agent. Of course, the agent's body has to be relatively intact for this chem to work, and the nanites do an imperfect job of repairing the body, so a revived agent is never quite as healthy as he was before his unfortunate death.

Boosters: Never

Requirements: –10 to –30 wound points

Benefits: If injected into an agent who has been dead no more than one hour, and who hasn't been reduced to less than –30 wound points, Kickstart repairs his internal injuries within 10 minutes, restoring the agent to 1 wound point and 1 vitality point. Kickstart does not cause an overdose if administered to an agent using another chem treatment.

Drawbacks: Kickstart cannot completely reverse the trauma of death. As a result, the agent suffers 2 points of permanent Constitution damage. This lowers the agent's total wound and vitality points. Kickstart cannot save an agent who dies from a chem overdose.

Muscle

Muscle is a light blue liquid injected into the spine at the base of the neck. This chem greatly stimulates rapid muscle and bone growth, increasing the user's size and strength over time. However, Muscle also retards mental development, making it difficult for the user to learn new skills. Worse, if the user stops taking the chem, he can suffer brain damage, or death.

Boosters: Monthly

Requirements: Str 13+

Benefits: Upon receiving his first treatment, the agent immediatly gains a permanent +2 bonus to his Strength and grows 6 inches taller. For every 3 agent levels he advances after his first treatment, he gains another +1 bonus to Strength and grows another 3 inches taller. These bonuses are gained whether he takes subsequent chem treatments or not. If the agent ever reaches 8 feet in height, his size category changes to Large, allowing him to wield a Large weapon in each hand, increasing his lifting and carrying limits to twice those of Medium-size agents, and increasing his fist attack damage to 1d4 plus his Strength modifier.

Drawbacks: Once an agent has taken this chem, the number of skill points he receives at the start of each new level is reduced by 1. Worse, if the agent misses a chem treatment, he suffers 1 point of permanent Intelligence damage. If this reduces his Intelligence to 0, he dies as his brain dissolves. Finally, his growth may eventually cause him problems – should he ever reach 8 feet in height, his size category changes to Large, which applies a –1 size penalty to his attack rolls and Defense, and a –4 size penalty to his Hide checks.

Rush

Rush is a viscous brown fluid injected through the temple. This chem makes the agent's synapses fire faster, greatly improving his reaction speed and ability to think on his feet. However, sometimes the acceleration process goes wrong, triggering an epileptic seizure.

Boosters: Every two weeks

Requirements: Dex 13+

Benefits: Once per scene, the agent may choose to activate his Rush treatment as a free action. He then rolls a d6. If he rolls a 6, he suffers an epileptic seizure *(see Drawbacks, below)*. Otherwise his treatment activates and lasts for a number of rounds equal to the number rolled on the d6 (e.g. the treatment lasts for 4 rounds if the agent rolls a 4). While the treatment is active, the agent receives an extra half action at the end of each round, after everyone else has performed their actions.

Drawbacks: When activating his Rush treatment, there's a chance that the agent suffers an epileptic seizure. If this occurs, the agent falls to the ground and cannot act for 1d6 rounds. In addition, if not restrained from hurting himself, the agent suffers 1d3 wound points of damage. Worse, every time he misses a treatment, his odds of suffering a seizure increase by 1 in 6 until he receives his treatment. Thus, an agent who has missed 3 Rush treatments suffers a seizure when activating his ability if he rolls a 3 or higher. Once he has had his treatment, his odds of suffering a seizure return to normal.

Sharpen

Sharpen is a watery golden chemical injected into the medulla oblongata at the base of the brain. This chemical contains a retrovirus designed to implant certain animal genes into the user, enhancing each of his senses without externally altering his appearance. Unfortunately, the process is imperfect, leading to irregular burning headaches that Sharpen users refer to as brainfire.

Boosters: Monthly

Requirements: Wis 13+

Benefits: The agent receives a +5 bonus to Spot, Listen, and Search checks, as well as to any Survival checks made to find or follow tracks.

Drawbacks: The Game Control may, once per game session, spend an action die to cause the agent to suffer a brainfire attack that lasts for 1d6 rounds. During the attack, the agent receives a –4 penalty to all rolls he makes. For every treatment the agent misses, the Game Control may cause an extra brainfire attack, every game session until the agent receives his treatment (after which the number of times the GC may trigger a brainfire returns to normal). Thus, if an agent has missed 3 treatments, the Game Control can cause him to suffer 4 brainfire attacks every session until he gets a Sharpen treatment, after which the attacks return to once per session.

Talon

Talon is an orange liquid injected into the bone marrow in several points along the agent's arms and hands. Talon causes the growth of retractable bone claws along the back of the agent's hands and arms that can cause significant damage in hand-to-hand combat. However, when the claws are extended, his hands are forced to clench into fists, and he cannot hold anything in them.

Boosters: Every two months

Requirements: Con 11+

Benefits: When the agent's claws are extended, any unarmed attacks he makes using his arms or hands receive a +2 bonus to their damage rolls. This bonus increases by +1 for every 4 agent levels the Talon user gains after receiving his first treatment.

Drawbacks: When the agent's claws are extended, he cannot hold anything in either of his hands, and he receives a –6 penalty for anything that the Game Control determines to require fine manipulation, or to any Disguise check. If the agent misses a treatment, his bone claws lock in the extended position until he receives another Talon treatment.

These talons are an integral part of the character's forearm musculature and cannot be removed. Even surgically removing the talons does not unlock the agent's fists, nor does it remove the associated –6 penality.

Chems and the Mastermind System

If a GC would like his villains to have access to chems, he may purchase the option at a base cost of 5 MP, then spend 1 MP per chemically augmented mastermind or henchman, or plus 2 MP per chemically augmented minion or foil. Chems purchased in this way are available at the start of the season, and may be used as desired by the villain in question. The base cost of 5 MP is part of the mastermind's organization cost, and is only paid once per season, while the cost of 1 MP per chemically augmented NPC is paid for each character affected.

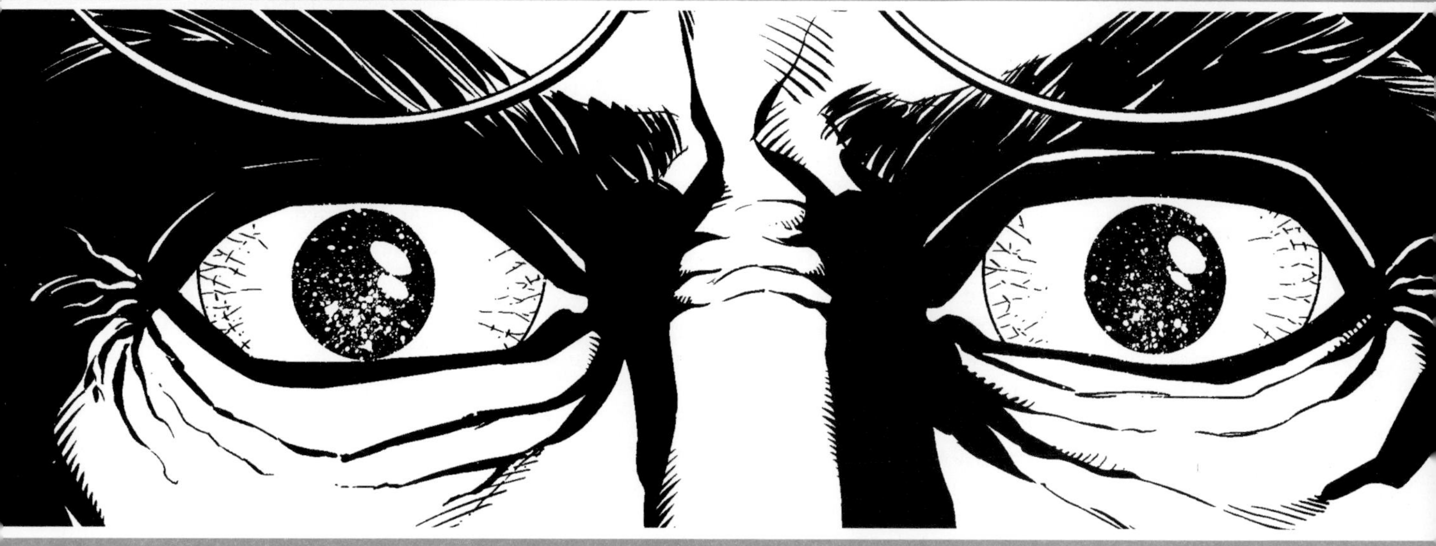

*"Watch the eyes.
When the pupils bleed out, run."*
*– Advice given to Conspiracy operatives,
for how to deal with Shop mentalists*

PSIONICS

One Step Beyond

The development of the human mind has made radical strides in the last hundred years, raising psionic powers from an idealistic concept to an amazing reality. Today, brilliance walks among us – "psions" capable of mental leaps beyond (and often altogether outside) the realm of rational scientific explanation, controlling and manipulating their bodies on a molecular level, and invading the thoughts and emotions of others.

But these shining beacons of progress are not unprecedented. They are genetic throw-backs, linked to civilizations that existed tens of thousands of years ago. Their origins, even the true identity of their progenitors, are unknown to us, but their presence reverberates in evach incredible act they perform for the common good – or the greatest evil.

Psionics and the World

Like mysticism and the chemical "aberrations" devised by P.E.R.I.L.'s scientists (many of whom are mentalists), the existence of psionics remains a secret. The vast majority of those outside the hidden struggle to protect the world have no idea that such remarkable abilities are real, let alone that they are so prevalent. Even most initiates into this fantastic world never realize how far-reaching and powerful psionics have become in the 21st century.

There are, however, those whose position, power, or influence ensures a certain understanding of the truth. High-ranking politicians – especially those from governments allied with the Archer Foundation, most global spy organizations, and unaligned psions whose powers have manifested without formal training – all see the world through different eyes than the general public. They also accept the fact that some secrets are best left out of the hands of the unprepared.

How long this precarious balance can be maintained, and the secret kept from prying eyes, remains to be seen.

The New Order

The science of psionics is not completely understood, but the information available follows a rigid pattern. All powers fall into one of three families, each a genetic strain passed down through the centuries, each the focus of one brand of modern psion training.

All psionic powers are the result of genetic psionic potential expanded through medical tampering or mental discipline, and all psionic powers manifest as chemical triggers are "flipped" in those with latent potential. The original triggers for psionic ability were the three prime strains discovered at ancient burial sites around the world. The recipients of these strains – Conrad Archer, Avery Schillingsfield (a.k.a. Helix), and the Demagogue – became human "factories" for serums used to awaken psion powers in others, and the remains of the last two (held by the Archer Foundation and the Hand of Glory, respectively) are perhaps the most cherished scientific samples anywhere in the world. Conrad Archer's body, never found after his disappearance in 1945, has become one of the most sought-after relics of the 20th century, and untold theories about its whereabouts abound, sparking wild theories and "urban legends" within the intelligence community.

Ultimately, however, the serums proved too dangerous to develop long-term psions, destroying the minds and bodies of test subjects within a matter of years, sometimes months or even weeks. With the mapping of the human genome, new avenues of psion research appeared, and sceintists developed more humane methods of producing psions. Today, psions are almost universally the result of careful screening, cultivated study, genetic therapy, and mental focus.

It has been proven that not everyone has the latent potential to develop psionic powers, and those who do seem predisposed to develop certain abilities in lieu of others. As yet, the reasons for this remain a mystery.

Further, some psions have developed powers from two of the three families, though to date only one person – the Archer Foundation's Control, "Two" *(see page 60)* – has manifested all three. Outside the fact that he was seemingly engineered as a psion experiment, the causes of this limitation remain unknown.

But that is where the facts end and speculation and field experience begin. With new information about the human genome available every day, and new psion abilities cropping up without warning, the Foundation and its allies can only wonder about the future direction of human evolution.

Playing a Psion Agent

Playing an agent with psionic powers requires several additional steps, which may be undertaken at any time in your career; there are no first-level requirements for psion agents.

1. Raise Your Psion Level

Your psion level represents how much raw psionic strength you possess. Agents normally begin with a psion level of 0.

You can raise your psion level in two ways.

- Take a level in a psionic class, such as the mentalist, physical adept, or telepath. This raises your psion level by 1. Thus, a 1st-level physical adept has a psion level of 1.
- Take a feat that raises your psion level, such as Psion Prodigy *(see page 179)*. The feat you take explains how your psion level is affected.

All multiclassing rules apply to psion classes normally, with one exception – agents who already possess levels in two psion classes may not gain levels in a third.

2. Take One or More Psionic Feats

You may only take psion feats from a family you have a class level of 1 or more in (i.e. you must have at least one level as a telepath to select a telepathic psion feat; likewise for physical adepts and mentalists).

Psionic feats do one of three things for you.

- Some psionic feats, such as Adrenal Basics, ESP Basics, and Telekinetic Basics give you access to a group of psion skills.
- Other psionic feats, such as Electrokinesis, Expanded Horizons, and Sympathetic Healer offer you a single powerful ability.
- Finally, several basic psionic feats *(seen on the next page)*, such as Quicken Power, modify one of your other psionic abilities, in this case reducing the time and concentration it takes you to use one of your psion skills.

3. Buy Ranks in Your Psion Skills

Just because you have access to one or more psion skills doesn't mean you automatically gain ranks in them. You must still buy ranks in your psion skills using skill points, just as if they were ordinary class skills. For instance, if you take the Adrenal Basics feat, you are allowed to purchase ranks in the Body Sculpting skill, but if you don't invest any skill points in it, then you can't use that skill nor any of the powers listed in its description.

Ranks in psion skills factor into the skill bonus for powers associated with that skill, just as normal skill ranks factor into the skill bonus for using the psion skills in question. For instance, three ranks in Poltergeist adds +3 to the skill bonus for using powers described under the Poltergeist skill.

Normal skills may only be used to augment checks if the pertinent description indicates a synergy bonus. Psion skills are an entirely new branch of agent training, which rarely overlaps with the other knowledge agents acquire.

Table 5.1: Psion Bonuses

	Psion Level																								
Skill Check Result	1	2	3	4	5	6	7	8	9	10	11	12	13	14	15	16	17	18	19	20	21*	22*	23*	24*	25*
up to 10	+1	+1	+1	+1	+1	+1	+2	+2	+2	+2	+2	+2	+3	+3	+3	+3	+3	+3	+4	+4	+4	+4	+4	+4	+5
11-15	+1	+1	+1	+1	+2	+2	+2	+2	+3	+3	+3	+3	+4	+4	+4	+4	+5	+5	+5	+5	+6	+6	+6	+6	+7
16-20	+1	+1	+1	+2	+2	+2	+3	+3	+3	+4	+4	+4	+5	+5	+5	+6	+6	+6	+7	+7	+7	+8	+8	+8	+9
21-25	+1	+1	+2	+2	+3	+3	+4	+4	+5	+5	+6	+6	+7	+7	+8	+8	+9	+9	+10	+10	+11	+11	+12	+12	+13
26-35	+1	+2	+2	+3	+4	+4	+5	+6	+6	+7	+8	+8	+9	+9	+10	+11	+11	+12	+13	+14	+14	+15	+16	+16	+17
36+	+1	+2	+3	+4	+5	+6	+7	+8	+9	+10	+11	+12	+13	+14	+15	+16	+17	+18	+19	+20	+21	+22	+23	+24	+25

* Agents cannot achieve more than 20 levels in a psion class, but core abilities or feats may increase the agent's psion level to above 20.

No combination of modifiers may raise a character's psion level (temporarily or permanently) above 25.

How to use this table: Find your psion level listed across the top and your psion skill check total along the side, then cross-reference to find the actual bonus your psion skill check grants you. Apply this bonus to the psionic power or ability that directed you here.

USING YOUR PSIONIC POWERS

Psionic powers are granted either by a feat or a skill. Each power granted by a feat is different – the feat itself explains everything you need to know about the power.

Powers granted by psion skills, on the other hand, must obey certain uniform rules. You must pay a certain number of vitality points in order to activate one of these powers (as described under the power), plus 1 for every non-psion level you have gained since your last psion level. This vitality cost acts just like damage suffered during combat, with one exception. If activating the power would take you to 0 or fewer remaining vitality points, then you are too exhausted to use that power and cannot activate it. Once you've paid the cost to activate a power, you make a skill check, and usually look the result up on a table to determine the power's strength and duration.

Some psionic powers may logically continue for longer than their listed duration, without interruption. In such cases, you must pay the listed vitality cost and roll against the listed DC at the start of each use of the power. Failure to pay the vitality point cost, or failure with the skill check, interrupts the use of the power.

Finally, if you are successfully attacked during the same round you intend to use a psionic power, before you make the skill check to activate the power, you must also make a Concentration check with a DC equal to the total damage you suffer from all attacks this round. If you fail this Concentration check, you may not activate the power this round (though you still pay the power's vitality point cost).

Basic Psion Feats

Unless otherwise noted, these feats may be taken by any agent who has an open generic (i.e. non-specified) feat slot.

ANTI-PSI TRAINING

You have received training that allows you to mentally interfere with psionic powers targeting you.

Prerequisites: European Commonwealth agents only; psion level 0 only.

Benefit: The DC to affect you with any psionic ability is increased by 2, and you receive a +2 bonus to any saves to resist psionic abilities. Also, you have damage reduction 2/– against damage caused by psionic abilities.

Special: You may never raise your psion level above 0 once you have taken this feat.

COMBAT PSION

You have been trained to focus your psionic powers even in the chaos of combat, which gives you an edge when things get dicey.

Prerequisites: Psion level 1+.

Benefit: You receive a +4 psionic bonus to Concentration checks made while activating any of your psionic abilities.

DEADLY POWER

You can use the powers listed under one of your psion skills to much deadlier effect than most psions.

Prerequisites: Combat Psion, psion level 2+.

Benefit: Choose one of your psion skills. Powers or psionic attacks listed under that skill that inflict damage to others now receive a +2 psionic bonus to their damage. In addition, the threat range of attacks made with those powers is increased by 1 (e.g. if the power had no threat range before, its threat range is now 20).

Special: You may take this feat multiple times. Each time you take the feat, it applies to a new psion skill.

EFFICIENT POWER

You can activate powers listed under one of your psion skills with much less effort than most psions.

Prerequisites: Psion Level 4+.

Benefit: Choose one of your psion skills. Powers listed under that skill now cost 2 less vitality to activate (minimum 1). If used in conjunction with Extended Power *(see below)*, apply the effects of Extended Power first, then apply this feat.

Special: You may take this feat multiple times. Each time you take the feat, it applies to a new psion skill.

EXTENDED POWER

You can activate powers listed under one of your psion skills for longer than most psions.

Prerequisites: Psion Level 2+.

Benefit: Choose one of your psion skills. When you activate powers listed under that skill, you may choose to pay 150% of the normal vitality point cost (e.g. a cost of 2 becomes 3) in order to double the power's duration. If used in conjunction with Efficient Power *(see above)*, apply the effects of this feat first, then Efficient Power.

Special: You may take this feat multiple times. Each time you take the feat, it applies to a new psion skill.

MASTERED POWER

You have mastered one of your psion skills and can control its powers more easily than most psions.

Prerequisites: Psion Level 2+.

Benefit: Choose one of your existing psion skills. When you activate powers listed under that skill, you receive a +4 psionic bonus to any skill check required.

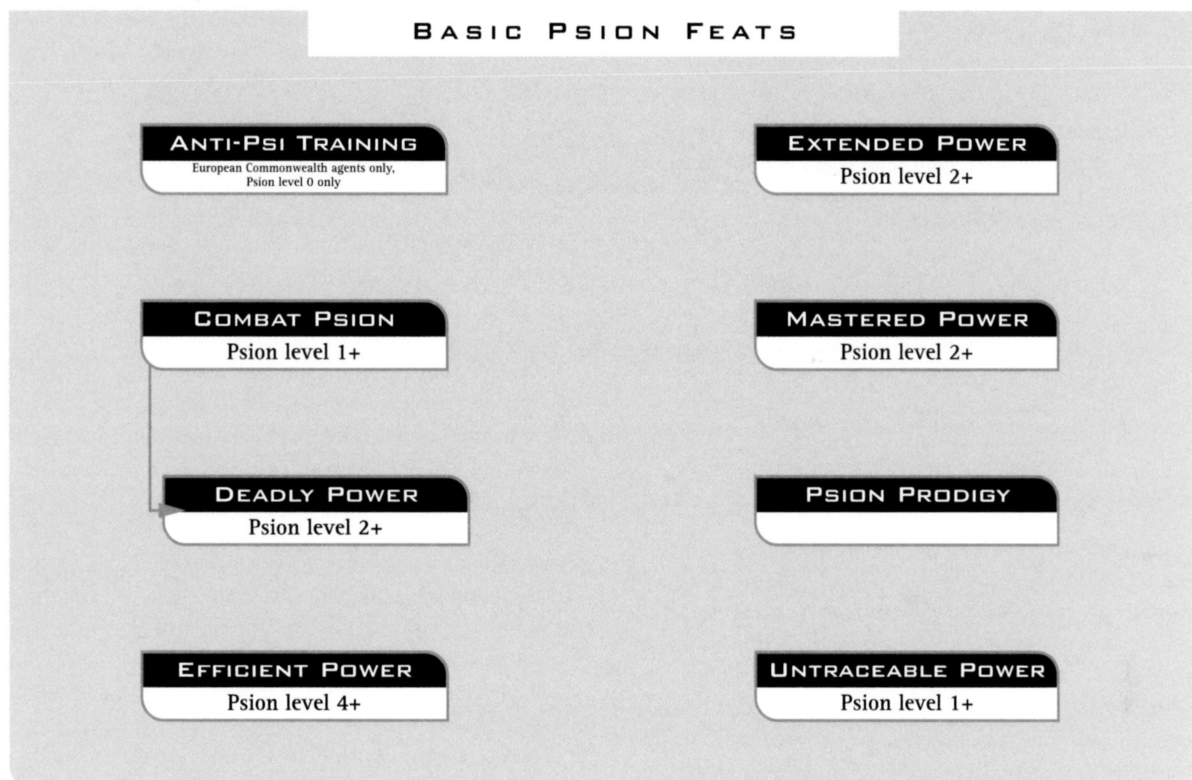

Special: You may take this feat multiple times. Each time you take the feat, it applies to a new psion skill.

Psion Prodigy

You have powerful, if untrained, psionic potential.

Benefit: Your psion level is increased by 1. This allows you access to the various psionic feats, or increases your psionic power if you already have access to these feats.

Special: You can gain this feat two times, increasing your psion level by 1 each time.

Untraceable Power

You may activate powers listed under one of your psion skills without leaving a trace of your activities.

Prerequisites: Psion Level 1+.

Benefit: Choose one of your psion skills. When you activate powers listed under that skill, you do not give off any of the psychic residue that enables other psions to detect your power use, either during or after the fact.

Special: You may take this feat multiple times. Each time you take the feat, it applies to a new psion skill.

Normal: You emit psychic residue when using your powers. This can be sensed by certain psychic powers and PsiTech gadgets during – or even days after – the psionic power use.

The Mentalist

Where physical adepts focus on the body and telepaths reach into the minds of others, mentalists enhance the powers of their own minds.

Abilities: A mentalist should have high Wisdom and Intelligence scores. Not only are a mentalist's class abilities primarily intellectual in nature, but these two abilities are key to every single class skill the mentalist receives. Constitution is also important for powering the mentalist's various (and often draining) powers.

Vitality: 1d8 plus Constitution modifier per level

Class Skills

The mentalist's class skills, and the key ability for each, are listed below:

Class Skill	Key Ability
Computers	Int
Concentration	Wis
Craft	Int
Cryptography	Int
Electronics	Int
Hobby	Wis
Knowledge	Int

Mechanics	Int
Profession	Wis
Sense Motive	Wis

Skill Points at 1st level: (8 + Int modifier) × 4.
Skill Points at each additional level: 8 + Int modifier.

Class Features

All of the following are class features of the mentalist.

Psionic Class: The mentalist is a psionic class. Levels gained in this class increase your psion level.

Class Feats: The mentalist begins play with the following feats.

Armor Proficiency (Light)
Weapon Group Proficiency (Melee)
Weapon Group Proficiency (Handgun)

Insightful: Whenever the mentalist spends an action die to add to a mental psion skill check, the results of that die are also added to his psion level (to a maximum of 25) to determine the effectiveness of the power for that skill check only (e.g. a 1st-level mentalist who spends an action die and rolls a 3 adds +3 to his skill check result and increases his psion level by 3 for the purposes of that skill check). This is the mentalist's core ability.

Mental Psion Feats: At 1st level, the mentalist may begin choosing feats from the mental psion feats category. The mentalist must still have the slots free for any feats he selects, and must still meet all prerequisites for any feat chosen.

Bonus Feat: At 1st level, the mentalist receives a bonus gear or mental psion feat. The mentalist must still meet all prerequisites for a feat, including ability score and base attack bonus minimums. At 4th level, and every 4 levels thereafter, the mentalist receives an additional bonus gear or mental psion feat.

Mental Leap: Starting at 2nd level, once per game session as a free action, the mentalist may add half his psion level (rounded down) to his Intelligence or Wisdom for ten rounds. This does not increase the number of skill points or languages the mentalist possesses. This power is so exhausting that when it wears off, the mentalist must rest for a full round, taking no actions and using no psion skills. This ability's duration may be cut short at the player's discretion, but the agent suffers the full round exhaustion penalty, regardless. At 11th and 19th level, the mentalist may use this ability one additional time per game session.

Psi Mastery: Starting at 3rd level, the mentalist chooses a mental psion skill that he has at least 1 rank in. He receives a +2 psionic bonus to all skill checks

Table 5.2: The Mentalist

Lvl	Base Att Bon	Fort Save	Ref Save	Will Save	Def Bon	Init Bon	Budg Pts	Gadg Pts	Special
1	+0	+0	+1	+2	+1	+1	2	1	Mental psion feats, bonus feat, *insightful*
2	+1	+0	+2	+3	+1	+1	4	2	Mental leap 1/session
3	+1	+1	+2	+3	+2	+2	6	3	Psi mastery
4	+2	+1	+2	+4	+2	+2	8	4	Bonus feat
5	+2	+1	+3	+4	+3	+3	10	5	Psi mastery
6	+3	+2	+3	+5	+4	+4	12	6	Skill bonus
7	+3	+2	+3	+5	+4	+4	14	7	Psi mastery
8	+4	+2	+4	+6	+5	+5	16	8	Bonus feat
9	+4	+3	+4	+6	+5	+5	18	9	Psi mastery, skill bonus
10	+5	+3	+5	+7	+6	+6	20	10	More toys (+3)
11	+5	+3	+5	+7	+6	+6	22	11	Mental leap 2/session, psi mastery
12	+6	+4	+6	+8	+7	+7	24	12	Bonus feat, skill bonus
13	+6	+4	+6	+8	+8	+8	26	13	Psi mastery
14	+7	+4	+6	+9	+8	+8	28	14	Masterpiece
15	+7	+5	+7	+9	+9	+9	30	15	Psi mastery, skill bonus
16	+8	+5	+7	+10	+10	+10	32	16	Bonus feat
17	+8	+5	+8	+10	+10	+10	34	17	Psi mastery
18	+9	+6	+8	+11	+11	+11	36	18	Skill bonus
19	+9	+6	+8	+11	+11	+11	38	19	Mental leap 3/session, psi mastery
20	+10	+6	+9	+12	+12	+12	40	20	Bonus feat, more toys (+6)

with that skill. For every 2 levels after 3rd, the mentalist selects an additional mental psion skill to receive this bonus, choosing a different skill each time.

Skill Bonus: At 6th level, the mentalist receives an extra 4 skill points. For every 3 levels after 6th, the mentalist receives an additional 4 extra skill points.

More Toys: Starting at 10th level, the mentalist gains an additional +3 gadget points during the Gearing Up phase of each mission. Also, gadgets which may be customized may include one more option per housing than normal *(see the PsiTech Gadgets and Usual Refinements sections in this book and the Spycraft Espionage Handbook for more).* At 20th level, the mentalist gains three more gadget points (for a total of +6), and all of his gadgets may exceed the choice per housing limit by 2. This ability may be used for standard gadgets and vehicular gadgets, as the mentalist desires.

Masterpiece: At 14th level, the mentalist may declare one gadget of his creation to be his "masterpiece." All of this device's statistics (ammunition, range, speed, etc.), damage, and bonuses are doubled. If the gadget increases a DC, the bonus to the DC is doubled, not the total DC (e.g. if the gadget offers a DC modifier of +3, the modifier becomes +6). Defense bonuses are considered DC modifiers (so if a gadget offers its user a +2 bonus to Defense, this ability increases the bonus to +4).

Mental Psion Feats

You must have a mentalist level of 1 or more to take any feats from this category.

Control Junction

You have learned to link your psychokinetic and telekinetic powers together to create a union of strength and grace. This provides you with unusual control over your psionic attacks.

Prerequisites: Telekinetic Mastery, Psychokinetic Mastery, psion level 10+.

Benefit: You receive a +1 bonus to all of your telekinetic and psychokinetic skills when you gain this feat, not to exceed your normal skill limits. In addition, you receive a +2 bonus to all of your attack rolls when making psionic attacks.

Energy Junction

You have learned to link your psychoinventive and psychokinetic powers together to enhance the energy you create with your mind. This strengthens your psionic attacks.

Prerequisites: Psychoinventive Mastery, Psychokinetic Mastery, psion level 10+.

Benefit: You receive a +1 bonus to all of your psychokinetic and psychoinventive skills when you gain this feat, not to exceed your normal skill limits. In addition, you receive a +1 bonus to each die of damage you do when making a psionic attack (e.g. 3d6 becomes 3d6+3).

Evolved Mind

Through your advancing mastery of mental psionic powers, new vistas have been opened to your mind, allowing you to see and understand connections between events in the world that others can only sense.

Prerequisites: Int 13+, Psychokinetic Mastery, Telekinetic Mastery, Psychoinventive Mastery, psion level 14+.

Benefit: You receive 12 skill points. In addition, all skills that aren't barred to you are now considered class skills.

Electrokinesis

You can read and manipulate certain electronic pulses, allowing you to mentally interface with computers and generate small electromagnetic pulses with your touch.

Prerequisites: Room 39 agents only, psion level 1+.

Benefit: You may use this ability in one of two ways. The first allows you to mentally interface with a computer as a free action simply by touching it with your bare hand. The computer must be turned on in order for you to interface with it. You receive a +2 psionic bonus to any Computers skill checks you make while touching the computer for every 5 psion levels you have gained (rounded up). Alternately, as a half action, you may touch an unshielded electronic device with your bare hand and release a small electromagnetic pulse into it. If the device is turned on, its circuits instantly fry, utterly ruining the device and destroying all data it contains. You may use these two abilities a total of once per game session for every 5 psion levels you have gained (rounded up).

Instinct Junction

You have learned to link your psychoinventive and telekinetic powers together to speed your mental processes a hundredfold. This provides you with the ability to make decisions incredibly quickly under stress.

Prerequisites: Telekinetic Mastery, Psychoinventive Mastery, psion level 10+.

Benefit: You receive a +1 bonus to all of your telekinetic and psychoinventive skills when you gain this feat, not to exceed your normal skill limits.

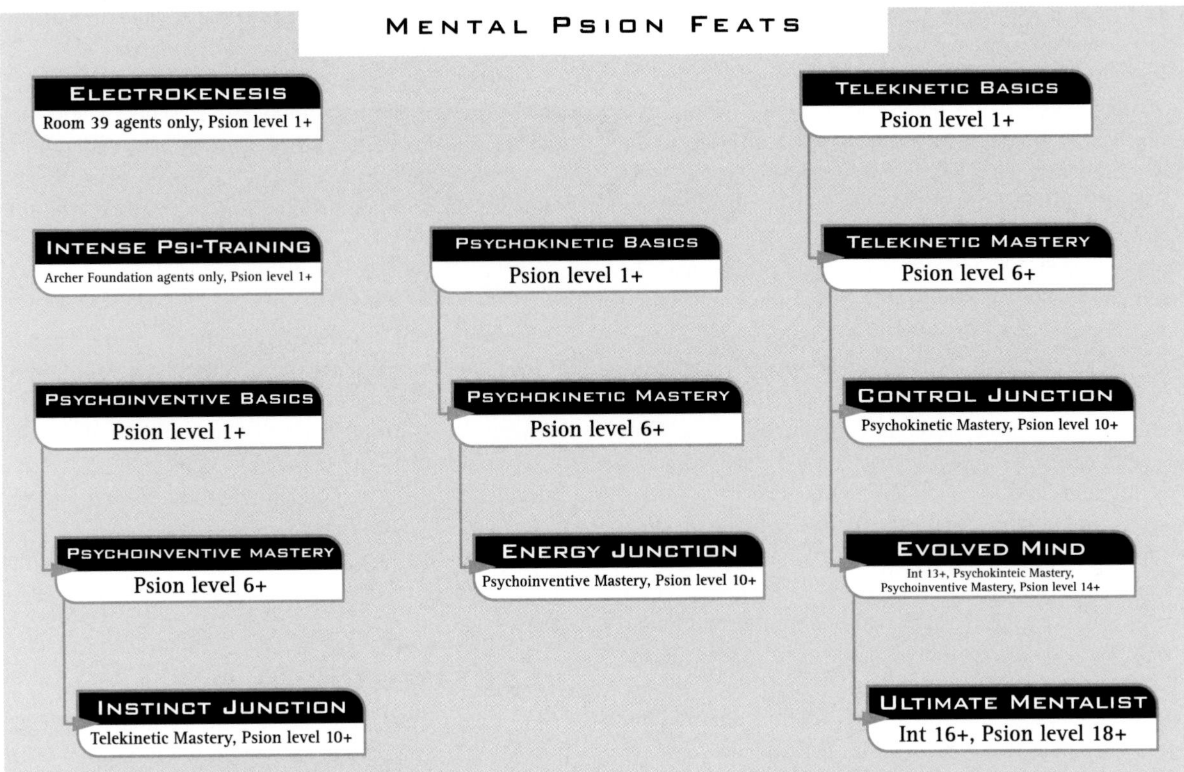

In addition, when making an initiative check, your die roll is considered to be at least a 10 unless you roll a natural 1.

Intense Psi-Training

You have undergone the Archer Foundation's intensive course to unlock your psionic potential.

Prerequisites: Archer Foundation agents only, psion level 1+.

Benefit: You receive a +1 psionic bonus to all of your psion skill checks.

Psychoinventive Basics

Your mind is capable of incredible leaps of intuition, logic, and imagination, and generates more creative energy than a normal human mind.

Prerequisites: Psion level 1+.

Benefit: You may learn psychoinventive psion skills as though they were class skills.

Normal: Without this feat, you may not learn psychoinventive psion skills.

Psychoinventive Mastery

You have spent a great deal of time and effort perfecting your psychoinventive psion skills.

Prerequisites: Psychoinventive Basics, psion level 6+.

Benefit: You may take 10 when using psychoinventive psion skills, even if stress and distraction would normally prevent you from doing so. In addition, you may make up to three inspiration checks per game session without spending an action die.

Psychokinetic Basics

You can manifest the power of your mind as various forms of energy. You are able to direct this energy and shape it into devastating attacks to use against your enemies.

Prerequisites: Psion level 1+.

Benefit: You may learn psychokinetic psion skills as though they were class skills.

Normal: Without this feat, you may not learn psychokinetic psion skills.

Psychokinetic Mastery

You have spent a great deal of time and effort perfecting your psychokinetic psion skills.

Prerequisites: Psychokinetic Basics, psion level 6+.

Benefit: You may take 10 when using psychokinetic psion skills, even if stress and distraction would normally prevent you from doing so. In addition, you gain a +4 psionic bonus to all saves against energy-based attacks and temperature-related effects when you take this feat.

TELEKINETIC BASICS

You can move and redirect objects using the power of your mind.

Prerequisites: Psion level 1+.

Benefit: You may learn telekinetic psion skills as though they were class skills.

Normal: Without this feat, you may not learn telekinetic psion skills.

TELEKINETIC MASTERY

You have spent a great deal of time and effort perfecting your telekinetic psion skills.

Prerequisites: Telekinetic Basics, psion level 6+.

Benefit: You may take 10 when using telekinetic psion skills, even if stress and distraction would normally prevent you from doing so. In addition, your speed is increased by 5 and your weight is reduced by 50% for purposes of setting off traps when you take this feat.

ULTIMATE MENTALIST

You have forged a perfect union between your psychokinetic, telekinetic, and psychoinventive abilities, and awakened the innermost powers of the human mind. This is the pinnacle of psion achievement for a mentalist, and one of the most powerful feats ever discovered.

Prerequisites: Int 16+, Evolved Mind, psion level 18+.

Benefit: You receive 24 skill points. In addition, when you make a skill check of any sort, your die roll is considered to be at least a 10 unless you roll a natural 1.

MENTAL PSION SKILLS

These psion skills allow you to push your mind beyond normal human limitations to create physical changes in the world around you. Psychoinventive, psychokinetic, and telekinetic skills are all considered mental psion skills.

PSIONIC ATTACKS

Some mental psion skills, such as Cryokinesis or Pyrokinesis, give you the ability to attack others with the power of your mind. Psionic attacks are an ability gained through the use of psionic powers – they are not psionic powers in and of themselves. You don't pay vitality points to make a psionic attack, and you can't use the Quicken Power feat (for instance) to make psionic attacks as a free action. Instead, Quicken Power would allow you to activate your flame jet power (for instance) as a free action, allowing you to use the fire attack ability it gives you without first spending a half action to turn the power on in the first place.

You may only have one power which provides a psionic attack active at one time. You must wait for that power to expire or deliberately cancel it before you may prepare and use another. You may not make more than one psion attack per round.

MAKING PSIONIC ATTACKS

Psionic attacks take a half action and add your Intelligence modifier to the attack roll rather than Strength or Dexterity. When a psionic attack hits, you add the modifier for the skill's keyed ability to the damage roll.

Example: The Static Charge skill offers an agent the Lightning Blast attack. When a lightning blast is used, the agent applies his Intelligence modifier to the attack roll and the modifier for Static Charge's keyed ability (Dexterity) to his damage roll.

The range increment for a psionic attack depends on the type of energy employed, and is defined in each attack description. Psionic attacks have a maximum range of five increments.

PSIONIC BACKLASH

When an agent scores a critical failure using a psionic attack, he suffers psionic backlash as the intense mental energy he is trying to focus turns on him. The amount of damage taken is listed under each psionic attack. Psionic backlash is normal damage and may not be reduced by damage reduction.

PHYSICAL PSIONIC ATTACKS

Some psionic attacks have a physical effect (such as fire, electricity, and the like), rather than consisting of purely mental force. Psionics cannot create something from nothing – these powers augment minute traces of existing elements to manifest dramatic physical attacks. Lightning attacks, for instance, manifest from the natural static charge of the human body. Cold attacks freeze the moisture in surrounding air, and fire attacks add thermal energy to the surrounding air until the ambient nitrogen oxidizes (ignites). This limitation is the reason why psions are normally unable to create large ice structures, wield fireballs, or cause electrical storms. Very powerful psions can manipulate large volumes of existing elements to create these astounding effects (and much more). Rules for such advanced powers will be presented in the upcoming *Archer Foundation* sourcebook.

PSYCHOINVENTIVE PSION SKILLS

You must have the Psychoinventive Basics feat in order to take ranks in any psychoinventive psion skill.

FOCUS THE MIND (INT; TRAINED ONLY)

Requires the Psychoinventive Basics feat.

You may enter a meditative trance that focuses your mind completely on a single problem, giving you a much better chance of coming up with a solution.

Check: A Focus the Mind check requires a full action and adds a psionic bonus to certain die rolls for a number of minutes equal to 5 times your psion level. The result of the Focus the Mind check *(see Table 5.1)* determines the bonus, and the power you choose from the list below determines which die rolls receive the bonus. You can have more than one of these powers active at the same time, but you must pay the vitality point cost for each.

Inspire: By throwing open the gates of your imagination, you can gain the listed bonus to your inspiration checks.

Recall: By psionically scanning your own memories, you can gain the listed bonus to your education checks.

Prepare: By entering a special trance state, you can gain the listed bonus as a one-time modifier to the next Intelligence- or Wisdom-based skill check you make. This power ends when used or when its duration runs out, whichever comes first.

Vitality Point Cost: 2

GADGETEER (INT; TRAINED ONLY)

Requires the Psychoinventive Basics feat.

You are capable of building, modifying, and analyzing PsiTech gadgets.

Check: A Gadgeteer check allows you to activate one of the following powers. You can have more than one of these powers active at the same time.

Build Gadget: Given the proper materials and a set of tools, you can build any gadget your GC allows in the game (not including vehicles or vehicular gadgets). This ability may not be used to build standard gear, or to modify any use of the Mechanics or Electronics skills. You must spend action dice equal to the device's gadget point cost, and your psion level must equal or exceed this cost in order for you to build the gadget. Your Gadgeteer check determines how long it takes you to build the device.

Result	Time Spent Building Gadget
up to 15	5 hours × (gadget point cost)
16–20	4 hours × (gadget point cost)
21–25	2 hours × (gadget point cost)
26–30	1 hour × (gadget point cost)
31+	30 minutes × (gadget point cost)

Devices created by agents in the field are submitted to R&D for testing as part of the mission debriefing – they do not become part of any agent's personal gear.

Modify Gadget: Starting with an existing gadget and given the proper materials and a set of tools, you may add any modification (not including vehicles or vehicular gadgets) your GC allows in the game. You must spend action dice equal to the modified device's total gadget point cost, and your psion level must equal or exceed this cost in order for you to modify the gadget. Your Gadgeteer check determines how long it takes you to build the device.

Result	Time Spent Building Gadget
up to 15	4 hours × (gadget point cost)
16–20	2 hours × (gadget point cost)
21–25	1 hour × (gadget point cost)
26–30	30 minutes × (gadget point cost)
31+	15 minutes × (gadget point cost)

This ability may not be used to modify standard gear, or to modify any use of the Mechanics or Electronics skills.

Analyze Gadget: As a full action, you can analyze a gadget you've never seen before in order to identify a number of its functions determined by your Gadgeteer check. Your psion level must be equal or higher than the device's gadget point cost in order to analyze it. You may only use this ability once with any given gadget, but it costs you nothing to do so.

Result	Number of Functions Determined
up to 15	1
16–20	2
21–25	3
26–30	4
31+	5

This ability may not be used to analyze standard gear, or to modify any use of the Mechanics or Electronics skills.

Vitality Point Cost: 1/2 GP cost of gadget (rounded up); Minimum 1.

STATIC CHARGE (DEX; TRAINED ONLY)

Requires the Psychoinventive Basics feat.

This offensive skill allows you to focus your body's natural static charge into electrical attacks and offers you the ability to electromagnetically disable high-tech items.

Check: A Static Charge check allows you to activate one of the following powers. You can have more than one of these powers active at the same time.

Lightning Blast: While this power is active, you gain the lightning attack ability, described below. The duration of this power depends on the result of your Static Charge check.

Result	Duration
up to 15	1 round
16–20	2 rounds
21–25	3 rounds
26–30	4 rounds
31+	5 rounds

Lightning Attack: Once per round as a half action, you may hurl a bolt of lightning at an opponent as a psionic ranged touch attack. The range increment of the attack is 25, its error range is 1, and its threat range is 20. You add your Intelligence modifier to your attack roll, and if you hit, you roll 2d4 damage, plus an additional 1d4 for every three psion levels you have, adding your Dexterity modifier to the final result (e.g. a mentalist with psion level of 6 and a +2 Dexterity modifier deals 4d4+2 damage). This damage is treated as electrical and psionic, and the target may make a Reflex save (DC 10 + your psion level) to suffer only half damage rounded down.

If you suffer a critical miss when using this ability, you suffer 2d4 points of psionic backlash damage and your lightning blast power immediately ends.

Scramble Mind: While this power is active, you gain the scramble attack ability, described below. The duration of this power depends on the result of your Static Charge check.

Result	Duration
up to 15	1 round
16–20	2 rounds
21–25	3 rounds
26–30	4 rounds
31+	5 rounds

Scramble Attack: Once per round as a half action, you may fire a blast of mental energy at an opponent as a psionic ranged touch attack. The range increment of the attack is 5, and it has no error or threat range, nor can it ever gain one. You add your Intelligence modifier to your attack roll, and if you hit, your target must make a Will save (DC 10 + your psion level) or be unable to act for 1d3 rounds.

Inhibit Device: When you activate this power, you target a small (hand-held) electronic device or gadget with a gadget point cost no higher than your psion level. While this power persists, that gadget cannot be used. The duration of this power is decided by the result of your Static Charge check.

Result	Duration
up to 15	1 round
16–20	2 rounds
21–25	3 rounds
26–30	4 rounds
31+	5 rounds

Vitality Point Cost: 4 for lightning blast or scramble mind, 2 for inhibit device.

PSYCHOKINETIC PSION SKILLS

You must have the Psychokinetic Basics feat in order to take ranks in any psychokinetic psion skill.

CRYOKINESIS (CHA; TRAINED ONLY)

Requires the Psychokinetic Basics feat.

You may lower the temperature of the air nearby, allowing you to stay cool on a hot day, hurl shards of ice at your enemies, or freeze an object solid.

Check: A Cryokinesis check requires a half action (except when activating Chill Air, which is a free action), and allows you to activate one of the following powers. You may have more than one of these powers active at the same time.

Chill Air: You may activate this power as a free action. Once activated, all heat or fire damage you receive for a number of minutes equal to 5 times your psion level is reduced according to the result of your Cryokinesis check.

Result	Damage Reduction
up to 15	5/–
16–20	10/–
21–25	15/–
26–30	20/–
31+	25/–

Ice Shards: While this power is active, you gain the ice attack ability, described below. The duration of this power depends on the result of your Cryokinesis check.

Result	Duration
up to 15	1 round
16–20	2 rounds
21–25	3 rounds
26–30	4 rounds
31+	5 rounds

Ice Attack: Once per round as a half action, you may hurl shards of ice at an opponent as a psionic ranged attack. The range increment of the attack is 15, its error range is 1, and its threat range is 19-20. You add your Intelligence modifier to your attack roll, and if you hit, you roll 2d4 damage, plus an additional 1d4 for every two psion levels you have, adfing your Charisma modifier to the final result (e.g. a mentalist with psion level of 4 and a +2 Charisma modifier deals 4d4+2 damage). This damage is treated as cold and psionic, and the target may make a Reflex save (DC 10 + your psion level) to suffer only half the damage, rounded down. A target who fails this save suffers frostbite as described under Cold on page 229 of the *Spycraft Espionage Handbook.*

If you suffer a critical miss when using this ability, you suffer 2d4 points of psionic backlash damage. In addition, your ice shards power immediately ends.

Freeze Object: By touching a non-living object, you can cause its temperature to plunge to below freezing. This power lasts for a number of rounds equal to five times your psion level. Your skill check determines how large an area you can affect per round.

Result	Size Affected
up to 15	5 foot × 5 foot area
16–20	10 foot × 10 foot area
21–25	15 foot × 15 foot area
26–30	20 foot × 20 foot area
31+	25 foot × 25 foot area

The freezing effect spreads outward from your touch in a circular pattern. Once frozen, an area becomes slippery with a thin sheen of ice *(see Ice on page 230 in the Spycraft Espionage Handbook for the effects of this),* and any flames in the area are extinguished. In addition, metallic surfaces that are frozen become brittle, halving their hardness. You cannot use this power on an object held or worn by a person.

Vitality Point Cost: 2 for chill air or freeze object, 4 for ice shards.

Photokinesis (Wis; Trained Only)

Requires the Psychokinetic Basics feat.

You can control the light around you, enabling you to create blinding flashes of light, dim a room to better conceal yourself in the shadows, or create a simple glowing image on a surface.

Check: A Photokinesis check requires a half action, and allows you to activate one of the following powers. You may have more than one of these powers active at the same time.

Dim: By dimming the light in an area and lengthening the shadows, you may add a psionic bonus to your Hide skill, as determined by the result of a Photokinesis check *(see Table 5.1).*

Flash: While this power is active, you gain the flash attack ability, described below. The duration of this power depends on the result of your Photokinesis check.

Result	Duration
up to 15	1 round
16–20	2 rounds
21–25	3 rounds
26–30	4 rounds
31+	5 rounds

Flash Attack: Once per round as a half action, you may create a bright flash of light around your body. Anyone looking in your direction must make a Fortitude save (DC 10 + your psion level) to look away in time. Targets who fail this save are blinded *(see page 177 of the Spycraft Espionage Handbook)* for 1d4 rounds.

If you suffer a critical miss when using this ability, you are blinded by your own power for 1d4 rounds and your flash power immediately ends.

This attack may not be performed in total darkness; any amount of light allows it to work normally.

Image: You may cause an object to brightly phosphoresce wherever you touch it, allowing you to draw a pattern or message on the object, or even to turn it into a makeshift light by illuminating the entire object (resulting in a glow as bright as a flashlight). To determine how long the object glows, make a Photokinesis check and consult the table below.

Result	Duration
up to 15	5 minutes × (your psion level)
16–20	10 minutes × (your psion level)
21–25	15 minutes × (your psion level)
26–30	30 minutes × (your psion level)
31+	1 hour × (your psion level)

Lase: While this power is active, you gain the laser attack ability, described below. The duration of this power depends on the result of your Photokinesis check.

Result	Duration
up to 15	1 round
16–20	2 rounds
21–25	3 rounds
26–30	4 rounds
31+	5 rounds

Laser Attack: Once per round as a half action, you may focus ambient light into a fine beam, directed at an opponent as a psionic ranged attack. The range increment of the attack is 30, its error range is 1, and its threat range is 20. You add your Intelligence modifier to your attack roll, and if you hit, you roll 2d4 damage, plus an additional 1d4 for every three psion levels you have attained, adding your Wisdom modifier to the final result (e.g. a mentalist with psion level of 3 and a +2 Wisdom modifier deals 3d4+2 damage). This attack ignores the first three points of damage reduction or hardness possessed by the target. This damage is treated as laser and psionic, and the target may make a Reflex save (DC 10 + your psion level) in order to suffer only half the damage, rounded down.

If you suffer a critical miss when using this ability, you suffer 2d4 points of psionic backlash damage *(see page 183)*. In addition, your lase power immediately ends. The vitality cost for this action is 5, not 2 as listed for all other uses of this power.

Vitality Point Cost: 2

Pyrokinesis (Cha; Trained Only)

Requires the Psychokinetic Basics feat.

You may raise the temperature of the air nearby, hurl jets of flame, and cause objects to burst into flame.

Check: A Pyrokinesis check requires a half action (except when activating warm air, which is a free action), and allows you to activate one of the following powers. You may have more than one of these powers active at the same time.

Warm Air: You may activate this power as a free action. Once activated, all cold or ice damage you receive for a number of minutes equal to 5 times your psion level is reduced according to the result of your Pyrokinesis check.

Result	Damage Reduction
up to 15	5/–
16–20	10/–
21–25	15/–
26–30	20/–
31+	25/–

Flame Jet: You may activate this power as a half action. While this power is active, you gain the fire attack ability, described below. The duration of this power depends on the result of your Pyrokinesis check.

Result	Duration
up to 15	1 round
16–20	2 rounds
21–25	3 rounds
26–30	4 rounds
31+	5 rounds

Fire Attack: Once per round as a half action, you may shoot a jet of flame at an opponent as a psionic ranged attack. The range increment of the attack is 10, its error range is 1–2, and its threat range is 19–20. You add your Intelligence modifier to your attack roll, and if you hit, you roll 2d6 damage, plus an additional 1d6 for every two psion levels you have, adding your Charisma modifier to the final result (e.g. a mentalist with psion level of 4 and a +2 Charisma modifier deals 4d6+2 damage). This damage is treated as fire and psionic, and the target may make a Reflex save (DC 10 + your psion level) to suffer only half damage, rounded down. A target who fails this save catches fire as described under Fire on page 230 in the *Spycraft Espionage Handbook.*

If you suffer a critical miss when using this ability, you suffer 2d6 points of psionic backlash damage. In addition, your flame jet power immediately ends.

Heat Object: By touching a non-living object, you can rapidly excite the molecules around it, igniting the air immediately above the object's surface. you may contain this flame as a single curl of fire hovering above the object (never touching or harming the object, if that is your wish), or will it to expand out across the surface at a rate of (1 foot × your psion level) per round. you determine whether the flame burns the objects and surfaces it spreads across or not. Finally, there must be enough oxygen in the area for the fire to burn naturally or this power cannot be activated.

This power lasts for a number of rounds equal to five times your psion level. Your skill check determines the size of the area you may affect per round.

Result	Size Affected
up to 15	5 ft. × 5 ft. area
16–20	10 ft. × 10 ft. area
21–25	15 ft. × 15 ft. area
26–30	20 ft. × 20 ft. area
31+	25 ft. × 25 ft. area

The heating effect spreads outward from your touch in a circular pattern. Once heated, an area becomes hot to the touch (inflicting 1d4 damage to anyone who touches it with bare skin), and any combustibles in the area are automatically ignited. You cannot use this power on an object held or worn by a person.

Vitality Point Cost: 2 for warm air and heat object, 6 for flame jet.

Telekinetic Psion Skills

You must have the Telekinetic Basics feat in order to take ranks in any telekinetic psion skill.

Kinetic Shield (Con; Trained Only)

Requires the Telekinetic Basics feat.

You can temporarily raise a telekinetic shield around yourself that deflects attacks.

Check: A Kinetic Shield check requires a half action and increases your damage reduction for a number of rounds equal to 2 times your psion level. The result of the Kinetic Shield check determines how much your damage reduction is increased.

Result	Bonus
up to 15	+2/–
16–20	+3/–
21–25	+4/–
26–30	+5/–
31+	+6/–

Special: If you possess the Telekinetic Mastery feat, you may target another character to receive this benefit. Doing so halves the duration (to 1 times your psion level in rounds). Your target must be within 10 feet when you activate the power, and if he ever moves more than 10 feet from you the power is immediately terminated.

Vitality Point Cost: 6

Levitation (Wis; Trained Only)

Requires the Telekinetic Basics feat.

You can float straight up and down using your this power. You cannot actually maneuver when levitating, but you can push off of walls or along ceilings.

Check: Using Levitation is a half action. When activated, you can levitate up or down as if moving normally for a number of rounds equal to 5 times your psion level. The speed at which you can move is determined by the result of your Levitation check.

Result	Speed
up to 15	15
16–20	20
21–25	30
26–30	40
31+	60

Special: If you have the Telekinetic Mastery feat, you may take your 5-ft. step each round while levitating, even if there are no available surfaces to push off from.

Vitality Point Cost: 2

Poltergeist (Dex; Trained Only)

Requires the Telekinetic Basics feat.

You can move objects with the power of your mind.

Check: A Poltergeist check requires a half action, and allows you to activate one of the following powers. You can have more than one of these powers active at the same time.

Grab: By activating this power, you can psionically "grab" an object within your line of sight and quickly pull it to your hand. The object may be up to five feet away from you for every psion level you have gained.

If the object is held in place by another object or person, you must win an opposed Strength check to seize the object. Your effective Strength for this check is determined by the result of your Poltergeist check – you must be able to lift an object using this Strength value in order to affect it with this power.

Once you've grabbed an object, it flies straight to your hand, making only slight detours to avoid obstacles. Once successfully grabbed, an object moves too quickly to be intercepted by anyone else. This power ends as soon as the object reaches your hand.

Result	Effective Strength
up to 15	5
16–20	10
21–25	15
26–30	20
31+	25

Hurl: When this power is activated, you receive a psionic bonus to your attack and damage rolls when using a hurled or projectile weapon for a number of rounds equal to your psion level. The bonuses you receive are determined by the result of your Poltergeist check.

Result	Attack Bonus	Damage Bonus
up to 15	+0	+1
16–20	+1	+3
21–25	+2	+5
26–30	+3	+7
31+	+4	+9

Catch: If this power is active when you would normally be hit with a ranged weapon (type determined by your Poltergeist check, *see below*), you may make a Reflex save (DC 17 + attacker's base attack bonus – your psion level) as a free action. If you succeed, you telekinetically repel the attack. This power lasts for one round, but may be maintained indefinitely by paying the vitality point cost at the start of every round. When you continue using this power from round to round, you do not need to make another Poltergeist check – you keep the total you rolled when you activated the power. This power is useless against psionic or other non-physical ranged attacks.

Result	Avoidable Ranged Weapon Attacks
up to 15	Small hurled weapons
16–20	Hurled weapons, small projectile weapons
21–25	Hurled/projectile weapons, small firearms
26–30	Hurled/projectile weapons, firearms
31+	Any

Fling: While this power is active, you gain the debris attack ability, described below. The duration of this power depends on the result of your Poltergeist check.

Result	Duration
up to 15	1 round
16–20	2 rounds
21–25	3 rounds
26–30	4 rounds
31+	5 rounds

Debris Attack: This ability requires the presence of several loose objects (a modest pile of gravel, a stack of crates, etc.) within your line of sight. Once per round as a half action, you may fling these objects at an opponent as a

psionic ranged attack. Objects may be reused from round to round, or new ones launched, at the agent's discretion. The range increment of the attack is 20, its error range is 1, and its threat range is 20. You add your Intelligence modifier to your attack roll, and if you hit, you roll 2d6 damage, plus an additional 1d6 for every three psion levels you have attained, adding your Dexterity modifier to the final result (e.g. a mentalist with psion level of 3 and a +2 Dexterity modifier deals 3d6+2 damage). This damage is psionic and treated as if it were inflicted by a hurled weapon. The target may make a Reflex save (DC 10 + your psion level) to suffer only half the damage, rounded down.

If you suffer a critical miss when using this ability, you suffer 2d6 points of psionic backlash damage. In addition, your fling power immediately ends.

The vitality cost for this action is 6, not 4 as described for every other use of this power.

Vitality Point Cost: 4

The Physical Adept

Psions who specialize in body-affecting powers are called physical adepts. They are capable of a variety of superhuman feats that make them extremely valuable to any team.

Abilities: Most of the physical adept's powers augment his normal physical prowess, and so he must be in excellent physical condition to make the best use of his abilities. This is especially true of Constitution and Intelligence, which supply the necessary vitality and skill points to fuel his powers.

Vitality: 1d10 plus Constitution modifier per level.

Class Skills

The physical adept's class skills, and the key ability for each, are listed below:

Class Skill	Key Ability
Balance	Dex
Climb	Str
Concentration	Wis
Craft	Int
Driver	Dex
Handle Animal	Cha
Hobby	Wis
Intimidate	Str or Cha
Jump	Str
Knowledge	Int
Move Silently	Dex
Profession	Wis
Sense Motive	Wis
Sport	Str or Dex
Swim	Str

Skill Points at 1st level: (6 + Int modifier) × 4.
Skill Points at each additional level: 6 + Int modifier.

Class Features

All of the following are class features of the physical adept.

Psionic Class: The physical adept is a psionic class. Levels gained in this class increase your psion level.

Class Feats: The physical adept begins play with the following feats.

Armor Proficiency (Light)
Armor Proficiency (Medium)
Weapon Group Proficiency (Handgun)
Weapon Group Proficiency (Hurled)
Weapon Group Proficiency (Rifle)
Weapon Group Proficiency (Archaic)

Zen: Whenever the physical adept spends an action die to add to a physical psion skill check, the results of that die are also added to his psion level (to a maximum of 25) to determine the effectiveness of the power for that skill check only (e.g. a 1st-level physical adept who spends an action die and rolls a 3 adds +3 to his skill check result and increases his psion level by 3 for the purposes of that skill check). This is the physical adept's core ability.

Physical Psion Feats: At 1st level, the physical adept may begin choosing feats from the physical psion feats category. The physical adept must still have the slots free for any feats he selects, and must still meet all prerequisites for any feat chosen.

Bonus Feat: At 1st level, the physical adept receives a bonus basic combat or physical psion feat. The physical adept must still meet all prerequisites for a feat, including ability score and base attack bonus minimums. At 4th level, and every 4 levels thereafter, the physical adept receives an additional bonus basic combat or physical psion feat.

Superhuman: Starting at 2nd level, once per game session as a free action, the physical adept may add half his psion level (rounded down) to his Strength, Constitution, or Dexterity for ten rounds. This power is so exhausting that when it wears off, the adept must rest for a full round, taking no actions and using no psion skills. This ability's duration may be cut short at the player's discretion, but the agent suffers the full round exhaustion penalty, regardless. At 11th and 19th level, the physical adept can may this ability one additional time per game session.

Psi Mastery: Starting at 3rd level, the physical adept chooses a physical psion skill that he has at least 1 rank in. He receives a +2 bonus to all skill checks with that skill. For every 2 levels after 3rd, the physical adept selects an additional physical psion skill to receive this bonus.

Ability Bonus: At 6th level, the physical adept raises an ability score of his choice by 1. For every 3 levels after 6th, the physical adept raises another ability score by 1. The same ability score may be raised more than once.

Complete Focus: Starting at 10th level, once per game session, the physical adept may use one psion skill of his choice, ignoring all vitality point costs normally associated with the skill. At 20th level, the physical adept may use this ability twice per game session.

Reduced Vitality Cost: Starting at 14th level, the vitality point cost of all the physical adept's physical psion skills is reduced by 2 (minimum 1).

Physical Psion Feats

You must have a physical adept level of 1 or more to take any feats from this category.

Adrenal Basics

You can externally alter your body to perform many incredible feats, like temporarily increasing your strength or reshaping your face.

Prerequisites: Psion level 1+.

Benefit: You may learn adrenal psion skills as though they were class skills.

Normal: Without this feat, you may not learn adrenal psion skills.

Table 5.3: The Physical Adept

Lvl	Base Att Bon	Fort Save	Ref Save	Will Save	Def Bon	Init Bon	Budg Pts	Gadg Pts	Special
1	+0	+2	+0	+2	+1	+0	2	0	Physical psion feats, bonus feat, *zen*
2	+1	+3	+0	+3	+1	+1	4	1	Superhuman 1/session
3	+2	+3	+1	+3	+2	+1	6	2	Psi mastery
4	+3	+4	+1	+4	+2	+2	8	3	Bonus feat
5	+3	+4	+1	+4	+3	+2	10	3	Psi mastery
6	+4	+5	+2	+5	+4	+2	12	4	Ability bonus
7	+5	+5	+2	+5	+4	+3	14	5	Psi mastery
8	+6	+6	+2	+6	+5	+3	16	6	Bonus feat
9	+6	+6	+3	+6	+5	+4	18	6	Ability bonus, psi mastery
10	+7	+7	+3	+7	+6	+4	20	7	Complete focus 1/session
11	+8	+7	+3	+7	+7	+4	22	8	Psi mastery, superhuman 2/session
12	+9	+8	+4	+8	+7	+5	24	9	Ability bonus, bonus feat
13	+9	+8	+4	+8	+8	+5	26	9	Psi mastery
14	+10	+9	+4	+9	+8	+6	28	10	Reduced vitality cost (–2)
15	+11	+9	+5	+9	+9	+6	30	11	Ability bonus, psi mastery
16	+12	+10	+5	+10	+10	+6	32	12	Bonus feat
17	+12	+10	+5	+10	+10	+7	34	12	Psi mastery
18	+13	+11	+6	+11	+11	+7	36	13	Ability bonus
19	+14	+11	+6	+11	+11	+8	38	14	Psi mastery, superhuman 3/session
20	+15	+12	+6	+12	+12	+8	40	15	Bonus feat, complete focus 2/session

ADRENAL MASTERY

You have spent a great deal of time and effort perfecting your adrenal psion skills.

Prerequisites: Adrenal Basics, psion level 6+.

Benefit: You may take 10 when using adrenal psion skills, even if stress and distraction would normally prevent you from doing so. In addition, you receive a +2 psionic bonus to your Defense when you take this feat.

COORDINATION JUNCTION

You have learned to link your adrenal and sensory powers together to create a union of your senses and reflexes. This provides you with uncanny speed and awareness.

Prerequisites: Adrenal Mastery, Sensory Mastery, psion level 10+.

Benefit: You receive a +1 bonus to all of your adrenal and sensory skills when you gain this feat, not to exceed your normal skill limits. In addition, you receive an extra half action every other round, starting in the second round of any combat you engage in.

EQUILIBRIUM JUNCTION

You have learned to link your adrenal and metabolic powers together to create a powerful equilibrium of the body.

Prerequisites: Adrenal Mastery, Metabolic Mastery, psion level 10+.

Benefit: You receive a +1 bonus to all of your adrenal and metabolic skills when you gain this feat, not to exceed your normal skill limits. In addition, you receive an extra 2 action dice at the start of every game session.

HEIGHTENED INNER STRENGTH

Your psionic power constantly enhances your abilities.

Prerequisites: African Alliance agents only, psion level 1+.

Benefit: You receive a +1 bonus to one of your abilities. You receive another +1 bonus to one of your abilities (chosen each time) for every 5 additional psion levels you gain after acquiring this feat. You cannot choose to increase any attribute more than twice using this feat.

METABOLIC BASICS

You can make internal changes to your body and the bodies of those you touch to perform such feats as holding your breath for extended periods or healing wounds that an ally has suffered.

Prerequisites: Psion level 1+.

Benefit: You may learn metabolic psion skills as though they were class skills.

Normal: Without this feat, you may not learn metabolic psion skills.

METABOLIC MASTERY

You have spent a great deal of time and effort perfecting your metabolic psion skills.

Prerequisites: Metabolic Basics, psion level 6+.

Benefit: You may take 10 when using metabolic psion skills, even if stress and distraction would normally prevent you from doing so. In addition, once per game session as a half action, you may heal yourself or someone you are touching of a number of wound points equal to half your psion level (rounded up).

OVERCHARGE POWER

You may use your psionic powers as if your psion level were higher than it really is.

Prerequisites: Psion level 1+.

Benefit: When activating one of your psionic powers with a vitality point cost, you may choose to pay double its normal cost. Doing so lets you activate that power as though your psion level were 1 higher than it truly is, and gives you a +2 psionic bonus to the psion skill check.

PERFECT HARMONY

You have learned to link your adrenal, metabolic, and sensory powers together to create a near-perfect harmony of the mind and body.

Prerequisites: Wis 13+, Adrenal Mastery, Metabolic Mastery, Sensory Mastery, psion level 14+.

Benefit: You receive 10 extra vitality points. In addition, you receive a +1 bonus to Strength, Dexterity, Constitution, Wisdom, Intelligence, and Charisma when you gain this feat.

QUICKEN POWER

You can activate powers listed under one of your psion skills much faster than most psions.

Prerequisites: Psion level 3+.

Benefit: Choose one of your psion skills. Powers listed under that skill that normally require a full action to activate now require only a half action to activate, and powers that took a half action to activate are now free actions for you.

Special: You can take this feat multiple times. Each time you take the feat, it applies to a new psion skill.

RECUPERATION JUNCTION

You have learned to link your metabolic and sensory powers together, giving you a heightened sense of your own well-being and a remarkable healing factor.

Prerequisites: Metabolic Mastery, Sensory Mastery, psion level 10+.

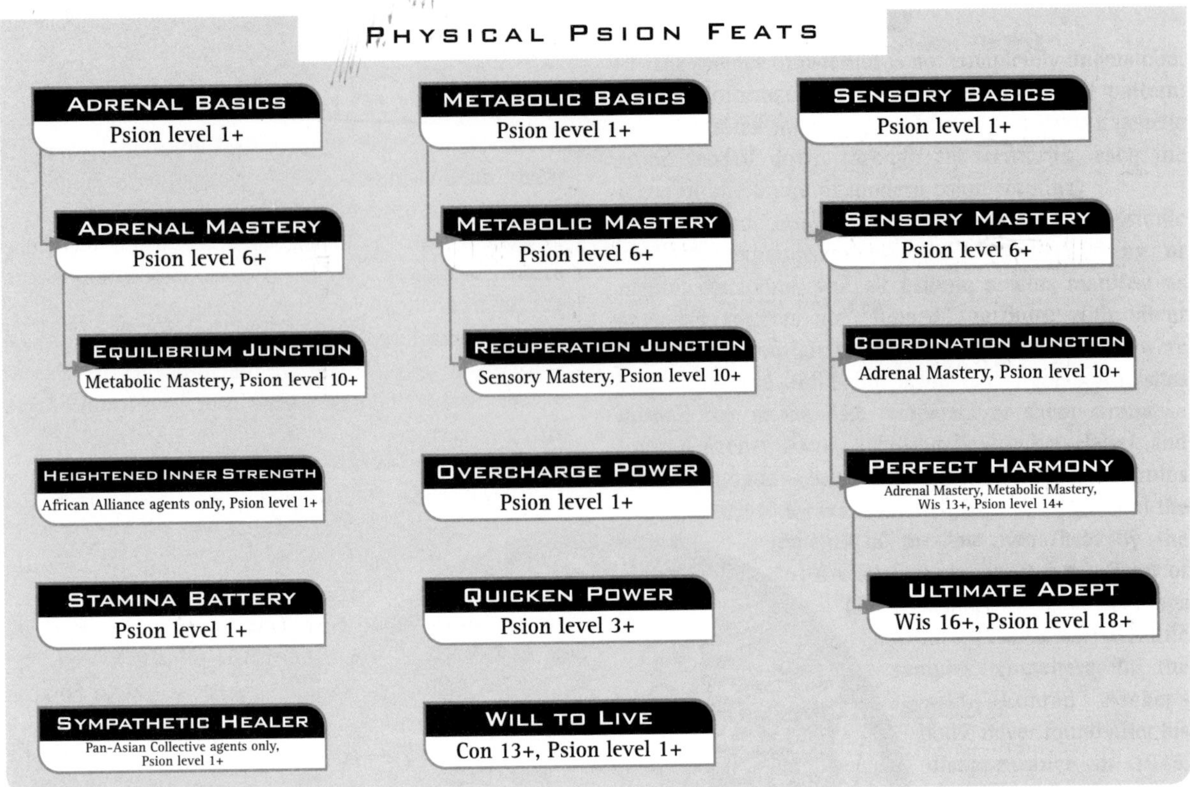

Benefit: You receive a +1 bonus to all of your metabolic and sensory skills when you gain this feat, not to exceed your normal skill limits. In addition, you gain the ability to regenerate 1 wound point every 6 hours.

Sensory Basics

You can enhance or modify your senses to perform such feats as seeing in the dark or surviving in the extreme pressure found at the bottom of the ocean.

Prerequisites: Psion level 1+.

Benefit: You may learn sensory psion skills as though they were class skills.

Normal: Without this feat, you may not learn sensory psion skills.

Sensory Mastery

You have spent a great deal of time and effort perfecting your psionic sensory skills, allowing you to narrowly escape many dangerous situations.

Prerequisites: Sensory Basics, psion level 6+.

Benefit: You may take 10 when using sensory psion skills, even if stress and distraction would normally prevent you from doing so. In addition, once per game session, you automatically succeed at any one Reflex, Fortitude, or Will save of your choice. Announce that you are using this power instead of rolling the dice.

Stamina Battery

You have a hidden reserve of psionic power that you can call upon in times of need.

Prerequisites: Psion level 1+.

Benefit: Each game session, you receive a number of vitality points equal to your psion level. These vitality points may only be spent activating psionic powers – you can't use them to absorb damage like normal vitality points.

Sympathetic Healer

You can heal others by absorbing their wounds into your own body.

Prerequisites: Pan-Asian Collective agents only, psion level 1+.

Benefit: You may, as a half action, transfer a number of your wound or vitality points to an ally by touching them. You may give a number of your vitality or wound points equal to 5 times your psion level in a single half action. This restores an equal number of the same type of points (vitality or wound) to the ally. You may not increase your ally's vitality or wound points past their normal maximum, nor may you reduce your own vitality or wound points below 0.

ULTIMATE ADEPT

You have forged a perfect union between your adrenal, metabolic, and sensory abilities, and awakened the innermost powers of the human body. This is the pinnacle of psion achievement for a physical adept, and one of the most powerful feats ever discovered.

Prerequisites: Wis 16+, Perfect Harmony, psion level 18+.

Benefit: You receive 10 extra wound points. In addition, you receive a +2 bonus to Strength, Dexterity, Constitution, Wisdom, Intelligence, and Charisma when you gain this feat.

WILL TO LIVE

You are particularly hard to kill. When severely wounded, you are likely to keep going.

Prerequisites: Company agents only, psion level 1+, Con 13+.

Benefit: Before your first roll to stabilize when reduced to negative Wound Points, you may make a Fortitude save with a DC of 5 + the number of wounds you are below 0 (6 for –1, 10 for –5, etc.). If the roll succeeds you automatically stabilize. Only one Fortitude save may be made using this feat each time you fall below 0 Wound Points.

PHYSICAL PSION SKILLS

These psion skills allow you to push your body beyond normal human limitations. Adrenal, metabolic, and sensory skills are all considered physical psion skills. Due to early research by Room 39 and (after World War II) the Archer Foundation, many more options are currently open to physical adepts than mentalists and telepaths. These options, and each Chambers' attempts to correct this discrepancy, will be featured in upcoming sourcebooks for each Chamber.

ADRENAL PSION SKILLS

You must have the Adrenal Basics feat in order to take ranks in any adrenal psion skill.

BODY SCULPTING (DEX; TRAINED ONLY)

Requires the Adrenal Basics feat.

You can contort your body in unnatural ways, allowing you to escape from tight spots, blend into the background, or disguise yourself.

Check: A Body Sculpting check requires a half action and adds a psionic bonus to one of your skills for a number of minutes equal to 5 times your psion level. The result of your Body Sculpting check determines the bonus *(see Table 5.1)*, and the power you choose from the list below determines which skill receives the bonus. You can activate more than one of these powers at once, but you must pay the vitality point cost for each.

Triple Jointed: By stretching yourself out unnaturally, you may gain the listed bonus to your Escape Artist skill.

Chameleon: By rapidly changing the color of your skin and clothing, you may gain the listed bonus to your Hide skill.

Clay Face: By changing the appearance of your face and your build, you may gain the listed bonus to your Disguise skill.

Vitality Point Cost: 2

ENERGY BURST (STR; TRAINED ONLY)

Requires the Adrenal Basics feat.

You can send a surge of energy through your body, using hidden reserves to jump farther, swim harder, or smash obstacles in your way.

Check: An Energy Burst check requires a half action and adds a psionic bonus to certain die rolls for a number of minutes equal to 5 times your psion level. The result of your Energy Burst check determines the bonus *(see Table 5.1)*, while the power you choose from the list below determines which die rolls receive the bonus. You may activate more than one of these powers at once, but you must pay the vitality point cost for each.

Bounding Leap: By sending a surge of energy through your legs, you may gain a bonus to your Jump checks and temporarily ignore the normal maximums for jumping distance.

Crushing Blow: By focusing a surge of energy through your fist, you may gain a bonus to Strength checks (for breaking down doors and the like).

Strong Swimmer: By focusing a surge of energy through your arms and legs, you may gain a bonus to Swim checks.

Vitality Point Cost: 2

SPEED CONTROL (DEX; TRAINED ONLY)

Requires the Adrenal Basics feat.

You can temporarily boost your speed and reflexes, allowing you to run faster, fall farther, or act more often during a round of combat.

Check: A Speed Control check requires a free action, and it allows you to activate one of the following powers.

Improve Speed: When you activate this power, your speed is increased for a number of rounds equal to 5 times your psion level. Your speed is increased according to the result of your Speed Control check.

Result	Bonus
up to 15	+5
16–20	+10
21–25	+15
26–30	+20
31+	+25

Graceful Fall: When you activate this power, all falling damage you receive for a number of minutes equal to 5 times your psion level is reduced according to the result of your Speed Control check.

Result	Damage Reduction
up to 15	5/–
16–20	10/–
21–25	15/–
26–30	20/–
31+	25/–

Burst of Speed: When you activate this power, you receive an extra half action at the end of each round while it lasts, after everyone else has performed their actions. If more than one psion uses this power in the same round, then each psion receives his extra action in initiative order. If more than one psion with the same initiative total uses this power in the same round, then each psion receives his extra action in Dexterity order. If there is still a tie, randomly determine the order in which the psions receive their extra action. This power is so exhausting that you may only use it once per combat. The duration of this power depends on the result of your Speed Control check.

Result	Duration
up to 15	1 round
16–20	2 rounds
21–25	3 rounds
26–30	4 rounds
31+	5 rounds

Vitality Point Cost: 2 for improve speed or graceful fall, 8 for burst of speed.

Metabolic Psion Skills

You must have the Metabolic Basics feat in order to take ranks in any metabolic psion skill.

Control Metabolism (Wis; Trained Only)

Requires the Metabolic Basics feat.

You can slow your body's metabolism to a crawl, allowing you to hold your breath for long periods of time, resist extreme temperatures, or pretend to be dead.

Check: A Control Metabolism check requires a half action and allows you to activate one of the following powers. Your Control Metabolism check determines how long the power remains active. You may activate more than one of these powers at once, but you must pay the vitality point cost for each.

Result	Hold Breath	Temp. Dur.	Feign Death Dur.
up to 15	5 minutes	1 minute	10 days
16–20	15 minutes	2 minutes	20 days
21–25	30 minutes	4 minutes	40 days
26–30	60 minutes	8 minutes	80 days
31+	2 hours	16 minutes	160 days

Hold Breath: By reducing your body's need for oxygen, you may increase the length of time you can hold your breath by the duration of this power. You may only use this power once each time you have an opportunity to replenish your breath.

Resist Temperature: By speeding up or slowing down your metabolism, you may create or bleed off excess heat. This gives you Damage Reduction equal to 3 times your psion level against heat- and cold-based attacks while this power is active.

Feign Death: By slowing your heartbeat and other bodily functions almost to a standstill, you may enter a state of suspended animation in which you appear to be dead. You need no food or drink, are unaware of your surroundings, and may take no actions while feigning death. When you use this power, you may choose how long you wish to wait before awakening, or you may set a specific condition under which you will awaken. Additionally, another person can use First Aid to tell that you're still alive (DC 10 + your psion level) or to wake you up prematurely once they've realized that you're alive (DC 25).

Vitality Point Cost: 4

Control Pheromones (Cha; Trained Only)

Requires the Metabolic Basics feat.

You can control the pheromones your body emits, allowing you to subtly manipulate the emotions of those around you.

Check: A Control Pheromones check requires a half action and adds a psionic bonus to one of your skills for a number of minutes equal to 5 times your psion level. The result of the Control Pheromones check determines the bonus *(see Table 5.1)*, while the power you choose from the list below determines which skill receives the bonus. You may activate more than one of these powers at once, but you must pay the vitality point cost for each.

Entice: By giving off attractive pheromones, you may gain a bonus to your Bluff skill when attempting to seduce someone.

Enrage: By giving off pheromones that agitate others, you may gain a bonus to your Taunt attempts.

Frighten: By giving off pheromones that inspire fear in others, you may gain a bonus to your Intimidate skill.

Vitality Point Cost: 2

Pain Transmission (Int; Trained Only)

Requires the Metabolic Basics feat.

Simply by touching an opponent, you can send a blast of blinding pain through his body, causing nerve damage or possibly death.

Check: In order to make a Pain Transmission check, you must first perform a successful touch attack against an opponent. You may then activate this power as a free action to deal damage to the touched opponent. The result of the Pain Transmission check determines how much damage you deal to your target. Damage reduction is not subtracted from damage caused by this power. You may only activate this power once per successful touch attack, and you cannot score critical hits using this power.

Result	Damage
up to 15	1d6 + psion level
16–20	1d8 + psion level
21–25	2d6 + psion level
26–30	2d8 + psion level
31+	3d6 + psion level

Vitality Point Cost: 4

Sensory Psion Skills

You must have the Sensory Basics feat in order to take ranks in any sensory psion skill.

Combat Sense (Int; Trained Only)

Requires the Sensory Basics feat.

Your awareness of your surroundings is sharp enough that you can sense surprise attacks.

Check: A Combat Sense check requires a half action and activates one or more of the following powers for a number of minutes equal to 5 times your psion level. The result of the Combat Sense check determines which powers are activated.

Result	Powers Activated
up to 15	Sense ambush
16–25	Sense ambush, sense flanker
26+	Sense ambush, sense flanker, sense trap

Sense Ambush: By enhancing your sensitivity to light levels and air currents, you may retain your Dexterity bonus to Defense even when flat-footed or struck by an unseen opponent for the duration of this power.

Sense Flanker: By enhancing your sensitivity to vibrations and air currents, you may become immune to flanking attacks for the duration of this power.

Sense Trap: By enhancing your sensitivity to sudden movement and air currents, you may automatically succeed at all Reflex saves against traps for the duration of this power.

Vitality Point Cost: 6

Enhance Senses (Wis; Trained Only)

Requires the Sensory Basics feat.

You can sharpen your senses, allowing you to see and hear more acutely. In addition, you can enhance your sense of smell, allowing you to track like a bloodhound.

Check: An Enhance Senses check requires a half action and adds a psionic bonus to one of your skills for a number of minutes equal to 5 times your psion level. The result of the Enhance Senses check determines the bonus *(see Table 5.1)*, and the power you choose from the list below determines which skill receives the bonus.

Deft Hands: By enhancing your hand-eye coordination, you gain a psionic bonus to your Open Locks and Sleight of Hand checks for a number of minutes equal to 5 times your psion level. The result of the Sensitive Touch check determines the bonus *(see Table 5.1)*.

Keen Eyes: By enhancing your eyesight, you may gain a bonus to your Spot checks.

Keen Hearing: By enhancing your hearing, you may gain a bonus to your Listen checks.

Bloodhound: By enhancing your sense of smell, you may gain a bonus to Survival checks made to find or follow tracks.

Vitality Point Cost: 2

Extended Visual Spectrum (Wis; Trained Only)

Requires the Sensory Basics feat.

You can see into visual spectra that most people are unable to detect. This allows you to see in the dark, or extend your sight into the infrared or ultraviolet spectra.

Check: An Extrnded Visual Spectrum check requires a half action and activates one or more of the following powers for a number of minutes equal to 5 times your psion level. The result of the Extrnded Visual Spectrum check determines which powers are activated.

Result	Powers Activated
up to 15	Low-light sight
16–20	Night sight
21–25	Night sight, infrared spectrum
26+	Night sight, infrared spectrum, sense invisible

Low-light Sight: You can see twice as far as a normal person in poor lighting, and can distinguish details and colors under such conditions. In addition, you ignore concealment penalties caused by up to moderate darkness, and near total darkness provides only one-half concealment to your targets.

Night Sight: You can see normally even in total darkness, and concealment provides no benefit to your targets.

Infrared Spectrum: You can see heat, giving you a +5 psionic bonus to Spot checks when you are trying to find a warm-blooded creature, and a +5 psionic bonus to Search checks when looking for an item that is a different temperature than its surroundings (these modifiers are cumulative with one another). In addition, you gain a +5 psionic bonus to Survival checks when tracking a warm-blooded creature, as long as the trail isn't more than 10 minutes old.

Sense Invisible: You can see any objects or beings that are invisible as if they were visible.

Vitality Point Cost: 2

The Telepath

No other psion is as feared or as misunderstood as the telepath. The earliest telepath serums were derived from the blood of the Demagogue, and that terrible era has permanently scarred the reputation of this field of psionic research and training. Further, the idea of mental intruders, who can steal deeply held secrets or command obedience without an agent's knowledge, is terrifying to secret agents, who live and die by the information they keep locked away in their minds.

Regardless, telepaths have proven one of the Foundation's greatest tools in the secret war to save humanity from dire threats they cannot see, Whether as tools of interrogation, investigation, or brainwashing, telepath's are the cutting edge of psion development in the information age.

Abilities: A telepath should have high Charisma and Wisdom scores. Force of personality is key to the telepaths active abilities while Wisdom supports their perceptive skills. Like all psionic agents, a high Constitution provides additional vitality to power their abilities.

Vitality: 1d10 plus Constitution modifier per level

Class Skills

The telepath's class skills, and the key ability for each, are listed below:

Class Skill	Key Ability
Bluff	Cha
Concentration	Wis
Craft	Int
Diplomacy	Cha
Driver	Dex

Electronics	Int
Gather Information	Cha
Handle Animal	Cha
Hobby	Wis
Intimidate	Str or Cha
Knowledge	Int
Languages	Wis
Profession	Wis
Sense Motive	Wis
Sport	Str or Dex

Skill Points at 1st level: (6 + Int modifier) × 4.

Skill Points at each additional level: 6 + Int modifier.

Class Features

All of the following are class features of the telepath.

Psionic Class: The telepath is a psionic class. Levels gained in this class increase your psion level.

Class Feats: The telepath begins play with the following feats.

Armor Proficiency (Light)
Armor Proficiency (Medium)
Weapon Group Proficiency (Melee)
Weapon Group Proficiency (Handgun)

Sensitive: Whenever the telepath spends an action die to add to a telepathic psion skill check, the results of that die are also added to his psion level (to a maximum of 25) to determine the effectiveness of the power for that skill check only (e.g. a 1st-level telepath who spends an action die and rolls a 3 adds +3 to his skill check result and increases his psion level by 3 for the purposes of that skill check). This is the telepath's core ability.

Telepathic Psion Feats: At 1st level, the telepath may begin choosing feats from the telepathic psion feats category. The telepath must still have the slots free for any feats he selects, and must still meet all prerequisites for any feat chosen.

Bonus Feat: At 1st level, the telepath gets a bonus basic or telepathic psion feat. A telepath must still meet all prerequisites for a feat, including ability score and base attack bonus minimums. At 4th level, and every 4 levels thereafter, the telepath receives an additional bonus basic or telepathic psion feat.

Force of Will: Starting at 2nd level, once per game session as a free action, the telepath may add half his psion level (rounded down) to his Charisma or Wisdom for ten rounds. This power is so exhausting that when it wears off, the telepath must rest for a full round, taking no actions and using no psion skills. This ability's duration may be cut short at the player's discretion, but the agent suffers the full round exhaustion penalty, regardless. At 11th and 19th level, the telepath may use this ability one additional time per game session.

Psi Mastery: Starting at 3rd level, the telepath chooses a telepathic psion skill that he has at least 1 rank in. He receives a +2 psionic bonus to all skill checks with that skill. For every 2 levels after 3rd, the telepath selects an additional telepathic psion skill to receive this bonus, choosing a different skill each time.

Psychic Escape: The telepath has an uncanny ability to escape harm. At 6th level, the telepath receives a +1 psionic bonus to all Fortitude, Reflex and Will saving throws. For every 3 levels after 6th, the telepath's psionic bonus to all saves increases by +1.

Blind Spot: Starting at 10th level, once per game session, the telepath may use his powers to create a "blind spot." One object or individual of up to the Large-size or smaller becomes effectively invisible to all minds within the telepath's Imprint skill range *(see page 201)*. This increases the DC of all Spot checks to notice the target a number equal to the telepath's psion level. Mechanical devices are unaffected but living minds relying on such devices (such as a guard watching a TV

Telepaths: The Bogeymen of the Spy Business

In the world of *Shadowforce Archer,* telepaths are a conundrum. During World War II, the rise of the Demagogue demonstrated with tragic clarity the influence that telepaths could have on the minds of millions – and the very course of history. All subsequent telepaths were created with formulae distilled from the Demagogue's blood, and the memory of those terrible events still taints the world's view of all mental psions.

Since the earliest days of the Archer Foundation, it has been been something of an open international secret that psionic powers exist. But since the number of agents with the skill and training to consistently resist the powers of a skilled telepath are few and far between, the Foundation has kept most sensitive information about them from outside agencies. So while everyone in the intelligence business knows telepaths exist, only a select few truly know their capabilities.

All this has earned telepaths a reputation as the bogeymen of the shadow community. Many telepaths play upon this fear, hinting that they can rip thoughts from people's minds and take over people's bodies like their counterparts of classic science fiction.

Certainly within the shadowed halls of the Foundation itself, high-ranking telepaths observe security briefings and conduct "loyalty inspections," though in reality this reputation is at best half true. Telepaths *can* override bodily impulse. Incredibly poweful and skilled telepaths can even pick up surface thoughts... sometimes. But only the greatest minds begin to approach the capabilities evidenced by the Demagogue.

monitor) ignore the evidence of their senses if they are within the telepath's Imprint skill range (suffering the DC penalty described above). If an individual does spot the hidden object or person, he is no longer affected by this use of the blind spot ability, but any attempt to aid others in spotting the target automatically fails. This ability may last for up to one hour, and costs the telepath one vitality point per minute it is in effect. At 20th level, the telepath may use this ability twice per game session.

Mind Wipe: Perhaps the most dreaded of all telepath abilities, mind wipe allows the telepath to selectively erase recent memories from the minds of one or more individuals. Starting at 14th level, once per session, the telepath may spend an action die to force an agent to make a Will save with a DC of 15 plus the telepath's psion level. If the save succeeds, the target is unaffected and the power is not considered to have been used this session. Regardless of the save's result, the action die is spent, and the telepath may not target the same individual again this session.

If the target fails, the telepath may selectively erase any memories the target has gained during the last hour. This does not allow the telepath to plant new memories so care must be taken if the telepath does not wish the target to notice the gaping holes in his recall. Additional individuals may be affected by spending one action die per additional target, but the same events or knowledge must be erased from all of the targets' memories as one action.

Mind Wipe takes a full round per target, requires line of sight, and has a maximum range of 50 feet.

Telepathic Psion Feats

You must have a telepath level of 1 or more to take any feats from this category.

Connection Junction

Your abilities to sense and project thoughts have become so intertwined that you can now communicate by classic telepathy.

Prerequisites: ESP Mastery, Imprint Mastery, psion level 10+.

Benefit: You receive a +1 bonus to all of your ESP and imprint skills when you gain this feat, not to exceed your normal skill limits. In addition, characters you have contacted via imprint skills are now considered to have the equivalent skills and abilities to converse with you, allowing true two-way communication with non-telepaths.

Table 5.4: The Telepath

Lvl	Base Att Bon	Fort Save	Ref Save	Will Save	Def Bon	Init Bon	Budg Pts	Gadg Pts	Special
1	+0	+0	+2	+1	+0	+1	3	0	Telepathic psion feats, bonus feat, *sensitive*
2	+1	+0	+3	+2	+1	+2	6	1	Force of will 1/session
3	+1	+1	+3	+2	+1	+3	9	2	Psi mastery
4	+2	+1	+4	+2	+2	+3	12	3	Bonus feat
5	+2	+1	+4	+3	+2	+4	15	3	Psi mastery
6	+3	+2	+5	+3	+2	+5	18	4	Psychic escape (+1)
7	+3	+2	+5	+4	+3	+6	21	5	Psi mastery
8	+4	+2	+6	+4	+3	+6	24	6	Bonus feat
9	+4	+3	+6	+4	+4	+7	27	6	Psi mastery, psychic escape (+2)
10	+5	+3	+7	+5	+4	+8	30	7	Blind spot 1/session
11	+5	+3	+7	+5	+4	+9	33	8	Force of will 2/session, psi mastery
12	+6	+4	+8	+6	+5	+10	36	9	Bonus feat, psychic escape (+3)
13	+6	+4	+8	+6	+5	+10	39	9	Psi mastery
14	+7	+4	+9	+6	+6	+11	42	10	Mind wipe
15	+7	+5	+9	+7	+6	+12	45	11	Psi mastery, psychic escape (+4)
16	+8	+5	+10	+8	+7	+14	48	12	Bonus feat
17	+8	+5	+10	+8	+7	+14	51	12	Psi mastery
18	+9	+6	+11	+8	+7	+14	54	13	Psychic escape (+5)
19	+9	+6	+11	+8	+8	+15	57	14	Force of will 3/session, psi mastery
20	+10	+6	+12	+9	+8	+16	60	15	Blind spot 2/session, bonus feat

ESP Basics

You pick up impressions and other subtle clues about your environment.

Prerequisites: Psion level 1+.

Benefit: You may learn ESP psion skills as though they were class skills.

Normal: Without this feat, you may not learn ESP psion skills.

ESP Mastery

Your sensitivity to psychic impressions has steadily improved, allowing you to sense things even without entirely meaning to.

Prerequisites: ESP Basics, psion level 6+.

Benefit: You may take 10 when using ESP psion skills, even if stress and distraction would normally prevent you from doing so. Further, you may now use your ESP skills on objects and people within line of sight rather than having to touch them.

Expanded Horizons

Your awareness of events present and future has become so precise that you seem almost inhumanly calm and ready at all times. Life holds few surprises for you anymore.

Prerequisites: Cha 13+, ESP Mastery, Imprint Mastery, Intuitive Mastery, psion level 14+.

Benefit: Whenever you have the opportunity to make a save in order to suffer half damage or a reduced negative effect, you instead suffer no damage or effect with a successful save. In addition, all of your telepathic psion skills have a range equal to your psion level times your Charisma modifier in miles.

Imprint Basics

By force of will you are able to force your thoughts or feelings into the minds of others.

Prerequisites: Psion level 1+.

Benefit: You may learn imprint psion skills as though they were class skills.

Normal: Without this feat, you may not learn imprint psion skills.

Imprint Mastery

Practice has sharpened your skills, greatly improving the effectiveness of your imprint psion skills.

Prerequisites: Imprint Basics, psion level 6+.

Benefit: You may take 10 when using imprint psion skills, even if stress and distraction would normally prevent you from doing so. Further, you may now use your imprint psion skills on objects and people within line of sight rather than having to touch them.

Insinuation Junction

You have learned to use your intuition to guide your telepathy, allowing you to breach the mental defenses of others far more easily.

Prerequisites: Intuitive Mastery, Imprint Mastery, psion level 10+.

Benefit: You receive a +1 bonus to all of your imprint and intuitive psion skills when you gain this feat, not to exceed your normal skill limits. Further, the DC of all saving throws against your psion skills and class abilities is increased by +4.

Intuitive Basics

You are subject to flashes of insight, hints about the future or a nagging sense of what is to come.

Prerequisites: Psion level 1+.

Benefit: You may learn intuitive psion skills as though they were class skills.

Normal: Without this feat, you may not learn intuitive psion skills.

Intuitive Mastery

You have spent a great deal of time and effort perfecting your intuitive psion skills.

Prerequisites: Intuitive Basics, psion level 6+.

Benefit: You may take 10 when using intuitive psion skills, even if stress and distraction would normally prevent you from doing so. Further, you gain the fixer's evasion ability: whenever you have the opportunity to make a Reflex save in order to suffer half damage from an effect (such as a grenade), you instead suffer no damage with a successful save.

Premonition Junction

Your psychic senses begin to merge with your intuitive side, giving you critical moments to act before disaster strikes.

Prerequisites: ESP Mastery, Intuitive Mastery, psion level 10+.

Benefit: You receive a +1 bonus to all of your ESP and intuitive skills when you gain this feat, not to exceed your normal skill limits. Further, you never suffer the penalties of being caught flat-footed.

Sustained Link

You are able to keep a power active for extended periods of time.

Prerequisites: Psion level 6+.

Benefit: While using any psion skill with a variable duration, at the end of that duration you may spend vitality to activate the power again for the same duration without rolling the skill check a second time.

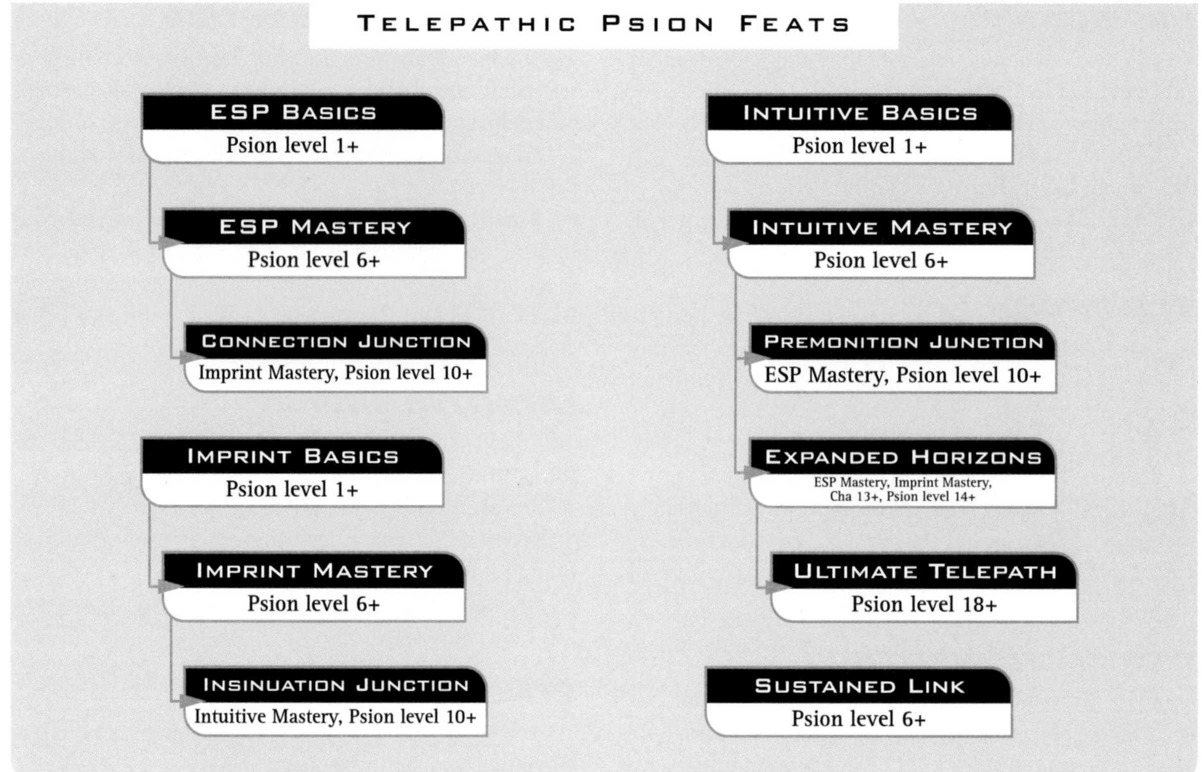

ULTIMATE TELEPATH

The strength of your will can reach around the world to touch the minds of anyone, anywhere.

Prerequisites: Expanded Horizons, psion level 18+.

Benefit: Whenever you have the opportunity to make a save in order to suffer half damage or a reduced negative effect, you suffer half damage or reduce effect even if you fail your save. Further, your ESP and imprint psion skills may reach out to 1000 miles, and by spending an action die you may reach anywhere on the globe or in near orbit.

TELEPATHIC PSION SKILLS

These psion skills allow you to touch the world in many subtle ways and expand your ordinary senses. ESP, Imprint, and Intuitive skills are all considered telepathic psion skills.

ESP PSION SKILLS

Many telepaths can pick up clues from other minds as well as their environment. This ESP makes the telepath a remarkable investigator and interrogator. The range of these skills is severely restricted for less powerful telepaths, beginning at touch and slowly expanding as the agent gains feats which increase his range.

You must have the ESP Basics feat in order to take ranks in any ESP psion skill.

CLAIRSENTIENCE (WIS; TRAINED ONLY)

Requires the ESP Basics feat.

You are able to "throw" your senses outward, experiencing other areas from a remote location. Initially you may only project your point of view up to one 5-foot square away, though this is often enough to peek past closed doors or through walls, floors, and ceilings. When you gain the ESP Mastery feat, this range increases to 50 feet. The Expanded Horizons and Ultimate Telepath feats extend the range of this skill as described in those feats.

Check: Using this feat requires you to spend one full round concentrating before its effects begin. The duration of the remote viewing is equal to 1 round plus a number of rounds equal to the bonus generated on Table 5.1. You cannot move your point of view while using this skill – you must stop and focus for another round before projecting to a new point. While using this skill, you are considered flat-footed. Being injured while using this skill ends the effect unless you succeed with a Concentration check (DC equal to 10 + the damage taken).

Observe: This is a full sensory experience: you see in full color, hear normally, and can smell and even feel by touch (though you cannot move objects in any way). You do not benefit from any artificial viewing aids. For example, if you are wearing night vision goggles and use this skill to perceive a darkened room, the goggles offer you no benefit.

Remote Focus: With additional effort you may use clairsentience as a guide for other psion skills that require line of sight.

Vitality Point Cost: 1 per round to Observe, 3 per round when using it to Remote Focus.

Empathy (Cha; Trained Only)

Requires the ESP Basics feat.

You are skilled at reading the emotional states of others. This does not allow you to read their thoughts, but is very useful in determining their true feelings and forming "gut" reactions during interviews and interrogations.

Soothsayer: You are extraordinarily adept at sensing falsehood. The DC for someone to deceive you (e.g. with Bluff) is increased by the result of your Soothsayer check *(see Table 5.1)*. Also, you receive the same bonus to all checks to see through disguises. If the target is aware of your telepathic abilities, he may attempt to resist by making a Will save against a DC of 10 plus your psion level. If he is successful, you lose your bonus against the target for the remainder of the session.

Sympathy: By carefully monitoring a target's responses, you can tailor your words and actions to gain greatest effect. This allows you to add a psionic bonus to the result of all your Bluff, Diplomacy, and Gather Information skills, according to the result of your Empathy check *(see Table 5.1)*. If the target is aware that you are a telepath, he may attempt to suppress his reactions by making a Will save against a DC of 10 plus your psion level. If he succeeds, you lose your bonus against him for the remainder of the session.

Vitality Point Cost: 3 per minute.

Psychometry (Wis; Trained Only)

Requires the ESP Basics feat.

By touching an object, you can gain a sense of strong emotions that have been felt and events that happened around it.

Object History: By handling an object for three full rounds and making a Psychometry check, you may learn the following information about the item's last owner. Ownership is defined as possession for one month or more – an object possessed by someone for less than a month may only be tapped for information about the last person who possessed it for one month or more. An object with no previous owner reveals no information.

Result	Knowledge
up to 15	Last owner's gender
16–20	Last owner's age (within 5 years)
21–25	Last owner's highest class level
26–30	Last owner's emotional state right now
31+	Current direction of last owner now

Rolls higher than 15 gain not only the knowledge mentioned, but all entries prior (for instance, if use of this ability reveals the last owner's class or classes, it also reveals the last owner's age and gender).

Object Memory: By handling an object for one full round, you may gain a brief visual "flash" of recent events surrounding it. Declare a one-hour time period you wish to witness and make your Psychometry check, consulting the table below for the DC. Success grants you a six-second visual replay of the most important event that occurred within the item's "line of sight" during the specified time period. This flash consumes the psion's next half action, as he focuses on the image replaying in his mind. The GC determines the most important event during the specified time period, and any future Psychometry checks to see the same time period yield the same information.

Time period is...	DC of Skill Check
Within last hour	10
Within last day	15
Within last week	20
Within last month	25
Within last year	30
Each additional year	+1

Vitality Point Cost: 3

Imprint Psion Skills

Use of an Imprint skill requires a touch attack against unwilling recipients (applying the agent's Intelligence modifier rather than his Dexterity modifier). The range of these skills begins at touch. Telepaths with the Imprint Mastery feat may use their Imprint skills along line of sight, making a ranged touch attack to target unwilling recipients (again, applying their Intelligence modifier). If they have feats that extend their range beyond this limit they no longer need to make attack rolls to target any character within their range, but they must still know the target's location to within 25 feet to target them with Imprint skills.

You must have the Imprint Basics feat in order to take ranks in any imprint psion skill.

Dominion (Cha; Trained Only)

Requires the Imprint Basics feat.

You can enter the mind of someone else and implant a powerful compulsion to perform a single action.

Check: Using Dominion requires you to concentrate solely on the power for one full round. You cannot move and are considered flat-footed while concentrating. Using Dominion does not require you to speak to the target, but many telepaths do so out of habit. The DC of your target's Will save to resist the compulsion is 5 plus a bonus determined by the result of your Dominion check *(see Table 5.1)*. With a successful save, the target resists the Dominion attempt and is immediately aware that someone is tampering with his mind. With a failed save, you may activate one of the following effects.

Command: Through brute mental force you control the target's actions and may dictate his physical actions for one full round. The target will not take any action to injure or kill himself or those he considers allies (according to his disposition). You may compel the target to speak, but only words you choose; this ability may not be used to force a target to divulge information unknown to you.

Plant: You may create simple memories of up to 1 minute in length in the target's mind. Because the target's mind fills in the details and helps "set" the memory within the context of his own experience, you only need to describe the new memory in general terms for it to be effective.

Suggestion: By placing subtle mental urges, you may coerce the target's weaker mind into doing your bidding. You may suggest a course of action (limited to a sentence or two) which does not place the target at obvious risk or incapacitate him (e.g. you cannot put someone to sleep using this power). The target pursues the course of action until completed or a number of minutes equal to your psion level has elapsed. The target instantly puts aside the suggested task to defend himself if attacked. A target may be the subject of only one suggestion at a time.

Vitality Point Cost: 7

Project Thought (Int; Trained Only)

Requires the Imprint Basics feat.

You can send silent messages that are heard only in the minds of those you contact.

Check: Using Project Thought allows you to send thoughts to another individual within your range. Each additional person you contact beyond the first applies a –4 penalty to the result of your check.

Result	Duration
up to 15	1 round
16–20	2 rounds
21–25	3 rounds
26–30	4 rounds
31+	5 rounds

Speech: You may speak to the individual normally without vocalization.

Scream: By unleashing a blast of concentrated thought you may stun a target's mind. Once each round as a half action, you may inflict 1d4 subdual damage on any target within your range. The target must also make a Will save with a DC of 10 + your psion level or suffer 1d4 temporary Intelligence damage. This damage is recovered at the rate of 1 point per round after this power's duration expires.

Vitality Point Cost: 3

Telempathy (Wis; Trained Only)

Requires the Imprint Basics feat.

You may carefully focus your emotions and impress them upon another, compelling them to feel as you do.

Check: A telempathy check allows you to activate one of the following powers. You may only have one of these powers active at any time. The duration of the emotional influence is equal to 1 round plus a number of rounds equal to the bonus generated on Table 5.1. Each target beyond the first applies a –4 penalty to your telempathy check.

Calm: The target gains a +4 psionic bonus to all Concentration checks for the duration of this power.

Friendship: You encourage the target to act in a more agreeable manner. The target must make a Will save with a DC of 10 + your psion level or his disposition toward you is improved by one category for the duration of this power.

Revulsion: You disrupt the target's equilibrium. The target must make a Fortitude save with a DC of 10 + your psion level or suffer a –4 penalty to all attacks, damage, and skill rolls for the duration of this power.

Vertigo: You confuse and overwhelm the target with sensory input. The target must make a Fortitude save with a DC of 10 + your psion level or suffer 1d4 Wisdom damage. This damage is recovered immediately after this power's duration expires.

Vitality Point Cost: 4

Intuitive Psion Skills

Telepaths frequently display abilities that continue to baffle even the most advanced researchers at the Archer Foundation. While mentalists can unlock the powers of the conscious, thinking mind, telepaths seem to be able to draw on the dark pool of the subconscious.

You must have the Intuitive Basics feat in order to take ranks in any intuitive psion skill.

Catalyst (Con; Trained Only)

Requires the Imprint Basics feat.

More than any other type of psion, the telepath seems to be hooked into the underlying nature of all psionic abilities. Those with the catalyst skill are able to influence the very nature of psionic abilities.

Aid: You may provide some of the energy for another agent's psion powers. Makes a Catalyst check to determine how many points you may contribute.

Result	Bonus
6 or less	failure (0 vitality)
7-15	1 vitality
16-20	2 vitality
21-25	3 vitality
26-30	4 vitality
31+	5 vitality

Counter-psi: As a half action, you may make a Catalyst skill check with a DC of another psion's skill roll to cancel their skill use. This may be done to skills with a duration at any point during that duration.

Dampen: You are able to generate a field that 'grounds' the use of psionic energy. The vitality costs of any psionic abilities that require the expenditure of vitality points are doubled when activated or maintained inside the field. This field has a radius equal to 5 feet times your psion level, and lasts for a number of minutes determined by your Catalyst check.

Result	Duration
up to 15	1 minute
16-20	2 minutes
21-25	3 minutes
26-30	4 minutes
31+	5 minutes

Vitality Point Cost: The cost for Aid is equal to the number of points given +3. Counter Psi costs the number of points spent on the canceled skill +3. Dampen costs 5 vitality points.

Precognition (Wis; Trained Only)

Requires the Intuitive Basics feat.

You are able to sense the flow of future events. While this does not render concrete results, it can provide guidance and considerable short term advantage.

Augury: You may attempt to get a feel for an immediate (one round) course of action you might take, to tell if it will have positive or negative effects. Indicate the action you are considering and spend one half action concentrating. The GC makes a secret Precognition check for you (DC 10, 15 if another member of your team will be taking the action). If the check succeeds, the GC informs you the action is "beneficial," "detrimental," "both," or "neither." If the check fails, the GC informs you the action is "neither." Either way, the GC doesn't tell you whether the check succeeded.

Combat Precog: Your future-sense guides you away from dangerous consequences. As a free action, you may make a Precognition check and add the results from the following table as a psionic bonus to your Defense. This bonus lasts for a number of rounds equal to half your psion level (rounded up).

Result	Bonus
6 or less	failure (no Defense bonus)
7-15	+1 Defense
16-20	+2 Defense
21-25	+3 Defense
26-30	+4 Defense
31+	+5 Defense

Vitality Point Cost: 4

Synthesis (Int; Trained Only)

Requires the Intuitive Basics feat.

You are capable of making subconscious connections between events and information, allowing you to piece together puzzles that confound others.

Sleep On It: You may allow your subconscious to attack a problem for you. By getting 8 hours of sleep after determining the nature of a problem, you may make a Synthesis check to gain a psionic bonus to a single inspiration or education roll you make to resolve that problem *(see Table 5.1)*.

"Something's Missing...": After a failed Gather Information or Search check, you may make a Synthesis check against the same DC to try and discern the information indirectly.

Vitality Point Cost: 3

PsiTech Gadgets

In the *Shadowforce Archer* setting, gadgets are created by mentalists, psions with the gift of thinking outside the box of conventional science. This does not mean that mentalists can betray the laws of physics, or that they're capable of bending time, converting matter, or creating life. They are not magicians (though they are often referred to as such). They are merely capable of envisioning and building technologies that mundane culture would not get around to for years.

Most mentalists work with or for the Shop, and most gadgets constructed in the *Shadowforce Archer* setting originally came from the Shop. Unfortunately for the Foundation, the Shop left some "surprises" behind when they left, not all of which have been found yet. When an agent scores a critical failure using a Shop device, the GC may rule that it has been booby-trapped... and let the agent suffer the consequences.

CONCEPT

Mentalists look at the world in a different way than other people. Where we look at a pen, for example, and see a writing instrument, they see thousands of other possibilities. We might *imagine* those possibilities, but only mentalists actually *see them on a mechanical level.* This is what makes them special.

DESIGN

Mentalists speak in their own language, using a sophisticated techno-jargon only faintly related to scientific terms. Their blueprints are mazes of assumptions that they couldn't explain to their non-mentalist peers if they tried. The rest of the world is simply not prepared for the information they take for granted.

CONSTRUCTION

Mentalists are restricted in one important respect: they must work with the same basic building materials as everyone else. They can fabricate parts, of course, but ultimately they are limited to metals, chemicals, and particles already known to science. This works to the Foundation's advantage, however, since most items designed by their mentalists at least *look* like something familiar to the world at large...

REQUISITIONING GADGETS

Agents requisitioning gadgets from the Archer Foundation use the gadget points system from the *Spycraft Espionage Handbook*. That section contains all rules concerning gadgets, including building multiple gadget options into a single housing, and definitions of special gadget-only traits like "experts only" and "super-science."

ANTI-PSI TECHNOLOGY

Only used in the most dire of circumstances, anti-psi technology emits an electro-magnetic pulse that disrupts the use of psion powers. Anti-psi technology has significant drawbacks, however; it can permanently injure both psions and non-psions, scrambling their thoughts or punching "holes" in their minds (effectively eliminating knowledge or memories).

Anti-Psi Grenade: This is a one-shot "burst" weapon that wipes out psion use within a 20-foot radius. These are the most "dirty" of all anti-psi weapons. Anti-psi grenades are normally disguised as standard flash grenades.

Gadget Point Cost: 1 each.

Weight: 1/2 lb.

Spot DC: 20 (experts only, super-science).

Mechanics: Anyone caught in the grenade's radius of effect finds his psionic feats and skills disabled for 1 hour. In addition, everyone in the blast radius (even those without psion abilities) must make a Will save (DC 10) or forget everything that happened during the last 10 minutes.

Safety Field: Commonly concealed within simple jewelry or clothing, this gadget emits a low-power anti-psi field around the agent, extending out 5 feet.

Gadget Point Cost: 1 each.

Weight: –

Spot DC: 30 (no housing, super-science).

Mechanics: The wearer of this gadget gets a +2 to all saves against psionic abilities, and the DC to affect him with any psionic ability is increased by 2.

Sappers: When sprinkled onto a target's skin, these tiny flakes slowly absorb psion ability. They are too small to cause permanent harm.

Gadget Point Cost: 1 per use.

Weight: –

Spot DC: 30 (no housing, super-science).

Mechanics: Until washed off, the vitality cost of all of the target's psion skills is increased by 2.

CELL PHONE MODELS

Cell phones contain many options and have proven a godsend to agents in the field. You may take the standard cell phone option on its own, or take the standard option and then take more options from those below at the additional costs listed (e.g. taking a standard cell phone equipped with a remote control unit costs a total of 2 gadget points). You may have a maximum of three options (including the standard option) in any single cell phone.

Standard: The standard agency cell phone is protected through a variety of complex message filters. Agents of the Foundation frequently use dedicated encrypted cell phones during short-term, isolated operations.

This gadget (or another standard cell phone gadget) must be purchased as a housing first before you can add any of the options listed below.

Gadget Point Cost: 1 each.

Weight: 1/2 lb.

Spot DC: 25 (experts only).

Mechanics: Add +15 to the DC of any checks made to intercept calls from this phone.

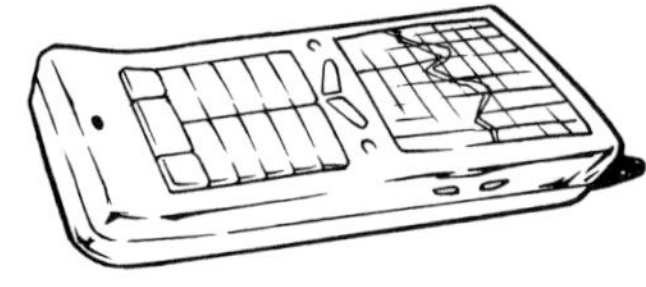

Remote Control: With enough time and parts (plus the know-how), practically anything can be linked to a cell-phone remote control. Vehicles and weapons are long-time agent favorites.

Gadget Point Cost: +1.

Weight: –

Spot DC: -5.

Mechanics: The agent must determine what the cell phone is linked to when requisitioning the gadget. As a half action, the agent can activate and – in the case of a vehicle – steer the linked device. All skill rolls using the remotely operated device suffer a -4 interface penalty due to the awkward nature of the disguised controls.

Slip-Away Unit: When triggered, a sensitive ultrasonic emitter located in the earpiece of this cell phone causes immense pain in anyone within 30 feet without ear plugs or similar protection.

Gadget Point Cost: +2.

Weight: –

Spot DC: +0.

Mechanics: Those within the area of effect must make Will saves (DC 15) or be stunned for 1d3 rounds. This unit comes with enough earplug filters for the agent's whole team. The unit uses a great deal of power and must be recharged at headquarters after each use.

New Clothing Options

Chameleon Bodysuit: The chameleon bodysuit is designed to both visually conceal the diver and protect him from the rigors of the ocean depths. The suit is easily damaged, however, after which it loses these abilities *(see below)*. A surface variant is currently in development.

Gadget Point Cost: +8.

Weight: –

Spot DC: 25 (when not in use, experts only).

Mechanics: As a free action, the wearer of this suit may turn invisible (giving him total concealment – *see the Spycraft Espionage Handbook, page 171*). He may take any actions he desires, including attacking, without revealing himself. Environmental conditions, such as heavy rain or sand, may reveal his position, however (reducing his concealment to three-quarters or one-half, at the GC's option). Characters who can see in the infrared or ultraviolet spectrums (by virtue of gear, abilities, or other effects) can see agents wearing a chameleon suit normally, and their attack rolls suffer no concealment modifier from the suit's invisibility effect.

The suit's ability may be used for a total of 10 minutes (60 rounds) a day, after which it must recharge until the next day. The suit may be turned on and off at the agent's leisure, so long as the total time it remains in use does not exceed 10 minutes.

Finally, if the wearer suffers more than 10 points of damage from a single hit, the suit's camouflage ability shorts out for the rest of the day until its self-repair circuits can fix the damage.

Disguise Enhancer: Usually employed by Pan-Asian Collective deep cover agents, the disguise enhancer projects false sensory impressions into the minds of others. These false impressions fool all five of the victim's senses. With this gadget, the practical restrictions of disguise (such as a 6 ft., 4 in. man disguising himself as a small child) do not apply. This gadget is usually incorporated into a piece of clothing, such as a shirt or jacket, though other items, such as personal radios, are sometimes used.

Gadget Point Cost: +5.

Weight: Per housing.

Spot DC: 20 (modified by housing – per GC, super-science).

Mechanics: When an agent is using the disguise enhancer, NPCs may not make a Spot check to see through his disguise. Instead, they must make a Will save with a DC equal to 15 plus the agent's rank in the Disguise skill.

"Void" Pocket: Generally incorporated into a real pocket, this device allows an agent to hide items he would not normally be able to conceal on his person. When the void pocket wraps around such an item, any unsightly bulge is concealed.

Gadget Point Cost: +2.

Weight: –

Spot DC: 20 (super-science).

Mechanics: A void pocket can conceal one item from sight completely. When an NPC makes a Spot or Search check to find the item, they only succeed with a critical success. The void pocket has no effect on electronic means of detection, such as a metal detector or using a thermal imager to find an item that is warmer than its surroundings.

Diving Equipment

Diving equipment may include many options. You may take the standard diving suit option on its own, or take the standard option and then more options from those below at the additional costs listed (e.g. taking a standard diving suit equipped with the chameleon option costs a total of 2 gadget points). You may have a maximum of three options (including the standard option) in any single diving suit. When more than one option offers the same benefit (such as maximum diving depth), only the highest benefit is applied.

Standard: The standard "snake-suit" protects its wearer from the rigors of greater ocean depths than its mundane counterpart. Aquatica personnel *(see page 56)* are all provided personal snake-suits.

This gadget (or another standard diving suit gadget) must be purchased as a housing first before you can add any of the options listed below.

Gadget Point Cost: 1 each.

Weight: 20 lb.

Spot DC: 25 (experts only).

Mechanics: The snake-suit allows its wearer to breathe underwater for up to six hours at depths up to 500 ft. without suffering pressure damage, the bends, or euphoria.

Fluid Breath Tanks: This option allows the diver's lungs to sustain the added pressure of great depths.

Gadget Point Cost: +1.

Weight: +15 lb.

Spot DC: 15 (experts only).

Mechanics: This option increases the standard diving suit gadget's depth tolerance to an incredible 1500 feet.

Oxygenated Chewing Gum: This device appears and tastes like a normal pack of chewing gun. In reality, chewing it provides the agent with a 10 minute supply of oxygen.

Gadget Point Cost: +1.

Weight: +15 lb.

Spot DC: 30 (obvious, super-science).

Mechanics: The agent is unaffected by drowning or gases for 10 minutes. This option includes 6 sticks of gum.

Propellers: Many diving suit gadgets are equipped with micro-propellers (mounted along the diver's flanks or on his shoulder blades), allowing him to get around quickly. Movement is possible in any direction except directly backward.

Gadget Point Cost: +1.

Weight: +5 lb.

Spot DC: Automatic.

Mechanics: When swimming as a half action, the agent may move at half his normal speed. When swimming as a full action, the wearer may move at his full normal speed.

New Evidence Analysis Items

These gadgets (sometimes called "sniffers") work like rudimentary chemical analysis kits. When one picks up trace gases, it breaks them apart and identifies their components. This has two significant uses. First, stains and other evidence can often be analyzed without the need for complex chemical comparisons, greatly aiding field investigations. Second, various smells (including human perspiration) can be used to track and identify suspects, even people disguised with advanced materials such as memory flesh *(see page 211)*.

Dedicated Unit: The dedicated model can only be programmed to identify one smell at a time.

Gadget Point Cost: 1 each.

Weight: 2 lb.

Spot DC: 25 (often no housing).

Mechanics: As the external unit (below), except that it takes 10 minutes to program the unit to detect a new smell.

External Unit: This sniffer model has the most utility, with a built-in micro-computer containing the particulars of thousands of smells and precision cross-reference software.

Gadget Point Cost: 3 each.

Weight: 2 lb.

Spot DC: 25 (often no housing).

Mechanics: This gadget is capable of identifying trace elements in the air nearby, and can be used like a bloodhound, adding +6 to skill checks made to identify gases and Survival checks made for tracking.

Nasal Implant: This sniffer surgically replaces the agent's natural sense of smell, making it ideal for agents who wish to remain discreet.

Gadget Point Cost: 6 each.

Weight: –

Spot DC: 30 (experts only, super-science).

Mechanics: As the external unit. A failed save against a gas-based attack burns the implant out for 1 day, leaving the agent without a sense of smell for the duration.

This gadget is kept by the agent after being requisitioned, but it must be replaced once a year (at the full cost) as its power cells wear out. This implant cannot be detected through normal medical examinations – a medical professional must look for it.

Ear Implants

Though far from "cybernetic," some gadgets are improved versions of existing medical implants, including these inner-ear devices.

Ear implants may contain many options. You may take the standard implant option on its own, or take the standard option and then more options from those below at the additional costs listed (e.g. taking a standard ear implant equipped with a blindman unit costs a total of 9 gadget points). You may have a maximum of two options (including the standard option) in any single ear implant.

Standard: The standard ear implant among most Archer teams is the sub-cochlear implant, a two-way transceiver which amplifies and transmits low whispers.

This gadget (or another standard ear implant) must be purchased as a housing first before you can add any of the options listed below.

Gadget Point Cost: 4 each.

Weight: –

Spot DC: 30 (experts only, super-science).

Mechanics: This device transmits whispered messages to and from all similar devices on the same frequency in a 1 mile radius. The frequency is adjusted with an infrared programming device – typically, all members of a team have their implants set to the same frequency before a mission.

This gadget (and all extra options installed into it) is kept by the agent after being requisitioned, but it must be replaced once a year (at the full cost of the standard option, plus all extra options installed into it) as its power cells wear out. This implant cannot be detected through normal medical examinations – a medical professional must look for it.

Blindman Unit: This enhancement improves the agent's spatial awareness, allowing him to sense his surroundings in dimly lit or unlighted areas.

Gadget Point Cost: +5.

Weight: –

Spot DC: +0.

Mechanics: The agent ignores concealment bonuses granted by darkness.

Danger Unit: With this enhancement, the agent can sense subtle movements around him, allowing him to notice when danger looms.

Gadget Point Cost: +4.

Weight: –

Spot DC: +0.

Mechanics: The agent receives a +2 bonus to all checks to avoid surprise.

Polygraph/Voice Stress Analyzer: An excellent aid for diplomats and deep cover agents, this ear implant enhancement helps to detect minute variances in voice patterns, revealing stress or lies.

Gadget Point Cost: +4.

Weight: –

Spot DC: +0.

Mechanics: The agent receives a +2 bonus to all Sense Motive checks.

ICON PROSTAR 7

This device, distributed to Archer agents through the Gemeinschafft Consortium's Icon Entertainment front company, provides a hand-held operations center to agents in the field. Unless activated through voice and palm-print authentication, it appears to be a mundane portable PDA.

Gadget Point Cost: 4 each.

Weight: ½ lb.

Spot DC: 20.

Mechanics: The ProStar 7 establishes a satellite connection with the home office within 1 minute (3d20 seconds). Missions are often coordinated through this device, as are backup requests and emergency warnings to the Foundation.

In addition, agents can access the Overwatch satellite system to download local maps and recent satellite photos of the area, and track linked agent teams anywhere in the world.

OMNID CARDS

OmnID cards appear to be ID cards from the region of the agent's choice, and may contain many options. You may take the standard OmnID card option on its own, or take the standard option and then more options from those below at the additional costs listed (e.g. taking a standard OmnID card equipped with a backup ID costs a total of 2 gadget points). You may have a maximum of two options (including the standard option) in any single OmnID card.

Standard: The standard OmnID card can record audio and video messages for later playback.

This gadget (or another standard OmnID card) must be purchased as a housing first before you can add any of the options listed below.

Gadget Point Cost: 1 each.

Weight: –

Spot DC: 25.

Mechanics: This device stores up to 2 hours of video or 6 hours of audio.

Backup ID: By rapidly tapping an OmnID card's corner, the name, photo, and details shift to a preset backup.

Gadget Point Cost: +1 each.

Weight: –

Spot DC: +0.

Mechanics: Uses the Forgery skill at +20.

Duplication: Any ID card can be duplicated by pressing it against the OmnID card.

Gadget Point Cost: +2.

Weight: –

Spot DC: +0.

Mechanics: Uses the Forgery skill at +15.

Electronic Lockpick: OmnID cards act as master keys for all electronic key card locks Archer has encountered.

Gadget Point Cost: +1.

Weight: –

Spot DC: +0.

Mechanics: Uses the Electronics skill at +10, but only to open electronic locks.

Warning Signal: If slid through any credit card reader in the world, the OmnID card immediately alerts the home office with the name and location of the agent, and elevates his current mission to Code: Black *(see the Spycraft Espionage Handbook, page 203)*.

Gadget Point Cost: +1.

Weight: –

Spot DC: +0.

Mechanics: There is a time delay of 1d6×10 minutes before headquarters can respond (not including travel and prep time).

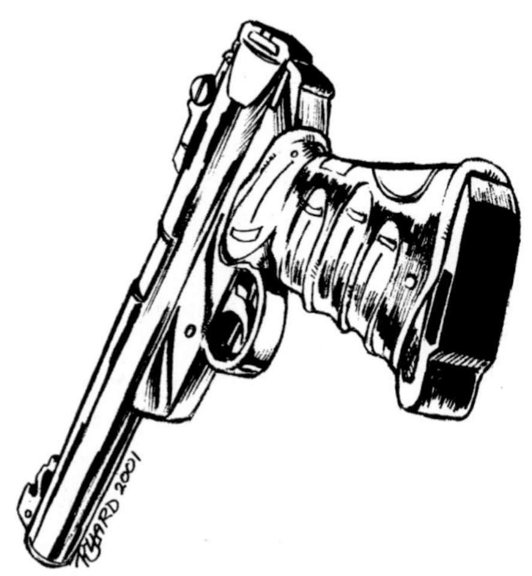

PALMPRINT IDENTIFIERS

Agents are quite protective of their sidearms. These pistol enhancements offer significant reassurance by verifying their identity when they grip the weapon.

You may take the standard palmprint identifier option on its own *(see Mark I Model, below)*, or take the standard option by paying the base cost and then include more options from those below at the additional costs listed (e.g. taking a standard palmprint identifier equipped with a "Backfire" option costs a total of 3 gadget points). You may have a maximum of two options (including the standard option) in any single palmprint identifier.

All of these gadgets may be installed on any weapon unless otherwise noted.

Mark I Model (Standard): This non-lethal model simply locks the weapon up when held by someone other than the programmed owner. This gadget is built into a firearm (which must be requisitioned separately additional budget or gadget points), and must be purchased as a housing first before you can add any of the options listed below.

Gadget Point Cost: 1 each.

Weight: –

Spot DC: 25 (super-science).

Mechanics: The firearm does not fire unless the hand gripping it matches the palmprint it has been programmed with. The palmprint may be faked with a Forgery check and a proper delivery method (such as smart-skin – *see page 211*), but the palmprint identifier has a +10 bonus against attempts to fool it.

"Backfire" Edition: When activated by an unrecognized palmprint, this lethal option discharges the weapon backward, into the person holding it.

Gadget Point Cost: +2.

Weight: –

Spot DC: 25 (super-science).

Mechanics: As the standard option, but in addition to locking up for regular use, the firearm attacks the person holding it with a +15 attack bonus.

"Blowback" Edition: This lethal option detonates the weapon when it doesn't recognize the palm holding it.

Gadget Point Cost: +1.

Weight: –

Spot DC: 25 (super-science).

Mechanics: As the standard option, except that the firearm is destroyed, and explodes as a fragmentation grenade.

Tracking Modification: When the weapon is picked up by someone other than the programmed owner, a warning signal is sent to the Foundation, who can track it.

Gadget Point Cost: +1.

Weight: –

Spot DC: 25 (super-science).

Mechanics: Telemetry from the stolen weapon can be forwarded in real-time to a team of agents in the field if they have a way to communicate with headquarters.

PATCHES

Patches are stored in the lining of clothing and in other areas where they can be reached quickly during combat. When needed, the agent simply rips the seal from the chemical pad and presses it firmly onto an area of exposed skin.

Mechanics for all patches: All patches have a Spot DC of 10 (no housing). Unless otherwise stated, a successful melee touch attack is required to use a patch on an unwilling target.

Adrenaline Patch: This patch offers a short-term burst of energy and temporarily increase one's reflexes.

Gadget Point Cost: 1 each.

Weight: –

Mechanics: Use of this patch allows the agent to take an additional half action each round for the next 1d4 rounds. However, he suffers 1d10 points of damage when it wears off. An agent may only use one of these patches per day. Further patches have no effect.

Brainscanner Patch: This patch is a mundane electroencephalograph (EEG), used to monitor the electrical impulses in the brain, which can help to diagnose disease.

Gadget Point Cost: 1 per 3.

Weight: –

Mechanics: The agent gains a +2 bonus to First Aid checks when treating a person wearing this patch.

Caffeine Boost Patch: This patch helps fatigued agents stay awake.

Gadget Point Cost: 1 per 2.

Weight: –

Mechanics: Use of this patch allows the agent to ignore the effects of fatigue *(see the Spycraft Espionage Handbook, page 178)* for 2d8 rounds. This does not counteract the effects of drugs or poisons designed to knock the agent unconscious.

Calm Emitter Patch: This patch combats panic and restores lucidity. Applying it to non-frenzied targets produces profound euphoria.

Gadget Point Cost: 1 per 2.

Weight: –

Mechanics: Use of this patch grants the agent a +4 bonus when resisting Intimidation checks or making Will saves against fear or terror-induced effects.

Coagulant Patch: This patch speeds up blood clotting.

Gadget Point Cost: 1 per 2.

Weight: –

Mechanics: Use of this patch stanches the flow of blood from any wound breaking the agent's skin. Additionally, the agent recovers 1d4 wound points.

Deepsleep Patch: When placed on a subject's forehead, this patch releases chemicals that lull him to sleep.

Gadget Point Cost: 2 each.

Weight: –

Mechanics: Use of this patch for 1 full minute causes the target to fall into a coma-like state. He cannot wake up under any circumstance until the patch is removed, or until 24 hours have passed, whichever comes first.

Endorphin Patch: This patch promotes endorphin release, helping the subject to ignore pain.

Gadget Point Cost: 1 per 2.

Weight: –

Mechanics: Use of this patch immediately heals 2d6 vitality points. An agent may only use three of these patches per day. Further patches have no effect.

Psitector Patch: This patch monitors a subject's brain waves, detecting the presence and strength of psion ability, including latency.

Gadget Point Cost: 1 each.

Weight: –

Mechanics: A successful Sleight of Hand check, opposed by a Spot check made by the target, allows the agent to slip this patch onto a sleeping person's forehead without waking them up. Use of this patch detects the presence of psionic ability and determines the user's psion level. The patch has a simple digital display which can be read easily with no ambient light.

Panic Emitter Patch: Placing this patch on an enemy alters his brain chemistry, causing panic and fear.

Gadget Point Cost: 1 per 2.

Weight: –

Mechanics: The wearer of this patch suffers a –4 penalty when resisting Intimidation checks or making Will saves against fear or terror-induced effects.

Telestatic Emitter Patch: Similar to anti-psi technology (though chemical in nature), this patch prohibits low-level psion ability.

Gadget Point Cost: 1 per 2.

Weight: –

Mechanics: This patch reduces the psion level of the wearer by 2 as long as it is worn. If this eliminates prerequisites for any skills or powers, they cannot be used until the patch is removed.

SUPERLUMINAL Patches: Russian Confederacy mentalists have adapted Foundation patches to administer their SUPERLUMINAL serums *(see page 140)*. These patches drastically change the subject's brain chemistry, effectively rewiring his mental functions; applying more than one patch cuts his reduced life span in half, with no additional benefit.

Note: Only Russian Confederacy agents may requisition these patches without Game Control approval.

Gadget Point Cost: Per GC approval (usually 5 or more each)

Goliath Mechanics: Use of this patch immediately grants the agent 1 psion level, a free psionic feat, and 4 skill points to spend on psion skills. However, the agent dies in 1d6+10 months. There is no known cure for this treatment once administered.

Cronus Mechanics: Use of this patch immediately grants the agent 2 psion levels, a free psionic feat, and 8 skill points to spend on psion skills. However, the agent dies in 1d6+5 months. There is no known cure for this treatment once administered.

Hyperion Mechanics: Use of this patch immediately grants the agent 3 psion levels, a free psionic feat, and 16 skill points to spend on psion skills. However, the agent dies in 1d6+10 weeks. There is no known cure for this treatment once administered.

PROSTHETICS

Losing a limb is usually a one-way ticket out of the espionage game, but Shop developments countered the loss, and in some cases turned it into an opportunity for improvement. With the addition of memory flesh, prosthetics can look nearly identical to the original limb.

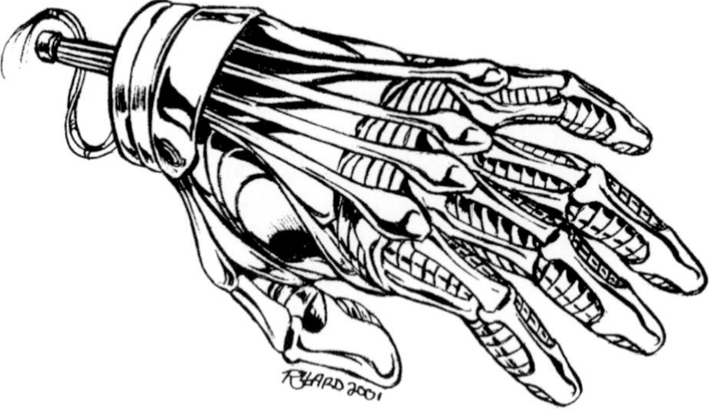

You may take the standard prosthetic option on its own, or take the standard option and then more options from those below at the additional costs listed (e.g. taking a standard prosthetic equipped with a strongman limb option costs a total of 8 gadget points). You may have a maximum of three options (including the standard option) in any single prosthetic. When more than one option offers the same benefit (such as increased hardness), only the highest benefit is applied.

Standard: This replacement limb (or another standard prosthetic option) must be purchased as a housing first before you can add any of the options listed below.

This gadget (and all extra options installed into it) is kept by the agent after being requisitioned, but it must be replaced once a year (at the full cost of the standard option, plus all extra options installed into it) as its power cells wear out. This implant is automatically detected by medical professionals.

Gadget Point Cost: 4 each.

Weight: –

Spot DC: 10 (normally) or 20 (with memory flesh)

Mechanics: Replaces a lost limb.

Strongman Limb: One of the most common prosthetics is a simple equivalent of the original, only stronger.

Gadget Point Cost: +4.

Weight: +10 lb.

Spot DC: +0.

Mechanics: The agent adds +4 to his Strength when using the limb to perform a task.

Weapons Limbs: Most small melee weapons and firearms can be fitted inside prosthetics, though doing so reduces the limb's standard utility.

Gadget Point Cost: +5.

Weight: Per weapon.

Spot DC: –5.

Mechanics: A Small melee or ranged weapon is mounted inside the limb. It can be wielded or fired as normal (no modifiers), and holds up to 15 rounds of ammo (if it uses ammo). The wearer can reload the limb as a full action.

RINGS

A wide variety of gadgets are disguised as rings, some of which are peculiar to certain Chambers of the Conspiracy.

Foundation Rings: Beyond identifying agents of Archer's central faction, these devices also effectively conceal psionic ability without hampering it. Foundation rings recognize their owners on a chemical level, and cannot be used by others.

Note: Archer Foundation agents only.

Gadget Point Cost: 5 each (requires GC approval)

Weight: –

Spot DC: 25.

Mechanics: No known device or psionic ability can sense the psionic abilities of a person wearing one of these rings. In addition, the wearer's psionic use leaves no traceable psionic residue. After being keyed to a specific individual, these rings cannot be used by others.

'irif Rings: As described on page 102, these rings make their owners aware of anyone else wearing an 'irif band within 50 feet.

Note: Guardians of the Whispering Knife only.

Gadget Point Cost: 2 each (requires GC approval)

Weight: –

Spot DC: 25.

Mechanics: Anyone wearing this ring becomes instantly aware of every other person wearing such a band, including distance and direction.

Hologram Projector: When the jewel setting on this ring is twisted one-quarter turn clockwise, a lifelike hologram is projected out to a 5-foot radius. The hologram is not transparent, and appears real, though it cannot move, and close inspection or touch reveals the ruse. An interesting use of this ring is to program it with the image of an eye to fool retina scanners.

Gadget Point Cost: 1 each.

Weight: –

Spot DC: 25.

Mechanics: A Spot check is required (DC 20) to spot the hologram for what it is.

NEW SURVEILLANCE GADGETS

"Bugs" are just what they sound like – these mobile devices are ingeniously disguised as common insects. Bugs can be programmed with very simple instructions (up to 25 if-then clauses) or manually piloted (which requires the Piloting skill).

Houseflies (Standard): The standard Bug model, houseflies are fast and agile, with no weapons or defenses.

To purchase one of the Bugs listed below, you must buy the standard version first, and then upgrade it to another type.

Gadget Point Cost: 1 each.
Weight: –
Spot DC: 30.

Mechanics: A housefly Bug is a tiny flying device with 1 wound point, a hardness of 0, a range increment of 10 feet, and a Defense of 20. It transmits sight and sound up to 1 mile away.

Mosquitoes: Mosquitoes are capable of either injecting user-defined toxins into a target or releasing a 10-foot radius toxic gas cloud.

Gadget Point Cost: 2 (upgrade).
Weight: –
Spot DC: 30 (super-science).

Mechanics: As a housefly, except that it can land on a target (Spot check at DC 15 to notice) and inject a pre-loaded poison (the target is allowed a second Spot check at DC 10 to notice the sting). This attack deals no damage except for the poison. Alternately, the mosquito may release a 10-foot cloud of poison gas *(see the Spycraft Espionage Handbook, page 128)*. Either way, the mosquito only has enough poison for one use.

Roaches: Roaches are nearly impervious to physical harm, making them excellent in hostile areas.

Gadget Point Cost: 1 (upgrade).
Weight: –
Spot DC: 30.

Mechanics: As a housefly, except that the roach has a hardness of 5 and 5 wound points. The agent must pay the cost of any poison gas loaded into the bug.

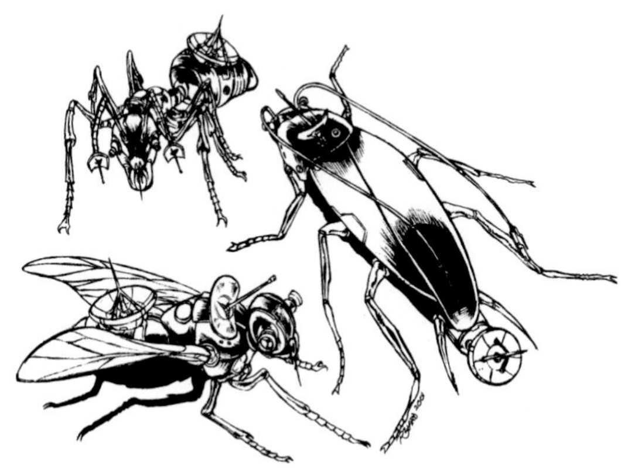

SYNTHETIC SKIN

Synthetic skin is incredibly popular with the super-spies of today, who utilize it in many ingenious ways.

Ballistic Flesh: This subdermal skin layer contains a thin mesh of special alloys designed to absorb the impact of concussive attacks and even – to a small degree – protect from high-speed projectiles (like arrows and bullets).

Gadget Point Cost: 15.
Weight: 5 lb.
Spot DC: 20 (sometimes automatic, super-science)

Mechanics: Ballistic flesh works like a built-in steel-weave vest that cannot be removed *(see the Spycraft Espionage Handbook, page 124)*. Agents wearing ballistic flesh gain both their class Defense bonus and the gadget's armor Defense bonus (+1). Metal detectors do not register the ballistic flesh, but anything more than a cursory medical exam automatically discovers it. This gadget is kept by the agent after being requisitioned.

Grafters: These patches of synthetic skin bond with a wound, instantly sealing most small injuries.

Gadget Point Cost: 1 each.
Weight: –
Spot DC: 10 (no housing).

Mechanics: Grafters restore 1d3 wound points to an injured agent. They may also be used as flesh "pockets" to hide an object of 1 cubic inch or smaller. The DCs of Search checks made to find such objects are increased by 20.

Memory Flesh: This industrious design can be "molded" into a near-perfect likeness of any individual by pressing it against his face; once set, it can be worn by an agent impersonating him. Also, CAD programs can be used to generate new identities from scratch, which are imprinted on memory flesh by laser.

Gadget Point Cost: 2 each.
Weight: –
Spot DC: See below.

Mechanics: When used to impersonate a specific individual, a memory flesh mask adds +5 to Disguise checks.

Smart-Skin: This thin, translucent membrane may be smoothed over your face, a glass, your palm (or the back of your hand), or on any other largely flat surface. When someone else touches it, the smart-skin "records" their fingerprints. The smart-skin may then be transferred to your own fingers, replacing your prints with those of the person who touched the smart-skin first.

Gadget Point Cost: 2 each.
Weight: –
Spot DC: 20 (no housing).

Mechanics: Agents using smart-skin to bypass palm or fingerprint scanners or other print-based security receive a +10 bonus to their Electronic checks (assuming the smart-skin has recorded the right person's prints).

NEW VEHICLES

Archer's Spring 2002 offerings include...

The Battle Bus: The battle bus is a semi *(see the Spycraft Espionage Handbook, page 148)* converted to handle any number of tasks according to the Foundation's needs. The basic unit is well armored and equipped with one or more modular bays, shown below.

The battle bus has the following statistics.

Gadget Point Cost: 10.

Size: Gargantuan.	*Handling:* –7.
Speed: 400 ft.	*MPH:* 40/80.
Defense: 5.	*Wound Points:* 200.

Hardness: 11.

Once you have requisitioned the battle bus, you may requisition battle suites from the list provided *(see next column)*. Each of these battle suites has an additional cost, which must be paid in addition to the cost fot the battle bus itself (e.g. taking a standard battle bay equipped with a garage suite option costs a total of 17 gadget points). You may have a maximum of two battle suites (including the standard option) in any single battle bus. When more than one suite offers the same benefit (such as a Mechanics skill bonus), only the highest benefit is applied.

Battle buses have a Spot DC of 25 unless someone looks inside (in which case their Spot check succeeds automatically).

The Sagittarius: The best-selling high-end sports car for the last three years has been Equinox Motors' flagship design, the Sagittarius. While well outside the budget of the average consumer, the Sagittarius has nonetheless captured the interest of the popular market, where it has been featured in magazine ad campaigns, album covers, and the blockbuster "Wildcat" action-adventure series *(see page 93)*. Secretly, the Sagittarius is also issued to many agents of the Archer Foundation, usually with many of "the usual refinements."

The Sagittarius has the following statistics.

Gadget Point Cost: 7.

Size: Large.	*Handling:* +6.
Speed: 1,000 ft.	*MPH:* 100/200.
Defense: 16.	*Wound Points:* 100.

Hardness: 5.

The Usual Refinements: The Sagittarius automatically comes with 2 gadget points worth of vehicular refinements of the agent's choice, at no cost. Additional refinements may be installed by paying their standard gadget point costs. Up to 15 vehicular refinements may be installed in a Sagittarius.

Battle Suites

The following suite options are available for the Battle Bus *(see previous column)*. The cost of each is paid in addition to the cost for the Battle Bus itself.

Battle Bay (Standard): This jack-of-all-trades refinement converts a semi's cargo container into an all-purpose bay holding four bunk beds, a mini-hospital for emergency field surgery, a computer system with surveillance capability, and a basic mechanics bay.

Gadget Point Cost: +4.

Mechanics: All Computers, First Aid, Mechanics, and Surveillance checks made using these facilities enjoy a +5 bonus.

Garage Suite: In addition to providing space for two Medium-sized vehicles or one large vehicle, this refinement allows mechanics to fix vehicles on the fly with the speed and efficiency of a Daytona 500 pit crew.

Gadget Point Cost: +3.

Mechanics: All Mechanics checks made using these facilities enjoy a +10 bonus. The garage suite must be situated at the rear of the container to accept cars over the ramp. Optionally (and at the cost of 1 extra gadget point), the garage suite may include a hydraulic lift with roof access for helicopters and other VTOL vehicles.

Medical Suite: This bay contains a mini-operating room, isolation tanks to contain biohazardous patients, a well-stocked pharmacy, and the latest medical diagnostic software.

Gadget Point Cost: +3.

Mechanics: All First Aid checks made using these facilities enjoy a +10 bonus.

Props Suite: This bay includes a firearms rack, prop and costuming section, and weapon-cleaning room. There is also a station to analyze and help replicate forged documents.

Gadget Point Cost: +3.

Mechanics: All Disguise and Forgery checks made using these facilities enjoy a +10 bonus, as do skill checks to clean or repair weapons.

Surveillance Suite: This bay includes state-of-the-art surveillance equipment and a dedicated satellite link, wire-tap capabilities, full spectrum video analysis including x-ray imaging, and a chemical analysis station.

Gadget Point Cost: +3.

Mechanics: All Surveillance checks made using these facilities enjoy a +10 bonus. Further, any standard-issue or gadget-based surveillance gear may be linked to this suite with a successful Electronics check (DC 15) and one hour of work. The range of linked devices is doubled and agents using them gain a cooperation bonus when any agent with the Surveillance skill at 1 or more is manning this suite.

"Lesser men have forgotten us, and in their murder of history have nearly destroyed the mystic world. But we shall see it rise again, and stride over the shattered remains of this new age."

– Eva Kraus

THE MYSTIC WORLD

Echoes of the Ancients

Shadowforce Archer is not merely a world of cloak and dagger. It is a world of mystery laced with faith in the divine, with powers that guide us through the ages. Our history is a road map leading us to uncharted realms of understanding, where anything is possible. But it is also a shield, protecting us from the ravages of corruption, the pitfalls of villainy and vice.

If we're not careful, we may stumble...

Manifestations

The mystic world is difficult to fathom. It is not "magic" or "alchemy," which can be predicted and prompted (though its physical forms are often mistaken as such). Rather, it is a lens which magnifies the power of the human spirit and gives it shape and form. It reflects the power within everyone, honed until it can be directed like a weapon. This appears three different ways, each another shard of a world now lost.

Rituals and Rites

The Ancients understood how to focus the human spirit through great communal rituals drawing on the faith of hundreds or thousands. These rituals were capable of incredible feats, from shifting weather to raising the dead. But they came with a great price – the risk of addiction to the powers they offered. The Ancients understood this, and hid their knowledge away from the prying eyes of their enemies... and from the uninformed who might blunder into obsession and brutality.

Artifacts and Relics

The Ancients also imbued items with the forces they wielded, or fashioned them directly from the raw strength of their own spirits, sacrificing themselves as an eternal nexus of faith. These items – commonly artifacts and relics of enormous cultural significance, such as the Ark of the Covenant and the Spear of Destiny – are mystic powers in their own right, but they are without soul. They cannot choose between right or wrong. In the hands of the virtuous, they can be weapons or great good, but the greedy, vindictive, and ambitious can also use them for great evil.

Spirits and Entities

We are not alone in the world. Human spirits have survived the death of centuries, waiting to be unleashed on the modern age. Some are trapped by rituals of the Ancients, which can be undone with the right key and enough followers dedicated to the cause. Others are bound to protect the Ancients' secret caches of power. Still others wander lost or insane, now incorporeal shades, searching for a way to regain their forms or complete tasks they left behind with their mortal shells. We know these spirits and entities as ghosts, goblins, and the shadows we can never pin down at the edge of our vision. Occasionally they are more.

The Enlightened

At present, two primary groups know of the mystic world: one dedicated to guarding its secrets and the other to exploiting them. Many more people in the world have peripheral knowledge of the forces around them, though most write them off as "luck," "fate," and "happenstance." Only the most naturally gifted learn to channel the insights they glean through their window into the world of the Ancients.

The Guardians of the Whispering Knife (page 100)

The fabled Guardians of the Whispering Knife rank among the last remaining holy warriors to protect their discoveries – and the last to understand them. On occasion, they seek out and train the gifted, particularly when such candidates show promise with disciplines the Guardians seek to control, such as the ability to sense when the spirits of the dead are near, or speak with them.

Mysticism and Religion

While *Shadowforce Archer* makes no attempt to represent the religions of the real world, certain parallels can be drawn between mystic abilities and the miracles of ancient times. It is entirely possible within the *Shadowforce Archer* setting for certain clergymen to be "blessed" with the ability to perform rites or even rituals as implied by the articles of their faith (in the form of having the appropriate mystic feats). This is, however, extraordinarily rare. Such mystic accomplishments involve focusing the spirits of the faithful rather than drawing upon mystically-bonded followers, and as such are much more spontaneous and infrequent than the system proposed in this chapter.

For Game Controls wishing to introduce such a rare occurrence into their game, we suggest allowing the individual leading a rite to utilize their Knowledge (Theology) skill in place of Knowledge (Occult), and that the GC specifically choose such events in keeping with the faith in question. As always, care, discretion, and respect should be extended to the sensibilities of your playing group.

The Hand of Glory (page 154)

The Hand of Glory's fanatic hunt for rituals and relics to use in their quest for global domination is fueled by the obsession of a living god trapped inside Eva Kraus. The gifted are little more than tools for the Hand, to be collected, exploited, and discarded with little consideration. Unfocused mystics are dominated and bonded by force until the time comes for them to be consumed as components in powerful and malignant rituals. Those with potential as mystic warriors are trained as brutal sorcerers.

Playing a Mystic Agent

The basis of all serious mystic study is the Mystic feat. This serves as an entry point into the unseen world. It in turn opens up other possibilities and leads to the next great discovery, the Initiate feat. At that degree of discipline, it becomes possible for an agent to perform mystic rites, embodying the simplest of spiritual powers. Further dedication to the mystic arts may allow an agent to achieve the stature of Magus (when he selects the feat of the same name). Such agents can enact massive mystic rituals, and gather truly awe-inspiring power. But the dangers are greater for high-level mystics as well, as rituals contain the seeds of temptation within their power. Agents who perform rituals must measure themselves against the perils of the "Thirst," a flaw in human nature that leads many advanced mystics to their doom. Finally, if the agent continues to seek out mystic knowledge, he must make a decision between even greater levels of ritual might, or the prospect of immortality through a sort of mystic transmogrification, forever foreswearing the greatest heights of raw power in exchange for eternal life.

Mysticism is not inherently a class-based pursuit. At present, no base classes offer additional mystic feats, so those who wish to become a mystic do so using their level-based feat choices. While mystically oriented prestige classes (and threats) will appear in forthcoming supplements, particularly the *Guardians of the Whispering Knife* and *Hand of Glory* sourcebooks, it is possible for a dedicated student to achieve great power solely by using his level-based feats for choices from the mystic feat tree.

Special Note: Throughout this chapter, we refer to rites and rituals, jointly, as "invocations." Whenever something refers to an invocation, it refers to both rites and rituals.

Learning Rites & Rituals

Before an agent can perform an invocation, he must research it in ancient texts or learn it from another mystic. Typically, texts that contain mystic rituals date back to ancient civilizations such as the Toltecs, Babylonians, or Assyrians. Once such a text (or a teacher) has been acquired, the mystic may make one Knowledge (Occult) skill check per month of study in an attempt to learn the invocation. The invocation studied determines the DC of this check, and the agent may add one-half his teacher's Knowledge (Occult) skill as a bonus to his skill check if learning from a teacher rather than a book. A mystic may study only one invocation at a time.

Performing Rites & Rituals

To perform an invocation, a mystic must fulfill three requirements:

- He must have learned the invocation with a successful Knowledge (Occult) check, as described above.
- He must meet the invocation's minimum Knowledge (Occult) skill requirement *(see page 222)*.
- He must harvest spiritual energy from a number of his bonded followers *(see the Bond Follower rite, page 222)*. The number of followers required to produce the desired effect is listed in the rite or ritual description.

If the mystic meets all three of these requirements, the invocation is automatically completed unless somehow disrupted during the invocation (e.g. the mystic is killed or his followers are driven off).

Mysticism: Good vs. Evil

Throughout the design of the mystic world, we've tried to draw clear lines between good and evil, but the morality of mystic powers ultimately depend on how they are used. The majority of the material presented in this book is geared for use by NPCs – particularly villains – but ingenious players will undoubtedly find ways to apply even the darkest invocations to positive ends. We recommend experimenting, and having fun. Find what works for your team, and run with it.

Future supplements will delve further into the background of the mystic world, and present new mystic prestige classes, feats, invocations, and relics. Watch for them in the *Archer Foundation, Hand of Glory* and *Guardians of the Whispering Knife* sourcebooks, and elsewhere throughout the *Shadowforce Archer* release schedule.

The Shadespeaker

For the Guardians of the Whispering Knife, belief is not faith, but fact. Of all the Chambers of the Archer Conspiracy, the Guardians, steeped in occult history and legend, undoubtedly have the closest ties to the mystic world. The shadespeaker is perhaps the most profound example of this, a living link to the world of the dead.

The title shadespeaker is a label given by the Archer Foundation in an attempt to classify this ancient tradition. The Guardians themselves have another name for this respected position: *khatib bidal maiyit* – literally, "speaker for the dead."

Abilities: A shadespeaker deals in matters of faith and the occult, which require a high Wisdom vital. As the Guardians' culture relies so heavily upon melee combat – specifically the use of knives, as both a mode of combat and a focus for many social rituals – high Strength is also common.

Vitality: 1d12 plus Constitution bonus per level

Requirements

To become a shadespeaker, an agent must meet all of the following requirements.

Agent Level: 5+
Chamber: Guardians of the Whispering Knife
Wisdom: 13+
Feats: Sixth Sense

Class Skills

The shadespeaker's class skills and key abilities are listed below:

Class Skill	Key Ability
Balance	Dex
Concentration	Wis
Craft	Int
First Aid	Wis
Gather Information	Cha
Handle Animal	Cha
Hobby	Wis
Jump	Str
Knowledge	Int
Languages	Wis
Listen	Wis
Sense Motive	Wis
Spot	Wis
Survival	Wis
Tumble	Dex

Skill Points at Each Level: 4 + Int modifier.

Class Features

All of the following are class features of the shadespeaker.

Class Feats: The shadespeaker gains the following feats at 1st level.

Armor Proficiency (Light)
Weapon Group Proficiency (Melee)
Weapon Group Proficiency (Hurled)

Dedication: Shadespeakers are known for their extremely fierce dedication to the ideals of their order. Such focus allows them to exceed the limits of the ordinary. The agent receives an additional action die at the start of each session. This is the shadespeaker's core ability.

The Call: At 1st level, the shadespeaker can not only see and speak with the dead, but attract them to his location.

When people die, their spirits tend to remain in locations important to them in life. However, many are bound to more than one such location, and spend different periods of time in different locations (such as a spirit's home and workplace).

This ability calls forth all spirits who have even a partial connection to the shadespeaker's current location, allowing him to question the spirits for specific information regarding the location. Using this ability, the shadespeaker may ask the GC one question about his current location, such as "What is the access code to the locked door?" or "Where are the sensitive documents kept." Since the spirits only know what they knew in life, the GC may refuse to answer by spending one action die per question ignored. Questions cannot be repeated or rephrased at the same location in a single session. This ability may be used a number of times per session equal to the agent's shadespeaker class level.

At 5th level, the shadespeaker's will is sufficient to focus the thoughts of the dead and grant an illusion of normal interaction. The agent may converse in a (mostly) normal fashion with a dead person's spirit. The spirit rarely understands its condition, and is prone to irrational anger and raving, thus making its disposition one grade worse than what it would normally be in life. The shadespeaker must be in the presence of the spirit's corpse to achieve this level of rapport, and the target may not have died more than 3 days prior. This ability is brutally tiring for the shadespeaker, and drains him of 10 vitality at the beginning of each minute of use.

At 9th level, the shadespeaker may suffer 1 wound (by cutting himself with his *washaif blade* – see below) to render a spirit he has called visible to others. The spirit appears solid in all respects (including any injuries it was aware of at the time of its death), but cannot physically influence the world of the living. It can move strongly mystic objects. This ability is usually invoked so that the spirit may convince someone of the veracity of the shadespeaker's insight, and does not increase or change the information that can be gained from use of the Call ability. This effect lasts no more than one minute, and cannot be used on the same spirit more than once per session.

Deathwatch: The shadespeaker's connection to the realm of the dead increases, and he may now sense things about the bodies of the spirits he communicates with. At 2nd level, as a half action, he may locate with precision any corpse within 10 feet per agent level, and immediately knows the body's age at death, the amount of time that has passed since its death, and its basic physical cause of death. This ability also conveys a general sense of the deceased's emotional state at the time of death. Oddly, this ability is strictly limited to human remains, and the remains of some humans badly warped by medical experiments or chems may slip through unnoticed (per the GC's discretion).

At 7th level, the shadespeaker can sense a nearby death. The GC must notify the shadespeaker whenever someone in the vicinity dies, out to a distance equal to the agent's shadespeaker class level in miles. A momentary chill wracks the shadespeaker with each death, as well as a strong sense of the deceased's emotional state, allowing the agent to identify untimely deaths.

The shadespeaker may disable this ability when it might become distracting, such as in a hospital. Alternately, he can focus the ability by voluntarily limiting its range to as tight an area as he wishes.

Bonus Feat: At 3rd level, the shadespeaker gains a bonus mystic or melee combat feat. He must still meet prerequisites for this feat as normal. The agent gains an additional feat from the mystic tree at 5th, 7th, and 9th levels.

The Sleep: At 4th level, the shadespeaker understands the ties that bind us to life. As a full action, he may enter a state of hibernation akin to death. Any examination reveals no vital signs – the shadespeaker is, for all intents and purposes, dead, and does not require necessities such as food, water, or oxygen. All physical functions are suspended, except for the aging process.

Unfortunately, as the shadespeaker remains extremely vulnerable in this state, any physical damage done to him applies directly to his wound points, rather than his vitality. Further, in order to rouse himself, the shadespeaker must make a Will save (DC 20). If another helps him to wake up, the shadespeaker receives an additional +5 bonus to his roll. In any event, such a recovery requires one full round, during which the shadespeaker is considered to be flat-footed.

As a full action, once the shadespeaker has entered the sleep, he may elect to sever all ties to his life. The shadespeaker is killed, and may not be resurrected by any means. This is rarely done, except at the end of a shadespeaker's natural life, when he ritually enters the sleep rather than become a burden upon his family.

Washaif Blade: At 4th level, the shadespeaker may receive a *washaif* blade. These blades are forged in the unseen world beyond death. Delivered into this world by spirits made visible with the power of the shadespeakers. Each *washaif* blade is forged expressly for its owner. The spirits delivering the blade are those closest to the shadespeaker who have already passed onto the realm of the dead – the shadespeaker may not receive his blade until he has experienced personal loss, forever bonding him with the spirit realm.

The shadespeaker and the delivering spirits perform a complex ritual in solitude, during which the shadespeaker accepts the blade's first cut into his own flesh. This ritual bonds the shadespeaker to his weapon, after which it always returns to him when he needs it,

Table 6.1: The Shadespeaker

Lvl	Base Att Bon	Fort Save	Ref Save	Will Save	Def Bon	Init Bon	Budg Pts	Gadg Pts	Special
1	+1	+1	+0	+2	+1	+1	1	0	The call (questions), *dedication*
2	+2	+2	+0	+3	+1	+2	2	1	Deathwatch (corpse sense)
3	+3	+2	+1	+3	+2	+3	3	1	Bonus feat
4	+4	+2	+1	+4	+2	+3	4	2	Washaif blade (marking)
5	+5	+3	+1	+4	+3	+4	5	2	Bonus feat, the call (converse)
6	+6	+3	+2	+5	+4	+5	6	3	Resolute aura
7	+7	+4	+2	+5	+4	+6	7	3	Bonus feat, deathwatch (death sense)
8	+8	+4	+2	+6	+5	+6	8	4	Cloaked in the Fringe, washaif blade (blooding)
9	+9	+4	+3	+6	+5	+7	9	4	Bonus feat, the call (appear)
10	+10	+5	+3	+7	+6	+8	10	5	Channel

by traveling through the unseen world. The shadespeaker is always considered to be carrying the knife, even if it is found and removed during a search. He simply reaches into the folds of his cloak (or into a pocket or behind his back, if wearing contemporary clothes), and draws out the blade.

Damage	Error	Threat	Weight
2d4	1	18-20	1 lb.

At 8th level, the shadespeaker may undergo the blooding, a ritual in which he further attunes himself to his blade. At this level, the threat range of the agent's weapon is increased by two, and the damage increased by 1d4.

Resolute Aura: At 6th level, the shadespeaker learns to draw great personal willpower from the Guardians' centuries of tradition, becoming an unstoppable, implacable combatant. He may add his shadespeaker class level to all Intimidate skill checks and saves vs. fear.

Cloaked in the Fringe: Powerful shadespeakers are rumored to stand partially within the spirit world themselves, slightly beyond the reach of enemies grounded in the mortal world. This is likely just a myth spread by the Guardians to frighten the superstitious, but at 8th level, after the shadespeaker is successfully attacked (but before damage is rolled), he may give up an action (or a ready action) to cause the attacker to roll a d20. On a roll of 1-10, the attack misses, regardless of the original attack roll. Attacks thus prevented seemingly pass through the shadespeaker without effect. Most who have seen this effect discount it as a trick of the light, or a clever use of the shadespeaker's voluminous robes to distract from an extremely adept dodge. This ability may be used a number of times per session equal to the agent's shadespeaker class level.

Channel: At 10th level, as a full action, the shadespeaker may spend an action die to channel a spirit's knowledge and physical memory through his body. In so doing, the shadespeaker gains a skill of his choice (including specialized skills such as Craft and Hobby, for which he must select a specific focus, per the skill description). The shadespeaker may channel any skill not restricted by the Game Control – he merely identifies the skill he desires and it is assumed he is able to channel a spirit possessing it. The skill's rank is equal to the shadespeaker's agent level.

Alternately, the shadespeaker may gain a feat (again, any feat is allowed, pending the Game Control's approval). The shadespeaker need not have any feats listed as prerequisites for the feat he desires, though he must still meet all the feat's other prerequisites (such as a minimum base attack bonus or ability score).

The skill or feat may be used normally for a number of minutes equal to his Wisdom modifier.

Mystic Feats

As mentioned under Playing a Mystic Agent *(page 215)*, the three critical "nexus" feats for mystic advancement are Mystic, Initiate, and Magus. Most other feats in this section have one or more of these feats as prerequisites.

Blade Master

As an agent of the Guardians, you have received intense training with melee weapons, particularly knives.

Prerequisites: Guardian agents only, Str 13+, Dex 13+.

Benefit: +2 bonus to all damage rolls when using any melee weapon with a blade.

Blood of the Phoenix

Any lingering imbalances from your days as a mortal have been flushed from your system. You are now truly eternal.

Prerequisites: Agent level 20+, Philosopher, Talented (Knowledge (Occult)), Knowledge (Occult) skill 24+.

Benefit: While your outward appearance does not change, you ignore any and all penalties for age. You may still die from violence or accident. Your maximum wound points are doubled. You cannot be affected by critical hits.

Ceremony

Your understanding of ceremony offers you special insight into the mechanics of mystic events.

Prerequisites: Magus, Knowledge (Occult) Skill 15+.

Benefit: By choosing a time rich with symbolism, meticulously preparing the setting, and indoctrinating your followers with special care, you can augment the energies available for an invocation. You must spend $10 for every follower (possibly producing a money trail others may notice) at least one month and not more than one year before the invocation is to take place. Your GC may have other requirements as well, based on the invocation in question, the location, the time of year, and other factors.

By fulfilling the requirements above, each of your regular followers (excluding those with mystic feats that increase their value) is counted twice towards the number of followers available to perform the invocation. You may only prepare a follower for a single invocation at any time; his energies are not doubled for any other invocation you perform.

DISCIPLINE OF THE BODY

You have extraordinary control over your body.

Prerequisites: Str 13+, Con 13+.

Benefit: You may add your Strength modifier to your initiative rolls. Further, you may spend an action die to use one of the following abilities.

Endure: You gain 5 points of damage reduction against heat and cold damage for 1 minute.

Hold Breath: You may go without breathing for a number of minutes equal to your Constitution modifier while performing actions, or for a number of hours equal to your Constitution modifier while remaining still.

Withstand: When you spend an action die to add to a Fortitude save, two dice are added instead of one (e.g. if you would normally roll 1d4, you roll 2d4 instead). The action die spent to use this power counts as the action die spent to add to the Fortitude save.

DISCIPLINE OF THE MIND

Your studies into the basic nature of thought have unlocked many unusual abilities.

Prerequisites: Dex 13+, Int 13+, Discipline of the Body, Initiate.

Benefit: You may add your Intelligence modifier to your initiative rolls. Further, you may spend an action die to use one of the following abilities.

Focus: You automatically succeed with one Concentration skill check.

Ignore Pain: You gain 5 points of damage reduction against subdual damage for 5 minutes. This damage reduction stacks with DR from all other sources.

Quick Reflexes: When you spend an action die to add to a Reflex save, two dice are added instead of one (e.g. if you would normally roll 1d4, you roll 2d4 instead). The action die spent to use this power counts as the action die spent to add to the Reflex save.

DISCIPLINE OF THE SPIRIT

You have come to understand much about the nature of the spirit, and how to channel its power.

Prerequisites: Cha 13+, Wis 13+, Discipline of the Mind, Magus.

Benefit: You may add your Charisma modifier to your initiative rolls. Further, when you spend an action die, you also gain the following benefits:

Complete the Circle: You may spend the action die mentioned above to activate someone else's critical success.

Prevent Strife: When you spend the action die mentioned above to add to your Defense, two dice are added instead of one (e.g. if you would normally roll 1d4, you roll 2d4 instead).

Resist Temptation: When you spend the action die mentioned above to add to a Will save, two dice are added instead of one (e.g. if you would normally roll 1d4, you roll 2d4 instead).

ENLIGHTENED

You see the unseen world clearly now, and its vast powers are yours to command!

Prerequisites: Agent level 18+, Magus, Knowledge (Occult) skill 20+. You must have at least six other mystic feats before you may take Enlightened.

Benefit: There is no limit to the number of followers you may harness for your invocations *(see page 222)*. You count as 20 bonded followers when participating in any mystic event (including one you are performing).

Special: You may not take the Philosopher feat after gaining the Enlightened feat.

FAITH HEALING

You are able to soothe the injuries of others.

Prerequisites: Initiate.

Benefit: By placing your hands upon a willing target for one full round, you may heal a number of wound points equal to 1d6 + the number of mystic feats you have. Alternately, you may heal a number of vitality points equal to 2d6 + the number of mystic feats you have. You may use this ability on yourself. No character (including you) may benefit from this ability more than once per day (i.e. 24-hour period).

GLIMPSE

You have flashes and occasional visions about the future.

Prerequisites: Mystic, Knowledge (Occult) skill 1+.

Benefit: Once per session, during a session in which you or your team will face a life-threatening challenge, the Game Control must secretly make a Knowledge (Occult) check for you with a DC of 20. If the roll succeeds, he must describe the challenge as a simple 1-3 second flash of what is to come. The GC may be as vague and misleading as he wishes, but cannot lie about the challenge. The GC may spend one of his action dice to forego this roll for this session.

GUARDIAN PRESENCE

Sometimes it seems as if... something... is watching out for you.

Prerequisites: Cha 13+, Mystic.

Benefit: At the start of each session, you may give one action die to the Game Control to hold for you. At any time during the session, he may decide that your agent is in great peril and secretly add the maximum value of the held action die to one of your rolls. The maximum value of the action die must have an impact on the result of your roll or the GC may not use it for you. If the die is not used by the end of the session you gain two additional action dice at the beginning of the next session.

INITIATE

Through diligent study and force of will you can tap into the primal mystic forces of the universe.

Prerequisites: Agent level 5+, Knowledge (Occult) skill 1+. You must have the Mystic feat and at least one other feat from the mystic tree before you may take Initiate.

Benefit: You may attempt any mystic rites that you have learned. You may combine the energies of up to 40 followers to enact your rites. You may begin to learn mystic rituals. You count as 5 bonded followers when participating in a mystic event (including one you are performing).

Normal: Agents with the Knowledge (Occult) skill may learn mystic rites but cannot perform them without the Initiate feat. Agents cannot comprehend mystic rituals until they gain this feat.

MAGUS

Your knowledge of the unseen world allows you to gather tremendous spiritual power and shape it into grand displays of mystic force. Your mastery may even match that of the mythical Ancients!

Prerequisites: Agent level 10+, Initiate, Knowledge (Occult) skill 10+. You must have at least four other mystic feats before you may take Magus.

Benefit: You may perform mystic rituals that you have learned. You may combine the energies of up to 1,000 followers when you enact invocations. You count as 10 bonded followers when participating in a mystic event (including one you are performing).

MASKED ENERGIES

You are able to dampen any "overflow" of energies as you perform invocations.

Prerequisites: Magus, Knowledge (Occult) skill 12+.

Benefit: All attempts to detect your invocations suffer a +4 DC modifier and the effective range at which you may be detected (using the Quickening feat or a similar ability) is reduced to one quarter of normal (rounded down).

MYSTIC

The forces of the unseen world have peculiar resonance for you.

Benefit: Your action dice are considered one die type larger than you normally receive for your agent level (e.g. d4s become d6s, d8s become d10s). Further, you count as 2 bonded followers when participating in any mystic event (including one you are performing).

MYSTIC SURGE

You are able to accelerate the process of performing an invocation by devoting excess energy to it.

Prerequisites: Magus, Knowledge (Occult) skill 15+.

Benefit: Each time you make a Knowledge (Occult) skill check to perform an invocation, you may use the energy of 50 bonded followers to add +10 to the result of your roll. This energy is no longer available to determine the effects of the invocation (as described under Effect).

PHILOSOPHER

Through exploration of the unseen world, you have reached equilibrium. You have achieved an enduring balance with yourself and with the world.

Prerequisites: Agent level 16+, Magus, Knowledge (Occult) skill 15+.

Benefit: You cease to age, and ignore all age penalties. You may still die from violence or accident.

Special: You may not take the Enlightened feat after gaining the Philosopher feat.

THE QUICKENING

You are able to sense gathering mystic energies.

Prerequisites: Initiate.

Benefit: You automatically become aware of the performance of any mystic invocation within one mile for every 25 followers (or fraction thereof) involved in the event. If you are within half that distance from the event, you may sense the general direction of such activities. Finally, if you come within one quarter that distance, you can determine the exact location of the event.

SECOND SIGHT

You are sensitive to the presence of mystic relics.

Prerequisites: Mystic.

Benefit: When you are within 20 feet of one or more mystic relics, the GC secretly rolls a d6. With a result of 1, you become aware of the relic's presence. You may automatically determine if an object is a mystic relic simply by handling it, and once you have identified a relic, you may sense its direction up to 5 miles away.

SIXTH SENSE

Sometimes you have glimpses into the unseen world, visions of past lives and unquiet spirits. Guardians of the Whispering Knife take a particular interest in those with the Sixth Sense ability, and often track them down and "collect" them for special training. This is one of the rare instances where outsiders are welcomed into the Guardians without question – those who can sense the dead are simply too important to let go, regardless of their background and disposition.

Prerequisites: Wisdom 13+.

Benefit: You see dead people. Whenever you are near the site of a person's death, there is a chance that you experience an "echo" of their soul. Such an echo cannot speak to you or interact in any way, but may replay the events of its demise or pantomime events it has left unfinished.

To witness a death-echo, you must deliberately open yourself to the spirit world, taking a full round and making a Will save against a DC based on the following conditions about the spirit.

Conditions	DC*
Died today	8
Died in the last three days	10
Died more than three days ago	12
Died more than a year ago	16
Died more than a century ago	20
Died more than a millennium ago	24
Died peacefully	+0
Died violently	–2
Has "unfinished business"	–5
Knows it was murdered	–5

*If the DC is reduced to 0 or less, you automatically succeed.

With a successful save, you gain a vision as described above. Otherwise, you are shaken and disturbed by the forces you allowed into yourself and suffer a –1 to all skill checks and attack rolls for a number of hours equal to the Will save DC.

Invocations

After an explanation of the format for rites and rituals are the rite and ritual descriptions, respectively. This section ends with rules for "the Thirst."

Rite/Ritual Descriptions

The format for all rites and rituals follows.

Rite or Ritual Name

Each invocation's name is followed by a general description it s function, following by these entries.

Learning DC: The DC of the Knowledge (Occult) skill check required to learn this invocation. A mystic may only make one such check per month, and he cannot study more than one invocation at once.

Thirst DC: The DC against which the mystic must make a Will save to avoid the corrupting power of the mystic world. Applies only to rituals.

Minimum Knowledge (Occult) Skill: The mystic leading the invocation must have at least this many ranks in his Knowledge (Occult) skill.

Bonded Followers: The mystic must harvest the energy of this many bonded followers *(see the Bond Follower ritual, opposite)* to perform the invocation.

Complex Check: The DC for casting the invocation, and how often it may be attempted – *see Complex Skill Use on the opposite page.*

Effect: The effects of successfully completing the invocation.

Mystic Rites

Many individuals draw strength from the observation of simple rites, from weddings to holiday celebrations to funerals. Ceremony gives form and substance to our social lives. Many of these practices echo the traditions of ancient mystic rites – ceremonies that gather the spiritual force of the faithful and channel it as a palpable force for the good of their group or the aims of their leader.

Agents with the Initiate feat may attempt to perform any rites they know as a complex check using their Knowledge (Occult) skill. Rites generally require 5 or more linked followers on the scene to lend their spiritual strength to the undertaking, though the mystic's feats usually cover lower numbers. The initiate may utilize his own energies in his ritual, but like any follower, may only do so once per day.

Bolt

Bolt allows the mystic to channel his followers' energy into a missile of destructive force. This rite is often used to fight off intruders or as a show of power to remind followers where their loyalties lie. Powerful mystics often perform Steal Soul *(see page 225)* enough times to be able to power this rite on their own, without any followers nearby to harvest from.

Learning DC: 20

Minimum Knowledge (Occult) Skill: 5

Bonded Followers: 10 per 1d6 damage, up to 20d6

Complex Check: 25 – 1 half action

Effect: This rite launches a bolt from the mystic's hands targeted at one person within the mystic's line of sight. The bolt deals 1d6 damage for every 10 followers nearby for the mystic to harvest, up to a maximum of 20d6 damage. There is no attack roll required for this rite. Instead, the target may attempt a Reflex save to suffer half damage from the bolt.

Bond Follower

Bond Follower is used to harness the spiritual energy of the mystic's loyal followers for use in other invocations. During this process, the follower swears allegiance to the mystic in a ceremony designed to cement the mystic's authority. This varies from mystic to mystic, but often involves a show of loyalty and the creation of a visual reminder of the follower's subservience, such as a tattoo or even a brand.

Learning DC: 12

Minimum Knowledge (Occult) Skill: 5

Bonded Followers: 5

Complex Check: 25 – 1 minute

Effect: The mystic may only harvest the spiritual energy of followers he has bonded with this rite. In addition, these followers must be physically present at an invocation he performs to donate their energy to it. A single follower may only donate his energy to one invocation per day, requiring a full night's rest to replenish his power before he may be tapped again.

Followers must at least marginally understand the process of performing invocations and have developed their mystic potential to be of any use to a mystic. As such, a follower must have at least 5 ranks in Knowledge (Occult) to be bonded; any less and the Bond Follower rite fails.

The mystic may bond followers with mystic feats as well, though they only count as one bonded follower when they participate in rituals the mystic performs, even if they have feats and abilities which increase the energy they convey to invocations of their own (such as Mystic, Initiate, and Magus).

If the mystic bonds a follower who has followers of his own, each of those followers adds their energy to invocations he performs – assuming they're present when the invocation is enacted, of course.

Followers who are already bonded to one mystic may not be bonded to another, and bonded followers may not be stolen by another mystic. Bonded followers may be transferred to a new mystic, however, if both mystics agree.

Followers may not be bound against their will.

Bonded followers are immune to the Steal Soul ritual except when performed by the mystic to whom they are bound.

Should a follower ever leave the mystic he is bonded to (voluntarily or not), neither party suffers adverse effect (other than the fact that the follower can't contribute to the mystic's invocations). However, the bond between mystic and follower remains – the mystic gains a +4 bonus to his Listen, Search, Spot, and Surveillance checks when the follower is within a number of feet equal to ten times the mystic's Wisdom modifier. The mystic may also make an inspiration check (DC equal to 5 + the follower's level) to glean the current direction to the follower at any time, at any range.

If the mystic dies (or his soul is stolen), the bond with his followers dissolves and the followers may be bonded to another mystic, using the standard rules.

Complex Skill Use

Certain tasks are reliable in nature but require a long and variable period to complete. These occasions call for a complex skill check. The check comes in two parts – a DC and an interval. The DC works much like a normal skill check: it represents the number an agent must reach with his skill roll. The interval indicates how often the agent may make a skill roll (each roll coming at the end of one interval).

What makes complex checks different is that the results of each skill roll are cumulative. If the first roll does not reach the DC (and it usually won't due to the very high DCs associated with most complex skill checks), the agent may continue to work towards that goal, making another check after another interval has elapsed and adding it to his previous total. The agent may continue to work towards the DC until the task is accomplished, he gives up, or he is interrupted for a period equal to half of one interval (after which he must begin again, with a cumulative total of 0).

A threat adds the total of the roll to the complex skill check (as normal), while a critical success adds the total of the roll to the skill check and *reduces the time before the next roll only by one half* (rounding up). An error subtracts the total of the roll from the complex skill check (to a minimum of 0), while a critical failure cancels the entire attempt and uses up any materials or resources devoted to the complex skill check (such as the energy of bonded followers).

Complex skill checks require total concentration. When making one, you are considered flat-footed. Being injured while making a complex skill check interrupts the effect, though the agent may normally return to it as his next action if the interval is more than 1 round. If the interval lasts 1 round or less, any interruption ends the check and requires that the agent start the skill check over with a cumulative total of 0 unless he succeeds with a Concentration check (DC equal to 10 + the damage taken).

You may not take 10 or 20 when making a complex skill check.

Example: Eva Kraus wishes to put a squad of enemies to sleep. The complex check for the Mass Slumber ritual is "25 – 1 minute," so she makes her first Knowledge (Occult) skill check after performing the ritual for 1 minute with a DC of 25. After 1 minute, she makes her first skill check, scoring a total of 21, not enough for the ritual to work – yet. Eva continues to concentrate for another minute (a total of 2 minutes have elapsed), after which she makes another skill check. This time, the total is 24. Added to her previous total of 21, her cumulative total is 45, more than enough for the ritual to succeed.

Invocations and the Mastermind System

If a GC would like his villains to know invocations, he may purchase them at a base cost of 5 MP, then spend 1 MP per rite and 3 MP per ritual, per villain who knows the invocation. Invocations purchased in this way are known at the start of the season, and may be used as desired by the villain in question. Paying the base cost for invocations also allows the GC to purchase relics (*see page 231*). The base cost of 5 MP is part of the mastermind's organization cost, and is only paid once per season, while the cost of specific invocations is paid for each invocation known.

Borrow Power

Borrow Power transfers spiritual energy from the mystic's followers to a single person. This can make the person extremely strong, agile, or tough for a short period of time. Once this surge wears off, however, the benefactor becomes quite weary, requiring immediate rest.

Learning DC: 28
Minimum Knowledge (Occult) Skill: 13
Bonded Followers: 40 per +2 *(see below)*
Complex Check: 45 – 1 round

Effect: The mystic selects one person (including himself, if he so desires) to receive its benefit. For every 40 bonded followers harvested for energy, the target receives a +2 bonus to his choice of his Strength, Constitution, or Dexterity. These bonuses may be spread out among the three abilities (e.g. the power of 90 followers could provide a +4 to each ability, or +12 to just one of them). This power lasts for a number of rounds equal to the mystic's Knowledge (Occult) skill. After it wears off, the person affected by the ritual falls into a deep sleep for 8 hours.

Control Animals

The mystic can exert supernatural control over animals. While this ritual is in effect, the mystic can see through the animals' eyes and control their every move. The mystic would be wise, however, not to instruct an animal to attack one of its close companions.

Learning DC: 20
Minimum Knowledge (Occult) Skill: 8
Bonded Followers: 20
Complex Check: 35 – 1 round

Effect: The mystic seizes control of a number of animals within a 1 mile radius. He may only control a number of animals whose total vitality dice total does not exceed his Knowledge (Occult) skill. The mystic may control non-sentient species. There are only two limits to this control: 1) Controlled animals are still afraid of fire and refuse to pass through it, and 2) Controlled animals cannot be forced to attack anyone they share a close emotional bond with, such as a beloved owner. Attempting either of these things breaks the mystic's control over the animal, after which it is likely to be very angry with him.

Curb Violence

This rite renders a single weapon absolutely harmless to living beings. Modern weapons refuse to function, while melee weapons slide harmlessly off of flesh. This is a popular rite with 'white' initiates, as it can quickly bring all hostilities to a close, allowing a moment for reason to settle in.

Learning DC: 15
Minimum Knowledge (Occult) Skill: 5
Bonded Followers: 20
Complex Check: 35 – 1 round

Effect: The mystic renders harmless one weapon of his or her choice within line of sight. This effect lasts for one hour or until the weapon leaves the mystic's presence. This rite confers no immunity to unarmed attacks of any kind, and weapons may still be used to damage inanimate objects.

Curse

This rite takes the form of a blight of bad luck inflicted upon one of the mystic's enemies. Things begin to go spectacularly wrong for the afflicted person – guns jam, gadgets malfunction, small items go missing, etc. Close friends and family almost immediately notice the difference and wonder what's wrong. Fortunately, a curse wears off over time, gradually growing weaker until it fades away altogether. Alternately, this rite can be used to remove a curse before it has run its course.

Learning DC: 27
Minimum Knowledge (Occult) Skill: 11
Bonded Followers: 25 per –1 *(see below)*
Complex Check: 40 – 1 round

Effect: The mystic targets one person within his line of sight to be the victim of the curse. That person receives a Will save (DC equal to the mystic's Knowledge (Occult) skill). Success negates the rite entirely. Failure, however, indicates that the victim suffers a –1 penalty to all die rolls for every 25 bonded followers harvested during the rite, up to a maximum of –5. This penalty decreases by 1 every Saturday until it has faded away entirely. A friendly mystic may remove the curse earlier by performing this rite and making an Knowledge (Occult) skill check (DC equal to the Knowledge (Occult) skill of the mystic who laid the curse).

HEALING

This rite heals an injured person's wounds – torn muscles mend, broken bones knit, and bleeding stops.

Learning DC: 23

Minimum Knowledge (Occult) Skill: 11

Bonded Followers: 20 +5 per level of injured person

Complex Check: 50 – 1 round

Effect: One person whom the mystic is touching is healed of all vitality and wound point damage. This rite has no effect on the dead (those at -10 wound points or less).

INVISIBILITY

Invisibility causes one person to fade from sight, rendering him completely transparent to the visible, infrared, and ultraviolet spectra, allowing him to move about unmolested and bypass certain types of security.

Learning DC: 24

Minimum Knowledge (Occult) Skill: 9

Bonded Followers: 40

Complex Check: 40 – 5 minutes

Effect: One person – either the mystic or someone he designates – is rendered invisible. This offers the target total concealment *(see page 171 of the Spycraft Espionage Handbook)* and makes it easy for him to surprise others, as long as they aren't alerted by noise or smell. The Extended Visual Spectrum psion skill counteracts this invocation, allowing the psion to see the mystic clearly. Security devices based on light, such as cameras and electronic eyes, cannot sense the target. Security devices based on more exotic principles, such as air currents, still detect him, as do animals that rely on scent such as guard dogs. The target remains invisible for 5 minutes per rank the mystic has in the Knowledge (Occult) skill.

SHIELD

Shield creates a bubble of power around the mystic that protects him from all forms of ranged attacks, including bullets. This ritual is typically used in self-defense, forcing attackers to close to hand-to-hand combat with the mystic, where the Killing Touch ritual can be used to deadly effect.

Learning DC: 16

Minimum Knowledge (Occult) Skill: 5

Bonded Followers: 5 per round of duration

Complex Check: 25 – 1 half action

Effect: The mystic becomes immune to all ranged attacks for one round per 5 followers he harvests. In addition, any object (such as a grenade) propelled into the mystic's square automatically rebounds towards the person who threw it, traveling 1d6 squares in his direction. This rite confers no immunity to melee attacks of any kind.

STEAL SOUL

Steal Soul is the dark side of Bond Follower. Only the most evil mystics use the rite, since it requires a human sacrifice, but the power it offers tempts all those who know of it. Unlike Bond Follower, the sacrifice need not be a willing subject. Best of all (from the mystic's point of view), the mystic permanently absorbs the spiritual energy of the sacrifice and may thereafter call upon it as though it were an extra follower.

Learning DC: 35

Minimum Knowledge (Occult) Skill: 15

Bonded Followers: 80

Complex Check: 150 – 4 hours

Effect: When the mystic performs the sacrifice, he automatically slays the victim with a single blow. The mystic is then considered to have two or more extra followers present at all times (see below), whom he may harvest once per day. This rite may be performed multiple times, granting the mystic one or more extra followers each time.

The mystic may only steal the souls of those who have the Mystic feat, and each stolen soul contributes to the mystic's invocations as if he were performing them (e.g. a stolen mystic's soul contributes 2 followers' worth of energy, while a stolen initiate's soul contributes 5 followers' worth of energy, and a stolen magus' soul contributes 10 followers' worth of energy.)

Finally, stolen souls fade after one year (their energies do not add to the mystic's follower total beyond that time).

MYSTIC RITUALS

Beyond the power of rites are truly mighty examples of mystic power – rituals. A mystic must be at least an initiate to learn a ritual. Like rites, rituals are consistently successful as long as the mystic gathers sufficient followers and is allowed to perform the ritual without undue interruption. Each ritual lists the minimal number of bonded followers required and the DC and interval for the complex Knowledge (Occult) skill check required to perform them. Unlike rites, rituals involve a certain degree of risk in the form of the Thirst. This dreadful peril is detailed on page 229.

CONTROL WEATHER

This ritual makes it possible to control the currents of weather. The mystic may call up rainstorms, or cause droughts. Hail, sleet, and snow are all possible as well. Given enough followers, a mystic can even cause hurricanes, tornadoes, or an ice age.

Learning DC: 38 **Thirst DC:** 35

Minimum Knowledge (Occult) Skill: 20

Bonded Followers: Varies *(see below)*

Complex Check: 200 – 4 hours

Effect: Although the ritual's DC remains the same no matter how severe the desired weather effect, the number of followers required greatly increases as the impact of the effect spreads to cover a wider area (see below). In addition, the GC may rule that summoning an effect out of season requires even more followers.

Once the ritual is completed, the mystic concentrates on the desired effect and chooses a spot in his line of sight where the weather effect originates. The game effects of each type of weather are described on page 232 of the *Spycraft Espionage Handbook*.

Weather Effect	Followers	Duration
Call light wind	15	6 hours
Call severe wind	25	6 hours
Call a rainstorm	30	1 hour
Call sleet or hail	50	1 hour
Call a snowstorm	50	1 hour
Call blizzard	150	6 hours
Cause drought	250	1 week
Call a tornado	500	1 hour
Call a hurricane	1,000	1d6 days
Change local climate	10,000	1 year
Cause an ice age	100,000	10 years

Create Anchor Node

This ritual turns an ordinary circle of stones into an anchor node which can be used with the Teleport ritual. This ritual was frequently used in pagan Britain, resulting in the numerous stone circles found there.

Learning DC: 35 **Thirst DC:** 35
Minimum Knowledge (Occult) Skill: 18
Bonded Followers: 1000
Complex Check: 300 – 4 hours

Effect: This ritual may only be performed on a solstice, and requires a circle of stones, each of which must weigh at least 500 pounds. Once the ceremony is complete, the circle becomes an anchor node to which mystics can transport matter with the Teleport ritual. The anchor node may be eliminated if more than half of the stones are removed or destroyed. The mystic who creates an anchor node is automatically familiar with it, and does not need to spend 3 hours there in order to use it (per Teleport).

Destroy Technology

This ritual creates a field of mystic energy that interferes with any technology more complicated than a bow. Guns are more likely to jam or misfire, cars and planes stall at a critical moment, and computers begin to act erratically. During WWII, this strange effect was observed by American pilots and jokingly referred to as "gremlins." Little did they realize that this was a real phenomenon, and not an imagined one.

Learning DC: 40 **Thirst DC:** 35
Minimum Knowledge (Occult) Skill: 21
Bonded Followers: 500 per mile radius (see below)
Complex Check: 350 – 4 hours

Effect: An anti-technology "field" is created, centered on the mystic's current location. This field is one mile in radius for every 200 followers the mystic harvests for the ritual, and it lasts for one month. The error range of all weapons, vehicles, and devices within this field are doubled, so long as their original error range is at least 1. Thus, an error range of 1–2 would become 1–4.

Killing Touch

The Killing Touch is one of the most potent weapons a mystic has at his disposal. It does just what its name implies – it instantly and painfully kills the first person the mystic touches after performing the ritual. A red palm print is left where the touch was delivered.

Learning DC: 31 **Thirst DC:** 40
Minimum Knowledge (Occult) Skill: 15
Bonded Followers: 50
Complex Check: 40 – 1 round

Effect: The mystic's hands begin to glow red. This glow lasts a number of rounds equal to the mystic's agent level. While his hands are glowing, a successful touch attack against a target forces the target to immediately make a Fortitude save (DC equal to the mystic's Knowledge (Occult) skill) or be instantly reduced to -10 wound points. The effects of this ritual wear off immediately after a life is claimed.

Mass Slumber

Mass Slumber can cause a large number of people to fall into a deep sleep for up to 8 hours. This ritual works best on ordinary people; those who have been trained to guard their thoughts, such as agents, present much more difficult targets.

Learning DC: 22 **Thirst DC:** 25
Minimum Knowledge (Occult) Skill: 12
Bonded Followers: 30
Complex Check: 25 – 1 minute

Effect: Everyone targeted by the mystic (up to 5x his Knowledge (Occult) skill within line of sight) may fall into a deep slumber for 8 hours. Minions and unimportant NPCs receive no saving throw – they simply fall asleep. Everyone else (i.e. agents, henchmen, villains, and important supporting characters) must make a Will save (DC equal to the mystic's Knowledge (Occult) skill) or fall asleep as well. Any rough handling (such as attacking or shaking) wakes a sleeping person, but loud noises do not.

Mass Suggestion

Mass Suggestion can hypnotize a large number of people to believe or do a certain thing – even to forget something they've seen or done. Like Mass Slumber, this ritual also works most effectively on untrained minds.

Learning DC: 29 **Thirst DC:** 30

Minimum Knowledge (Occult) Skill: 15

Bonded Followers: 80

Complex Check: 75 – 5 minutes

Effect: The mystic gives a command consisting of a number of words equal to or less than his Knowledge (Occult) skill. All minions and unimportant NPCs within line of sight receive no saving throw – they simply obey. Everyone else within line of sight (i.e. agents, henchmen, villains, and important supporting characters) must make a Will save (DC equal to the mystic's Knowledge (Occult) skill) or obey as well. Victims may not be given a suggestion that results in their death – even the meekest person naturally resists such a command.

Move Earth

This extremely powerful ritual alters the earth itself. Mountains can be raised or islands dropped into the ocean if enough followers are harvested. Perhaps most frightening of all, buildings in the area of such massive upheavals are sure to collapse, killing or trapping everyone inside.

Learning DC: 37 **Thirst DC:** 35

Minimum Knowledge (Occult) Skill: 19

Bonded Followers: 400 per square mile *(see below)*

Complex Check: 100 – 4 hours

Effect: The mystic targets an area within his line of sight to raise or lower. He may affect 1 square mile for every 150 followers he has harvested, raising or lowering the land to a maximum of 100 feet for every square mile affected. Thus, if a mystic harvests the power of 1500 followers, he can affect 10 square miles, raising or lowering the land a maximum of 1000 feet. Any buildings in the affected area automatically collapse The mystic may crudely shape the area he is affecting, but in general, only natural shapes are possible.

Plague

Plague creates a virulent disease that spreads far and wide, sparing only the mystic and his bonded followers from its nightmarish grip. The great epidemics of the past, such as smallpox, polio, and the bubonic plague, may have originated from the use of this ritual. Only the most insane mystics would dare to call up a Plague, for like the efreet of legend, once released it cannot be put back in its bottle.

Learning DC: 33 **Thirst DC:** 45

Minimum Knowledge (Occult) Skill: 18

Bonded Followers: 800

Complex Check: 350 – 4 hours

Effect: To perform this ritual, the mystic needs a minimum of 10 people who are not his bonded followers. These people must be restrained during the ceremony, because the ritual is very painful for them.

Once the ritual is completed, these people become infected with a deadly disease never before seen by man. Usually incoherent and hallucinating by this point, they are then released to spread the new plague in the nearest city. The GC determines the specifics of the plague, but it is ultimately fatal, and easily spread.

Vaccination sometimes works against the plague. Each time a doctor attempts to save a plague victim using practical medicine, he must make a First Aid check against the mystic's Knowledge (Occult) skill total.

Resurrection

The greatest power many mystics ever know, this ritual has the power to bring the dead back to life, no matter how long they've been deceased. It only works on sentient beings, however, and it requires the dead person's skull, and exacts a terrible price – another life, or the mystic's gift.

Learning DC: 45 **Thirst DC:** 45

Minimum Knowledge (Occult) Skill: 23

Bonded Followers: 5000

Complex Check: 1000 – 4 hours

Effect: The mystic must remain awake while performing this ritual (requiring a Fortitude save each day, against a DC of 20 plus the number of days he has remained awake past the first). Once the vigil is completed, the mystic places the deceased's skull in the center of a circle of his followers and performs the final chant. Lastly, the ritual comes with a price – either the mystic must perform a human sacrifice ("a life for a life") or he loses all bonded followers, as well as the ability to bond new followers ("the mystic's gift"). Once lost, his powers are gone and may never be reclaimed.

Scry

Scry allows the mystic to observe and listen to a distant person or place. To do so, he stares into a reflective surface while his followers repeat a chant. Then a vision of the thing he wishes to see appears in the reflective surface. This vision cannot show the past or future, only the present. Some extremely powerful mystics can use the vision to extend the reach of other invocations, but only at great personal cost.

Learning DC: 26 **Thirst DC:** 30

Minimum Knowledge (Occult) Skill: 12

Bonded Followers: 15

Complex Check: 50 – 5 minutes

Effect: The mystic is granted a vision of a distant place or person for a number of minutes equal to his ranks in the Knowledge (Occult) skill. The ritual requires a reflective surface, such as a pool of water, a crystal ball, or a mirror, to perform. In order to scry a person, the mystic must have a personal object. In order to scry a place, the mystic must have visited it before.

Each character scryed upon is allowed a secret Knowledge (Occult) skill check (DC 10 + scrying mystic's Knowledge (Occult) skill), rolled by the GC. With success, he is aware that someone is watching him.

Table 6.2: Invocations

Invocation Name	Learning DC	Thirst DC	Min. Knowledge (Occult) Skill	Bonded Followers	Complex Skill Check
Rites					
Bolt	20	–	5	10 per 1d6 damage	25–1 half action
Bond Follower	12	–	5	5	25–1 minute
Borrow Power	28	–	13	40 per +2	45–1 round
Control Animals	20	–	8	20	35–1 round
Curb Violence	15	–	5	20	35–1 round
Curse	27	–	11	25 per -1	40–1 round
Healing	23	–	11	20 + 5 per level	50–1 round
Invisibility	24	–	9	40	40–5 minutes
Shield	16	–	5	5 per round	25–1 half action
Steal Soul	35	–	15	80	150–4 hours
Rituals					
Control Weather	38	35	20	Varies	200–4 hours
Create Anchor Node	35	35	18	1000	300–4 hours
Destroy Technology	40	35	21	500 per mile radius	350–4 hours
Killing Touch	31	40	15	50	40–1 round
Mass Slumber	22	25	12	30	25–1 minute
Mass Suggestion	29	30	15	80	75–5 minutes
Move Earth	37	35	19	400 per square mile	100–4 hours
Plague	33	45	18	800	350–4 hours
Resurrection	45	45	23	5000	1000–4 hours
Scry	26	30	12	15	50–5 minutes
Teleport	29	30	14	50	Varies

A magus (but not a mystic or initiate) may perform other invocations using Scry to extend his line of sight (effectively sending the invocation through the vision to affect those depicted by it), but this severely weakens him. The magus collapses after completing the invocation, and must have one full day of rest for every bonded follower the "sent" invocation requires. The magus cannot do anything but rest during this time.

Teleport

This ritual instantly transports objects or people to an Anchor Node *(see page 226)*, no matter the distance. Anchor nodes are large open areas ringed with mystic focal devices (such as Stonehenge). A rapid form of this ritual can be used in an emergency, but it inflicts permanent harm on the mystic.

Learning DC: 29 **Thirst DC:** 30
Minimum Knowledge (Occult) Skill: 14
Bonded Followers: 50
Complex Check: 35 – 15 minutes or half action *(see below)*

Effect: Using this ritual, the mystic instantly transports 50 lbs. of living or non-living matter (including himself, if he so desires) for every rank he has in the Knowledge (Occult) skill. This matter is sent to an anchor node, which is a special area prepared with the Create Anchor Node ritual. Many of the stone circles that exist around the world actually serve as anchor nodes, and a mystic may use any of these as a receiving point as long as he has first visited the circle and spent at least 3 hours inside it attuning himself to its mystic energies.

In an emergency, a mystic may perform this ritual as a half action, but may only transport 25 lbs. of matter for every rank he has in the Knowledge (Occult) skill, and permanently reduces his Constitution by 1 point.

Unwilling passengers may be transported using this ritual if the mystic is touching them. They must make a Will save opposed by the mystic. Failure indicates that they are teleported with the mystic. Success indicates that they remain behind when the teleportation occurs. The mystic may remain behind after failing this roll, but the ritual is considered spent regardless, and whatever (and whomever) else the mystic was teleporting continues to the destination whether he goes with them or not.

Each character who teleports (including the mystic) must make a Fortitude save (DC 25 minus the mystic's agent level). Any who fail are stunned for a number of rounds equal to the difference between their roll and the DC.

The Thirst

"Power tends to corrupt; absolute power corrupts absolutely."

"Knowledge is Power."

Throughout the millennia, mystic traditions have drawn upon different facets of an unseen world as dangerous as it is illuminating. Every mystic knows in his heart that the knowledge they amass is not without price. The oldest texts and earliest whispered traditions call this price "the Thirst".

Man is not a native of the mystic world, and humans who tap into it tread on alien ground. Once a mystic can enact rituals, he must forever after guard himself against the seductive lure of even greater power – absolute power – and those who seize it from him.

Thirst Mechanics

Each time a mystic begins a ritual, he must make a Will save against the ritual's Thirst DC, +1 for every ritual he already knows. If the save is successful, he has conquered the seductive sway of the forces he wields. Otherwise, he suffers from the Thirst, gaining one Thirst level.

Thirst levels have the following effects.

Level 1: Ritual power fills the mystic with a surge of confidence and personal will. The mystic gains a +1 bonus when using any Charisma-based skill within a number of hours after successfully performing any invocation equal to the difference between his roll and the invocation's DC.

Level 2: The mystic's focused mind awakens to new vistas of ritual power. Whenever the mystic spends an action die to add to a complex skill check, two dice are added instead of one (e.g. a 1st-level mystic's bonus of 1d4 becomes 2d4). However, the mystic becomes uncomfortable and ill at ease when not studying or using mystic forces. The DCs of all his Will saving throws are increased by 2 (including future Thirst checks), except when he is learning a new invocation.

Level 3: The mystic is able to fathom nuances about the mystic world that are lost to others. He performs and learns rituals as if his Knowledge (Occult) Skill were 2 higher.

Level 4: The mystic's physical needs wane in favor of his ritual efforts – his Fortitude DCs for not consuming food or fluids begin at 5 instead of 10 *(see page 230 of the Spycraft Espionage Handbook)*, and he gains +1 vitality point per agent level for 24 hours after starting any ritual (not to exceed one such vitality boost per 24-hour period). The mystic's focus comes at the cost of

broader pursuits, however – he is distracted and listless when not seeking the means to greater power, and suffers a –2 penalty to all skill checks except those using the Knowledge (Occult) skill.

Level 5: The mystic performs and learns rituals as if his Knowledge (Occult) Skill were 4 higher.

Level 6: The mystic's mind reels with the incredible knowledge he's acquired, and his control over "lesser men" increases by the day. The mystic gains 1 point each of Intelligence, Wisdom, and Charisma. The mystic's body pays the price, however – he is physically ravaged by the Thirst, appearing noticeably ill and losing 2 points each of Strength, Dexterity, and Constitution when not using a mystic feat.

Level 7: The mystic's mental and empathic powers turn from personal charm to domination – the mystic gains an additional 1 point each of Intelligence, Wisdom, and Charisma (for a total increase of +2 to each ability).

Level 8: The mystic is driven mad by the Thirst as his mind awakens to the vast outer reaches of the mytic world. The madness may not be apparent to casual observers, but the mystic no longer thinks or reacts in a truly human manner. Rumors persist that this level of comprehension opens up entirely new vistas of untapped power, but proof of this "apotheosis" is limited to mythic accounts of god-kings who lorded over the world thousands of years ago. Only mystics who achieve this state of being know for sure, and they rarely survive for long after their ascension. If an agent reaches this state, the GC takes contol, turning him into an NPC (and perhaps a new mastermind).

All Thirst effects are cumulative.

Mystics see the Thirst as a living force of nature, craving human slaves the same way that they crave mystic power. It is their greatest enemy, preying on spirits drunk with the very forces of creation at their fingertips. As shown above, the Thirst lures unwary mystics with seemingly greater power, but eventually leads them to madness, spiritual ruin, and physical self destruction. And when a powerful mystic destroys himself, he rarely goes out alone.

Slaking the Thirst

The call of the mystic world does abate over time. On the days of the solstices and equinoxes (four times a year, *see below*), when the physical and mystic worlds are in greatest balance, all mystics may make a single Will save with a DC of 20 + their Thirst level to reduce their Thirst level by 1. Making this save requires two full hours of quiet contemplation, and may be attempted at any time during that designated day or following night.

Day	Date
Equinox, autumnal	September 23 or 24
Equinox, vernal	March 20 or 21
Solstice, summer	June 21 or 22*
Solstice, winter	December 21 or 22*

** In the Northern Hemisphere; in the Southern Hemisphere, these dates are reversed.*

This process likely explains why the mystic traditions place so much emphasis on the days of the solstice and equinox, as cautious mystics strive to balance their occult knowledge with the precarious temptation of the Thirst.

Mystic Relics

Mystic relics are the stuff of legend, stemming from historical anecdotes, mythology, folklore, and old wives' tales. Professional scholars consider most of these items fantasy, but mystics understand the truth – that legends are the part of the world's living history, and that the remnants of that history contain our purest link to the world of the Ancients.

Relics may not be requisitioned with budget or gadget points. Rather, they should only be encountered only during missions – under bizarre circumstances.

Game Control has final approval on all mystic relics.

Beowulf's Hilt

Long ago, the Dane king Hrothgar had a problem: the Grendel. Night after night, the Grendel feasted upon his livestock and men. No one could put an end to its assaults against Hrothgar's people. Hearing of the Dane's troubles, the Great Beowulf traveled to Hrothgar's side, and swore to destroy the Grendel.

When the Grendel returned, Beowulf tore off its arm, crippling it. The creature retreated quickly, but Beowulf wasn't finished. He tracked the Grendel to its lair in a nearby marsh, accompanied by the Dane Unferth. When they arrived, Beowulf saw he would have to dive underwater in order to reach the Grendel's cave. Unferth offered Beowulf his blood-hardened sword to fight the beast, but did not accompany him.

When Beowulf arrived in the Grendel's lair, he found not only the Grendel, but the Grendel's mother. His attack was fierce, but the Grendel's mother turned aside Unferth's sword. Undaunted, Beowulf seized a sword from the grip of a nearby skeleton and smote the Grendel's mother, killing her with one blow. He then made short work of the crippled Grendel.

As Beowulf swam back to the surface, however, his new sword melted, leaving only the hilt. He returned Unferth's sword without admitting how it failed him. Later, he presented the hilt of the sword that slew the Grendel and its mother to King Hrothgar as a gift. The Hilt currently resides in the Horsens Museum, located in Horsens, Denmark.

Mechanics: Beowulf's Hilt promotes strength and ferocity in combat. If an agent is carrying the hilt, his Strength, Dexterity, and Constitution are each increased by 2.

Dream Catchers

Dream catchers appear in the oral history of a number of Native American tribes. Traditionally, dream catchers are made of willow and sinew; the willow frames a pattern resembling a spider web, which is formed by the sinew. They are not meant to last. Eventually the willow dries out and the tension of the sinew collapses the item. This reflects the intended purpose of the dream catcher – to guard young children against nightmares. The shape of the dream catcher is dictated by the legend surrounding it.

In ancient stories, Asibikaashi, or Spider Woman, was one of the spirits responsible for returning the sun back to her people. It was said that if you were awake at dawn, you could find Asibikaashi's lodge, or web. In that lodge, you would see how she captured the sunrise as the light sparkled on the dew gathered there.

In honor of Asibikaashi, dream catchers are constructed to resemble spider webs, and in honor of the sun she returned to her people, they are woven onto a round frame. A small hole at the center of the web allows the good dreams through the dream catcher, while nightmares are trapped in the web. The nightmares are destroyed as the first rays of the sun shine through the dream catcher.

In many tribes, it was traditional to place a feather at the center of a dream catcher, representing breath, or air. A baby watching the feather dance in the air was both protected by the dream catcher while sleeping, and given a lesson about the importance of "good air" while awake. The specific feather used was often determined by the qualities parents wished to instill in their children (e.g. an owl's feather for wisdom, or an eagle's feather for courage).

While dream catchers can be easily found across the United States in craft shops and the like, only a few are truly powerful. Some argue that modern dream catchers are worthless because they substitute items such as gems for the traditional feather, while others claim a true dream catcher can only be made for each of Asibikaashi's people born. The truth is – and may remain – a mystery.

Relics and the Mastermind System

If a GC would like his villains to have access to relics, he may purchase them at a base cost of 5 MP, plus 3 MP per relic. If the GC wants more than one copy of a non-unique relic, he must pay the cost for each copy his threat possesses. Relics purchased in this way are available at the start of the season, and may be used as desired by the villain in question. Paying the base cost for relics also allows the GC to purchase invocations (*see page 224*). The base cost of 5 MP is part of the mastermind's organization cost, and is only paid once per season, while the cost of specific relics is paid for each relic possessed.

Mechanics: While carrying a mystic dream catcher, an agent is not only protected from bad dreams, but from psionics as well. Whenever the agent becomes the target of a psion skill or feat that allows a save, he gains a +5 bonus to his roll.

In addition, if the dream catcher is adorned with the feather of an owl, falcon, or eagle, the agent receives a bonus to all saves of a specific type, based on which feather is used. An eagle's feather grants +2 to Fortitude saves, a falcon's feather grants +2 to Reflex saves, and an owl's feather grants +2 to Will saves. These bonuses do not stack with the save bonus granted against psion skills and feats.

The Feather of Ma'at

The Egyptian god Anubis has been ascribed a variety of positions, ranging from the God of the Dead (a title later usurped by Osiris) to the son of Osiris, who stood at Osiris' left hand in judgment of the dead. In both of these capacities, Anubis was responsible for weighing a dead soul's heart against the Feather of Ma'at.

The heart and the feather were placed opposite each other on the "Scales of Truth." If the soul's heart was light, and the Feather of Ma'at outweighed it, the soul was presented to Osiris. If the heart was heavy, the soul was fed to Ammit (the "Eater of the Dead") and destroyed.

Quetzalcoatl's Thorn

Outside of this capacity, the feather first appeared in the study of the Greek scholar Peraius, noted for his analyses of contemporary Greek political figures. For Peraius, who wrote with a quill and ink, the Feather was his favorite implement. Through the ages, the Feather has been used in this capacity several times, most recently by the noted Italian biographer Alberto Mellini. Mellini died in December of 2001, without a will. In the absence of such guidance, his three children have been unable to determine who should inherit his various possessions, including the quill. The case is currently in litigation.

It is unknown if Mellini's children are aware of the quill's true history.

Mechanics: The Feather of Ma'at grants its owner tremendous insight concerning other people. An agent carrying the feather may, as a half action, spend an action die to determine the level and class of one NPC.

The Gordian Knot

When the king of Phrygia died, leaving no heir, the Oracle at Delphi prophesied their next king would arrive drawn by oxen. The emissaries who bore witness to the Oracle's words described what they had heard to the citizens of Phrygia upon their return. Soon after, a man named Gordius and his wife rode into town on their oxen-drawn wagon. In keeping with the Oracle's declaration, the elders made Gordius king.

Upon his coronation, Gordius dedicated his wagon to the Oracle. To remind himself of his humble beginnings, he tied the wagon to a post in front of his palace with an enormous knot.

Gordius ruled well, as did his son, Midas. However, when Midas stepped from the throne, he left no heir. The Oracle at Delphi prophesied once more, this time proclaiming that he who untied the Gordian Knot would rule not only Phrygia, but all of Asia.

Many years passed, and many men tried to untie the famous Gordian Knot. None succeeded until Alexander the Great. At first, like other men, he attempted to untie the knot by hand, but when it became apparent that his efforts would be in vain, he drew his sword and sliced it in two.

Thereafter, Alexander did indeed conquer Asia (as it was known to the classical world) and went on to become one of the most prominent rulers in all of known history. The Gordian Knot has ever been a symbol of his wisdom, but to the Sons of Alexander, a secret society bent on world domination, it has become a symbol of his power. The Sons already hold one half of the Gordian Knot, and are currently scouring the world for the other.

Mechanics: Despite the beliefs of the Sons of Alexander, the Gordian Knot's powers promote wisdom rather than world domination. Whenever an agent possesses one half of the knot, he may make an inspiration roll without spending an action die, once per session. If he controls both halves of the knot, the roll is automatically successful.

Guan Gong's Halberd

Relatively unknown outside of Asia, Guan Gong of the I-Kuan Tao pantheon personifies the virtues of the warrior: honor, loyalty, integrity, justice, courage, and strength. Historically, Guan Gong lived in China roughly 1700 years ago, during the period of the Three Kingdoms, an era overrun with strife and civil war.

Guan Gong's distinctive appearance is often misleading. His fiery red complexion and long beard stand out immediately, as does his unique weapon – a great blade mounted on a long handle, which never leaves his side. This image, particularly his red face, often leaves the mistaken impression that Guan Gong is a demon.

On the contrary, Guan Gong's red face represents his righteous anger. Legend claims that his complexion changed after he slew a bullying magistrate for accosting a girl. The change allowed him to slip past the guards unrecognized, thus escaping the city and embarking on his illustrious adventures.

Guan Gong's halberd is his ultimate legacy. For centuries, it has appeared in stories and legends, surrounded by tales of the righteous toppling evil men and corrupt empires, regardless of the odds against them. Curiously, the weapon has been described not only as a halberd, but also as a Chinese broadsword, a spear, and even a staff, depending on the context of the story.

Currently, the location of Guan Gong's Halberd is unknown, despite the Pan-Asian Collective's ongoing attempts to track it down. Unfortunately, the Chamber's efforts are hindered by the Chinese Communist government, who believe the relic to be a threat to their control of China.

Mechanics: Guan Gong's Halberd always manifests as a melee weapon of some sort, though the specifics of its appearance are dictated by the individual who finds it. The Halberd reshapes itself as a weapon useful to its owner. When the Halberd is located, if anyone present has the Weapon Master feat, the Halberd appears as the appropriate weapon. Otherwise it retains its original form. If more than one agent (or NPC) near the Halberd has the Weapon Master feat, each must make an opposed Strength check. The Halberd takes a form matching the Weapon Master feat of whichever agent or NPC makes the highest check.

Regardless of its appearance, the Halberd is a formidable weapon:

Damage	Error	Threat	Weight
3d8	–	18-20	10 lb.*

* *As halberd, otherwise, matches appropriate weapon.*

But there's a catch – if the wielder ever witnesses an innocent in danger when wearing the weapon (whether he is currently using it or not), he must make a Will save (DC 25) or be compelled to intervene. This could easily endanger the agent – and under the wrong circumstances, the Cloak.

Rod of the Scarab

MARDUK'S SIGNET

When the Babylonian gods learned the primeval being Tiamat was preparing to do battle with the young pantheon, they petitioned Marduk to be their champion. Marduk agreed to their request, but he set forth a condition. When he arrived before the assembled gods, he said "If indeed, I, your avenger, am to bind Tiamat and give life to you, then put in session an assembly, proclaim my destiny pre-eminent. Sit joyfully together in the hall of assembly, let me determine destinies by the utterance of my mouth instead of yours; so that whatever I myself create shall be unalterable; so that the word of my lips shall neither turn about nor be changed."

After private deliberation, the gods agreed to Marduk's terms, but they set a condition of their own. Before he became king of the gods, Marduk would demonstrate his power, that he might prove himself worthy to sit among them. They asked that he choose a star in the sky, make it disappear, then reappear once more. This Marduk did.

The gods bestowed upon Marduk kingship of the universe, and with his position came symbols of his rank, including a scepter and a signet ring. In his ensuing battle with Tiamat, his hand was severed from his wrist, yet he still vanquished the creature. Later, his grievous wound healed – subsequent renderings and legends depict him with two hands – but the ring upon his hand was lost.

Marduk's Signet reappeared in 1990 during an archaeological expedition to the Babylonian city of Mashkan-shapir (now Tell Abu Duwari, Iraq), though the team had no inkling of its true discovery. When the Gulf War cut the dig short, several of the artifacts – including the ring – were transferred to the State University of New York at Stony Brook for further study, where they remain.

Mechanics: The wearer of Marduk's Signet is imbued with a commanding presence, and seemingly impervious self-confidence. Each time the agent makes an Intimidate or Diplomacy skill check, he receives a free action die to spend on the roll (which may not be spent on any other roll). This bonus action die is lost if it is not spent on the roll for which it is granted. In addition, any use of the Intimidate skill directed at the agent automatically fails, unless a threat is rolled.

MJOLNIR

Thor, son of Odin and the Norse god of Thunder, commanded storms and lightning. He rode in a chariot drawn by two goats called Toothgrinder and Toothgnasher, and possessed the magical axe-hammer Mjolnir, forged by the dwarf Brok. Mjolnir would destroy anything it was thrown at, always returning subsequently to the hand of its wielder. Thor used Mjolnir to smite giants, the ancient enemies of the Norse gods, and where Mjolnir struck home, lighting and thunder leapt forth.

Though mighty, not even Thor was strong enough to wield Mjolnir without magical aid. He wore a belt that enhanced his strength, as well as magical gloves that would protect his hands from the tremendous heat shed by the enchanted hammer.

One day, when Thor cast Mjolnir, it did not return, but instead fell to the earth below. The reasons for this event remain a mystery. Now it lies at the bottom of the North Sea, causing some of the worst storms to ever plague the region. No one knows the mystic hammer's exact location – except Eva Kraus. The Hand of Glory has mounted several expeditions to retrieve the fabled axe-hammer. Thus far, none have returned.

Mechanics: An agent must have a Strength of at least 25 to lift this relic, and wielding it as a weapon is impossible. Nonetheless, Mjolnir is a powerful relic. It generates enough electrical power to perpetually light New York City and several small towns besides. Eva Kraus, however, covets the axe-hammer for its mystic might. When used to power the Weather Control ritual, Mjolnir counts as 50,000 bonded minions. When Mjolnir's power is harvested in this way, it requires a month to recharge before it may be used again.

THE NECRONOMICON

The Necronomicon's origins are shrouded in mystery and controversy; some claim the book was written by Abdul Alhazred, the mad poet of Sanaa, in 700 A.D. Others claim the book was an invention of famed horror author H.P. Lovecraft, and does not exist at all. Still others claim the book is actually much, much older than Alhazred, and much, much truer than anyone suspects.

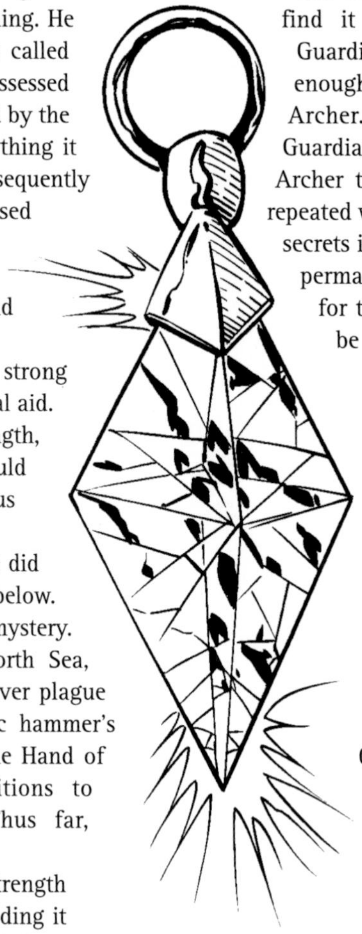

The original contents of the book are shrouded in mystery, thanks to the millennia long efforts of the Guardians of the Whispering Knife. Whatever secrets the book held, the Guardians decided long ago to make them disappear.

The only problem is, they haven't been able to find it since. During the early sixties, the Guardians' search for the book was intense enough to draw the attention of Raymond Archer. For reasons known only to the Guardians and Archer himself, they disclosed to Archer the contents of the book. He has never repeated what they told him, carrying the volume's secrets into retirement. He has, however, issued a permanent Code: Black open mission protocol for the return of the journal – so that it can be destroyed.

Mechanics: The contents of the Necronomicon are beyond the understanding of virtually everyone alive today, with the exception of a very few Guardians. And they aren't telling.

The Tears of Gethsemane

QUETZALCOATL'S THORN

An Aztec priest named Mahuizoh crafted this sacrificial dagger as a gift for the great feathered serpent Quetzalcoatl. Its careful design was meant to store the thoughts and knowledge of those it had slain, and to pass them on to its wielder, though history has proven that it also steals its victims' forms.

In the late 1500s the dagger was "liberated" and carried across the Atlantic Ocean by Bernal Diaz, a soldier formerly under the command of Hernando Cortes. In Spain, Diaz sold the relic to an enthusiastic nobleman.

For many months thereafter, Diaz suffered horrifying dreams of the dagger's true purpose, and he vowed to recover and destroy it. Diaz spent the rest of his days searching for the item, at last catching up with it outside a seedy tavern on the coast of Barbados. Its owner stabbed him sixty-three times.

The dagger has not made a public appearance since, though some speculated that Jack the Ripper wielded it during that bloody autumn in 1888. If the Ripper could use it, then certainly other serial killers may have possessed it as well; it currently rests in the hands of a vicious murderer known as Gemini *(see page 92)*.

Mechanics: When the wielder of the Thorn uses it to deliver the killing blow to an enemy, the knife absorbs the victim's form, allowing its wielder to perfectly impersonate the victim for up to 10 minutes per day (treat this as an undetectable disguise). In addition, the knife absorbs one rank of the victim's highest skill (wielder's choice if there is a tie). The Thorn's wielder may use all of the skill ranks that it has absorbed over the years, up to his own rank maximums. The GC determines which skills the Thorn contains when found.

Rod of the Scarab

In Ancient Egypt, the Pharoah's children played with small gadget scarabs which, when wound up, scuttled about and fluttered their wings. However, during the reign of Khufu (also known as Cheops), a high priest devised a ritual method of controlling them en masse, using an artifact imbued with the mystic power of armies, the Rod of the Scarab. The priests created and "blessed" thousands of the scarabs, and later used them to help build Pharaoh Ramses' greatest memorial, the Pyramids.

But when a disgruntled general named Djethutmose used the scarabs to destroy crops and lay waste to cities, the Pharaohs forbade the creation of more scarabs. Most remaining scarabs were confiscated and destroyed, but a few hundred may have survived.

Scarabs are especially adept at traversing difficult terrain and scaling walls. Their protective shell is almost impermeable, and they are strong enough to carry up to 500 times their own weight.

The notorious cat burglar Rhett Maguire may be using the Rod in his crimes following its theft from the British Museum of Natural History.

Mechanics: Once per day, the rod summons a swarm of 10d10 gadget scarabs with the following statistics.

Gadget Scarabs: SZ Diminutive; wp: 5; Init + 2 (+2 Dex); Spd 30 ft., fly 40 ft.; Def 16 (+4 size, +2 Dex); Atk: Bite +2 (1d2); Face 1 ft. by 1 ft.; Reach 0; SA None; SQ Immune to critical hits; SV Fort +6, Ref +3, Will +0; Str 12, Dex 14, Con 10, Int 10, Wis 10, Cha 10; Skills: Climb +12, Hide +8, Move Silently +7, Spot +7, Swim +3.

The wielder of the rod controls the scarabs for up to 10 minutes before they disperse.

The Rosetta Stone

Discovered at Rosetta, near the town of Rashid, in 1799, this relic dates back to 200 B.C. The stone is 3 feet tall, 27.5 inches wide, and 12 inches deep, and its engravings celebrate the coronation of King Ptolemy V in three different languages: Demotic, Egyptian, and Greek. At the time of its discovery, the Egyptian language was a mystery. But since the Rosetta Stone's text was identical in two other languages known at the time, it proved an invaluable tool in deciphering Egyptian hieroglyphics. In 1821, Jean-Francois Champollion used the stone to translate the Egyptian text, finally enabling archaeologists and historians to read the hieroglyphs found at various Egyptian digs.

However, while the remaining text allowed Champollion to interpret the dead Egyptian language, a portion of the Rosetta Stone was missing. Many have speculated the whereabouts of the missing section – all except the Guardians. Since they discovered the power of the Stone, they have held stewardship over the missing fragment, and kept a close eye on the main piece as well. The Stone has a strong connection with the mystic world – a connection not even the Guardians completely understand – and the missing fragment's powers of translation are formidable. The Guardians consider their dialect of Arabic sacred, and they have no wish for anyone – including the Archer Foundation – to use the Stone to interpret their language.

Mechanics: Thanks to its weight and volume, carrying the main section of the Rosetta Stone is impractical, at best. If an agent carries the "missing" fragment, however, he automatically understands all languages, whether spoken or written. The fragment does not grant the agent the ability to speak these languages, nor does the agent retain his understanding if he parts with the it. He does not learn the language in question; the fragment merely allows him to understand it. The agent should still make a Languages check each time he encounters a new language to see if he already knows it *(per the rules on page 58 of the Spycraft Espionage Handbook).*

Sedna's Knuckles

The sinister sea goddess of the Eskimos, Sedna was the daughter of giant parents, and had a voracious appetite. Once, she started eating the limbs of her parents as they slept, but they roused from their slumber. Horrified, they took her in a boat and cast her into the sea. Even then, she would not let go, and held on to the side of the boat. Ultimately, her father had to cut off her fingers one by one until she lost her grip. As the severed fingers touched the sea they became whales, seals, and shoals of fish, though her thumbs maintained their grisly form. The flesh was quickly consumed by the fish, leaving only the knuckles and bones.

Years later, an Eskimo boy discovered the knuckles, and carved them into a pair of dice. When he died, he was buried with the dice, in the hope that Sedna would look kindly upon him for returning her lost thumbs. The next day, the young man awakened in his igloo, alive and unharmed, though missing the dice.

Mechanics: Sedna's Knuckles have the miraculous (and rare) power to return the dead to life. If an agent is buried with one of her knuckles, he may make a Will save (DC 25) to return to life. If he is buried with both, the DC is lowered to 20.

In either case, if the save is successful, the agent wakes the next morning in his own bed, without the dice. If his grave is exhumed, it is found to be empty.

The Tears of Gethsemane

On the eve of Jesus' crucifixion, he sat at a table with his Disciples and shared the Passover meal. Judas, one of his Disciples, left the supper, and betrayed Jesus to the Romans for thirty pieces of silver. Jesus knew of Judas' actions, but didn't confront his betrayer. Instead, he left for a small garden just outside the city of Jerusalem: Gethsemane. He brought three of his Disciples into the garden with him, and asked them to watch over him as he prayed for God to let this cup pass him by, to spare him the suffering he knew would come.

When he finished his first prayer, he found his three Disciples asleep. He awoke his Disciples, and asked them again to remain on guard. When he returned to prayer, he cried. He was afraid, and seemingly very alone. When he returned to his Disciples, he found them asleep once more. This time, he did not awaken them. They had shown him God's will. He returned to prayer a third time, thankful that God had given him a sign, and that his choice was now clear. He cried once more, this time for joy that God had shown him the way.

The Wheel of the Ancients

At dawn, Jesus was betrayed and arrested, but his tears lingered in Gethsemane. Where his tears of fear and tears of joy mixed, they formed perfect diamonds.

Two thousand years later, these diamonds are owned by a private Israeli collector, Reuven Meir. He doesn't know the truth of what he has, and if the wrong people discover the secret, he won't live to find out.

Mechanics: The Tears of Gethsemane are only a half carat each, but are perfect in every way. On any market, they are priceless.

When worn or carried by an agent, they lend a sense of humility and purpose. Whenever the agent spends an action die on anything except an attack roll or damage roll, the die type rolled is one greater (e.g. if he spends a d4 action die, he rolls a d6).

The Wheel of the Ancients

A little over two thousand years ago, a group of Tibetan monks journeyed into what is now the Bamiyan province of Afghanistan. They were well received by the Buddhist monks of the region and, in a gesture of peace and friendship, helped craft this magical prayer wheel.

Like any Buddhist prayer wheel, this one rotates clockwise, constantly cycling the engraved mantra Om Mani Padme Hum to invoke the blessings of Chenrezig, the embodiment of compassion. But the outer designs reveal something subtle. Fueled by centuries of spinning spirituality, the wheel is actually a map that leads to other mystic relics in the region, relics that have been safely hidden through 50,000 years of religious history.

Somehow, an ambitious Afghani tribal leader has become aware of the wheel's power and is using it to find the treasures hidden in the region. Anything pre-Islamic is destroyed outright, as will the wheel be once it has served its purpose (unless someone saves it first).

The destruction of so many mystic artifacts has not gone unnoticed by the spiritually sensitive around the world, and plans are already under way by many to rectify the situation.

Mechanics: Once per month, the wheel can be spun. It then projects an image of the location of another mystic relic within 1,000 miles into the mind of the person who spun the wheel. That person receives no directions leading him to the location – he must follow an image which appears in his mind, like a flash photo.

*"Take pride in this moment, old friend, for this is a hollow victory.
My armies live on, and soon, they will march over
the remains of your precious protectorate.
Soon, the Conspiracy will be laid bare for the world to see."
– Helix, at his defeat in the bowels of the Lodge, 1975*

THREATS

THE CIRCLE OF HATE

The Circle of Hate

This short-season (3-serial) threat is appropriate for a team of 4th level agents.

The Circle of Hate is the brainchild of Gemini, who lost his brother to an Archer op *(see page 92)*. He has spent the last several years gathering like-minded individuals to form a conspiracy dedicated to destroying the Archer Foundation and its Chambers.

MP Cost: 275

Resources: 1 (26 BPs for minions; 41 BPs for henchmen and foils; 51 BP for mastermind)

Gadgets: 2 (2 gadget points per serial)

Loyalty: 4 (+4 to loyalty checks)

HQ Personnel: 5 **HQ Security:** 3

Serial Three: Gemini

Gemini's primary target is the Gemeinschafft Consortium, the group he blames for his twin brother's death.

Gemini, 4th-level pointman/4th-level physical adept (mastermind); CR 8. SZ M; v/wp: 139/15; Init +7 (+4 class, +3 Dex); Spd 30 ft.; Def 17 (+4 class, +3 Dex); Atk: Quetzalcoatl's Thorn +8 (1d6+3); Face 1 square; Reach 1 square; SA None; SQ None; SV Fort +8, Ref +6, Will +7; Str 16, Dex 16, Con 15, Int 15, Wis 9, Cha 11; Skills: Demolitions +7, Disguise +4, Hide +7, Intimidate +6, Knowledge (Occult) +8, Move Silently +7, Search +2, Sense Motive +8, Survival +2, Tumble +4. Feats: Overcharge Power, Power Attack, Sensory Basics. Psionic Skills: Combat Sense +8, Enhance Senses +5, Extra-Spectral Sight +5. Gear: Weapons, 11 BP. Gadgets and Vehicles: Magnetic flask. Mystic Artifact: Quetzalcoatl's Thorn *(see page 234)*.

The Many Faces of Hate: Those Gemini doesn't kill with Quetzalcoatl's Thorn to extract their memories and skills are "converted" to his cause, conditioned to believe that Archer's agents are the source of all evil, and worthy of no mercy.

The Many Faces of Hate, 3rd-level minions (squads of 5). CR 2. SZ M; v/wp: 3d8+3 (20)/13; Init +5 (+3 class, +2 Dex); Spd 30 ft.; Def 13 (+2 Dex, +1 armor); Atk: .38 Special revolver +5 (1d6+2) / fragmentation grenade +5 (2d10); Face 1 square; Reach 1 square; SA None; SQ None; SV Fort +4, Ref +4, Will +3; Str 12, Dex 14, Con 13, Int 12, Wis 14, Cha 13; Skills: Demolitions +4, Driver +6, Hide +4, Innuendo +5, Move Silently +5, Search +3, Tumble +6. Feats: Confident Charge, Jump Up. Gear: Weapons, kevlar with insert.

Serial Two: Hans Ironsfell

Hans is a former European smuggler duped by an Archer team into hiring them as couriers, for which his employer ordered his death. During the ensuing fight at a Munich steel factory, Hans' right hand was plunged into molten metal and the team left him for dead.

Rescued by Gemini, Hans endured extensive surgery which "sculpted" his right hand down to steel-plated bones, fused in place as a vicious raking claw. Once a symbol of his disgrace, it is now a reminder of his burning passion: to destroy those responsible for his failure, the Foundation.

Driven by madness and pain, Ironsfell collects his enemies as trophies, dipping them in molten metal while they are still alive and adding them to his private museum.

Hans Ironsfell, 7th-level soldier (henchman); CR 7. SZ M; v/wp: 92/18; Init +9 (+6 class, +3 Dex); Spd 30 ft.; Def 16 (+3 class, +3 Dex); Atk: Claw +13 (1d6+9) / .50 Magnum service pistol +10 (2d8); Face 1 square; Reach 1 square; SA None; SQ None; SV Fort +9, Ref +7, Will +1; Str 18, Dex 17, Con 18, Int 8, Wis 8, Cha 7; Skills: Intimidate +6, Move Silently +9,

Knowledge (Occult) +4, Spot +2. Feats: Ambidexterity, Improved Weapon Focus (Claw), Mobility, Sidestep, Swift Strike, Weapon Focus (Claw), Weapon Master (Claw). Gear: Weapons, 13 BP. Gadgets and Vehicles: 2 GP.

HQ Personnel: 7 **HQ Security:** 5

Sculptors: These twisted minions guard and staff Ironsfell's personal collection, often joining him in the field to capture enemies to be dipped.

Sculptors, 3rd-level minions (squads of 4). CR 2. SZ M; v/wp: 3d8+3 (20)/12; Init +4 (+3 class, +1 Dex); Spd 30 ft.; Def 12 (+1 class, +1 Dex); Atk: 7.62×39mm semi-automatic rifle +4 (2d8) / flash/bang grenade +4 (Special); Face 1 square; Reach 1 square; SA None; SQ None; SV Fort +4, Ref +3, Will +2; Str 12, Dex 12, Con 12, Int 11, Wis 12, Cha 11; Skills: Appraise +3, Balance +6, Jump +6, Spot +4, Tumble +6, Use Rope +7. Feats: Acrobatic, Endurance. Gear: Weapons, 4 BP.

Serial One: Fae

During his period of silence, Gemini had several traveling companions, including this disenfranchised smuggler who has since become his lover. Agents responsible for her death early in this season become direct targets of Gemini.

Fae, 5th-level fixer (henchman); CR 5. SZ M; v/wp: 29/10; Init +5 (+2 class, +3 Dex); Spd 30 ft.; Def 17 (+4 class, +3 Dex); Atk: 9mm service pistol +6 (1d10); Face 1 square; Reach 1 square; SA None; SQ None; SV Fort +3, Ref +7, Will +3; Str 12, Dex 16, Con 10, Int 15, Wis 14, Cha 13; Skills: Appraise +8, Bluff +6, Boating +9, Cultures +6, Diplomacy +3, Disguise +5, Driver +7, Electronics +7, Forgery +9, Gather Information +4, Hide +8, Intimidate +4, Knowledge (Underworld) +8, Sleight of Hand +7. Feats: Point Blank Shot, Precise Shot. Gear: Weapons, 23 BP. Gadgets and Vehicles: Hollow tooth.

HQ Personnel: 3 **HQ Security:** 3

Night Runners: These men take on roles as fishermen, coast guards, or others who won't draw attention to themselves when smuggling Fae's goods overseas.

Night Runners, 2nd-level minions (squads of 3). CR 1. SZ M; v/wp: 2d8 (12)/11; Init +3 (+2 class, +1 Dex); Spd 30 ft.; Def 12 (+1 class, +1 Dex); Atk: 5.56×45mm assault rifle +4 (2d8+2); Face 1 square; Reach 1 square; SA None; SQ None; SV Fort +3, Ref +3, Will +0; Str 10, Dex 12, Con 11, Int 11, Wis 11, Cha 14; Skills: Balance +5, Bluff +4, Boating +3, Disguise +4, Mechanics +2. Feats: Weapon Focus (5.56mm rifle). Gear: Weapons.

Foil (Any Serial): Cassandra

Cassandra gives Archer early warnings about the Circle of Hate. She contacts Archer via email to warn of Gemini's plans, and watches the resulting operation while disguised. Alternately, if the GC rolls under her loyalty level, she might be leading the agent team into one of Gemini's traps.

Cassandra, 5th-level snoop (foil); loyalty 4; SZ M; v/wp: 32/13; Init +4 (+3 class, +1 Dex); Spd 30 ft.; Def 15 (+4 class, +1 Dex); Atk: .38 Special revolver +3 (1d6+2); Face 1 square; Reach 1 square; SA None; SQ None; SV Fort +2, Ref +4, Will +4; Str 10, Dex 13, Con 13, Int 15, Wis 13, Cha 14; Skills: Bluff +5, Computers +9, Concentration +5, Cryptography +7, Cultures +4, Diplomacy +5, Disguise +6, Driver +4, Electronics +7, Gather Information +7, Innuendo +5, Listen +5, Move Silently +6, Read Lips +6, Spot +5, Surveillance +4. Feats: Mobility, Sidestep. Gear: Weapons, 30 BP. Gadgets and Vehicles: 2 GP (stolen – Archer allows her to keep these gadgets if her loyalty swings toward the agents).

Plot Hook #1

One of the agents begins to receive anonymous e-mails. Each e-mail contains details about the group Gemini is forming to take his revenge on the Gemeinschafft Consortium and the Foundation.

Possibilities

1. The messages are coming from Cassandra. She has been watching Gemini and his minions, and suspects they are on to her. She hopes the Foundation agents can bring down the Circle, in so doing, save her from retribution. Cassandra plans on parleying her assistance into a favorable relationship with the Foundation.
2. As above, but Cassanda is working with Gemini. She leads the agents to a steel refinery, where Hans Ironfell and a team of sculptors await.
3. Cassandra has fallen in love with Gemini, but she knows she can never have him while Fae lives. She leads the agents to Fae knowing Fae will kill herself rather than be captured. Once Fae is dead, Cassandra plans to kill the agents, with the help of Ironfell (who is unaware of Cassandra's true motives). She hopes to curry favor with Gemini by personally delivering Fae's killers to him.

Plot Hook #2

A recently retired Lord of the Archer Foundation has disappeared. The Foundation wants him located and retrieved.

POSSIBILITIES

1. The Lord in question was loyal to the Archer Foundation, until one day he realized just how many pawns he had sacrificed in his years as a Lord. He retired quickly, but not quickly enough to stave off his growing bitterness at the constant loss of life. Shortly after his retirement, Gemini contacted him and drew him into a web of treachery. It didn't take the Lord long to realize that he had become the enemy, and the cause of the very thing that drove him away from the Archer Foundation. Unfortunately, Gemini's retirement plan is not nearly as generous as Archer's....
2. The Lord was directly responsible for the assignment that lead to the death of Gemini's brother. Once the Lord retired, and was no longer under constant security, Gemini struck. The Lord is now a feature of Ironsfell's macabre scuplture gallery.
3. The Lord went into hiding, after his contacts at the Archer Foundation warned him he was Gemini's next target (as above). The agents must locate the Lord before Gemini claims another victim.

Dr. Fu and the Lung Triad

This short-season (4-serial) threat is appropriate for a team of 5th level agents.

Dr. Fu is a criminal mastermind with dreams of glory for China *(see page 120)*. He can trace his ancestry back to the last Ming Emperor, and now he schemes to acquire that title for himself. An annoying thorn in the side of the Archer Foundation, Dr. Fu has in the past attempted to foment a war between China and Russia by destroying Vladivostok, organized attempted annexations of Taiwan and Vietnam, and set off a bomb in Tokyo in retribution for Japanese atrocities during the Second World War.

MP Cost: 385
Resources: 2 (28 BPs for minions; 43 BPs for henchmen and foils; 53 BPs for mastermind)
Gadgets: 4 (4 gadget points per serial)
Loyalty: 6 (+6 to loyalty checks)
HQ Personnel: 6 (+extra HQ – 0/0)
HQ Security: 3

Serial Four: Dr. Fu

The PAC's greatest threat believes that the region can only benefit from open war. Of course, he wishes to rise from the ashes as Emperor.

Dr. Fu, 9th-level pointman (mastermind); CR 10. SZ M; v/wp: 66/13; Init +10 (+4 class, +2 Dex, +4 Improved Initiative); Spd 30 ft.; Def 16 (+4 class, +2 Dex); Atk: Katana +8 (1d12+2); Face 1 square; Reach 1 square; SA None; SQ None; SV Fort +5, Ref +6, Will +9; Str 14, Dex 15, Con 13, Int 19, Wis 17, Cha 14; Skills: Appraise +9, Bluff +12, Bureaucracy +7, Cryptography +9, Cultures +6, Gather Information +6, Innuendo +6, Intimidate +7, Knowledge (Asian History) +12, Knowledge (Underworld) +14, Languages +10, Perform (Public Speaking) +6, Sense Motive +11, Sleight of Hand +6, Spot +6. Feats: Darting Weapon, Expertise, Improved Disarm, Improved Initiative. Gear: Weapons, 33 BP. Gadgets and Vehicles: Palmprint identifier ("Backfire" Edition – electric charge) for katana, 1 GP.

Ninja: Dr. Fu claims that every one of his personally trained ninja bodyguards/assassins is a blood relative. If this is true, he must have an enormous family.

Ninja, 6th-level minions (squads of 3). CR 5. SZ M; v/wp: 6d8+12 (40)/15; Init +9 (+5 class, +4 Dex); Spd 30 ft.; Def 16 (+2 class, +4 Dex); Atk: Kama +8 (1d8+2) / 7.62x54mm sniper rifle +10 (5d4); Face 1 square; Reach 1 square; SA None; SQ None; SV Fort +7, Ref +7, Will +4; Str 15, Dex 18, Con 15, Int 15, Wis 15, Cha 13; Skills: Balance +12, Climb +10, Demolitions +6, Escape Artist +7, Jump +8, Move Silently +7, Tumble +12. Feats: Martial Arts, Kicking Arts, Throwing Arts. Gear: weapons.

Serial Three: Tze Chin

Archer has long suspected that Dr. Fu has accomplices in the Chinese government; this suspicion is correct. All of the mastermind's plans employ rogue Chinese generals and intelligence operatives. Tze Chin is one such military renegade.

Tze Chin, 8th-level soldier (henchman); CR 8. SZ M; v/wp: 70/14; Init +12 (+6 class, +2 Dex, +4 Improved Initiative); Spd 30 ft.; Def 15 (+3 class, +2 Dex); Atk: .45 service pistol +10 (1d10+2); Face 1 square; Reach 1 square; SA None; SQ None; SV Fort +8, Ref +6, Will +2; Str 14, Dex 14, Con 14, Int 14, Wis 10, Cha 10; Skills: Balance +8, Climb +6, Cryptography +6, Gather Information +4, Intimidate +5, Jump +7, Knowledge (Chinese Politics) +7, Pilot +5, Profession (Military) +4, Search +4, Surveillance +3. Feats: Dodging Arts, Dodging Mastery, Improved Initiative, Martial Arts, Punching Arts, Punching Mastery, Sidestep. Gear: Weapons, 9 BP. Gadgets and Vehicles: 2 GP.

HQ Personnel: 8 **HQ Security:** 2

Chinese Soldiers: Many of these Chinese Army veterans are aware that Tze Chin's loyalty is to a dissident body, but none know that he serves the infamous Dr. Fu.

Chinese Soldiers, 5th-level minions (squads of 3). CR 4. SZ M; v/wp: 5d8+5 (29)/13; Init +6 (+4 class, +2 Dex); Spd 30 ft.; Def 14 (+2 Dex, +2 armor); Atk: 7.62x39mm assault rifle +7 (2d8) / bayonet +7 (1d6+2); Face 1 square; Reach 1 square; SA None; SQ None; SV Fort +5, Ref +5, Will +2; Str 14, Dex 14, Con 13, Int 13, Wis 13, Cha 13; Skills: Craft (Gunsmithing) +6, Driver +7, Intimidate +6, Spot +6. Feats: Far Shot, Mobility, Point Blank Shot. Gear: Weapons, tuxedo liner.

Serial Two: Tommy Lung

See page 120 for more about Dr. Fu's contact in the Lung Triad.

Tommy Lung, 7th-level fixer (henchman); CR 7. SZ M; v/wp: 42/12; Init +4 (+3 class, +1 Dex); Spd 30 ft.; Def 17 (+6 class, +1 Dex); Atk: Nunchaku +7 (1d6+3); Face 1 square; Reach 1 square; SA None; SQ None; SV Fort +5, Ref +6, Will +5; Str 12, Dex 13, Con 12, Int 15, Wis 16, Cha 14; Skills: Appraise +11, Balance +11, Bluff +12, Diplomacy +7, Forgery +11, Gather Information +7, Innuendo +11, Knowledge (Underworld) +12, Move Silently +9, Open Lock +8, Use Rope +6. Feats: Sidestep, Weapon Focus (Nunchaku), Improved Weapon Focus (Nunchaku). Gear: Weapons, 23 BP. Gadgets and Vehicles: 2 GP.
HQ Personnel: 1 **HQ Security:** 2

Triad Elite: These minions are hand-picked to command the street warriors (opposite). They are the hub of the Lung Triad.

Triad Elite, 4th-level minions (squads of 3). CR 3. SZ M; v/wp: 4d8+4 (26)/13; Init +5 (+3 class, +2 Dex); Spd 30 ft.; Def 14 (+2 class, +2 Dex); Atk: Throwing knife +6 (1d4+1) / .45 service pistol +6 (1d10+2); Face 1 square; Reach 1 square; SA None; SQ None; SV Fort +5, Ref +4, Will +2; Str 13, Dex 14, Con 13, Int 14, Wis 13, Cha 11; Skills: Diplomacy +3, Disguise +3, Driver +6, Gather Information +3, Intimidate +5, Knowledge (Underworld) +5, Search +4, Tumble +7. Feats: Point Blank Shot, Precise Shot, Marksman. Gear: Weapons, 4 BP.

Serial One: King Ngai

Tommy Lung's second-in-command is a wild child, who regularly indulges in the Hong Kong nightlife.

King Ngai, 6th-level wheelman (henchman); CR 6. SZ M; v/wp: 45/12; Init +6 (+4 class, +2 Dex); Spd 30 ft.; Def 16 (+4 class, +2 Dex); Atk: Tiger claws +7 (Special) / flash/bang grenade (×2) +8 (Special); Face 1 square; Reach 1 square; SA None; SQ None; SV Fort +3, Ref +7, Will +4; Str 13, Dex 15, Con 12, Int 12, Wis 14, Cha 16; Skills: Balance +10, Bluff +7, Computers +4, Cryptography +4, Driver +11, Electronics +3, Jump +5, Mechanics +6, Sleight of Hand +4, Spot +7. Feats: Advanced Skill Mastery (Speed Demon), Dodging Arts, Martial Arts, Punching Arts, Speed Demon. Gear: Weapons, 12 BP. Gadgets and Vehicles: Motorcycle, standard belt, 1 GP.
HQ Personnel: 0 **HQ Security:** 3

Triad Street Warriors: The footsoldiers of Dr. Fu's campaign are recruited from the Chinese Triad.

Triad Street Warriors, 4th-level minions (squads of 2). CR 3. SZ M; v/wp: 4d8+4 (26)/12; Init +5 (+3 class, +2 Dex); Spd 30 ft.; Def 14 (+2 class, +2 Dex); Atk: .45 service pistol +5 (1d10+2); Face 1 square; Reach 1 square; SA None; SQ None; SV Fort +5, Ref +3, Will +2; Str 11, Dex 13, Con 12, Int 12, Wis 12, Cha 10; Skills: Balance +7, Climb +6, Disguise +3, Gather Information +2, Intimidate +5, Jump +6, Tumble +7. Feats: Point Blank Shot, Precise Shot, Ride Shotgun. Gear: Weapons, 6 BP. Gadgets and Vehicles: Motorcycles.

Plot Hook #1

Despite the Pan-Asian Collective's efforts to deal with the matter internally, Dr. Fu's arrangement with the Lung Triad has come to the attention of the rest of the Archer Foundation. Several Chambers (especially Room 39, due to England's former presence in the area), have made noise about putting their own teams into Hong Kong to deal with the problem, if the Collective can't.

Possibilities

1. King Ngai finds out that the agents are on his turf and decides to deal with them himself. His Triad street warriors attack the agents almost as soon as they arrive in Hong Kong. A rival triad, convinced the enemy of their enemy is their friend, comes to the agents' aid. The agents must navigate Hong Kong's seedy underbelly in order to foil Dr. Fu's alliance with the Lung Triad.
2. One of the Foundation's contacts in the Chinese government serves Tze Chin. He attempts to lead the agents astray. If that doesn't work, he warns Chin of the agents' arrival, who prepares an ambush for them.
3. Concerned the interference of other Chambers will expose several Collective deep cover agents, the Collective does everything in its power (stopping well short of violence) to distract the team, while simultaneously running their own investigation.

PLOT HOOK #2

Tommy Lung has decided to make his play for the Triad leadership. With Dr. Fu's backing, he thinks he can rise to the top spot in the Lung Triad organization.

POSSIBILITIES

1. Dr. Fu has no interest in Tommy or his petty personal ambitions. He betrays Tommy to the Triad in an attempt to win the favor of the current leadership. This way, he might better use them to accomplish his goals.
2. Dr. Fu believes that Tommy's little power play will be just the thing he needs to spark his private war. He uses the Triad conflict as cover to send his ninja to strike at key government officials, planning to fill the void in leadership with politicians subservient to him.
3. As above, but Dr. Fu also orders Tze Chin to coordinate an attack with Tommy; the streets of Hong Kong become a war zone almost overnight. Fu is certain he can take better advantage of the chaos than anyone else.

P.E.R.I.L.

This short-season (3-serial) threat is appropriate for a team of 7th level agents.

As the current controllers of Russia, the Project for Expansion, Retribution, Iniquity, and Lies (P.E.R.I.L.) poses a different kind of threat. They may perform operations Archer must counter, but most serials in which they appear should involve the Foundation prompting hostilities with them, rather than the other way around.

MP Cost: 320

Resources: 1 (27 BPs for minions; 42 BPs for henchmen and foils; 52 BPs for mastermind)

Gadgets: 2 (2 gadget points per serial)

Loyalty: 2 (+2 to loyalty checks)

HQ Personnel: 2 **HQ Security:** 2

Special Note: This threat does not include P.E.R.I.L.'s current leader, Davros Oleksandre *(see page 147)*, though it can easily be extended to include him.

SERIAL THREE: MADOX

Project PROMETHEUS has fielded several viable teams, but none have lasted longer (or achieved more success) than Team Madox, named after its commanding officer.

Madox, 11th-level pointman (mastermind); Department D-2 (Military Ops). CR 11. SZ L (8 ft. tall); v/wp: 124/18; Init +5 (+4 class, +1 Dex); Spd 30 ft.; Def 14 (+4 class, +1 Dex, –1 size); Atk: punch +14 (1d4+6) / .50 sniper rifle +10 (2d12); Face 1 square; Reach 2 squares; SA None; SQ None; SV Fort +12, Ref +6, Will +7; Str 22, Dex 12, Con 18, Int 14, Wis 11, Cha 7; Skills: Balance +6, Bureaucracy +0, Climb +13, Computers +8, Cryptography +8, Demolitions +9, Driver +8, Gather Information +3, Intimidate +8, Knowledge (P.E.R.I.L.) +14, Knowledge (Russian Politics) +10, Search +6, Spot +7. Feats: Ambidextrous, Improved Two-Weapon Fighting, Point Blank Shot, Two-Weapon Fighting. Gear: Weapons, 7 BP. Gadgets and Vehicles: Grafters (2). Chem Treatment: Muscle.

PROMETHEUS Soldiers: The rank and file of Team Madox have survived a rigorous training regiment that has killed 2 of every 3 volunteers.

PROMETHEUS Soldiers, 9th-level minions (squads of 2). CR 8. SZ M; v/wp: 9d8+31 (74)/17; Init +10 (+7 class, +3 Dex); Spd 30 ft.; Def 17 (+4 class, +3 Dex); Atk: 7.62x39mm assault rifle +12 (2d8) / .45 pistol +12 (1d10+2); Face 1 square; Reach 1 square; SA None; SQ None; SV Fort +11, Ref +7, Will +7; Str 17, Dex 17, Con 17, Int 14, Wis 14, Cha 11; Skills: Balance +6, Bureaucracy +2, Climb +7, Computers +6, Cryptography +6, Demolitions +6, Disguise +4, Driver +9, Hide +7, Intimidate +5, Search +6, Spot +5, Swim +6. Feats: Great Fortitude, Iron Will, Toughness. Gear: Weapons, 2 BP. Chem Treatment: Endure (5 damage reduction, including armor).

SERIAL TWO: QUICKSILVER

A former SMERSH assassin gone freelance after the fall of the Soviet Union, Quicksilver now works for the highest bidder. He is a remarkable marksman, and always leaves a silver bullet glimmering on his victims' bodies.

Quicksilver, 10th-level soldier (henchman); CR 10. SZ M; v/wp: 75/12; Init +15 (+8 class, +3 Dex, +4 Improved Initiative); Spd 30 ft.; Def 17 (+4 class, +3 Dex); Atk: 7.62×54mm sniper rifle with telescopic sight +13 (5d4); Face 1 square; Reach 1 square; SA None; SQ None; SV Fort +8, Ref +8, Will +6; Str 13, Dex 17, Con 12, Int 13, Wis 16, Cha 13; Skills: Balance +13, Bluff +5, Climb +6, Disguise +6, Gather Information +5, Jump +8, Move Silently +8, Spot +10. Feats: Extreme Range, Far Shot, Improved Initiative, Increased Precision, Marksman, Point Blank Shot, Precise Shot, Quick Draw, Sharp-Shooting. Gear: Weapons, 7 BP. Gadgets and Vehicles: Memory flesh (prepared identity).

HQ Personnel: 1 **HQ Security:** 2

SMERSH Wetworks Team: These Cold War veterans specialize in the art of killing. They've found no lack of employers in P.E.R.I.L.'s Russia.

SMERSH Wetworks Team, 8th-level minions (squads of 4). CR 7. SZ M; v/wp: 8d8+16 (56)/15; Init +11 (+6 class, +1 Dex, +4 feats); Spd 30 ft.; Def 15 (+3 class, +2 Dex); Atk: 9x19mm SMG +9 (1d10); Face 1 square; Reach 1 square; SA None; SQ None; SV Fort +8, Ref +5, Will +4; Str 15, Dex 13, Con 15, Int 14, Wis 13, Cha 14; Skills: Disguise +7, Electronics +6, Hide +5, Innuendo +5, Listen +6, Move Silently +5, Search +6, Spot +5, Tumble +5. Feats: Improved Initiative, Point Blank Shot. Gear: Weapons, 9 BP.

Serial One: Professor Dalia Creed

The head of SUPERLUMINAL research at the moment is Professor Dalia Creed. Her breakthrough discoveries have been fueled by her desire to cure her inherited congenital psion defect, which is wasting her mind away.

Professor Dalia Creed, 9th-level snoop (henchman); CR 9. SZ M; v/wp: 70/14; Init +7 (+5 class, +2 Dex); Spd 30 ft.; Def 19 (+7 class, +2 Dex); Atk: 9mm service pistol +6 (1d10); Face 1 square; Reach 1 square; SA None; SQ None; SV Fort +7, Ref +8, Will +8; Str 12, Dex 14, Con 14, Int 13, Wis 14, Cha 13; Skills: Bluff +7, Bureaucracy +13, Computers +13, Concentration +14, First Aid +12, Gather Information +9, Knowledge (Biochemistry) +13, Knowledge (Psionics) +13, Listen +10, Sense Motive +12. Feats: Great Fortitude, Iron Will, Lightning Reflexes, Surge of Speed. Gear: Weapons, DNA analyzer, portable chem lab (disguised as a doctor's bag). Gadgets and Vehicles: SUPERLUMINAL patches of various types (2 GPs' worth).

HQ Personnel: 1 **HQ Security:** 2

SUPERLUMINAL (Cronus) Agents: Dalia Creed's personal army of enhanced superspies.

SUPERLUMINAL (Cronus) Agents, 8th-level minions (squads of 2)—based on physical adept rather than soldier. CR 7. SZ M; v/wp: 9d8+27 (67)/17; Init +6 (+5 class, +1 Dex); Spd 30 ft.; Def 16 (+5 class, +1 Dex); Atk: punch +5 (1d3+1) / .38 Special revolver +5 (1d6+2); Face 1 square; Reach 1 square; SA None; SQ None; SV Fort +9, Ref +3, Will +6; Str 12, Dex 12, Con 16, Int 16, Wis 11, Cha 11; Skills: Balance +6, Climb +6, Concentration +5, Cryptography +8, Demolitions +8, Electronics +8, Gather Information +5, Hide +6, Intimidate +8, Listen +5, Open Lock +6. Feats: Adrenal Basics, Metabolic Basics. Psion Skills: Body Sculpting +12, Deadly Hands +12, Invigorate +12, Pain Transmission +14. Gear: Weapons, steelweave vest, binoculars, various kits (10 BPs' worth).

Foil (Any Serial): Andrea Styles

No one is sure where Andrea Styles is from or who she works for. Given the state-of-the-art equipment she carries and her interest in both P.E.R.I.L. and those who hunt them, it is likely an agency with interests in Russia.

Andrea Styles, 8th-level snoop (foil); loyalty 3; SZ M; v/wp: 64/12; Init +7 (+5 class, +2 Dex); Spd 30 ft.; Def 18 (+6 class, +2 Dex); Atk: Stiletto blade +5 (1d6+1) / .40 service pistol +6 (1d12); Face 1 square; Reach 1 square; SA None; SQ None; SV Fort +4, Ref +6, Will +6; Str 13, Dex 14, Con 14, Int 15, Wis 15, Cha 15; Skills: Bluff +7, Boating +6, Computers +10, Cryptography +10, Disguise +7, Driver +7, Electronics +8, Gather Information +8, Hide +8, Languages +8, Listen +8, Move Silently +9, Pilot +6, Search +10, Spot +10. Feats: Expertise, Mobility, Sidestep. Gear: weapons, headset radio, disguise kit, electronics kit, lockpicking kit, liquid skin patches (2), assorted bugs (video and audio) – 4 BPs' worth.

Plot Hook #1

Several Foundation agents have gone missing after attending a highly respected spy school in Russia. The school denies any knowledge of the agent's current whereabouts, claiming the students departed after completing their training. The Foundation suspects foul play at the hands of P.E.R.I.L.

Possibilities

1. P.E.R.I.L. believes the Foundation agents were sent to spy on them and their training techniques. The agents were killed to discourage any further attempts at infiltration. Any agent sent to investigate would be in grave danger of suffering the same fate.
2. As above, but one of the agents defected to the side of P.E.R.I.L. When the agents locate him, he reports he was followed – doubtless until an opportunity to assassinate him presented itself – but managed to escape. He assumes whoever was after him killed the other missing agent. In reality, he was forced to kill the other agent as proof of his loyalty to P.E.R.I.L. If his lies are not uncovered then P.E.R.I.L. gains a valuable asset: a mole in the Archer Foundation.

3. P.E.R.I.L. had no knowledge of the missing agents' connection to the Archer Foundation, but used the students of the spy school as test cases for Dalia Creed's experiments. One by one, these victims are being transformed into chemical monsters, grim side effects of Professor Creed's latest advances.

PLOT HOOK #2

The Foundation has begun a new initiative: Operation: EAGLE TALON. The Foundation needs hard data on the current status of Project PROMETHEUS. The agents are to immerse themselves in the Russian Shadow community in any way they can, and assemble as much information as possible on P.E.R.I.L.'s agenda.

POSSIBILITIES

1. Within P.E.R.I.L., an intense rivalry exists between Project PROMETHEUS and Operation SUPERLUMINAL. The success of Madox and his team infuriates the obsessed Dalia Creed; Madox, for his part, wishes to secure continued support for his activities, at the Professor's expense. This heated (and sometimes violent) competition has drawn the attention of the Foundation, and led Archer to initiate Operation: EAGLE TALON.
2. As above, but Madox has hired Quicksilver to assassinate Professor Creed. He plans to absorb SUPERLUMINAL into his already powerful PROMETHEUS project.
3. Andrea Styles is investigating the events surrounding the transformation of the Phantom Brigade. This has garnered attention from several directions. Nikolai Petrovich, concerned with Styles' progress, has asked the Foundation for assistance in stymieing her investigation. On a more ominous note, Madox has noticed her poking around and sent Quicksilver to eliminate the problem.

THE SHOP

This short-season (3-serial) threat is appropriate for a team of 12th level agents.

As discussed on page 158, the Shop's ultimate goals are unknown at this time, but at least one part of the enemy organization is interested in sparking international conflicts and promoting war. In many cases (including their attempts to grind old axes in Europe, particularly between reunified Germany and its neighbors), these conflicts have been dormant for some time. Others, such as the renewed hostilities in the Middle East and tensions between China and America, serve merely as fuel for an already smoldering fire. Their ulterior motives remain a mystery; the Foundation is only aware of them through their global network of informants, and blind chance.

MP Cost: 395

Resources: 3 (37 BPs for minions; 52 BPs for henchmen and foils; 62 BPs for mastermind)

Gadgets: 20 (20 gadget points per serial)

Loyalty: 0 (+0 to loyalty checks)

HQ Personnel: 1 **HQ Security:** 1

Special Note: This threat does not include the Shop's current leader, Dennis Gray *(see page 159),* though it can easily be extended to include him.

SERIAL THREE: SAMANTHA ABBOT

Miss Abbot, as she is most often addressed, is an extremely high-powered and dangerous Mentalist. Even when the Shop served the Archer Foundation as its research and development arm, Abbot's loyalty was to Dennis Gray first, the Shop second, and the Foundation not at all. In fact, she holds a great deal of resentment toward the Archer Foundation – she feels the Foundation's secretive nature limited the scope of the Shop's research. She is directly responsible for the recent downing of an American E-3 spy plane over China, after its crew sighted a secret Shop facility in the area.

Samantha Abbot, 15th Level mentalist (mastermind); Department D-2 (Military Ops). CR 15. SZ M; v/wp: (99)/12; Init +11 (+9 class, +2 Dex); Spd 30 ft.; Def 21 (+9 class, +2 Dex); Atk: Cryokinesis +13 (9d4+1); Face 1 square; Reach 1 square; SA None; SQ None; SV Fort +6, Ref +9, Will +15; Str 9, Dex 15, Con 12, Int 19, Wis 18, Cha 13;
Skills: Concentration +19, Intimidate +10, Knowledge (psions) +20, Knowledge: Psionics +20, Profession (researcher) +18, Sense Motive +18. Feats: Control Junction, Deadly Power (Cryokinesis), Efficient Power (Cryokinesis), Efficient Power (Kinetic Shield), Efficient Power (Poltergeist), Intense Psi-Training, Iron Will, Psychokinetic Basics, Psychokinetic Mastery, Telekinetic Basics, Telekinetic Mastery.
Psion Skills: Cryokinesis +27, Kinetic Shield +23, Levitation +26, Photokinesis +24, Poltergeist +24, Pyrokinesis +23. Gear: 62 BP. Gadgets and Vehicles: Hologram projector ring, 13 GP.

Shop Controllers: These mysterious figures control much of the Shop's field operations from remote, unconnected bases around the globe. They are unaware of each other's locations or goals, acting on orders left before the break with Archer.

Shop Controllers, 12th-level minions (squads of 4). CR 11. SZ M; v/wp: 12d8 (58)/10; Init +11 (+10 class, +1 Dex); Spd 30 ft.; Def 16 (+5 class, +1 Dex); Atk: 9x19mm service pistol +13 (1d10); Face 1 square; Reach 1 square; SA None; SQ None; SV Fort +8, Ref +7, Will +8; Str 11, Dex 13, Con 10, Int 17, Wis 18, Cha 15; Skills: Bureaucracy +9, Computers +10, Concentration +9, Cryptography +10, Electronics +10, Gather Information +9, Innuendo +9, Intimidate +13, Sense Motive +11. Feats: None. Gear: Weapons, 24 BP. Gadgets and Vehicles: Attaché case (booby-trapped PC unit, +6 ranks with a built-in ENIGMA Plus machine), and anti-psi technology.

Serial Two: Kryptos (See Page 159)

A child prodigy with an obsessive-compulsive weakness for puzzles, Kryptos feeds his compulsion with daring plans pitting Foundation agents against casts of enemy spies, informants for both sides, foils, and innocent bystanders, and lethal death-mazes in the least likely locations (such as the interior of a derelict oil tanker or a crowded shopping mall).

Kryptos, 14th-level snoop (henchman); CR 14. SZ M; v/wp: 58/11; Init +9 (+8 class, +1 Dex); Spd 30 ft.; Def 22 (+11 class, +1 Dex); Atk: 9mm automatic pistol +8 (1d10); Face 1 square; Reach 1 square; SA None; SQ None; SV Fort +4, Ref +7, Will +9; Str 9, Dex 12, Con 11, Int 21, Wis 17, Cha 13; Skills: Bluff +10, Computers +22, Concentration +18, Craft (architecture) +25, Cryptography +23, Electronics +20, Gather Information +18, Hobby (Puzzles) +25, Intimidate +9, Knowledge (physics) +20, Knowledge (occult) +13, Open Lock +8, Profession (architect) +20, Sense Motive +20, Surveillance +20. Feats: Advanced Skill Mastery (ordinary past), Grand Skill Mastery (ordinary past), Mathematical Genius, Ordinary Past, Scholarly. Gear: Weapons, 39 BP. Gadgets and Vehicles: Laptop (+5 ranks with a built-in ENIGMA Plus machine), memory flesh, sappers, various tracers (4 GPs' worth).

HQ Personnel: 4 **HQ Security:** 2

Field Technician Team: These are the builders of the Shop, techno-wizards who once engineered the Foundation's gadgets.

Field Technician Team, 10th-level minions (squads of 4). CR 9. SZ M; v/wp: 10d6+10 (47)/12; Init +9 (+8 class, +1 Dex); Spd 30 ft.; Def 15 (+4 class, +1 Dex); Atk: Cigarette pistol +11 (1d6+1) / micro-burst gel +11 (1d10 per application); Face 1 square; Reach 1 square; SA None; SQ None; SV Fort +8, Ref +6, Will +4; Str 12, Dex 12, Con 12, Int 18, Wis 12, Cha 12; Skills: Climb +9, Computers +10, Concentration +7, Cryptography +10, Demolitions +12, Disguise +9, Electronics +10, Knowledge (Gadgets) +10, Mechanics +10. Feats: None. Gear: Weapons, 37 BP. Gadgets and Vehicles: Weapons (above), sub-cochlear implant (with all options), B.U.G.S., 3 GPs.

Serial One: Strik-9 (See Page 159)

Strik-9 was one of Archer's finest agents, but he was mortally injured on the cliffs of the Serengeti by an as-yet-unidentified criminal mastermind. Months later, he resurfaced as a killer for hire, reportedly rescued by a tribal mystic process that transformed him into a living factory for one of the most lethal poisons on the planet. Both the Shop and the Foundation wish to understand this process, for obviously different reasons.

Strik-9, 13th-level physical adept (henchman); Department D-5 (Black Ops). CR 13. SZ M; v/wp: 132/16; Init +12 (+8 class, +4 Dex); Spd 30 ft.; Def 22 (+8 class, +4 Dex); Atk: Claw gauntlets +10 (1d6 + lethal poison II); Face 1 square; Reach 1 square; SA None; SQ None; SV Fort +11, Ref +8, Will +9; Str 14, Dex 18, Con 16, Int 13, Wis 13, Cha 12; Skills: Balance +10, Climb +9, Escape Artist +10, Jump +9, Move Silently +11. Feats: Adrenal Basics, Adrenal Mastery, Assassin, Cleave, Equilibrium Junction, Metabolic Basics, Metabolic Mastery, Power Attack, Quicken Power (Invigorate), Weapon Finesse (gauntlet claws). Psion Skills: Control Metabolism +12, Flesh Armor +10, Invigorate +10, Psionic Purge +14, Speed Control +14. Gear: Weapons, 39 BPs. Gadgets and Vehicles: Danger sensor, spring-loaded weapon holsters.

HQ Personnel: 2 **HQ Security:** 2

Shop Strike Team: These are the men and women the Shop relies upon to counter Archer directly, with force. Their mission briefings are always "need to know," with many details left out until required in the field. Shop strike teams have thus become accustomed to dealing with the unforeseen, and are highly adaptable.

Shop Strike Team, 9th-level minions (squads of 4). CR 8. SZ M; v/wp: 9d8+9 (49)/12; Init +9 (+7 class, +2 Dex); Spd 30 ft.; Def 17 (+4 class, +2 Dex, +1 armor); Atk: 7.62x39mm assault rifle +11 (2d8); Face 1 square; Reach 1 square; SA None; SQ None; SV Fort +7, Ref +6, Will +3; Str 12, Dex 14, Con 12, Int 10, Wis 11, Cha 11; Skills: Balance +6, Bluff +4, Climb +6, Computers +4, Driver +6, Electronics +4, Mechanics +3, Tumble +7. Feats: None. Gear: Weapons. Gadgets and Vehicles: Ballistic flesh.

PLOT HOOK #1

Archer Foundation agents are being killed, one by one. At first the Foundation dismissed the deaths as unrelated incidents, but it has become increasingly apparent that they are linked. The agents must investigate and determine who is eliminating the Foundation's operatives – and why.

POSSIBILITIES

1. A mole from the Shop has infiltrated the Foundation. He is passing information about covert assignments to his Control in the Shop, which is being used to set up and eliminate Archer agents. The mole's advantages are two-fold: first, he is a veteran agent of the Archer Foundation, considered beyond reproach. When the Shop defected, he remained as a deep cover agent. Second, he's a telepath.
2. Strik-9 is pursuing a vendetta against the Foundation, which he blames for his near demise on the cliffs of the Serengeti. The Shop has decided to support him in his bloody cause. He intends to extract payment from the Foundation for his suffering, one agent at a time.
3. Kryptos is testing his latest death-maze, built into the engineering and operations decks of a Pacific cruise ship. Due to its constantly changing location, the Foundation has not yet realized this one ship was responsible for the deaths of so many agents.

PLOT HOOK #2

Recently, a US Government spy plane was downed in the Pacific. The agents must investigate, since an operative of the Foundation was among the crew. Archer suspects that he is now in the hands of the Shop.

POSSIBILITIES

1. The CIA has tasked a small army of analysts and field operatives to ferret out the Company's identity once and for all. Several highly placed US Government officials believe that there is some sort of conspiracy going on within the CIA. No one knows exactly where they get their information, but the task is coming dangerously close to discovering the truth.
2. The pilot is a CIA agent working as a double agent for the Shop. He's discovered the Foundation's involvement in the spy plane's mission, which the Foundation hoped would discover a Shop facility in the Pacific. He informed Samantha Abbot, which lead to the plane being shot down and the crew captured. The informant will do everything he can to hamper investigation of the matter.
3. A CIA mole provided Miss Abbot with advance warning of the spy plane's mission. She arranged for it to be downed over international waters, casting doubt on which Chamber has jurisdiction on the matter. She hopes the Foundation will put together a joint task force, consisting of operatives from several Chambers. Once again calling on her agent in the CIA, she will provide information leading the agents into a death-maze set up on a remote Pacific island by Kryptos.

THE HAND OF GLORY

This short-season (3-serial) threat is appropriate for a team of 16th level agents.

The Hand of Glory *(see page 154)* began in part with the wartime Abwehr, Cold War Stasi, and of course the Nazi espionage machine. It is ruthless, meticulous, and careful, biding its time for the perfect moment to strike. This patience is offset, however, by the power-hungry ambitions of the ancient entity within Eva Kraus, whose desire to see its goals achieved is only outdone by its agitation as the world's mystic roots come to light.

MP Cost: 455
Resources: 2 (33 BPs for minions; 48 BPs for henchmen; 58 BPs for mastermind)
Gadgets: 0 (0 gadget points per serial)
Loyalty: 7 (+7 to loyalty checks)
HQ Personnel: 6 **HQ Security:** 3
Special Note: This threat does not include The Hand of Glory's current leader, Eva Kraus *(see page 156)*, though it can easily be extended to include her.

SERIAL THREE: SYBILLE VALLENTIN

An expert in behavioral psychology, Sybille specializes in invoking and interpreting moods and emotions in her subjects. Her scientific approach garnered her a great deal of positive attention within the Hand of Glory. This attention has lead to several unique opportunities. Less than a year ago she was injected with an experimental serum that awakened telepathic powers within her. Since then, her advancement has been quite rapid. Recently she became one of the first to set up a test of the Green Lucifer *(see page 156)* in the field.

Sybille Vallentin, 14th-level faceman/5th Level telepath (mastermind); CR19. SZ M; v/wp: 109/11; Init +16 (+15 class, +1 Dex); Spd 30 ft.; Def 21 (+10 class, +1 Dex); Atk: Telempathy: Friendship; Face 1 square; Reach 1 square; SA None; SQ None; SV Fort +7, Ref +9, Will +12; Str 10, Dex 13, Con 11,

Int 16, Wis 17, Cha 19; Skills: Bluff + 26, Concentration +12, Diplomacy +26, Gather Information + 21, Innuendo +20, Intimidate +16, Knowledge (Psychiatry) +23, Knowledge (Psychology) + 23, Perform +12, Profession (Psychiatrist) +19, Profession (Psychologist) + 19, Search + 14, Sense Motive + 20, Spot +13.
Feats: Advanced Skill Mastery: Persuasive, Advanced Skill Mastery: Scholarly, ESP Basics, Grand Skill Mastery: Persuasive, Imprint Basics, Mastered Power: Empathy, Mastered Power: Telempathy, Perfect Skill Mastery: Persuasive, Persuasive, Scholarly.
Psion Skills: Empathy +14, Telempathy + 13.
Gear: 58 BP. Gadgets and Vehicles: Green Lucifer

Mystic Warriors: Eva Kraus *(see page 156)* selects certain "prime specimens" from among her lieutenants' prisoners to undergo a mystic physical transformation into members of her monstrous personal guard, a process which leaves them virtual zombies. Sybille has access to a limited number of these warriors.

Mystic Warriors, 15th-level minions (squads of 6). CR 14. SZ M; v/wp: 15d8+60 (123)/18; Init +16 (+12 class, +4 Dex); Spd 30 ft.; Def 20 (+6 class, +4 Dex); Atk: Sword +19 (1d8+4); Face 1 square; Reach 1 square; SA None; SQ None; SV Fort +13, Ref +11, Will +3; Str 18, Dex 19, Con 18, Int 7, Wis 7, Cha 8; Skills: None. Feats: Combat Instincts, Iron Will, Power Attack. Gear: Weapons, chain shirt, 7 BP. Gadgets and Vehicles: None.

Serial Two: Flashfire

A former professional fighter and one-time champion of the underworld bloodsport called "Arena," Flashfire is lean, fast, and deadly. An obsessive arsonist, Flashfire often uses flamethrowers and incendiary grenades.

Flashfire, 18th-level soldier (henchman); CR 18. SZ M; v/wp: 199/18; Init +17 (+14 class, +3 Dex); Spd 30 ft.; Def 20 (+7 class, +3 Dex); Atk: Flamethrower +21 (2d6+fire); Face 1 square; Reach 1 square; SA None; SQ None; SV Fort +17, Ref +11, Will +8; Str 19, Dex 16, Con 18, Int 11, Wis 14, Cha 8;
Skills: Climb +12, Concentration +4, Demolitions +11, Intimidate +14, Jump +14, Listen +6, Mechanics +5, Search +4, Survival +12. Feats: Blind-Fight, Blindsight 5 ft. Radius, Controlled Burst, Controlled Strafe, Endurance, Great Fortitude, Hail of Bullets, Lay Down Fire, Marksman, Point Blank Shot, Power Attack, Precise Shot, Quick Healer, Rapid Shot, Sharp-Shooting, Snap Shot. Gear: Weapons, 28 BP. Gadgets and Vehicles: None.
HQ Personnel: 4 **HQ Security:** 3

Relic Hunter Team: These individuals are sent on missions to obtain mystic artifacts and knowledge for the Hand of Glory. They are primarily scientists and historians.

Relic Hunter Team, 14th-level minions (squads of 4). CR 13. SZ M; v/wp: 14d6+14 (67)/13; Init +16 (+11 class, +1 Dex, +4 feats); Spd 30 ft.; Def 17 (+6 class, +1 Dex); Atk: .357 pistol +15 (2d4+1);
Face 1 square; Reach 1 square; SA None; SQ None; SV Fort +10, Ref +7, Will +7; Str 12, Dex 12, Con 13, Int 16, Wis 16, Cha 14; Skills: Appraise +8, Climb +6, Cultures +10, Gather Information +7, Knowledge (Occult) +10, Knowledge (History) +10, Languages +10, Search +8, Surveillance +9, Survival +8, Swim +7, Use Rope +6. Feats: Increased Initiative, Zen Focus, Zen Shot. Gear: Weapons, binoculars, camera (standard), laptop, floodlight, geiger counter, climbing kit, survival kit.

Serial One: Jackboot

A crude and opinionated soldier of the *SS Standarte Germania,* Otto von Stapp participated in the invasion and occupation of France during World War II. His brutality against his own men earned him several months in a military prison and a reassignment to the SS Sonderkommando Dirlewanger, a unit of poachers and convicts ordered to combat regional partisan units.

When von Stapp was critically injured in the autumn of 1944, former subordinates working at the hospital refused to treat him, leaving him to die. He nonetheless survived and returned to Berlin, where he slowly recovered as the war ground to a halt. Then, as the Russians approached the German capital, he voluntarily headed for Hitler's bunker, where he hoped to die defending the Demagogue and his wife.

Eva Kraus, noting Otto's tenacity as well as his innate bloodthirst, ordered him to follow as she pulled out of Europe. He has since become one of her closest lieutenants, vowing to resurrect her Nazi empire, or die trying.

Otto von Stapp actively practices runic magic, and has many potent mystic tattoos on his body. Unstable to begin with, his mental state has deteriorated further over the years, partially due to these tattoos and the mystic tampering Eva has conducted to lengthen his life. At times, he even believes himself to be a Nordic hero come to rescue the world through bloodshed.

Jackboot, 9th-level snoop/8th-level physical adept (henchman); CR 17. SZ M; v/wp: 139/16; Init +12 (+10 class, +2 Dex); Spd 30 ft.; Def 23 (+12 class, +2 Dex); Atk: Survival knife +10 (1d6+2) / .45 service pistol +10 (1d10+2); Face 1 square; Reach 1 square; SA None;

SQ None; SV Fort +12, Ref +8, Will +11; Str 15, Dex 14, Con 16, Int 12, Wis 13, Cha 10; Skills: Balance +7, Bureaucracy +6, Climb +6, Concentration +6, Cryptography +9, Demolitions +5, Diplomacy +5, Disguise +5, Escape Artist +7, Forgery +7, Gather Information +5, Hide +10, Innuendo +4, Intimidate +8, Knowledge (Occult) +6, Knowledge (History) +7, Languages +8, Listen +7, Move Silently +14, Open Lock +6, Search +6, Survival +5. Feats: Darting Weapon, Expertise, Flashing Weapon, Mobility, Quick Draw, Sidestep, Snake Strike, Swift Strike, Weapon Finesse (shoe-blade). Gear: Weapons, 19 BP.
Gadgets and Vehicles: None.

HQ Personnel: 4 **HQ Security:** 5

Mind Controlled Shock Troops: Eva's mind-control techniques have little impact on her troops' ability to wreak havoc.

Mind Controlled Shock Troops, 12th-level minions (squads of 6). CR 11. SZ M; v/wp: 12d8+36 (92)/17; Init +12 (+10 class, +2 Dex); Spd 30 ft.; Def 17 (+5 class, +2 Dex); Atk: 7.62x39mm assault rifle +14 (2d8); Face 1 square; Reach 1 square; SA None; SQ None; SV Fort +11, Ref +8, Will +5; Str 17, Dex 15, Con 17, Int 8, Wis 8, Cha 8; Skills: None. Feats: Iron Will, Lay Down Fire, Point Blank Shot. Gear: Weapons, 8 BPs. Gadgets and Vehicles: None.

PLOT HOOK #1

Shut down by the Archer Foundation in 1994, "Arena" is making a comeback. All previous victors have been invited to the new tournament, though new fighters must prove themselves in a series of "challenger circuits". Several deaths have occurred at these "minor league", events prompting an investigation.

Possibilities

1. During the investigation, the agents discover information about one of the returning champions. He calls himself Flashfire, a name the agents will certainly recognize from the Foundation's files on the Hand of Glory.
2. As above, but someone at the contest is posing as Flashfire. One of the hopeful entrants was eliminated at one of the "minor league" events, and disguised himself as Flashfire in order to get a second chance at being a champion. Of course, it is unlikely that the real Flashfire will approve of the impostor, and the agents may encounter him when he arrives to register his displeasure in person.
3. Flashfire cannot resist the chance to fight again and prove himself as the supreme Arena combatant. His motives are not entirely based on pride, however. "Arena's" foremost investor is a rich antiquities dealer, whose collection includes a particular artifact Flashfire has been assigned to procure – by any means necessary.

PLOT HOOK #2

A marked increase in gang violence near the agents' headquarters draws the Foundation's attention. Initially, the Foundation dismissed the problem as something best dealt with by local authorities, until a recent eye-witness report caught the attention of Archer analysts: a description of one of the gang leaders included tattooing which fit the description of Jackboot.

Possibilities

1. One of the gangs serves as a training ground for shock troops, and a Hand of Glory agent provocateur is stirring tensions in the area to provide an adequate challenge. He gives out tattoos that emulate those of Jackboot as a reward to gang members who perform particularly well. Once a gang member attains the desired level of ferocity, he is transformed into one of Eva Kraus' mind-controlled shock troops.
2. The gang leader described is actually a rival of Jackboot's, who uses similar tattooing techniques to amass power. He has a great deal of information for the agents regarding the tattoos, as well as Jackboot's specific abilities, since the two have faced each other on several occasions. Of course, since this man is working to gain control of the streets of the city, he will certainly be on the lookout for a deal.
3. A vigilante gang, patterning themselves after the Guardian Angels, is slowly gaining respect in the city. They speak out against hate crimes and act as vocal opponents to Nazism and all it stands for. Jackboot has taken personal offense at this, and decided to rectify the problem. Sybille Vallentin has given him a Green Lucifer to use during the mission, along with his normal shock troops.

GLOSSARY

Some of the following terms are exclusive to the *Shadowforce Archer* setting, and others are seen in the *Spycraft* roleplaying game as well. All deserve special explanation. Please see the index for reference locations throughout this book.

African Alliance: A Chamber of the Archer Conspiracy, located in southern Africa, which fields agents for missions; one of eight Chambers players may choose from when designing an agent in the *Shadowforce Archer* setting.

AGAMEMNON virus: The contagion that sparked Chemical Monsters.

Agency, the: The default organization for the *Spycraft* RPG; used if this book (or another world setting) is not.

Agent: A secret agent; a player character.

Alliance, the: See African Alliance.

Ancients, the: The mythical, possibly human entities which resided in the world centuries or millennia ago, and created many of the mystic invocations and relics recently unearthed.

AQUATICA: The Archer Conspiracy's first underwater base.

Archer Conspiracy: Blanket term used to describe the Archer Foundation and the other Chambers as a whole; the Foundation's mission.

Archer Foundation: The core Chamber of the Archer Conspiracy, located in Australia, which fields agents for missions; one of eight Chambers players may choose from when designing an agent in the *Shadowforce Archer* setting.

Archer Institute for the Sciences: A legitimate Australian think tank devoted to science; the Archer Foundation's public face.

Archer, Conrad: The founder of the Archer Foundation; the world's first physical adept; Raymond Archer's father.

Archer, Raymond: Retired head of the Archer Foundation; Conrad Archer's son.

Archive, the: The Archer Foundation's collected information about world events.

Artifact: An item, usually of historic significance, imbued with mystic power. Also known as a relic.

Bond, bonded: Refer to the process of a mystic linking followers to himself so he can call upon their spiritual energy when performing invocations.

Broken Seal, the: One half of Room 39, a Chamber of the Archer Conspiracy.

Chamber: A division of the Conspiracy.

Chem treatment: A chemical compound used to create chemical monsters. Created in, and mostly limited to, the Russian Confederacy.

Chemical monster: A person transformed or granted special powers through chem treatments.

Cleaners: Agents who cover botched missions up for the Archer Foundation; unofficially part of the Foundation Chamber.

Cloak, the: The veil of secrecy surrounding the Conspiracy and its operations; all Conspiracy agents are pledged to support the Cloak, or they face the Dagger.

Codes: Three tiers of importance (yellow, red, and black, from least to most pressing) given to missions undertaken by Conspiracy agents.

Codename: A cover identity (with no supporting documentation) given to an agent of the Conspiracy, to protect his real name.

Collective, the: See the Pan-Asian Collective.

Committee, the: See Janus Committee.

Commonwealth, the: See the European Commonwealth.

Company, the: A Chamber of the Archer Conspiracy, located in the U.S., which fields agents for missions; one of eight Chambers players may choose from when designing an agent in the *Shadowforce Archer* setting.

Confederacy, the: See Russian Confederacy.

Consortium, the: See the Gemeinschafft Consortium.

Conspiracy, the: See the Archer Conspiracy.

Control: The man in charge of a Chamber of the Conspiracy (also used to refer to the Chamber as a whole); the man in charge of a team of agents while they are on a mission.

Daedalus Division: A research facility located inside the Lodge, which explores the secrets of the base and builds gadgets for the African Alliance.

Dagger, the: The global protection network that the Conspiracy uses to keep itself from public eyes; backlash from piercing the Cloak.

Demagogue, the: Adolf Hitler, secretly held in suspended animation by Eva Kraus, the leader of the Hand of Glory.

Department: A division of the Agency *(see above);* a game term referring to the office that fields agents, and which provides game benefits, in the *Spycraft* RPG.

Entity: Any sentient being, including living humans, lingering spirits, animals, etc.

European Commonwealth: A Chamber of the Archer Conspiracy, located in Europe, which fields agents for missions; one of eight Chambers players may choose from when designing an agent in the *Shadowforce Archer* setting.

Eyes of Argus: A watchdog group dedicated to rooting out and exposing the Archer Conspiracy.

Faceman: An agent class in *Spycraft,* specializing in disguise and guile.

"Fade": An organized crime syndicate controlled by a mysterious shrouded vigilante; one half of the European Commonwealth, a Chamber of the Conspiracy; also the leader of that sub-faction.

Fixer: An agent class in *Spycraft,* specializing in subterfuge, theft, and acquisition.

Followers: A mystic's legions, who lend their spiritual energy to his invocations once they have been bonded.

Foundation, the: See Archer Foundation.

Fringe, the: The realm between the physical world and the spirit realm, normally invisible, which appears in the physical world when the physical world and the spirit realm overlap; a shadow realm inhabited by the spirits of the dead, to which have been attributed many strange phenomena throughout Archer's shadow history; a secondary arena for *Shadowforce Archer* roleplay.

Game Control: The player who runs the game; otherwise known as a Gamemaster; aka "the GC."

Game, the: Espionage; aka "The Great Game."

Gemeinschafft Consortium: A powerful business conglomerate; one half of the European Commonwealth, a Chamber of the Conspiracy.

Ghost: A human soul; aka "spirit."

Guardians of the Whispering Knife, the: A Chamber of the Archer Conspiracy, located in the Middle East and northern Africa, which fields agents for missions; one of eight Chambers players may choose from when designing an agent in the *Shadowforce Archer* setting; aka "The Guardians."

Hand of Glory, the: A criminal organization founded in the Third Reich, which exists to dominate the world and fulfill the mad schemes of its leader, Eva Kraus.

Helix: A criminal mastermind who attempted to wipe out mundane (non-psion) humanity and who built the Lodge; originally Avery Schillingsfield, the discoverer of the civilization responsible for awakening psionic powers.

Henchman: The middle rung on the villain ladder (they serve a mastermind), and the average foe agents face during the game; generally the ultimate challenge faced in a serial.

Home Office, the: Another name for an agent's Chamber or Department ("Let me call the home office").

Invocation: The joint name for rites and rituals, used when you wish to refer to both types of spells together.

Janus Committee: A philanthropic organization founded by Elias Graham (Control of the African Alliance), dedicated to bridging racial and other gaps in society.

Lodge, the: The headquarters of the African Alliance; originally built as a prison for enemy psion agents by Helix, a criminal mastermind.

Mastermind: The top rung on the villain ladder (above a henchman), and the strongest foe agents face during the game; generally the ultimate challenge faced in a season.

Mentalist: One of three types of psion, focusing on the power of mind over matter, allowing the creation of gadgets, telekinesis, and other abilities.

Minion: The lowest rung on the villain ladder (below henchmen), and the weakest foe agents face during the game.

Mystic: An agent type; also a designation for all the feats, invocations, and prestige classes which that agent type can learn.

Mysticism: The power of religious faith, the occult, and fringe beliefs all rolled into one amalgam, which grants power to the righteous and devout; the source of rituals (spells) and artifacts (magic items), which convey power if controlled; "good" mysticism tends to be a personal thing, controlled by only one individual, while "evil" mysticism tends to be group- or cult-based, controlled by crowds of like-minded, or like-dominated individuals.

Omnium Corporation: The public face of Room 39, located in London.

OVERWATCH: The Archer Conspiracy's first orbiting satellite network.

PAC, the: See Pan-Asian Collective

Pan-Asian Collective: A Chamber *(see above)* of the Archer Conspiracy, located in Asia, which fields agents for missions; one of eight Chambers players may choose from when designing an agent in the *Shadowforce Archer* setting.

P.E.R.I.L.: The Project for Expansion, Retribution, Iniquity, and Lies; a criminal organization which has subverted the Russian Confederacy, turning it against the Conspiracy.

Physical adept: One of three types of psion, focusing on physical (body) performance, usually of the "wire fu" variation, and other abilities.

Physical world: The real world, where living humans reside; the primary arena for *Shadowforce Archer* roleplay.

Pointman: An agent class in *Spycraft,* broadly trained, favoring versatility over specialization.

PROMETHEUS: The Russian Confederacy's top-secret chemical monster program.

Psion: A psionic agent.

PsiTech: Gadgets, created by mentalists.

Relic: An item, usually of historic significance, imbued with mystic power. Also known as an artifact.

Rite: A magical spell, or invocation, cast to create a desired effect, powered by faith and the essence of the divine (either good or evil). Distinguished from a ritual in that a rite is generally less powerful and easier to perform.

Ritual: A magical spell, or invocation, cast to create a desired effect, powered by faith and the essence of the divine (either good or evil). Distinguished from a rite in that a ritual is generally more powerful and much more difficult to perform.

Room 39: A Chamber of the Archer Conspiracy, located in Great Britain, which fields agents for missions; one of eight Chambers players may choose from when designing an agent in the *Shadowforce Archer* setting.

Russian Confederacy: A Chamber of the Archer Conspiracy, located in the former Soviet Union, which fields agents for missions; one of eight Chambers players may choose from when designing an agent in the *Shadowforce Archer* setting.

Scene: The smallest division of a serial, in which one or more encounters happen and the serial's story moves forward.

Season: A string of serials; a campaign.

Serial: An adventure; a mission.

Shadowforce Archer: The project name given by Argus *(see page 152)* to his continued effort to reveal the Archer Conspiracy to the world.

Serum: A powerful catalyst used to awaken psion powers by bonding with and mutating DNA.

Serum soldier: See Chemical monster.

Shadespeaker: An agent of the Guardians of the Whispering Knife whose abilities focus on sensing and communicating with lingering human spirits.

Shadow: An operative of the Archer Conspiracy, or an operative of one of their secret enemies.

Shadow Community: A collection of spies; any of the Chambers in the Shadowforce Archer setting and the territories they immediately protect.

Shadow History: The secret history of the world, some created by the Archer Conspiracy and the rest created by their enemies or neutral factions; the "news behind the news."

Shop, the: The Archer Conspiracy's research and development department, which has splintered off this year as a criminal organization.

Soldier: An agent class in *Spycraft,* specializing in combat.

Snoop: An agent class in *Spycraft,* specializing in computer espionage and intelligence gathering.

Spirit: A human soul; aka "ghost."

SUPERLUMINAL: The Russian Confederacy's top-secret serum soldier program.

Telepath: One of three types of psion, focusing on the power of mind over mind, allowing mental communication, and other abilities.

Thirst, the: The seductive lure of the mystic world, which corrupts even as it grants more and more power.

Threat: An enemy organization or group of enemies collected for a serial or string of serials.

ULTRACORPS: One half of Room 39, a Chamber of the Archer Conspiracy.

Wheelman: An agent class in *Spycraft,* specializing in driving, with minor combat abilities.

Author Afterword

Patrick Kapera

This project has been a labor of love from the day it was conceived in a small harborside restaurant in the Bay Area. Kevin and I have given more than two years of our lives to this book and the basic *Spycraft* game, dedicated to recapturing the excitement of gaming we knew in our youth, and bringing it to a new generation of roleplayers. During this time, many new games have been released, several of which have made good on this promise, including the phenomenal *D&D 3rd Edition,* by Monte Cook, Jonathan Tweet, and Skip Williams. We are proud to be part of this new generation, this bold new step into the world of fantasy and science fiction.

Thanks to John Zinser and Maureen Yates for supporting this project through thick and thin, and helping to shape it into what it is today. Maureen, you've been one of my closest friends through the last four years, and the most amazing boss I've ever known. John, your vision kept this project on the cutting edge, and your enthusiasm kept Kevin and me going, even when we thought there wasn't anything left to say.

Ryan Dancey has been one of the biggest influences in what we hope will be *Spycraft's* success. His work with the OGL and invaluable advice made this a gamer's game. Ryan, you're one of the original good ones. Don't ever change.

Les Simpson, my personal assistant in most endeavors and one of my dearest friends, has been with us almost since the beginning. He helped to shape the feature characters and world concepts, and brought us into the multimedia realm with the audio drama we're co-producing, based on this property. (Shameless plug: you can listen to it on www.shadowforcearcher.com.) Les, your vigilance, attention to detail, and boundless drive keep me sane, and never fail to illuminate when the spark of creativity is dim.

Scott Gearin was one of the greatest assets to this project. His dogged focus and keen sense of game balance made this book sing and the *Spycraft Handbook* crunch. Scott's offerings include (but are by no means limited to) the telepath class, disposition system, gambling rules, countless feats, and most of the mystic mechanics. He also revamped nearly every rules set in the game, most notably the *Spycraft* chase system, and helped during many, many world development talks.

Thanks also to the fiction, design, and playtest teams, whose tireless efforts turned my mad ramblings (and those of the infamous Drunken Monkey) into the shiny gold niblets of gaming goodness they are today. In case you were wondering who did what, the clear credit goes to:

B.D. Flory came up with the prestige classes and mystic relics seen in this volume, as well as numerous feats, and edited almost as much material as I have. B.D. remains a guiding force for the mechanics and *Shadowforce Archer* world – you'll be seeing a lot of him in the next couple years.

Sean Michael Fish reworked the threat plot hooks and NPC statistics at the 11th hour, and helped out with rules revisions almost until the CDs were burned for the printers.

Joe Fulgham and Steve Wallace designed all three versions of the website.

John Phythyon, Jr. wrote the PAC and Room 39 sections, as well as chunks of the *Spycraft* basic rules.

Les Simpson wrote the Guardians and Cleaners sections (save Jack Frost, who was mine from the start), the Hand of Glory, and many minor essays.

Heath Scheiman wrote the world sections of each Chamber (Government and Economy).

Lucien Soulban gave us the Middle East section of Contested Regions, as well as much personal support and friendship throughout.

Jim Wardrip injected a dose of reality into our gear and weapons sections.

Shawn Carman, Steve Crow, B.D. Flory, Iain McAllister, and John Phythyon, Jr. wrote nearly all of Chapter Four of the *Spycraft Handbook* and much miscellaneous material throughout the books elsewise.

Brendon Goodyear, Steve Hough, and Mark Jelfo are responsible for the fantastic layouts we wound up with. Brendo especially deserves mention, as he created many early graphics for the website, countless spot images, and helped to forge the mystic world and material to be seen in the upcoming *Archer Foundation* sourcebook.

Mary Valles kept this juggernaut from becoming a sluggish hippo, wading hip-deep in mud. Mary's one of the unsung heroes of AEG, who – like Maureen Yates – makes sure all the stuff that no one ever sees gets done.

Jim Pinto and Cris Dornaus were two-thirds of the equation in bringing our feature NPCs to life.

Everyone else you can find on the credits page – their contributions are pretty clear. Thank you all!

Finally, this work is dedicated to Raymond Joseph Kapera, who I'd like to think could have been a hero, and to Patsy June Lynch Kapera, who really was.

Kevin Wilson

I was eight years old when I bought the red boxed edition of Basic Dungeons and Dragons from J.C. Penney. Since then, I've played 1st Edition, 2nd Edition, and even a 3-year-long campaign in college using the Rules Cyclopedia and those wonderful Gazetteers. All told, I've played Mr. Gygax's and Mr. Arneson's groundbreaking game for just over 18 years. The creation of the OGL provided me with a welcome opportunity to work with the 3rd edition of the system I've grown up with and loved ever since I learned what "3d6" meant. It's an honor to be walking in those footsteps.

I would like to dedicate my part of this book to my grandparents, Leonard and Bobbie Barnwell. I can't imagine two kinder and gentler people in the whole world.

I would also like to thank Patrick Kapera for inviting me along on this project. It's been a blast working with you.

This afterword will self-destruct in 5 seconds...

INDEX